MW01631362

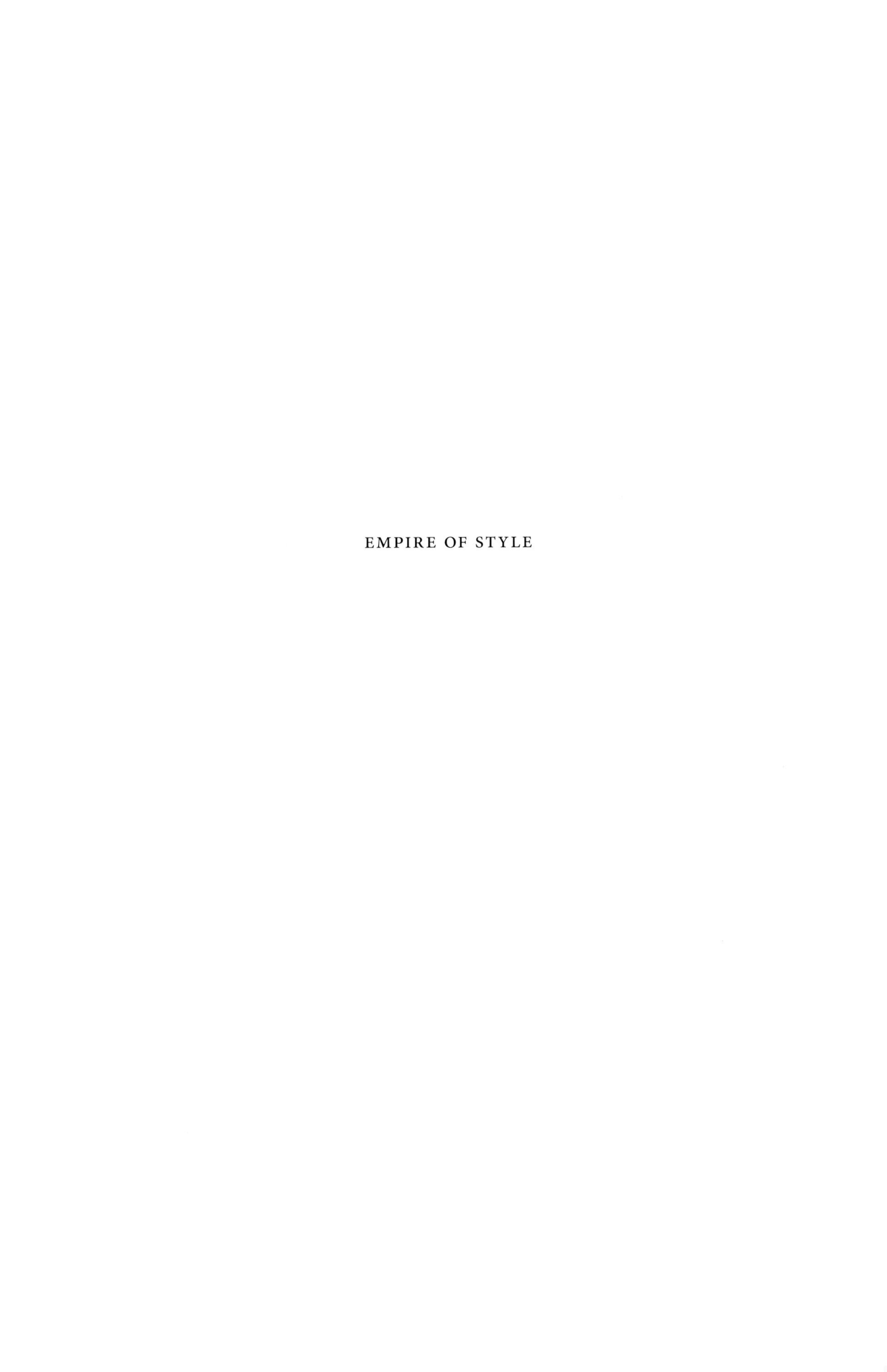

EMPIRE OF STYLE

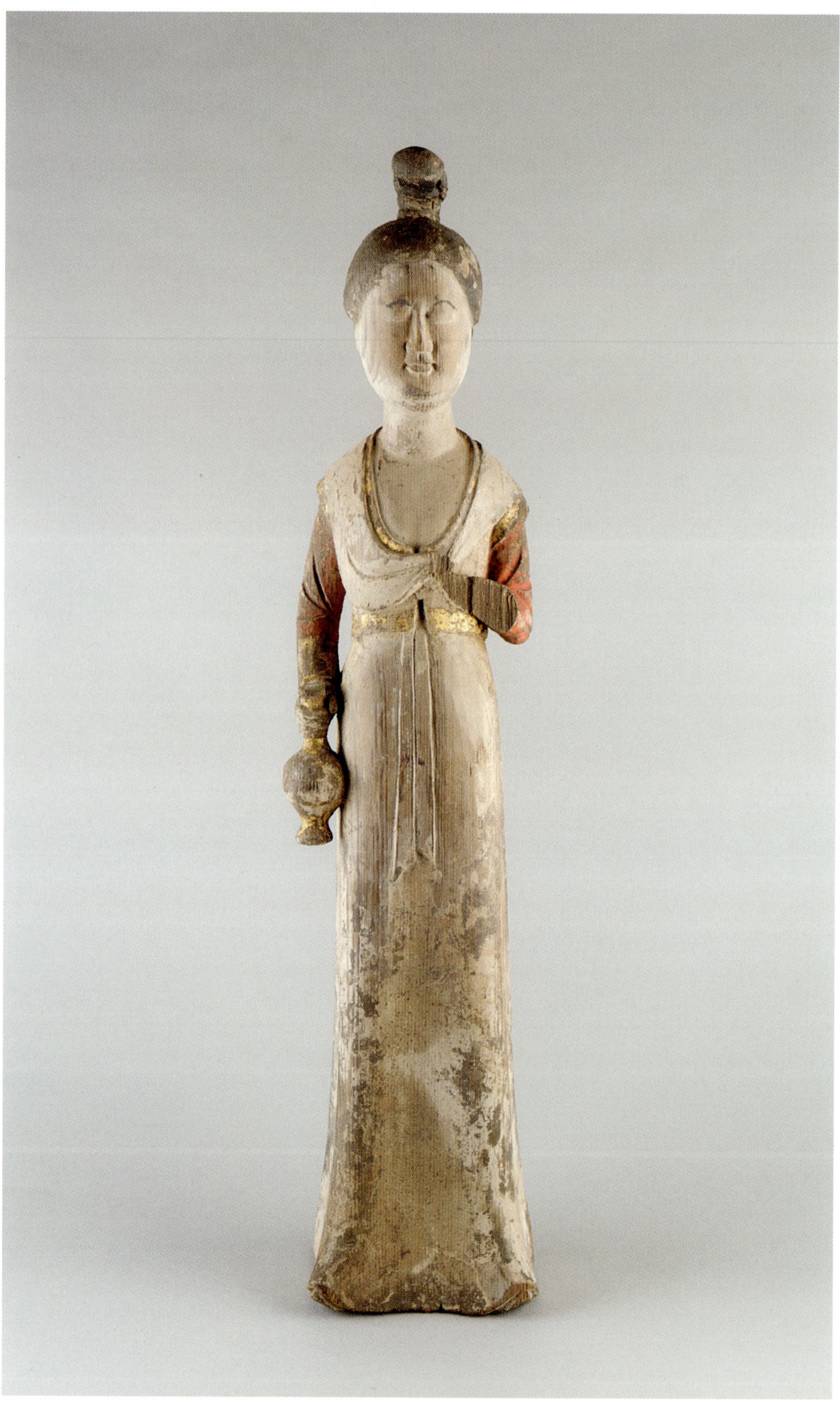

Empire of Style

Silk and Fashion in Tang China

BuYun Chen

UNIVERSITY OF WASHINGTON PRESS
Seattle

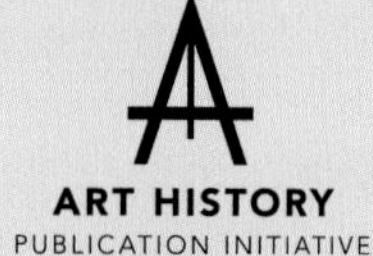

Empire of Style is made possible by a collaborative grant from the Andrew W. Mellon Foundation.

Additional support was provided by the Metropolitan Center for Far Eastern Art Studies, the Pasold Research Fund, the Hungerford Faculty Support Fund at Swarthmore College, and the Max Planck Institute for the History of Science.

Printed and bound in Korea

Design by Katrina Noble
Composed in Minion Pro, typeface designed by Robert Slimbach

FRONTISPIECE: Standing female attendant, late seventh or early eighth century. The figure is clothed in the basic ensemble: a slim-fitting, long-sleeved robe with a low neckline; a high-waisted skirt; a *banbi*, which features a gold-painted trim; and a shawl. Wood with pigments; H. 49.5 cm. Gift of Enid A. Haupt, 1997, Metropolitan Museum of Art, New York.

23 22 21 20 19 5 4 3 2 1

UNIVERSITY OF WASHINGTON PRESS
www.washington.edu/uwpress

LIBRARY OF CONGRESS CATALOGING-IN-PUBLICATION DATA

Names: Chen, BuYun, author.
Title: Empire of style : silk and fashion in Tang China / BuYun Chen.
Description: Seattle : University of Washington Press, [2019] | Includes bibliographical references and index.
Identifiers: LCCN 2018038430 | ISBN 9780295745305 (hardcover : alk. paper)
Subjects: LCSH: Clothing and dress—China—History—To 1500. | Fashion—China—History—To 1500. | Silk—China—History—to 1500. | Silk industry—China—History—To 1500. | China—History—Tang dynasty, 618-907.
Classification: LCC GT1555 .C5463 2019 | DDC 391.00951—dc23
LC record available at https://lccn.loc.gov/2018038430

The paper used in this publication is acid free and meets the minimum requirements of American National Standard for Information Sciences—Permanence of Paper for Printed Library Materials, ANSI Z39.48–1984.∞

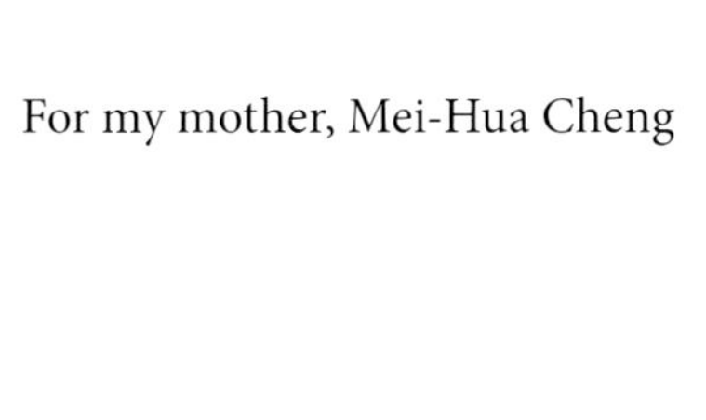

For my mother, Mei-Hua Cheng

CONTENTS

ACKNOWLEDGMENTS

This book is about fashion in Tang dynasty China, but it owes its genesis to the work of feminist theorists and historians, from whom I inherited a deep concern about the place of women in history. As a student, I was swept up by the efforts to restore women's long-absent voices to the analysis of non-Western societies and to present them as active agents, whose lives were far richer and more complex than past narratives had documented. When I embarked on the study of Chinese history, I did so with the resolve to uncover the political and moral autonomy of the female subject.

Dorothy Ko upended my world when she challenged my notion of women's agency as consubstantial with resistance to patriarchal domination, steering me away from my search for the active feminist consciousness. She opened my eyes to the productive lives of women in premodern China and showed me that it was possible to recover their knowledge cultures. Her lessons have accompanied this book throughout its formation. Words are an insufficient medium (as she often reminds me), especially here, to convey all the ways she enriches my life.

From our very first meeting, Robert Hymes has extended to me both his intellect and his magnanimity. Without his guidance, I would have remained a reluctant student of middle period Chinese history. He has been steadfast in his support and enthusiasm for my work, even as it ventures into areas outside premodern China. I have also incurred innumerable debts from teachers in other fields. Jonathan Hay has cultivated in me a love for objects and images, and continues to inspire how I look at a painting. Suzanne Cahill, whose translations of Yu Xuanji's poetry first sparked my interest in Tang studies, was an invaluable reader during the research phase. To the late Wu Pei-yi, I am indebted for instilling in me the discipline necessary to translate classical Chinese texts.

Teachers, colleagues, and friends have sustained me through this awkward enterprise we call academic life with their intellect, humor, and, above all, camaraderie. Dagmar Schäfer impressed upon me the importance of thinking boldly. Angela Sheng taught me about the rigor of textile studies through her own exemplary practice. I was lucky to find a fellow fashion historian in Rachel Silberstein. Anne Gerritsen and Carla Nappi gave the best pep talks. Conversations with Siyen Fei about gender were instructive and nourishing. Jacob Eyferth prompted me to think more critically about skill. Giorgio Riello read the entire manuscript during the final revision phase and buoyed me up with his encouragement.

Throughout the years, I have relied on the friendship of Talia Andrei, Andrew Liu, Joseph Scheier-Dolberg, Jenny Wang Medina, and Tom Wilkinson. With Talia's compassion, Andy's intellect, Joe's sharpness, Jenny's candor, and Tom's wit, I have found life both inside and outside the academe infinitely more pleasurable. In Philadelphia, Lara Cohen and Nina Johnson have become more like kin than friends. Jen Moore's warmth toward others is unparalleled. In Berlin, Emily Brownell, Alina-Sandra Cucu, Sebastian Felten, Xiaochang Li, Tamar Novick, and Julie Ren have become dear friends and valued interlocutors.

This book draws on research conducted with generous support from the Social Science Research Council, the Fulbright Program, and Swarthmore College. In 2009 and 2010, a research fellowship from SSRC and a Fulbright-IIE Grant allowed me to travel across China to see firsthand the artifacts that make up this book. When I struggled to gain access to museum collections, Qi Dongfang graciously wrote letters of introduction on my behalf. Thank you to Zhou Fang at the China Silk Museum and Shen Qinyan at the Shaanxi History Museum for granting me privileged entry into the museum vault. Funding from Swarthmore College enabled me to see key collections in Europe during the summer of 2014. I would also like to thank Helen Persson and Li Xiaoxin at the Victoria and Albert Museum, Lucy Carson at the British Museum, and Regula Schorta at the Abegg-Stiftung. Chris Hall kindly opened his collection to me; I am grateful to Eiren Shea for making the introduction.

I finished drafting the book while on a two-year fellowship from the Max Planck Institute for the History of Science in Berlin (MPIWG). During the first year of my leave, a Mary Albertson Faculty Fellowship from Swarthmore granted me a comfortable existence. My colleagues at Swarthmore, particularly in History and Asian Studies, have been steady supporters of my intellectual and pedagogical endeavors. My students at Swarthmore have reinforced for me the need for precision in thinking about theory and methodology.

I have been fortunate to work with Lorri Hagman and her team at the University of Washington Press. They have patiently assisted me through the completion of this book. I am thankful to the three anonymous readers, whose comments stressed to me the importance of clarity. Urte Brauckmann and Cathleen Paethe at the MPIWG have generously devoted their energy to the lengthy permissions process for the book. I am supremely grateful to Lu Pengliang for stepping in to help when all seemed hopeless. Che Qun shared her expertise with me and developed the base maps for the book. A Constance Hungerford Faculty Support Fund from Swarthmore helped subvent the considerable cost of image reproductions and permissions.

To my family, words are again insufficient. My brother, Brandon, has spurred me on with his unwavering confidence in my ability to succeed. His care, affection, and support has shored me up, and provided me with the freedom to move where my mind takes me. My father, Tan-Sheng Chen, did not survive the publication of this book, but he would have been excited to see it in print—for he never doubted my decision to pursue Chinese history. Without the labor of my mother, Mei-Hua Cheng, none of this would have been possible. Her mark on this book is indelible.

CHINESE DYNASTIES (WITH TANG REIGN PERIODS)

Xia, 2070–1600 BCE
Shang, 1600–ca. 1045 BCE
Zhou, ca. 1045–256 BCE
    Spring and Autumn period, 770–476 BCE
    Warring States period, 476–221 BCE
Qin, 221–206 BCE
Former (Western) Han, 206 BCE–8 CE
Later (Eastern) Han, 25–220 CE
Three Kingdoms, 220–280
Six Dynasties
    Western Jin, 265–317
    Eastern Jin, 317–420
    Southern and Northern dynasties, 420–589
Sui, 581–618
Tang, 618–907
    Gaozu, r. 618–626
    Taizong, r. 626–649
    Gaozong, r. 649–683
    Zhongzong, r. 684; 705–710
    Ruizong, r. 684–690; 710–712
Zhou, 690–705
Tang, continued
    Xuanzong, r. 712–756
    Suzong, r. 756–762
    Daizong, r. 762–779
    Dezong, r. 779–805
    Shunzong, r. 805
    Xianzong, r. 806–820
    Muzong, r. 820–824

Jingzong, r. 824–826
Wenzong, r. 826–840
Wuzong, r. 840–846
Xuanzong, r. 846–859
Yizong, r. 859–873
Xizong, r. 873–888
Zhaozong, r. 888–900; 901–904
Ai, r. 904–907

Five Dynasties and Ten Kingdoms, 907–979

Song, 960–1279
Northern Song, 960–1127
Southern Song, 1127–1279

Jin, 1115–1234

Yuan, 1271–1368

Ming, 1368–1644

Qing, 1644–1912

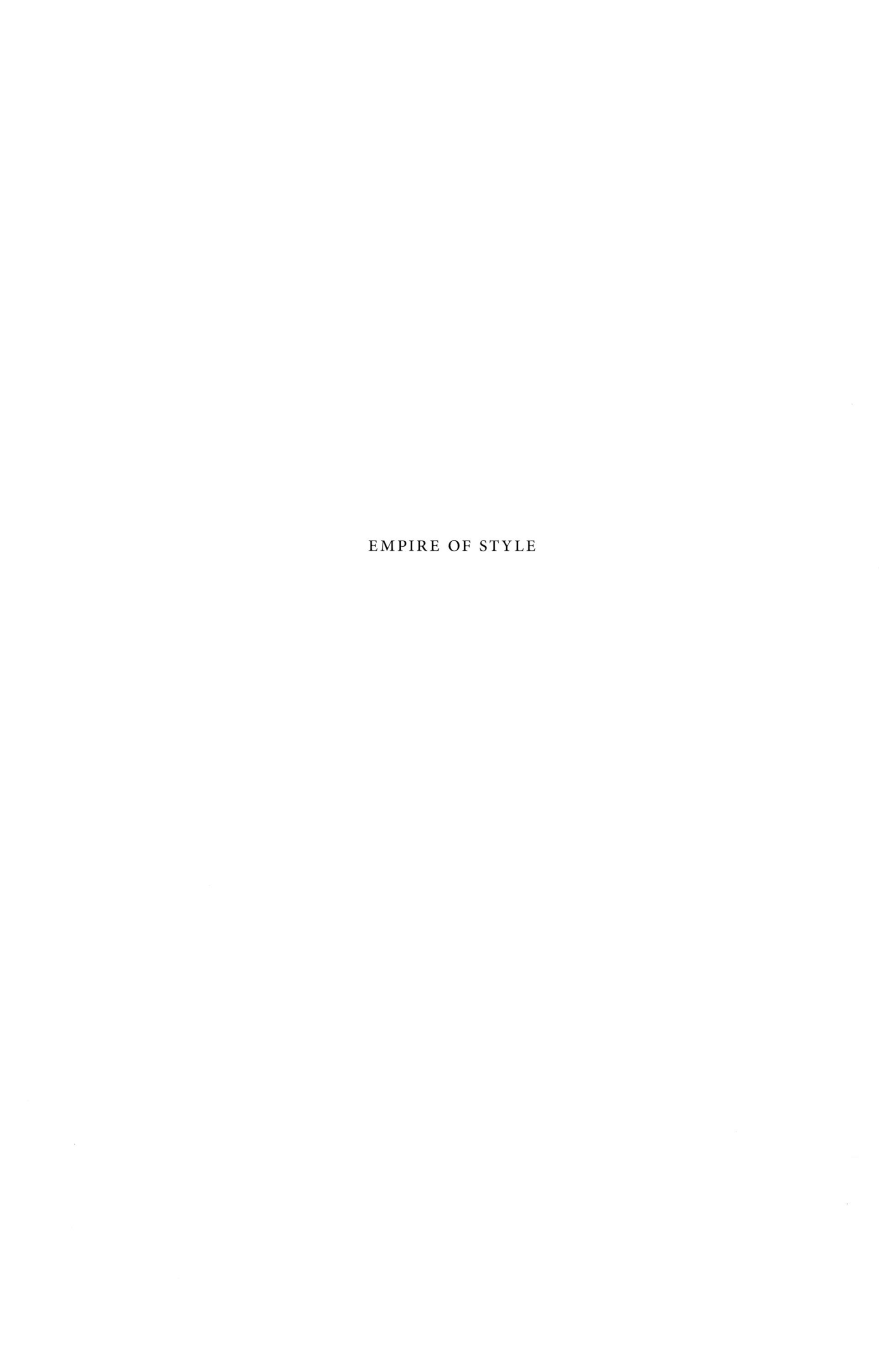

EMPIRE OF STYLE

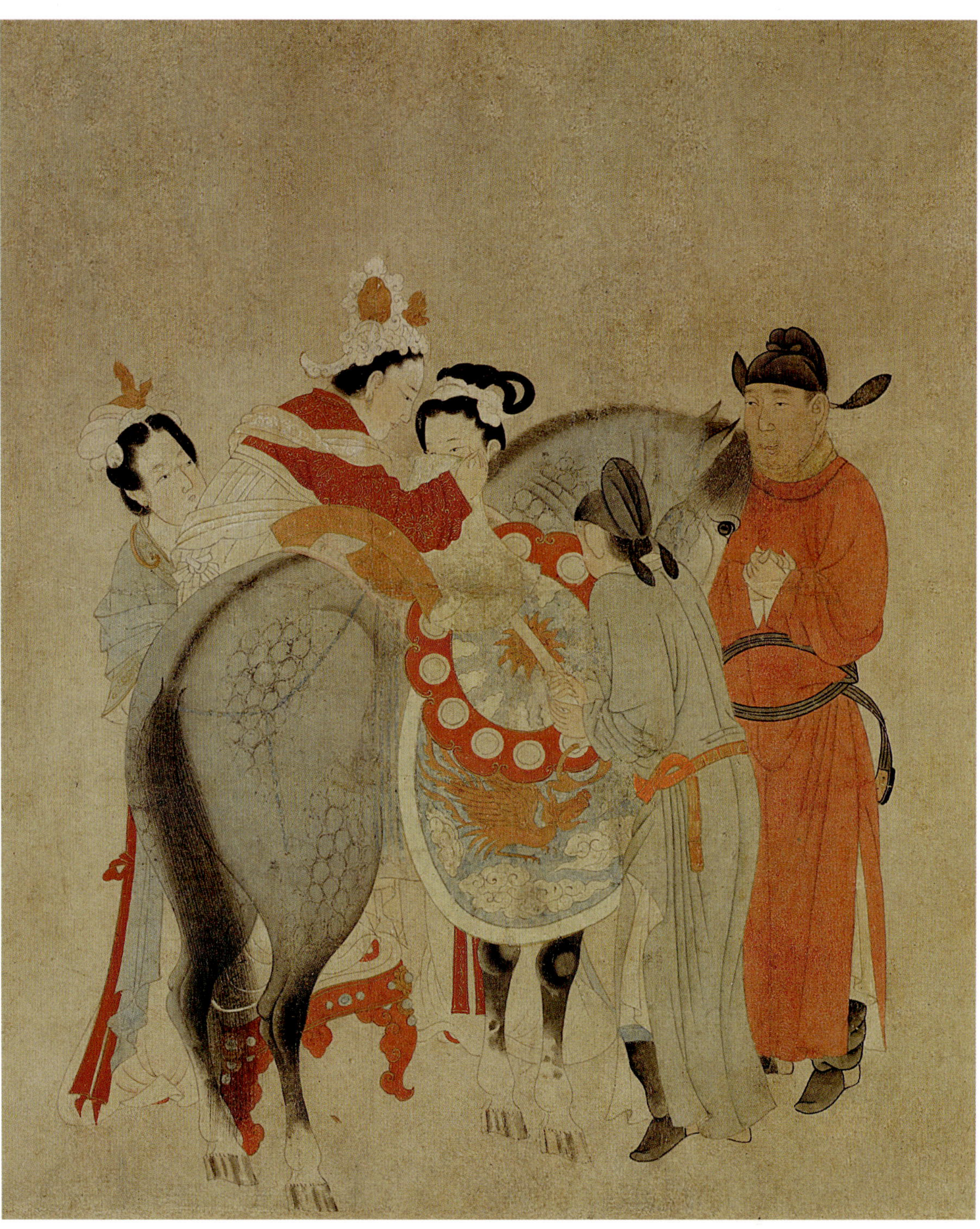

Introduction

TOWARD A DEFINITION OF FASHION IN TANG CHINA

IN DECEMBER 2014, A TELEVISION SERIES ABOUT THE LIFE OF WU ZETIAN (ca. 624–705), the only woman in Chinese history to rule as emperor of her own dynasty (the Zhou dynasty of 690–705), was taken off the air for purported technical reasons. The abrupt action was, however, actually a response to the low necklines of the Tang dynasty costumes that exposed too much cleavage for China's State Administration of Press, Publication, Radio, Film and Television. When the show returned in January, the footage had been crudely edited, and in place of widescreen shots, close-ups of the women's faces elided their bodies. The edited version prompted much criticism from viewers, who took to the Internet to debate whether or not the revealing necklines accurately represented Tang dynasty (618–907) dress styles. Now, as then, the dress practices of Tang women have invited censure.

In Tang China, officials were concerned not with women's cleavage, but something more troubling: the desire to dress according to personal tastes instead of one's station in life. To illustrate this point, let us consider an anecdote about the Taiping Princess (d. 713), the powerful daughter of Wu Zetian and Emperor Gaozong (r. 649–683). During a banquet held by Gaozong, the princess emerged wearing a purple robe outfitted with the accouterments of military officials, a jade belt, and a turban-like cap constructed from black silk gauze. She proceeded to perform a dance for the emperor and empress, who were both greatly amused by the spectacle. At the end of the dance, they

FIGURE I.1. Detail of figure I.5, *Consort Yang Mounting a Horse.*

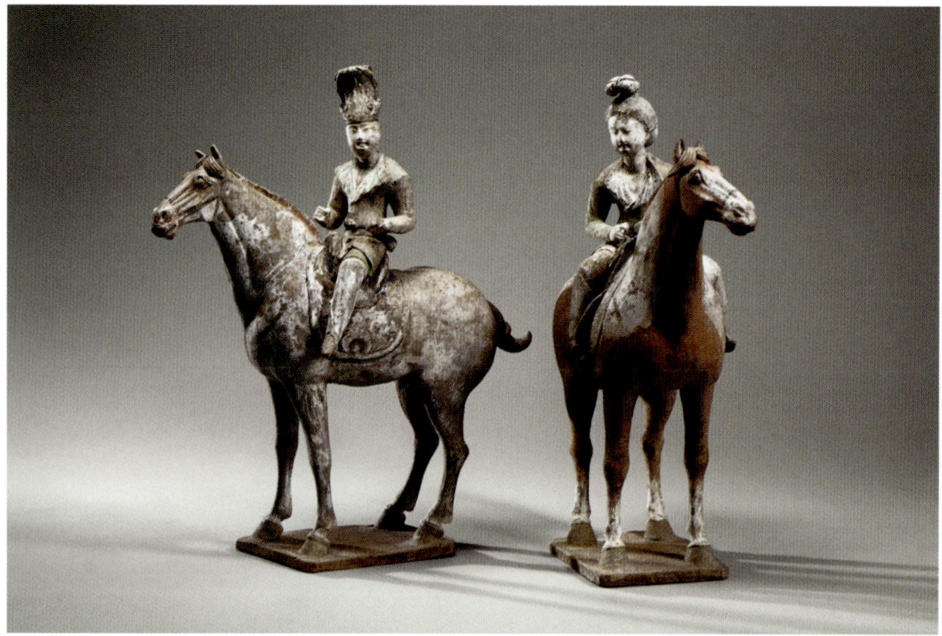

FIGURE I.2. Two equestrian figures, early eighth century. Both wear pointed boots, and their hands are positioned to hold the reins of the saddled horses on which they are mounted. Molded, reddish buff earthenware with cold-painted pigments over white ground. Left: male with a tall, embellished hat; H. 37 cm, W. 30.5 cm, D. 15.5 cm. Right: female with hair in a topknot; H. 36 cm, W. 31.5 cm, D. 13 cm. Harvard Art Museums/Arthur M. Sackler Museum, Gift of Anthony M. Solomon, 2003.207. Photo: Imaging Department © President and Fellows of Harvard College.

chided her, "Why dress this way, when girls cannot become military officers?"[1] The editors of *New Standard History of the Tang* included this story as one of the "sartorial anomalies" of the dynasty, a portent of the inversion of gender roles that would befall the empire when Wu Zetian ascended the throne as ruler. The story of the Taiping Princess's act of cross-dressing, and its transmission through the dynastic annals, is telling for two reasons: first, sartorial behavior was of political and moral concern and, thus, warranted documentation and interpretation; and second, modes of adornment gained meaning only through their attachment to and performance by a wearer in front of an audience. The princess was part of a rich symbolic and material world, in which what people wore and how they wore it, along with their depictions in image and text, were foundational to lived experience. By donning the attire of a military official, the Taiping Princess created and enacted a different image of herself, one that was rendered legible and meaningful through its connection to the gendered politics of her immediate context (fig. I.1). She exemplified the capacity for clothing to organize ideas about power, gender, and morality, exploiting dress to the fullest extent as a technique of *fashioning*.

The Tang men and women who populate this book belonged to a regime of fashion, one quite different from our regime of brand names and mass media, but fashionable nonetheless. Fashion, as epitomized by the story of the Taiping Princess, was first and foremost a meaning-making practice, in which a sense of being or selfhood was constructed in relation to social groups, through encounters with the material world, and conditioned by time and space. Tang China was fertile ground for fashion as a process of image- and self-making to take root, as ritual and official dress codes had opened up the space for thinking about the dressed body as a site of status performance. As such, fashion was implicated in Tang court culture, in the empire's finances, in visual culture, in textile technology, and in literary genres.

FASHION WITHOUT MODERNITY

Until recently, the equation of fashion with Western modernity has been the dominant view throughout the world. Fashion, as the German sociologist Werner Sombart proclaimed in 1902, is "the favored child of capitalism."[2] Sombart, of course, was only thinking of Europe—where a permanent revolution of taste, production, and consumption had taken place. For early twentieth-century theorists of fashion, the birth of an increasingly time-conscious world came about through the formation of a modern capitalist system, determined by the accelerated production and consumption of commodities. Viewing it as a symptom of modernity, these classical theorists of fashion agreed that it emerged in tandem with the development and intensification of a commodity culture in nineteenth-century western Europe. By the turn of the twentieth century, fashion had become synonymous with change and symbolic of the rapid turnover of capital. Its study has since been rooted in this Eurocentric formulation of fashion as a register of modernity, generated by the forces of industrial capital.[3]

Later twentieth-century historians like Quentin Bell and Fernand Braudel echoed Sombart's equation of fashion with Europe—so that dress in civilizations untouched by Western capitalism was merely a foil to a modern fashion system. Chinese dress, for these scholars, belonged to the realm of "costume," immune to restless change. From Bell's perspective, variations in Chinese dress were "of a kind that Western eyes would hardly notice."[4] For Braudel, China belonged to the timeless rest-of-the-world in which dress "scarcely changed in the course of centuries."[5] The myth of a static Chinese costume was part and parcel of a broad critique of an inert Chinese society immobilized by tradition that had as much to do with European self-perception as an industrializing force as it did with what Chinese people wore. This discourse of fashion as a peculiarly European phenomenon was also embraced by modern Chinese intellectuals, active during the first half of the twentieth century. In a 1943 article, the celebrated writer Eileen Chang wrote that "generation after generation of women wore the same sorts of clothes without feeling in the least perturbed."[6]

Recent scholarship has helped to overturn this Eurocentric view, showing that a desire for novelty, increased investment in material goods, and a widening distribution of consumption existed in medieval and early modern Europe, Ming China (1368–1644), and Tokugawa Japan (1603–1868).[7] These studies have worked to decenter Europe as the origin of consumer society and have turned the consumer revolution into a global phenomenon, characterized as a mark of the early modern world. By establishing shared patterns of consumption as the grounds for an early modernity, historians—particularly historians of China—aimed to call into question the parochial view that conflates modernity with industrial capitalism and the West.[8] Efforts to revise this narrative have dominated the field of Chinese history, which has been resolutely focused on disputing the distinctiveness of European modernity. This scholarship, while important and valuable, tends to fall into a trap of looking for "sprouts" or harbingers of the modern—defined in terms of the European experience—in historical contexts either contemporaneous to or preceding modern Europe. The search for modernity in China on these terms has fixed the European model as the standard by which to judge the Chinese experience. This also holds true for current studies on fashion in China.

While this study of fashion in Tang China is indebted to the interventions of these scholars, it diverges from their approaches to fashion as an expression of modernity. Instead, it focuses attention on the experience of dress and adornment as fundamentally one of meaning-making for the maker, wearer, viewer, and chronicler. It foregrounds fashion as an open-ended process that encouraged playing with self-formation by exploring the creative possibilities made feasible by the splendor of the material world and documented in ornate visual and literary modes of representation. This is not to suggest that fashion in Tang dynasty China was not related to change. On the contrary, dress and adornment were external trappings of a self and body that sought to square itself with social structures, the mutability of the material world, and political change. Meanings of textiles, garments, and accessories were relational and culturally constructed, such that a style of dress lost or gained meaning and value depending on its relevance to the wider fashion system. Subject to shifting interpretations, change in fashion had as much to do with perception as it did in the actual materials and cut of fabric. Pictorial representations of dress, for example, gave change a visual and material form. Through its association with the practices of representation, change was gradually reified as an aesthetic act, one that could be identified, scrutinized, and enacted.

In this negotiation of social belonging with one's exchanges with the images of clothed bodies and the materials of dress, the process of fabricating a self was intimately tied to historical time and place. By approaching fashion as processual and interactive rather than determinate, and as a system that is historically contingent rather than universal, we can allow for fashion to exist both with and without modernity—however the latter may be construed. The broader significance of this case study is to model an approach to fashion—one that brings together excavated visual and material evidence with the transmitted economic, political, legal, and literary texts—in the nonmodern, non-Western context of Tang China.

THE TACTILE AND PLAYFUL WORLD OF TANG FASHION

To understand the plural and contradictory practices that made up fashion in Tang China, we must, as Ann Rosalind Jones and Peter Stallybrass urged in their insightful study of clothing in Renaissance Europe, "undo our social categories, in which subjects are prior to objects, wearers to what is worn."[9] Commonly regarded as the cosmopolitan golden age of Chinese history, the Tang dynasty was marked by impressive economic growth, political innovations, the flourishing of art and literature, and increased contact with the outside world. At the height of Tang rule, the capital Chang'an was the largest city in the medieval world and home to over one million residents. The empire became a major sphere of influence within and beyond East Asia, absorbing and facilitating commercial, intellectual, religious, and artistic exchange across territories. The geographical and cultural contours of the Tang empire shifted continually around the local and mobile populations that were brought into its administrative framework. At the same time, the imperial court sought to impose traditional institutions of governance rooted in the classical ideal of a self-sufficient agrarian economy and stable social hierarchy onto this vast territory. The resulting tension between imperial expansion and the expectations of tradition was also mirrored in the fashion system that took shape in this era.

Fashion, as correlated with a desire for change, existed alongside the abiding conviction that clothing must cohere with the body underneath, and represent unequivocally the status of the wearer. Gaozong's response to the Taiping Princess's appearance in official military dress is a reflection of how dress was perceived to be constitutive of the person. That such a performance was undertaken by Taiping, or even narrated by the moralizing compilers of the dynastic records, however, suggests that clothing was also a site for contesting predetermined notions of status and gender. Whereas sumptuary codes aimed to regulate sartorial practices by prescribing and proscribing acceptable forms of dress according to status and rank, the creative possibilities opened up by innovations in textile production and encounters with foreign modes of adornment made fashion a force for change. By putting into conversation the visual and literary representations of elite dress, excavated textiles, and sumptuary legislation, this book shows the extent to which desire for material things structured fashion. Nowhere was this desire for sensuous materials more evident than in the demand for silk textiles (fig. I.2).

There were few, if any, areas of Tang dynasty life in which concerns were not voiced about textiles, their production, and use. As the ultimate store of value for personal and imperial use, textiles had a declared centrality to the realization of power, wealth, and status. Textiles were thus guaranteed visibility, and have accordingly survived as

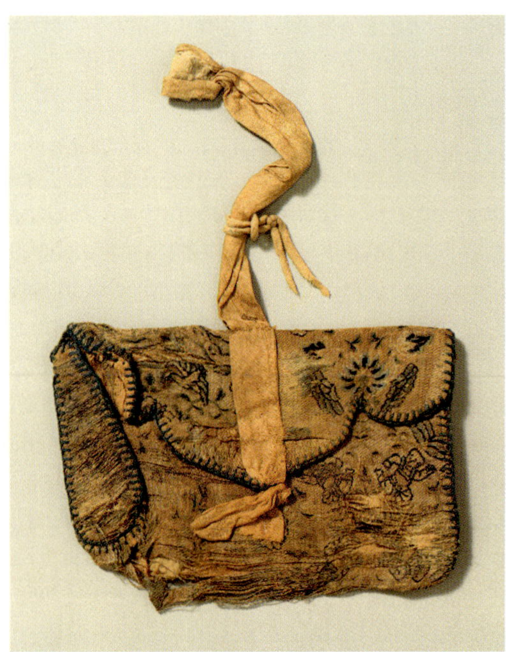

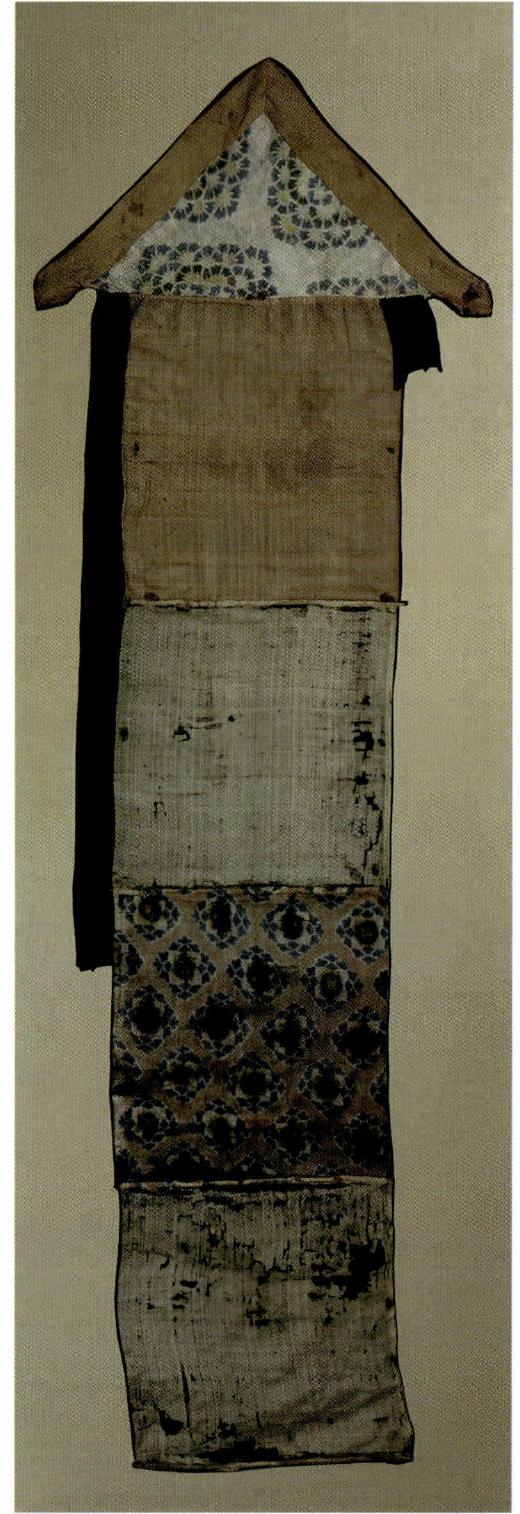

FIGURE I.3. (*Above*) Silk purse, eighth to ninth century. The outer textile is a weft-faced compound twill weave with a pattern of flora, birds, deer, and boys at play. H. 14.3 cm, W. 13.7 cm, D. 2.5 cm. Purchase, Eileen W. Bamberger Bequest, in memory of her husband, Max Bamberger, 1996, the Metropolitan Museum of Art, New York.

FIGURE I.4. (*Right*) Silk banner, ninth to tenth century. This is one of a group of eight clamp-resist dyed banners made up of textiles in the same arrangement, collected during Marc Aurel Stein's second Central Asian expedition (1906–8). Banners were an essential part of Buddhist worship: for the gaining of merit, for prayer, as a votive offering, or for use in ceremonial processions. As objects intended for display, the complexity and quality of the banner's decoration and material reflected both the donor's means and the banner's function. In this one, the banner face is a plain weave featuring clamp-resist dyed rosettes in lozenge shapes. The technique of clamp-resist dyeing was a late eighth-century Tang innovation. The other seven banners are part of the Victoria and Albert Museum's collection. H. 131.5 cm, W. 43.6 cm.; excavated from Cave 17, Mogao Grottoes. © Trustees of the British Museum.

fragments in elite tombs, as sutra wrappers and banners in the Dunhuang caves at the western frontiers of the empire discovered at the turn of the twentieth century, and as treasured artifacts in imperial repositories (fig. I.3).

Desire for such finery was regularly bound to the Tang women who inhabited the imperial court as princesses, consorts, dancers, and wives of ranking officials, and whose competition for sartorial distinction was derided as an agent of social disorder. The most infamous of these women was Yang Guifei (719–756), the darling of Emperor Xuanzong (r. 712–756), whose taste for sensuous pleasures cost him the throne. Xuanzong reportedly employed an additional seven hundred workers to weave and embroider for Yang Guifei and her retinue, while several hundred more craftsmen carved and molded precious ornaments. The prefects of Yangzhou, Yizhou, and Lingbiao even sought skilled workers to make rare things and unique clothing to offer to her.[10] Excoriated for causing the near ruin of the Tang ruling house, Yang Guifei and her fabled voluptuous body continued to dominate the popular imagination centuries after her death (fig. I.4).[11] Immortalized as an icon of the fallen empire, her plump frame and her desires came to embody an ideological narrative of the dynasty. Yang Guifei's legacy has much to reveal about the forces driving fashion in Tang China, as well as the inextricable relationship between women and material pleasures as propagated by male writers.

This book identifies and elaborates on two motors that powered fashion. One was the textile industry, which supplied an increasing variety of patterned, dyed, printed, and embroidered fabrics for clothing. Innovations in textiles were fueled by the imperial court's desire and need for silk, and by the expansion of frontiers that brought artisans into the empire. The growth of regional silk industries further stoked the desires for novel designs and weaves among disparate men and women. The other motor, interlinked to the first, was an ongoing engagement between Tang subjects and their visual and material world that I call aesthetic play.[12] The practices of fashion in the Tang were

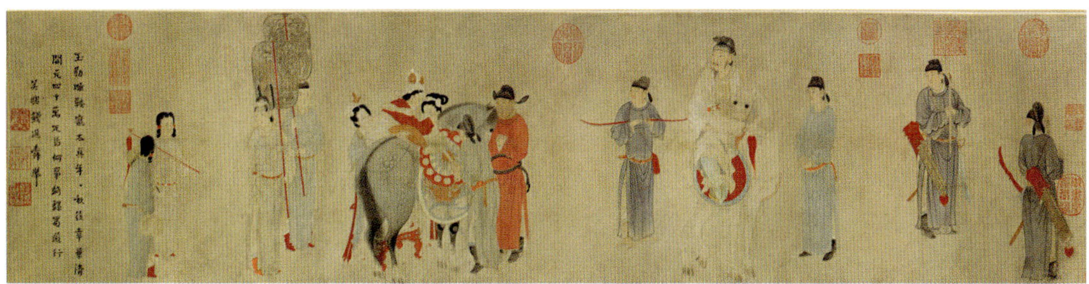

FIGURE I.5. Traditionally attributed to Qian Xuan (ca. 1235–before 1307), *Consort Yang Mounting a Horse*, Yuan-Ming dynasties, fourteenth century. The depiction of Yang Guifei mounting her horse with the aid of her attendants is an allusion to her legendary figure. Handscroll, ink and color on paper; H. 29.5 cm, L. 117 cm. Freer Gallery of Art and Arthur M. Sackler Gallery, Smithsonian Institution, Washington, DC: Purchase, Charles Lang Freer Endowment, F1957.14.

forms of aesthetic play, through which sensual desires were reconciled with formal social structures, and mediated by perception and the sensory experiences of the body.

The materiality of clothing mattered a great deal in this process of play: textiles shaped the body, decorated its surface, influenced posture and movement, and gave form to the body's mass.[13] Modifications in the fabrication, ornamentation, and shape of garments and the greater availability of such materials and accessories alongside changes in figural art contributed to an increasing awareness of style as historical. That is, through exploring the world visually and bodily, Tang men and women generated meaning from looking at others and being looked at, and gained a sense of being in a specific time and space. Aesthetic play thus describes an event engendered by the fundamental encounter between a self-body and the material world, which then produced acts of expression, such as practices of adornment and metaphoric thinking.

Dressing was a form of play that had to be brokered between a sumptuary protocol mired in classical ritual and a material world that offered novel silks and rare jewels for one to own and to assemble. Through play, a woman of the Tang court, for example, puts on nomadic dress (*hufu*) and ties her hair up into topknots. Having created this image of herself, she then uses it to represent her knowledge about styles of the cultural Other, as well as to demonstrate shared taste with and connections to the fellow women in her network. Aesthetic play involved experiencing the external world bodily and contemplatively. To dress or represent the world required looking at others as much as it entailed looking at the self. As this process recurs, in tandem with material change in the form of new fabrics, new modalities were created for self-presentation. Fashioning and image-making fostered presentations of a self that were constituted and reconstituted in relation to others, locking the "self" into an ongoing process of play. In this way, aesthetic play contributed to the experience of fashion as change.

To investigate fashion as a game of aesthetic play is to engage Tang writers, painters, weavers, and commentators as participants in the system of knowing and judging sartorial change. Silk artisans played through making, painters through fashioning, and writers through manipulating language. Membership in the fashion system did not require material possession and display, but instead demanded knowledge and awareness of changing styles. The two faces of Tang fashion, however, belonged to the palace woman and the poor weaver. This gendering of aesthetic play and material desire through the rival figures of the laboring woman weaver and the lavish palace woman was a discursive move by scholar-officials living during and after the Tang dynasty. By presenting women as the adherents—dressing in ways that did not accord with their station—and the victims—toiling away at the loom—of fashion, the critique emphasized the perilous frivolity of women rather than the weakness of the emperor to govern his empire—or the inappropriate aspirations of educated men. Tang writers positioned themselves as critics of a society upended by a widespread desire for play; in so doing, they sought to locate themselves outside the game. But their ability to document what they perceived to be a moral crisis required their participation in the fashion system as spectators. Poetic allusions and classical topoi constituted their materials for play, allowing them to articulate their enduring relevance to society.

What manifested in Tang China as the hallmarks of fashion—a desire for novelty and a game of imitation and emulation—was not borne by a controlled process of self-fashioning, but rather bespoke a continuous negotiation between the body, dress, and its social meanings. Appearances and their representation were thus intrinsic to social transformation.

ORGANIZATION

This study of fashion in Tang China is grounded in the wide range of textual, visual, and material sources of how people dressed and what others thought about it. Throughout the dynasty, there existed a tension between those who embraced the playful practice of dress and adornment and those who resisted the idea that sartorial practice should be linked to changing times rather than traditional values. The court continued to defend the notion that clothing should symbolize rank and status, even as its members violated the sumptuary codes. Examining these conflicting views within the broader economic, political, and aesthetic context of the Tang empire allows us to see how fashion was part of larger arguments about self, society, and history.

The shifting constellation of Tang fashion was made up of distinct but related events, which as a whole illuminate how practices of adornment were central to the lived experience of the empire. Organized thematically, this book first explores the symbiotic relationship between the politics of empire and the politics of fashion, and then turns to the forms of aesthetic play that characterized fashion as a meaning-making practice.

Chapter 1 sets the stage by describing key social and economic developments in Tang dynasty China through the rubrics of empire and cosmopolitanism. Imperial expansion and the subsequent building of a vastly expanded geographic and cultural sphere were as critical to fashion's development as the new materials and imported techniques themselves. Cultural and technological innovations, enabled by empire-building, brought men and women living in the inner empire into contact with a larger material world. Chapter 2 examines the discursive traditions in which sumptuary regulations were located to understand how and why sartorial practices mattered in Tang China. These laws are significant not as evidence of fashion's triumph over a static society, but for what they reveal about changes in the scale and technical infrastructure of cloth production that made luxury textiles increasingly available to those with the financial means to acquire them. The government's desire to uphold the status quo was at odds with its own imperialist ambitions: to pay for the conquest and maintenance of the extended frontier, the government pumped vast amounts of tax and tribute cloth into every outpost, paving the path of imperial glory with silk and hemp—and paving the way for fashion. By limiting the production and circulation of complex silks, while encouraging the making of plain textiles for tax, the government sought to maintain a monopoly over material resources that were critical to the empire's survival. In short, sumptuary laws emphasized the fundamental role of textile production in sustaining fashion and in preserving empire.

Shifting from received textual sources to the visual archive, chapter 3 shows how the garments of the Tang wardrobe were imagined to look on the body and explores the relationship between changes in pictorial style and fashion. Excavated murals and pottery figurines from Tang tombs provide the largest archive of visual evidence documenting the changes in the sartorial landscape. Representations of women and their dress reveal how women's clothing might have looked, but also how they were thought to look by the artisans and painters crafting the images. The visual archive provides important clues to understanding how perceptions of the female body and its relation to clothing changed over time. These changes are documented in tomb art and handscroll paintings, most notably in the creation of the Tang Beauty as a template to be fashioned, which show that artist–image makers depicted the relationship between a body and its adornment through the principle of aesthetic play.

Chapter 4 considers how increased silk production, enabled first by court investment and then further stimulated by the relocation of agriculture and commerce to the south in the latter half of the Tang, produced innovations in textile technology that propelled fashion to new heights. Records of tax and tribute goods show that the extension of silk weaving to the south led to new variations in the types of silks manufactured for elite consumption. Design of silk fabrics, expressed in considerations of color, motif, and scale, constituted the primary catalyst of sartorial change. Weavers, who were indispensable to the tax and tribute system, occupied a paramount position in the fashion system.

Chapter 5 surveys the basic lexicon for thinking and writing about fashion as change. The forging of a language of fashion developed in the poetry of the late eighth and ninth centuries, which linked forms of adornment to a desire for "keeping up with the times." The authors of these poems were the social critics of the era, for whom the desire to be current represented the emergence of a value system predicated on the accumulation of wealth and the obsolescence of things. In their critique, however, they—like the frivolous women they ridiculed—also embraced new styles to make their mark on the world. Male poets, through their emphasis on literary practice and style as the measure of value, were just as invested in claiming social distinction and contemporary relevance. The epilogue returns to the gendering of fashion in the Tang and the implications of this perpetuated legacy in the study of fashion and the history of Tang dynasty women. The key contention of this book is that fashion was central to the lives of all Tang subjects because the empire had placed cloth at the center of the structure of economic and moral values.

PART ONE

Traces

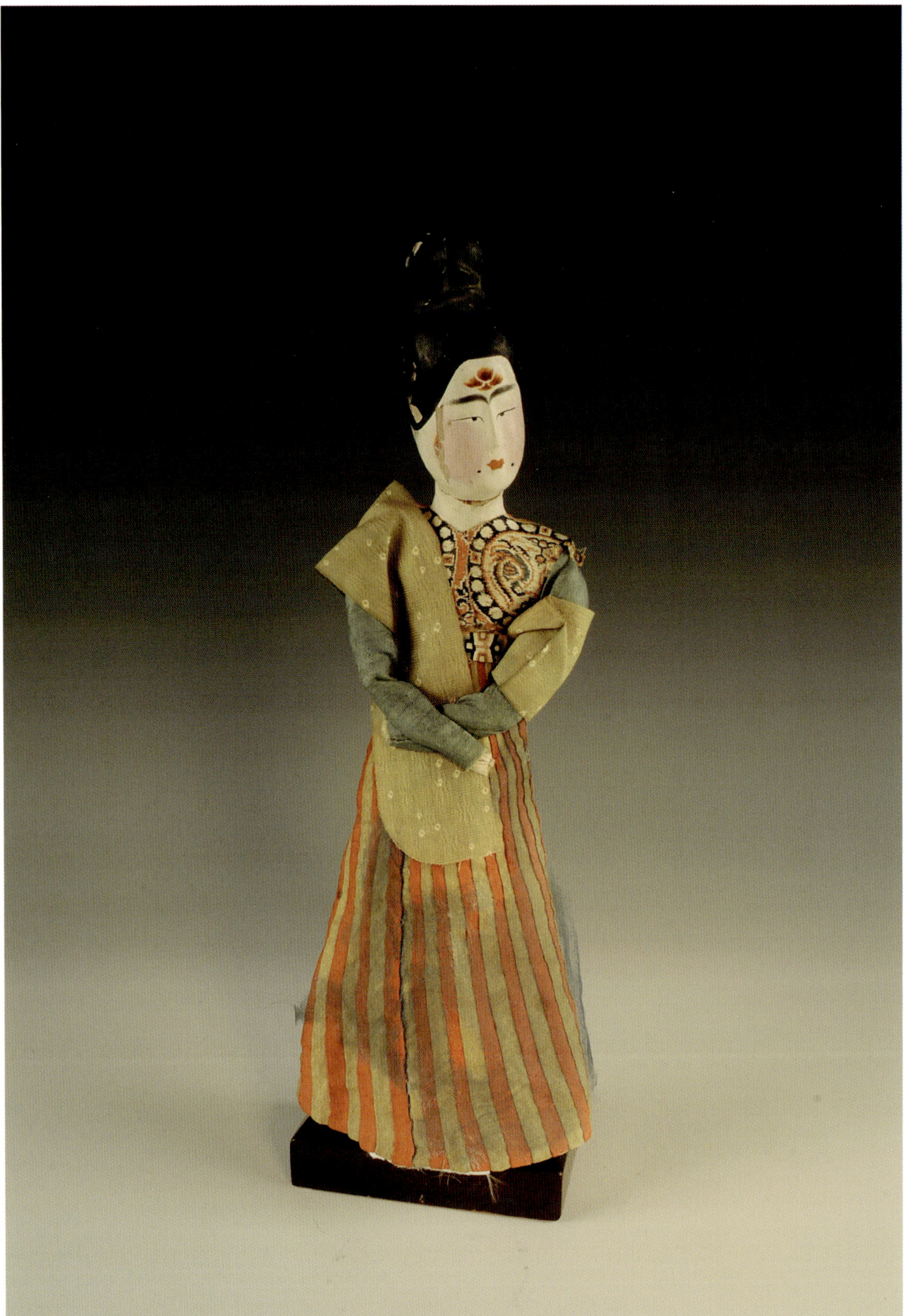

CHAPTER 1

History

CLOTH AND THE LOGICS OF COSMOPOLITAN EMPIRE

One of the central figures of this book is a late seventh-century figurine, a dancer whose silk sleeves contain many clues to the central place of textiles in economic life and fashion during the early Tang empire. Produced for the burial of Lady Qu of Turfan, an oasis city located along the Silk Road, the figurine was crafted in Chang'an (today's Xi'an) after her death in 688 (fig. 1.1).[1] Together with the other sumptuous figurines found in Lady Qu's tomb, this dancer traveled over a thousand miles from the capital to the western frontier of the empire to be buried in a joint tomb shared by Lady Qu's husband, Zhang Xiong (d. 633). Created to entertain Lady Qu in the afterlife, the figurine was dressed up in the fashionable silks of the late seventh century, including polychrome woven and resist-dyed silks. Nicknamed "Tang Barbie" by the Metropolitan Museum of Art staff when she was featured in the exhibition "China: Dawn of a Golden Age, 250–750" in 2004, the figurine is remarkable for her clothes, as well as for the materials that made up her body.[2]

FIGURE 1.1. Female dancer. The body is constructed from a wooden frame with paper padding, the head is formed from modeled clay and pigments, and the garments are composed of *jin* (a compound patterned weave; the term was used generally to refer to a wide range of polychrome fabrics in imperial China), tapestry, and resist-dyed silks. H. 29.5 cm. Excavated in 1973 from the tomb of Zhang Xiong and Lady Qu (dated 688), Astana, Turfan. Courtesy of Xinjiang Uyghur Autonomous Region Museum.

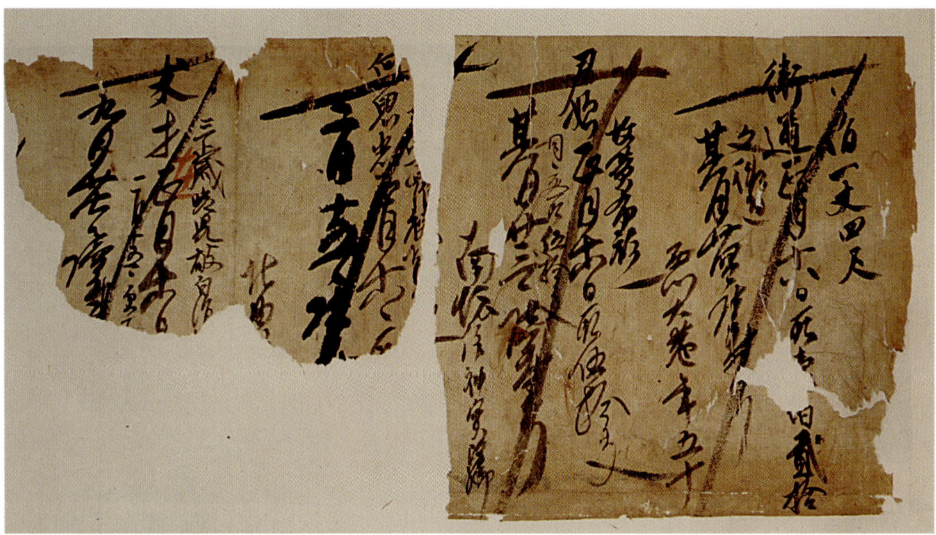

FIGURE 1.2. Pawnshop slip from the arms of the female dancer in figure 1.1. Excavated from the tomb of Zhang Xiong and Lady Qu, Astana, Turfan. Courtesy of Xinjiang Uyghur Autonomous Region Museum.

Standing at just under thirty centimeters, her frame was made from wood, while multiple slips of recycled paper were used in the construction of her arms. When she was unearthed in 1973, archaeologists discovered that the slips were from a pawnshop located in the capital.[3] Her paper arms are as instructive as her rich ensemble. The fifteen slips of paper unrolled from the figurine's arms document some fifty-four transactions at varying levels of completeness.[4] Each entry specified the item pawned, date, amount of money loaned, when the payment was returned, and the name and address of the borrower. Once the pawned item was reclaimed, a mark was made across the page (fig. 1.2). Twenty-nine names have survived, of which ten are assumed to have belonged to women.[5] Two of the borrowers were identified by occupation: one was a dyer and the other was a hairpin artisan. A few of the entries provide specific place-names, including Yanxing Gate, the southernmost gate on the east wall of the city, where Liu Niang lived (Borrower 14). Chen Guocan, a scholar of Turfan studies, has concluded that the pawnshop was established after 662, based on the record of He Qiniang's loan (Borrower 10), whose address was listed as the alley behind Guanyin Monastery. The monastery, located to the east of Xinchang Ward's south gate and just north of Yanxing Gate, was first founded in 582 as Linggan. Shut down in 621, the monastery was reopened four decades later as Guanyin Monastery. In 711, the monastery was renamed again to Qinglong.[6] This suggests that the accounts were drawn up between 662 and 688, before the pawnshop discarded the paper, selling them to a used paper vendor, who subsequently sold it to the workshop that made the figurine.

Pawnshops (*zhiku*) appear to have been a widespread business in the Tang capital.[7] The Taiping Princess (d. 713), the powerful and much-derided daughter of Empress Wu Zetian (ca. 624–705), reportedly operated pawnshops on her estate, and was famously ridiculed by her biographers for amassing a fortune that rivaled the imperial treasury. Following her death in 713, officials took several years to account for the all the wealth she had generated from her horses, sheep pastures, fields, and pawnshops.[8] By the ninth century, the money-lending business attracted sons of eminent families and officials alike. Upon learning of this, Emperor Wuzong (r. 840–846) decreed in 845 that they were forbidden to engage in the industry.[9] The pawnshop also figured in ninth-century fictional narratives about the capital. In "The Tale of Li Wa" (Li Wa zhuan), written by Bai Xingjian (776–826) in the ninth century, a young examination candidate falls for the eponymous courtesan shortly after his arrival in the capital. He successfully pursues her, takes up residence in the Li house, and within a year squanders his money. In one episode, the young examinee is deceived by Li Wa's "mother" into pawning some clothes for cash to purchase meat and wine for a sacrifice to the Spirit of the Bamboo Grove to pray for a son.[10] Soon after, having depleted his entire fortune, he is abandoned by Li Wa and her madam.

As narrated in "The Tale of Li Wa," clothes and more broadly, textiles, would have been the most common items pawned. Along with coins, textiles circulated as a standard of exchange and a preferred store of value within the multi-currency system of the Tang empire. All but two of the transactions recorded in the pawnshop slips of Lady Qu's figurine involved cloth, including ten skirts, several cut from twill-patterned silk (*ling*) and one resist-dyed, and ten shirts, most of which were of plain cloth. All of the garments were worn, some were even tattered, and few commanded high prices. The largest payment was made to Song Shoutian of the South Ward, who, in return for five items of clothing, received 1,800 coins. These documents offer a rare peek into the possessions that entered and departed the lives of Chang'an's residents and their wardrobes.[11] The body of this figurine, as well as her clothes and her travels, has much to reveal about the late seventh century.

Constructed from silk and paper, Lady Qu's tomb figurine embodies the broad themes that have long characterized the history of the Tang dynasty for modern scholars: empire and cosmopolitanism.[12] In the grand history of premodern China, the Tang dynasty stands out as an era marked by the cultural and technological innovations of an expansionist empire on the one end, and by the destruction of longstanding political institutions on the other. Paramount to the maintenance of empire—and the fashion system—was the movement of people and goods, first during an age of expanded frontiers and then during an era of political fragmentation. Nowhere was this mobility more apparent than in the excavated textiles woven for tax and elite use, which have brought to light the vast scale, complexity, and variation of cloth production under the Tang. Textiles, the prized materials of aesthetic play, were placed into circulation in local and distant markets by imperial expansion. The demand for and availability of sumptuous goods were coproduced by politics and fashion. Just as intensive textile production served the needs of empire, the desires of cosmopolitan Tang elites served craft technology and, in turn, the fashion system.

EMPIRE AND ITS FABRICATIONS

Lady Qu and Zhang Xiong's tomb was discovered in the burial grounds of Astana, a small village located near the ruins of the ancient city of Gaochang (today's Turfan).[13] The Gaochang Kingdom, established by the Qu clan around 502, governed a population that was predominantly Han Chinese and instituted political structures modeled after the Chinese state. Lady Qu herself was a member of the royal Qu clan of Gaochang. When Lady Qu's husband died in 633, Tang forces had yet to conquer the oasis. When she died in 688, Turfan had been under Tang rule for nearly half a century and her two sons had become officials in the bureaucracy. Her burial goods are a testament to how relations between center and periphery were constituted materially.

Since the late nineteenth century, Russian, German, British, Japanese, and Chinese scholars have led expeditions to the surrounding region in search of manuscripts and relics of the old Silk Road (fig. 1.3). Between 1959 and 1975, a team from the Xinjiang Uyghur Autonomous Region Museum and the Turfan Cultural Relics Preservation Office conducted further excavations at Astana and the adjacent grounds at Gaochang, resulting in the discovery of 456 tombs. The tombs date from the third century to the eighth century, spanning the Han (206 BCE–220) and Tang dynasties. Archaeologists have reconstituted nearly two thousand documents from over two hundred tombs.[14] Together with the textile finds, which comprised a significant portion of the excavated materials, the manuscripts provide a wealth of material about everyday life in the oasis. Discoveries from these tombs have served as evidence of the breadth of economic and cultural exchange along the Silk Road.

Coined in 1877 by German geographer Baron Ferdinand von Richthofen (1833–1905), *die Seidenstrasse* or "the Silk Road" has become a shorthand for the network of overland routes that linked Chang'an in the east to Antioch in the west.[15] In the Tang dynasty, the Silk Road stretched westward from Chang'an, across the Hexi Corridor, to the oasis-states along the Tarim Basin (map 1.1). At Dunhuang, a city situated in the western end of today's Gansu, travelers could take either the northern or southern route around the Taklamakan Desert into the Western Regions (Xiyu), which spanned Xinjiang, parts of modern-day Uzbekistan, and Tajikistan. The two routes converged in Kashgar, near the border of Tajikistan, from where travelers could continue to move west toward Samarqand or south toward India. From Samarqand, the route extended further west terminating in modern-day Turkey.

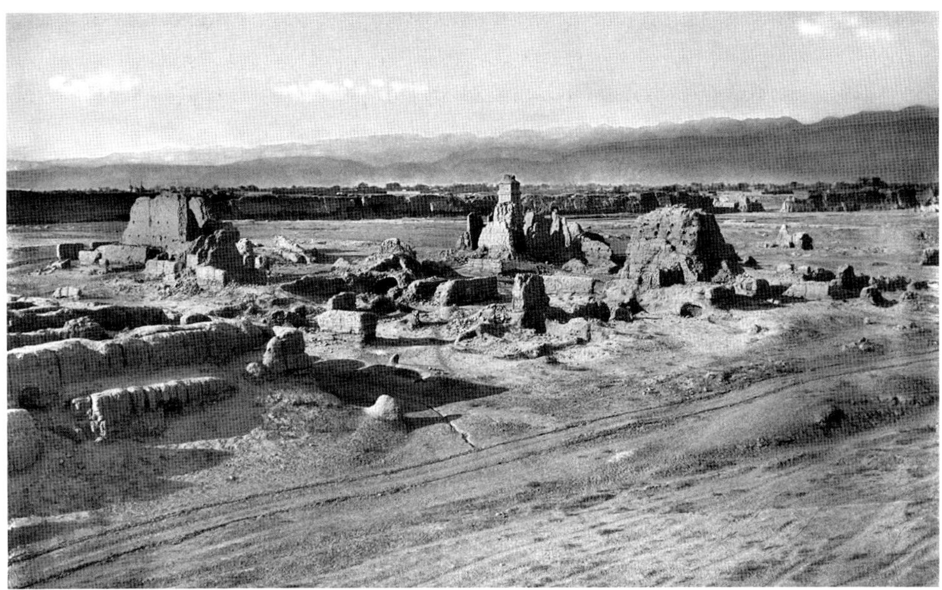

FIGURE 1.3. Ruins around Stupa Temple Gamma, Gaochang (Khocho). The German Turfan Expedition was initiated by Albert Grünwedel (1856–1935), who served as director of the Indian Department of the Museum für Völkerkunde. Between 1902 and 1914, four major expeditions to the Turfan Oasis and the northern Silk Road region were conducted under the leadership of Grünwedel and Albert von Le Coq (1860–1930). German Turfan Expedition Photographs, 1902–1914, Xinjiang, China, bpk / Museum für Asiatische Kunst, SMB (70231764).

The narrative beginning of the Silk Road was first documented in Sima Qian's (ca. 145–86 BCE) *Records of the Grand Scribe* (Shiji).[16] In 138 BCE, Emperor Wu (r. 140–87 BCE) of the Han dynasty (206 BCE–220) dispatched Zhang Qian (d. 113 BCE) on a mission to the Yuezhi people in the Fergana region of modern-day eastern Uzbekistan. Emperor Wu, concerned about the Xiongnu tribal confederation in the north, entrusted Zhang to persuade the Yuezhi into an alliance against their common enemy. During Zhang's journey through Xiongnu territory to the Yuezhi, he was captured and imprisoned for ten years. After his escape, he reached the land of the Yuezhi, but failed to secure an alliance. Zhang returned to court around 126 BCE and informed the emperor of all that he had heard and seen. His detailed report about the political system, military strength, local economy, and customs of the Western Regions laid the groundwork for Han expansion into the Hexi Corridor and further west.[17] As for Zhang himself, he was honored and ennobled as the Marquis of Bowang for "opening the road to foreign countries."[18] As the first written record of Han imperial interests in the Western Regions, Sima Qian's description of Zhang Qian's fateful embassy has become the locus classicus of Silk Road histories.[19]

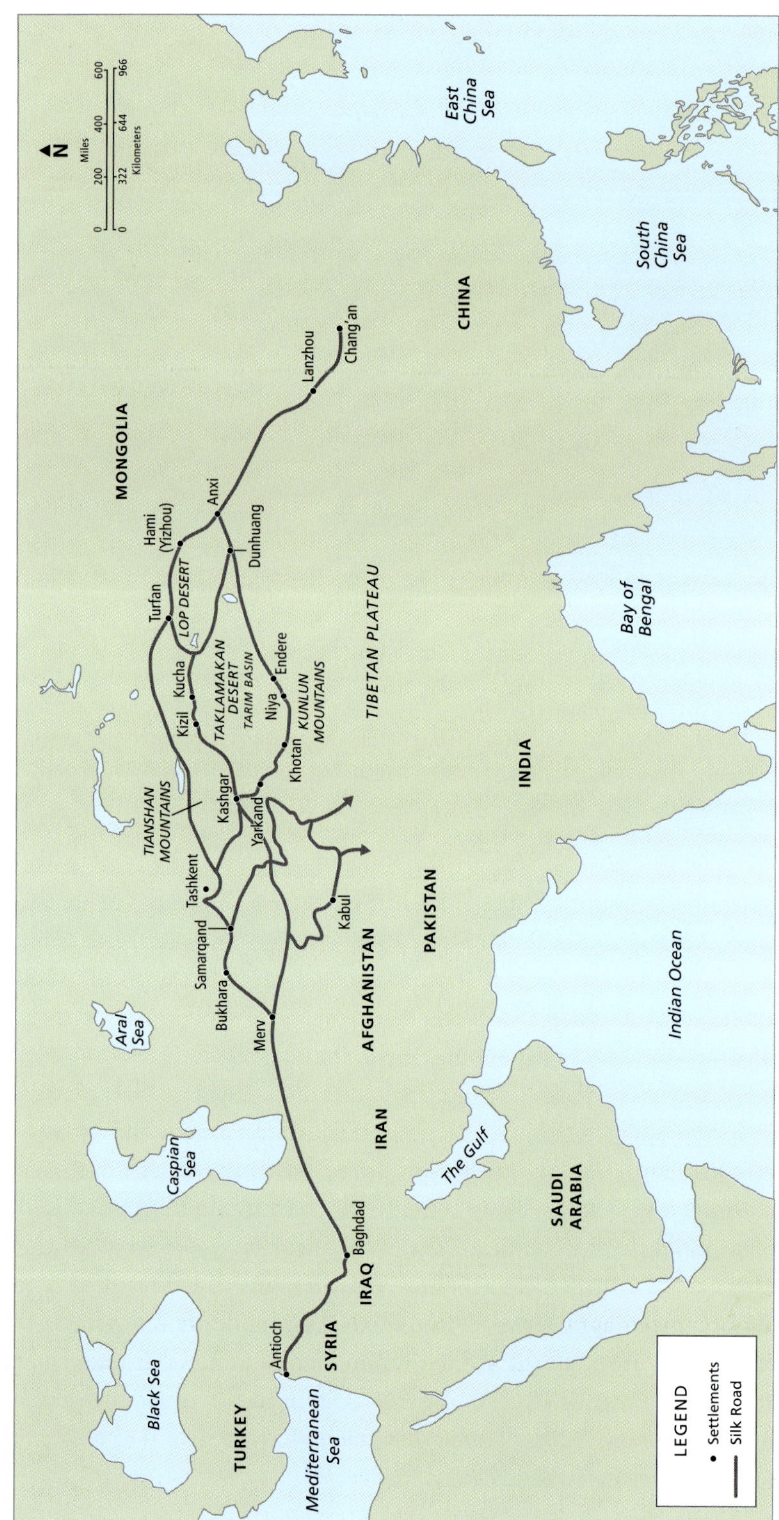

MAP 1.1. Routes along the Silk Road. Drawn by Jennifer Shontz.

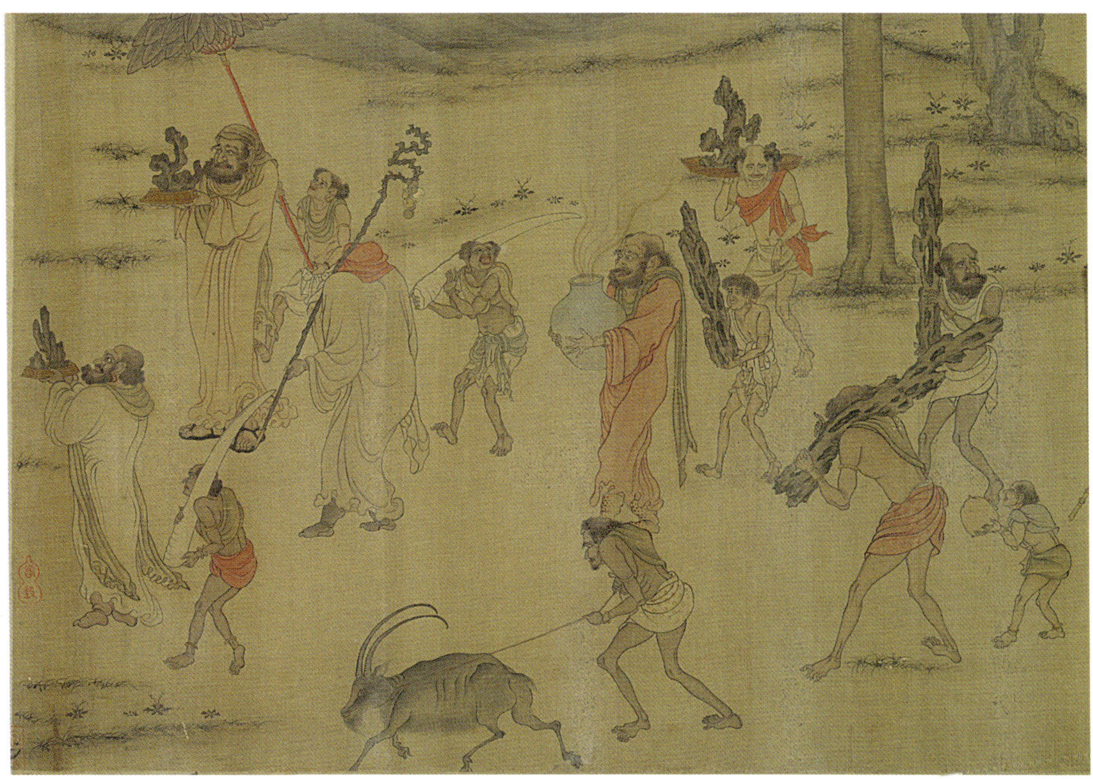

FIGURE 1.4. Traditionally attributed to Yan Liben (ca. 600–673), *Foreign Envoy with Tribute Bearers*. This painting depicts the procession of twenty-seven foreign tribute bearers in the capital of Chang'an in 631. Handscroll, ink and color on silk; H. 61.5 cm, W. 191.5 cm. The Collection of National Palace Museum, Taipei.

The fruit borne of Zhang's mission was the absorption of foreign peoples, labor, and goods into the tributary order. Sima Qian and Ban Gu (32–92 BCE) after him emphasized Emperor Wu's desire for rare and strange things, including "heavenly horses" (*tianma*) and grapes from Fergana, as Han imperialism's raison d'être.[20] Following Zhang's ennoblement, his fellow officers "all competed to submit reports that spoke of exotic marvels."[21] The dominant cultural paradigm of premodern China's political economy was the tribute system as delineated in canonical Confucian texts.[22] The model, derived from the legend of the ancient sage Yu, presented a centrally, hierarchically organized agrarian world order that symbolically reproduced the ruler's supreme authority through the annual submission of material tribute (*gong*). In the "Tribute of Yu" (Yu gong), Yu tamed a mythical deluge, restored order to the realm through the separation of land from water, and divided the world into nine provinces. He linked those regions to the political center through the institution of tribute, paid in locally produced agricultural goods (fig. 1.4). Yu then structured the world into five concentric zones that grew more barbaric the farther away they were from the central domain of the civilized ruler. This chapter preserved in the *Classic of Documents* (Shangshu), was included in the Confucian canon during the Han.[23] Such a worldview, with its neat division of people, land, and goods, may not have cohered with practice, but its representation of ruler and subject as tied together by material transactions and cultural influence became foundational to future ideological negotiations of imperial prerogative.

The Han dynasty's expansion of frontiers, bringing foreign lands, peoples, and goods into the tributary order, set the model for how successor dynasties envisioned and debated empire. During the four centuries following the fall of the Han, the lands of the former empire remained divided between the Northern and Southern dynasties (220–581). In the north, a succession of mixed Han Chinese and Xianbei (nomadic peoples who spoke either a Turkic or proto-Mongolic language) dynasties competed for power; while in the south, a series of Han Chinese regimes colonized the Yangzi River Valley region. In 589, the Sui dynasty successfully conquered the last of the Southern dynasties, reunified north and south, and revived the tributary system.[24] Under the second Sui emperor, the construction of a canal network that linked the northwest to the south, allowing for the provisioning of the political center with grain from south, completed the union.[25] The emperor's ambitions to extend Sui control into former Han territories in the northwest and into the Korean Peninsula, however, was ultimately disastrous as rebel forces sprouted up in the waning years of the dynasty.

One of these rebel forces was led by Li Yuan (566–635), born of mixed Han Chinese–Xianbei-Turkish ancestry, who belonged to a distinguished northern lineage that had dominated the northwest under the Sui.[26] In late 617, he marched on the Sui capital of Daxing. Six months later in the fifth month of 618, Li Yuan ascended the throne as Emperor Gaozu (r. 618–626) of the Tang dynasty. The dynasty was to endure for another three centuries, and would be commemorated alongside the Han dynasty as one of China's golden ages of empire.

Fashion was central to both the lived experience and memory of the Tang empire. The circulation of things and people, set into motion by the administrative and economic structures of Tang imperial expansion, spurred the desire for sensory pleasures offered by visual, material, and olfactory delights. Fashion's existence depended on this mutability of the material world as experienced and as epistemologically framed: the fluctuation of things was deeply entwined with the mobility of people across the social hierarchy and cultural boundaries that, in turn, fostered an understanding of style, innovation, and representation as tied to the progress of time. This development was crucial to the formulation of a historical self-consciousness. The administration of the Tang empire and its decline enabled fashion's rise as the dominant paradigm by which to engage with changes in both the material and social world.

Textual and archaeological sources confirm the indisputable fact that Tang imperialism increased the circulation of cloth across the empire. Collected as tax in kind and used as a form of currency, textiles were fundamental to all aspects of everyday life (fig. 1.5). Although the government began to mint new coins soon after the founding of the dynasty in 621, there was a continual shortage due to the high cost of manufacturing.[27] Silk was used for a variety of transactions: as payment for land and slaves, as imperial tribute from key silk-producing regions, and distributed as gifts in diplomatic exchanges by the emperor, or as payment for horses.[28] Armies also relied on textiles to purchase grain and equipment for its troops, and to pay their salaries. Shipments of textiles to the Western Regions swelled in the early eighth century as the frontier armies grew. By glutting the frontier with textiles from the interior, the Tang government linked the periphery to the imperial center through a shared demand and desire for silk and hemp.

Like their Sui predecessors, the early Tang emperors sought to expand the frontiers of their empire into old Han territories. The first century of Tang rule was marked by the aggressive imperialism of Emperor Taizong (r. 626–649) and his successor, Gaozong (r. 649–83). In 630, Taizong mobilized forces that conquered the Eastern Türks in

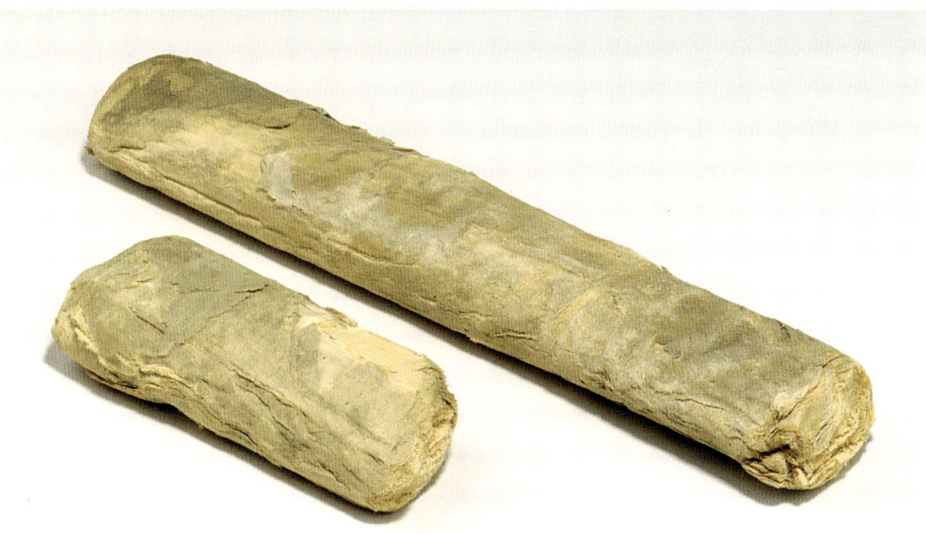

FIGURE 1.5. Bolt of plain white silk weave, broken into two sections (third to fourth century CE). This bolt was used as currency. L. 33.2 cm, W 5.8 cm. Excavated in Loulan, Xinjiang. © Trustees of the British Museum.

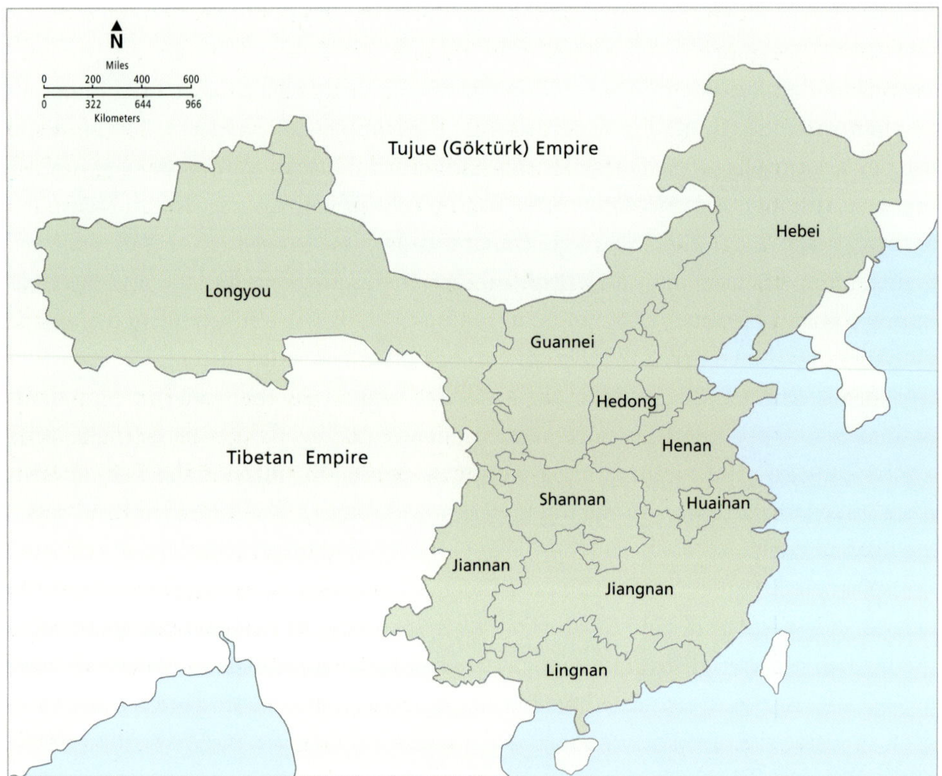

MAP 1.2. The Ten Circuits (*dao*), ca. 740. Under Emperor Gaozu, the empire was divided into a system of prefectures (*zhou*), governed by prefects (*cishi*). Each prefecture was separated further into counties (*xian*), headed by county magistrates (*ling*). Gaozu's successor, Emperor Taizong, carved up the empire afresh into ten administrative regions called circuits (*dao*): Guannei and Longyou in the northwest; Hedong and Hebei in the northeast; Henan, Huainan, Shannan, Jiannan in central China; and Jiangnan and Lingnan in the south. Developed from Robert Hartwell, "Hartwell China Historical GIS," 2015, doi:10.7910/DVN/29302, Harvard Dataverse, V2. Drawn by Jennifer Shontz.

Mongolia, a key victory in the recently enthroned emperor's bid for hegemonic dominance in the region.[29] The independent oasis kingdoms in the Tarim Basin were incorporated into the administrative, military, taxation, and tribute structures of his empire by the end of his reign. Under Gaozong, the Tang empire subjugated the Western Türk Khanate in 659 and Koguryŏ Kingdom in 668. A vast empire was taking shape and at its widest extent, encompassed regions of northern Korea, northern Vietnam, Mongolia, and Eastern Turkestan (map 1.2). These successful military campaigns into the Inner Asia borderlands secured the northern frontiers and facilitated the operation of local and long-distance trade, such as the market in funerary goods that brought Lady Qu's dancer from Chang'an to Turfan.[30]

Turfan was the first of the oasis states to fall to Taizong's armies.[31] Situated on the trade route along the northern edge of the Taklamakan Desert, Turfan was a key trading post and home to a majority of Han Chinese settlers and a substantial minority of Sogdians from the Eastern Iranian-speaking lands around Samarqand.[32] Beginning in the fifth century, Han Chinese migrants had settled in Turfan in increasing numbers and displaced the original inhabitants. Sogdians, whose homeland stretched between the two rivers, Amu Darya and Syr Darya (Transoxiana), were active traders on the Silk Road. In the seventh and eighth centuries, diaspora communities of Sogdians, fleeing the invading armies of the Umayyad Caliphate (661–750), settled in Turfan and Dunhuang, or moved further east into Chang'an and Luoyang.[33]

After Turfan was absorbed into the empire, the region was renamed Xizhou and was divided into five sub-prefectures, Gaochang, Jiaohe, Luzhong, Puchang, and Tianshan, under the Anxi protectorate. The expansionist regime organized foreign populations into "loose-rein area commands and prefectures" (*jimi fuzhou*). "Loose rein" was a metaphorical term invented by officials during the Han dynasty to refer to the empire's "loose" administrative strategies toward foreign peoples.[34] As the Tang continued to extend its borders, foreigners living along the frontier were grouped into loose-reign prefectures and area commands administered by their own chieftains. At the pinnacle of the Tang empire, there existed 856 loose-reign area commands and prefectures, most of them established between the reign of Emperor Taizong and the An Lushan Rebellion (755–763).[35] The creation of two parallel systems of governance sought to fix the boundaries between an inner and outer realm. In practice, however, the distinction was not always clear.

In strategic frontier areas like Turfan, loose-rein prefectures were placed under the supervision of protectorates (*duhu fu*), headed by chieftains, whose titles were hereditary and could be passed on within their clans.[36] By the early eighth century, a border of protectorates ran along the Tang's frontiers. The Anxi protectorate was followed by the establishment of Anbei (over the Uyghurs and other Tiele nomads), Andong (over the Khitan, Xi, and Koguryŏ), and Annam (over non-Chinese in what is now Vietnam).[37] The Tang military recruited non-Chinese soldiers to serve in frontier armies stationed in the borderlands and with increasing numbers as shifting power structures in the northwest brought instability to the Western Regions under the reign of Emperor Xuanzong (r. 712–756).[38] Along with the protectorates, these forces functioned as border defense and administration. To support the administration of these regions was an infrastructure of outpost garrisons, expeditionary armies, and networks of signal beacons and watch-posts. An empire-wide communication system that involved a postal relay service, long-distance relay horses, and travel permit checkpoints was also critical to the movement of information, people, and goods. Under the Anxi administration, four garrisons of Kucha, Kashgar, Khotan, and Karashahr were set up to maintain order in the newly conquered regions. Subjugation of these oasis cities broadened Tang imperial presence to almost all of the Tarim Basin by the late seventh century.

The primary function of the local administration was to collect revenue. The Tang continued the system of state-controlled land tenure, known as "equal-field" (*juntian*), in which the state distributed land to taxable subjects for the duration of their working life and according to their household size.[39] Lands planted with mulberry trees (*sangtian*) needed continuous cultivation to remain productive and thus belonged to a separate category of "hereditary land" (*shiye*). In return for a hundred-*mu* grant of land, each household was obligated to pay taxes and labor services. The system of direct taxation was referred to by the names of its three component taxes: *zu* (grain), *yong* (corvée labor), and *diao* (tax in kind). Each head of household was responsible for two piculs of grain and twenty days of corvée duty, which could be avoided by a payment in silk or hemp cloth. In silk-producing regions, tax in kind amounted to two decafeet of silk (approximately 62.2 cm) and three ounces of silk floss, while in areas that did not produce silk, two decafeet plus an additional five feet (approximately 77.7 cm) of hemp cloth and three pounds of hemp yarn were levied on the household.[40] The tax structure tied the work of men and women to the financial administration of empire and also functioned as a vehicle for social reproduction. Even though the official unit of taxation was the individual adult male (*ding*), the unit envisaged was the household of a married couple. Grain and cloth reinforced the ideal gender division of labor, "men till, women weave" (*nangeng nüzhi*), that had been canonized in the Han dynasty compilation, *Record of Rites* (Liji).[41] Through taxation, the Tang government not only institutionalized women's work (*nügong*) as the making of cloth, but more significantly, fixed gender difference to the division of labor.

The basic terms of the equal-field system and the *zu-yong-diao* taxes were stipulated in *Land Statutes* (Tianling) and *Taxation Statutes* (Fuyi ling) of 624, and enforced by specific sanctions written into the *Tang Code* (Tang lü), promulgated that same year.[42] During the founding year of the dynasty, an imperial commission was appointed to compile a comprehensive code of penal and administrative law. In 624, the commission presented the *Code* with the new set of administrative statues and ordinances to Gaozu. Between 624 and 737, the *Statutes* and *Code* underwent revision several times.[43] Effective implementation of the equal-field system and the collection of tax payments required that magistrates keep accurate and up-to-date registers of the local population. From the beginning, the system suffered from vagrancy and migration, the accumulation of land by wealthy and powerful families, and inconsistent local administration.[44]

Although the compilers of *New Standard History of the Tang* (Xin Tangshu) claimed that the loose-rein prefectures generally did not send tribute, taxes, and census records to the Board of Finance (Hubu), fragments of the *Taxation Statutes* have suggested otherwise.[45] Article six of the *Statutes* dated to 624 specified that, "All foreigners who have submitted and been registered should be divided into nine grades," and taxed accordingly. Tax payments from registered foreigners were assessed in goods produced in their local economies, such as sheep for the pastoral nomads.[46] In an article dating to 737, tax obligations of foreigners and Han Chinese were differentiated, such that the taxes and labor services of the various foreign tribes in the frontier and distant prefectures were to be estimated according to circumstances, and "need not be made identical with those of the Chinese [*huaxia*] themselves."[47] It is unclear if these foreigners were registered in the regular prefectures or if they lived in loose-rein areas.

Archaeological discoveries from the frontier have challenged the received historical sources on the social, political, and economic organization of the Tang empire, showing that the administrative reach of the central administration was greater than described in the official histories. Documents from Turfan confirm that the Tang government imposed the full range of its institutional system in Xizhou, including household registration for the equal-field system of land distribution, tax collection, and compulsory labor service.[48] The only evidence that the equal-field system existed, other than as policy, comes from the household registers and tax-textiles excavated at Turfan and Dunhuang. Each district (*xian*) was expected to compile household registers once every three years, based on household declarations (*shoushi*), in which each household head reported every year the head-count of his household and the ages of his family members, as well as his land-holdings. Household declarations were employed for levying tax duties and assigning corvée labor, as well as in the preparation of tax registers sent to the Department of Public Revenue (Duzhi) each year.[49] Surviving household declarations date from the fifth through tenth centuries, of which many coincide with Tang rule (640–769), and yield a more nuanced yet fragmentary look into the working lives of Turfan's residents. Women engaged in a wide range of activities outside of the home: as *da nü*, female household heads who shouldered tax-paying obligations, as guarantors on contracts, and as founders of Buddhist lay associations.[50]

The success of early Tang military campaigns was secured by the enormous quantities of plain and decorated textiles woven for payments to armies, negotiations with rival local powers, and salaries for officials dispatched to serve in the newly conquered territories. In a document found in the Kizil Grottoes, an artisan from Kucha was commissioned to weave a hundred feet of cloth to be cut into spring clothing for the local long-service troops (*jian'er*). Kucha, located west of Turfan on the northern edge of the Taklamakan Desert, was one of the four garrisons under the Anxi administration. The constant demand for cloth for uniforms and currency generated by Tang military expansion resulted in a more closely integrated center and periphery.[51] Like their counterparts in the inner empire, weavers, soldiers, and officials on the frontier were bound to the Tang court by cloth.

Tax-textiles discovered in the Astana graveyard during the 1972–73 excavations have provided material evidence for the large estimates of cloth shipped to the frontier found in textual sources, including *Compendium of Administrative Law of the Six Divisions*

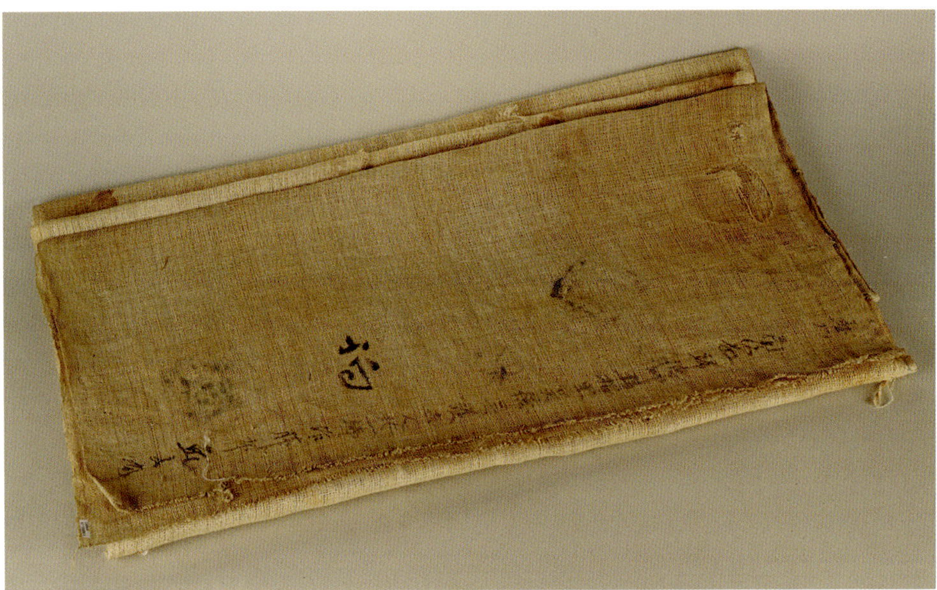

FIGURE 1.6. Tax textiles (*yongdiao bu*). Excavated from Astana, Turfan. Courtesy of Xinjiang Uyghur Autonomous Region Museum.

(Da Tang liudian), completed under the direction of Li Linfu (d. 752) in 738, and Du You's (735–812) *Comprehensive Institutions* (Tongdian), presented in 801 (fig. 1.6). The *Compendium* recorded that "coarse" (*gu*) goods were dispatched to the frontier: "All of the finest goods of nearby areas are to be presented to the imperial court, and will be designated for the Court of the Imperial Granaries, Court of the Imperial Treasury, Directorate for the Palace Buildings and Directorate for Imperial Manufactures. Goods of coarse quality and from the more distant areas are to be presented to the armies, and will be designated as goods for the frontier armies and for the various area commands and protectorates."[52] Grain and textiles made up the bulk of the "goods," which were inspected by local officials and marked with an inscription and a seal. A study of twenty tax-textiles found in Turfan, of which seventeen pieces were woven from hemp and three were from silk yarn, has shown how cloth from the inner empire was used and reused. All twenty pieces had been cut from the original bolt of fabric, except for one length of twill silk (*ling*) dated to 710.[53] Many of the hemp pieces were made into bed-sheets and one of the silk pieces, a red plain-weave tabby, had been cut into a skirt for a wooden figurine.

Among the tax-textiles were two burial shrouds with handwritten inscriptions that identified their place of production as Wuzhou prefecture in Zhejiang.[54] Woven hemp pieces with complete inscriptions give the date, place name, type of textile, the taxpayer's name, and quantity paid. Some of the inscriptions were composed after inspection, while a few recorded the transfer of the cloth to the central government. The inscriptions reveal that the tax cloths arrived in Turfan from six inner provinces: Henan, Shannan East, Shannan West, Jiangnan East, Jiangnan West, and Jiannan. These Tang provinces roughly correspond to the modern-day provinces of Henan, Shaanxi, Hubei, Hunan, Sichuan, Jiangsu and Zhejiang. All of the dated textiles were produced before the Tianbao era (742–756) of Emperor Xuanzong's reign. Twelve of the textiles have stamped impressions of one or more official seals in either red or black ink, except in the case of one fragment that displayed one seal in red and two in black (72TAM191:107). Red seals marked the inspection of tax cloth at the county and prefectural level, while black seals documented approval by the Treasury of the Left (Zuocang Shu), the office responsible for storage of tax income.[55] The textiles had been submitted in fulfillment of a range of tax obligations: annual tax cloth (*diaobu*), cloth paid in lieu of corvée service (*yongdiao bu* or *yongbu*), and transport tax cloth (*jiaobu*).[56] From a directive issued to the Department of Treasury (Jinbu) in 679, it is likely that all of the tax textiles were shipped from the Liangzhou Area Command (in today's Gansu), which served as the collection point for both the Hexi Corridor and the Western Regions, and transported on postal-station relay horses.[57]

In the following decades, instability on the frontier, changes in military organization, the creation of more military commands, and the concomitant surge in soldiers resulted in a sharp escalation of military costs. According to the *Old Standard History of the Tang* (Jiu Tangshu), annual expenditures for troops increased six-fold during the reign of Emperor Xuanzong: "There is a total of 490,000 men in the frontier armies with more than 80,000 cavalry horses. The annual expenditure is: 10.2 million bolts of silk and hemp [*piduan*] to clothe them, 1.9 million piculs to feed them, adding up to a total of 12.1 million [cloth and grain]. Before the Kaiyuan reign [713–741], border costs did not exceed two million per year. In the mid-Tianbao reign [742–756] the number reached this figure [of 12.1 million]."[58] What impelled this profound upswing in military costs was Xuanzong's reorganization of the Tang military from a militia model (*fubing*), in which conscripted soldiers were responsible for their own weapons, equipment, and rations, to professional armies composed entirely of long-service troops in 737.[59]

According to Du You's report on state finances during the Tianbao era in *Comprehensive Institutions*, average military expenditures included 12.6 million units of cloth, silk floss, strings of cash, and piculs of grain.[60] He calculated a total of 3.6 million bolts of tax cloth were set aside to purchase grain; 5.2 million bolts were marked for clothing provisions; 2.1 million (no unit given) for special payments; and 1.9 million piculs for additional rations. Based on Du's estimate of the Department of Public Revenue average intake of 57 million units of cloth, silk floss, strings of cash, and piculs of grain, military expenses amounted to over 20 percent of the state's total income.[61] Of the 10.2 million bolts of silk and cloth, the frontier commands received 2.7 million. The old transport of tax cloth by relay horses had to be abandoned in favor of a new system that appointed two officials, a journey overseer (*xinggang*) and a shipment supervisor (*guandian*), to travel to Liangzhou and pick up the loads.[62] These officials frequently hired merchants and commoners as transport convoys.

Vast quantities of cloth coursed through the frontier economies as currency and as fabric for clothing and furnishings. The influx of plain, patterned, and dyed twill and tabby silks influenced local textile production and bound local material needs to the imperial center, creating incentives for long-distance textile trade. A Turfan market register of prices dated to 742 list stalls of silk merchants selling bolts of plain-weave silks (*juan*), monochrome plain-weave silks dyed in purple (*manzi*) and scarlet (*manfei*), and weft-ribbed plain-weave silk (*shi*) from Henan.[63] A separate category of "colorful silk" vendors (*caibo hang*) sold *ling*-twill silks woven with threads of spun silk floss, dyed in either purple or scarlet, by the foot. These textiles were among numerous goods for sale, including local produce and livestock, and imports from further west.

Like the body of Lady Qu's dancer, the register is an artifact of Tang imperialism. They demonstrate that while military force conquered land and people, material exchanges were key to imperial success. The circulation of weft-ribbed plain-weave silk (*shi*) from Henan to Turfan, similar to the decorated silks worn by Lady Qu's dancer, forged coherence across the empire. Not only did textiles connect the frontier regions to the administrative and economic structures of the Tang empire, they also communicated a cohesive imperial identity through their universal use as currency, clothing, and furnishings for homes and temples. The market register further highlights how desire for colorful and patterned silks from the interior sustained, and even increased, the value of cloth. The pursuit of sumptuous, sensuous, and aesthetic pleasures across short and long distances was pivotal to the experience of the cosmopolitan empire and its decline.

For fashion to exist as a meaning-making practice, in which its participants could draw from their material world and perceive themselves as belonging to a particular time and place, attention to the traffic in things was essential. Imperial expansion facilitated both the discovery of and knowledge about novel pleasures across the empire, but most prominently in the capital. In Tang Chang'an, residents and travelers fell into a multitude of sensory entanglements that affirmed their perception of the metropolis as the city of fashion.

FASHION'S CAPITAL: CHANG'AN

One of the borrowers recorded in the pawnshop slips of Lady Qu's dancer was Liu Niang (Borrower 14), who lived near Yanxing Gate. North of Yanxing Gate, the southernmost gate on the east wall of Chang'an, was the East Central residential area and the East Market (map 1.3). During Taizong's reign, this district was home to several

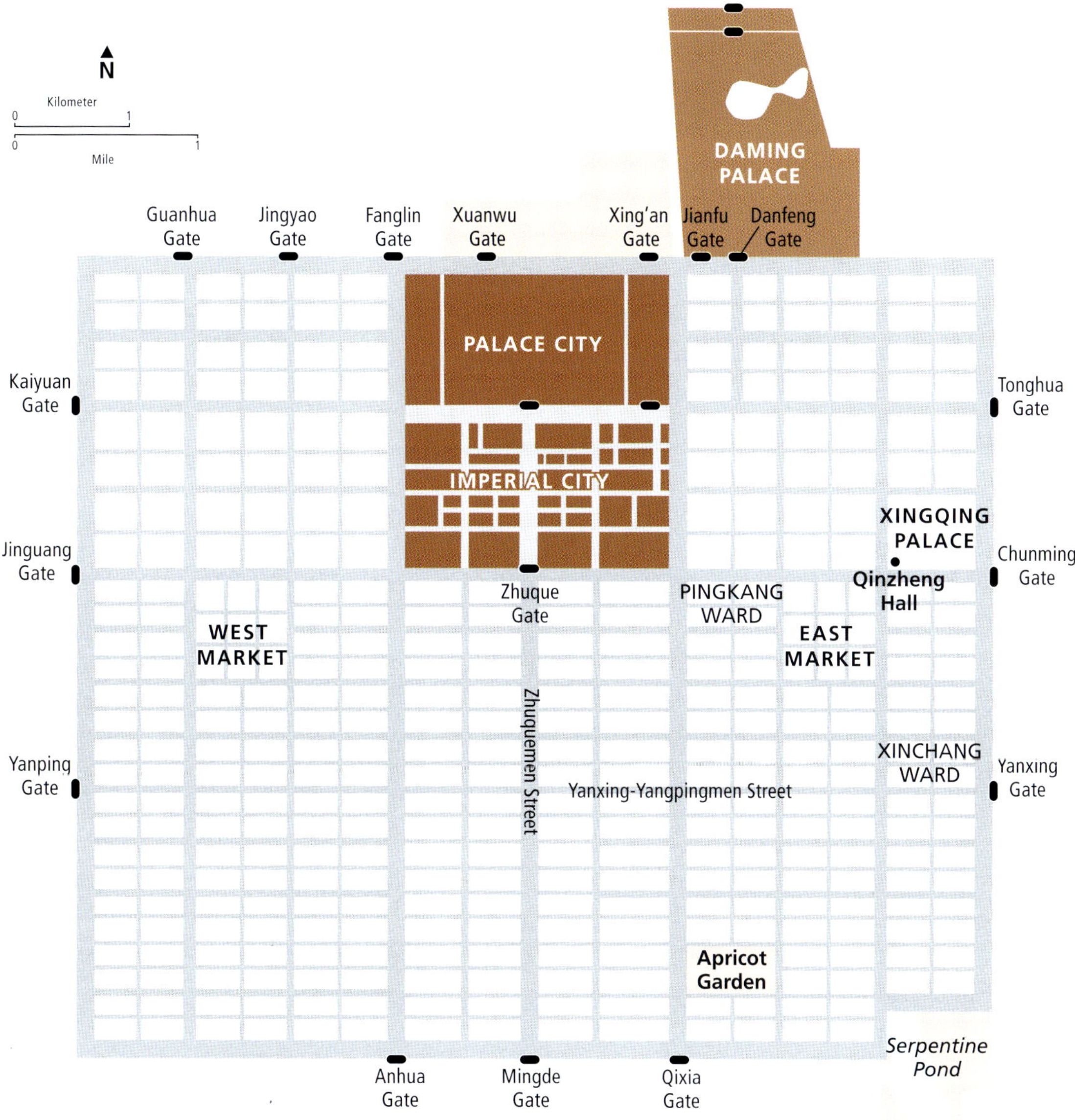

MAP 1.3. Tang Chang'an. Drawn by Jennifer Shontz.

prominent royal and official residents, including Hou Junji (d. 643), commander of the expeditionary force that captured Turfan.[64] It is, perhaps, more likely that Liu Niang lived south of the gate, in the Southeast residential quarter of the city. One of the smallest residential areas in Chang'an, the southeast corner was a popular destination among residents and travelers, who enjoyed Apricot Garden (Xingyuan) and Serpentine Pond (Qujiang Chi).

Yanxing Gate opened onto Yanxing-Yanpingmen Street, which stretched across to Yanping Gate on the west wall. Moving west on Yanxing-Yanpingmen Street and crossing the central north-south thoroughfare, Zhuquemen Street, we arrive in the West Central sector of the city. The West Market, in contrast to its counterpart in the east, was a bustling place where goods and peoples from beyond the inner empire could be found. The residential wards were less popular among the Chang'an elite.

Chang'an was a monumental capital city, extending about 9.7 kilometers from east to west and about 8.6 kilometers from north to south.[65] The city's layout was formed by twenty-five streets, comprising fourteen latitudinal (north-south) and eleven longitudinal streets (east-west) that divided the city into an axially symmetrical plan of over one hundred blocks. Residential wards constituted almost ninety percent of the city. Each ward was split into four quadrants by a central crossroad and each road led to one of four gates.[66] The four quadrants were further separated into sixteen subsections by a set of intersecting alleyways (*xiang*). Centrally situated in the northernmost part of Chang'an were the Palace City (*gongcheng*) and Imperial City (*huangcheng*), home to the imperial court and its bureaucracy, respectively. According to archaeologist Ma Dezhi, the Palace City measured approximately 2,820 meters wide by 1,492 meters, while the Imperial City was slightly larger at 2,820 meters by 1,844 meters.[67]

Situated in the Wei River valley, Chang'an was built in the old heartland of the Qin dynasty (221–206 BCE) and the Western Han (206 BCE–8 CE). In 582, about a year after the Sui came into power, Emperor Wen (r. 581–604) issued an edict calling for the construction of a new capital, Daxing, southeast of Han Chang'an. Beginning with the Palace City, the builders moved outward, adding the Imperial City and then the outer wall. By early 583, Daxing was complete. In 605, the second Sui ruler, Emperor Yang (r. 604–617), founded a secondary capital at Luoyang, east of Chang'an. The Tang inherited Daxing as its primary capital. In 634, Taizong launched the construction of a new palace, Daming Palace, northeast of the Palace City. Taizong intended the palace to serve as Gaozu's residence, but following his death a year later, construction was halted. Gaozong revived the project and the palace was finished in 663. Daming Palace was surpassed by Xuanzong's contribution, Xingqing Palace, built southeast of the Palace City in 714.[68] Daming Palace, however, remained the main imperial residence until it was destroyed during the rebellions that ravaged the city at the end of the dynasty.[69]

Under Emperor Xuanzong, Chang'an reached its apex of population growth. At the beginning of the Tianbao era, the capital prefecture area was home to 362,921 households and a population of nearly two million distributed among twenty-three counties with over 825,000 registered urban residents.[70] The addition of unregistered residents, including the royal family, palace attendants, foreigners, and monastic communities, who eluded the census, would have raised the total urban population to about one million. Located at the eastern terminus of the Silk Road, Chang'an had a diverse population, markets brimming with local and foreign goods, and a rich offering of entertainment and religious life.

Sound was a distinctive feature of Chang'an life. At dawn, drumbeats rang from the Chengtian Gate at the southern entrance of the Palace City, signaling the beginning of the day for city residents. At noon, three hundred drumbeats pulsated across the eastern and western sectors of the city, announcing the opening of the two markets. Before sunset, the markets were closed after the sounding of another three hundred strokes.[71] Once daylight ended, the drum at Chengtian Gate was struck four hundred times before the gate was locked. The drum was beaten again six hundred times, alerting the guards to close the gates to the residential wards. Between dusk and dawn, city residents were required by law to stay within their wards. A strict curfew forbade movement across the city after dark and violators were punishable by a flogging of twenty strokes.[72]

The central government restricted all commerce to the official markets (*shi*), established in the metropolitan centers of Chang'an and Luoyang, as well as in prefectural and county cities.[73] Shops were forbidden in residential areas. The Office for the Marketplaces of the Two Capitals, subordinate to the Court of Treasury (Taifu Si), administered the markets in both Chang'an and Luoyang. The Court of Treasury fixed the prices and standards of quality of goods traded in the markets, and required the registration of all shops and merchants. A market director (*shiling*) maintained a staff of two assistant directors (*cheng*), one managing clerk (*lushi*), three storekeepers (*fu*) responsible for the government warehouse, seven scribes (*shi*), and one clerk (*zhanggu*). In principle, these officials classified all the goods for sale, according to quality, into three grades. These values determined the price standards of the market and were updated every ten days. The Turfan market register of 742 is the only evidence that these procedures were implemented.

Excavation of Tang Chang'an's architectural remains between 1959 and 1962 has yielded rough estimates of the sizes of the two markets.[74] The West Market measured approximately 1031 meters (north-to-south) by 927 meters, and was split into nine sections by two sets of streets running north-south and east-west. Each section was further divided into four lanes according to *hang*, or category of trade.[75] Attempts to find the lane of coat shops (*dayi hang*), the location of which had been transmitted through historical sources, instead produced a large collection of hair ornaments, pearls, and agate. The East Market, which was not as well preserved, measured about 1000 meters by 924 meters, slightly smaller than its counterpart in the west.[76] Whereas the West Market attracted a large population of foreign merchants and sold a great variety of local and imported goods, the East Market was less bustling.[77]

Tales of the capital's landscape, residents, and urban delights have been transmitted via a variety of literary and historical sources, consisting of a fragmentary eighth-century source, *New Records of the Two Capitals* (Liangjing xinji) by Wei Shu (d. 757), *Gazetteer of Chang'an* (Chang'an zhi) compiled by Song Minqiu (1019–1079) in the Northern Song dynasty (960–1126), and *A Study of Urban Wards in the Two Tang Capitals* (Tang liangjing chengfang kao) by the Qing dynasty (1644–1912) scholar, Xu Song (1781–1848).[78] Poems, tales (*chuanqi*), jottings (*biji*), and miscellaneous accounts (*zashi*) form an additional archive of urban experience. Taizong himself expressed his experience of the capital in a series of ten poems, entitled, "The Imperial Capital: Ten Poems, with Preface."[79] A prolific writer, Taizong's composition was the first work on the Tang imperial capital. Each of the ten poems detailed an activity at a different site inside the imperial residence, from gazing "upon ancient scriptures and canons" in the Chongwen Academy (Poem Two) to the bewitching "gauzes and silks from Zhaoyang Palace" in the inner quarters of the palace (Poem Nine).[80] Drawing on these sources, historians have branded Tang Chang'an the "most cosmopolitan city in the world."[81] Archaeological excavations of the capital, neighboring imperial tombs, and steles have helped to uphold the view of Tang Chang'an as cosmopolitan.[82]

One of the first discoveries was a limestone monument serendipitously uncovered in the final decades of the Ming dynasty (1368–1644).[83] Standing about three meters high, the stone bore a long eulogistic inscription in both Chinese and Syriac, composed by a Nestorian (Jingjiao) priest named Jingjing, or Adam in Syriac, while a local official named Lu Xiuyan served as his calligrapher (fig. 1.7).[84] In the top register of the slab was the title "Stele Commemorating the Dissemination in the Middle Kingdom of the Illustrious Teaching [i.e., Nestorian Christianity] of the Great Qin" engraved in in large characters. According to the inscription, the priest Aluoben traveled from Da Qin (which loosely referred to the Roman empire), arrived in Chang'an in 635, and in 638 received permission from Emperor Taizong to proselytize Nestorian teachings.

With the support of Taizong and his successors, scriptures were translated into Chinese and monasteries were founded in Chang'an and in other cities. The stele, erected in 781, concluded with a celebratory ode, a short biography of Jingjing (Adam), and a list of sixty-seven priests in Syriac and sixty-one in Chinese. Historian Rong Xinjiang has identified one of the listed clergy as Li Su (741–817), who was a descendant of the Sasanid royal family and held an official post as a court astronomer.[85] On the stele, he was listed by his courtesy name (*zi*), Wenzhen, and his Syriac name Luqa. Now housed in the Forest of Steles Museum in Xi'an, the Nestorian stele is indeed a commemorative monument, one that celebrated the depth of Tang cosmopolitanism.[86]

The gathering of people, things and their display that made Chang'an cosmopolitan also established the city as the center of the Tang fashion system. Display and spectacle were central to the experience of the capital, as transmitted through writings about the literary elite. Chang'an, however, was also populated by a wide range of residents and itinerant groups who achieved visibility through the making and possession of material things. These communities located in the capital and in the greater empire were as

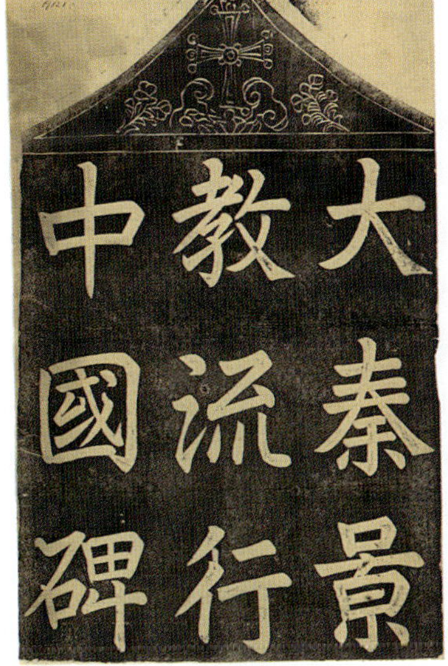

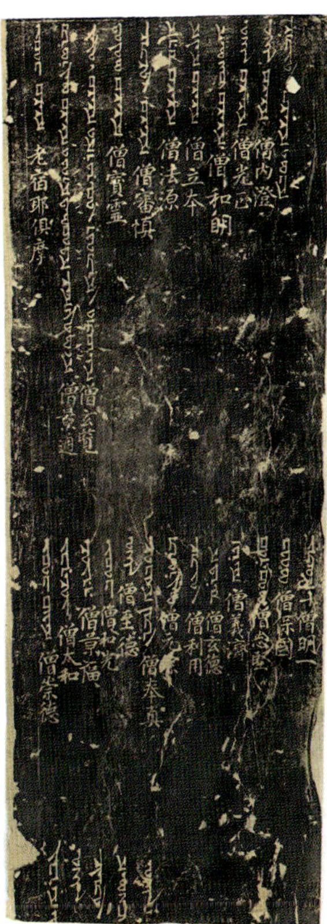

FIGURE 1.7. Ink rubbing taken from the Nestorian Stele, nineteenth century. The original stele was erected in 781 near Chang'an. (*Left*) The top of the monument reads "Stele Commemorating the Dissemination in the Middle Kingdom of the Illustrious Teaching [i.e., Nestorian Christianity] of the Great Qin" (Da Qin Jingjiao liuxing Zhongguo bei). H. 45 cm, W. 25 cm. (*Center*) The main text describes doctrinal matters and narrates the arrival of Nestorian teachings in the Chinese empire and its protection under the Tang emperors. H. 182 cm, W. 84.5 cm. (*Right*) A side column lists names of monks in Syriac and Chinese. H. 62.5 cm, W. 23 cm. Ink-squeeze rubbing, paper. Courtesy of Penn Museum, image nos. 255596, 255597, and 255602.

critical as their literate counterparts to the fashion system. The archaeological record reveals the significant role that material and technological exchanges had in driving aesthetic play.

CRAFTING COSMOPOLITANISM

Seventh- and eighth-century census registers from Turfan and Dunhuang show a minority of Sogdians lived and worked among the majority Han population as farmers and artisans. They also settled in Chang'an, Luoyang, and many other cities in the north between the sixth and eighth centuries.[87] The excavation of six tombs of a single Sogdian family, the prominent Shi lineage, in the southern suburbs of Guyuan (in today's Ningxia) has been key to the reconstruction of how Sogdians integrated into Sui and Tang society.[88] The funerary epitaphs claim that the family migrated to the Hexi Corridor in the fifth century and later settled in the northwestern borderland prefecture of Yuanzhou, near modern Guyuan. Shi Shewu (d. 610), a member of the fourth generation, became a military officer of the Sui. His elder son, Shi Hedan (d. 669) began his career as a local official under the Sui, but defected to the Tang around 618 and became a translator in the Imperial Secretariat. During his forty-year tenure as a court translator, he lived in a mansion near the Imperial City and the Western Market. After he retired, he moved to Yuanzhou and died at the age of eighty-six. Several of the tombs had been looted, but among the remaining artifacts were Sasanian coins and replicas of Byzantine coins that confirmed the family's connections to their western origins.[89]

Sogdian migrants, like the Shi family, traveled eastward toward the Sui-Tang court to pursue a range of livelihoods away from their homeland. One of the most celebrated Sogdians in the Sui court was He Chou (540–620), a master craftsman-official skilled in weaving *bosi* (Sasanian-Persian)-style silks, who also produced a kind of glass from green glaze used for ceramics.[90] Six-lobed greenish glass cups were recovered from three of the Shi family tombs, including Shi Hedan and his brother, Shi Daoluo (d. 658). The cups are remarkable not only for their form, but also the high lead oxide content of the glass.[91] High lead oxide content produced a translucent color finish typical of the hand-blown glassware of Sasanian or Eastern Roman empire origin. Migrant craftsmen from Central Asia likely transmitted these techniques for glassmaking into China during the fifth centuries.[92] The cups of the Shi family, which takes its form from Sasanian silverware, are representative of the influence foreign makers exerted on local craft culture.

The most significant, and substantial, proof of cultural and technological exchange was uncovered in Hejiacun, or Hejia village, a suburb of modern Xi'an. In 1970, local archaeologists dug up two clay pots and one silver pot that contained all together over one thousand pieces. Over two hundred gold and silver vessels and nearly five hundred gold, silver, and copper coins were buried alongside precious gems and medicines.[93] A consensus about the date and owner has yet to be reached by scholars.[94] A more pressing question deals with the identity and location of the artisans who made the vessels. Some of the treasure, such as the seven sapphires, two rubies, one topaz, and six agates, were imported as none of these stones could be mined within the Tang empire. The three octagonal cups, the gilt silver bowl with fourteen fluted lobes, and the eight-petal silver cup with gilt designs of women and hunters, in contrast, resist easy stylistic and typological identification.

The eight-petal silver cup features a composition of four scenes of women at leisure alternating with four scenes of men hunting on the outer body of the cup (fig. 1.8).

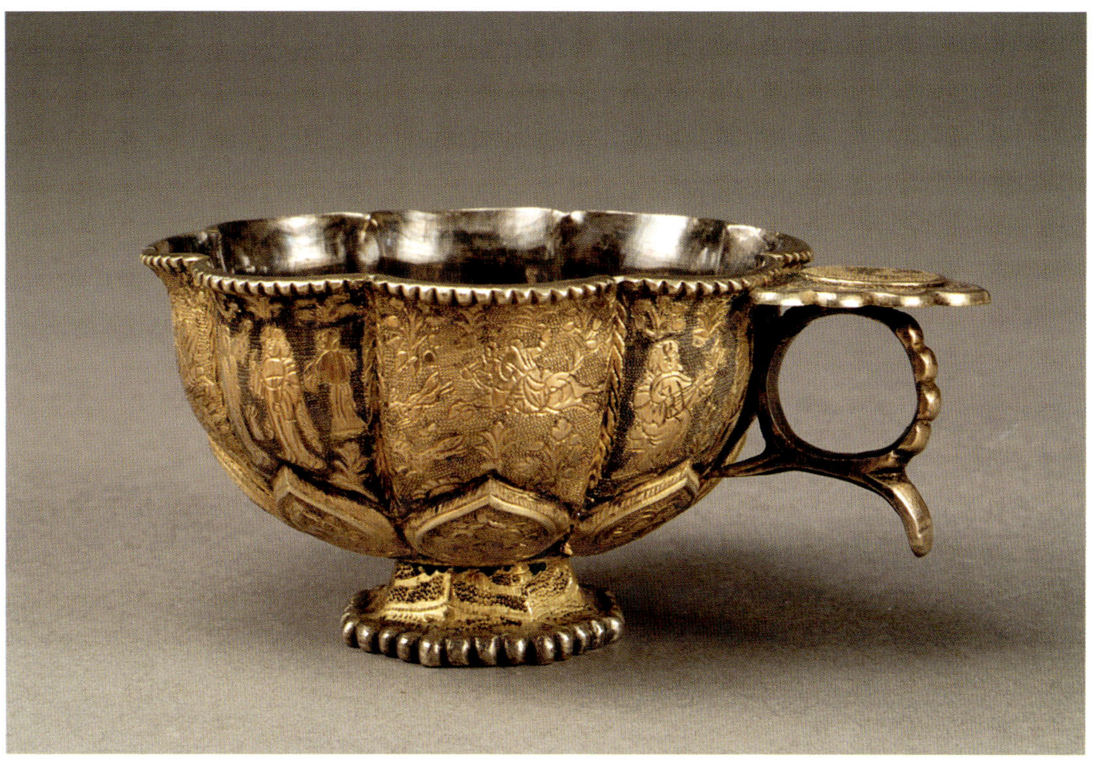

FIGURE 1.8. Eight-petal cup with pearl-border rim and thumb rest, eighth century. The exterior features alternating scenes of hunters on horseback and women dancing and playing instruments. Gilt silver; H. 4.5 cm. Excavated in 1970 in Hejiacun, south of Xi'an, Shaanxi Province. Courtesy of Shaanxi History Museum.

The striking resemblance to murals of palace women and hunting scenes found in Tang imperial tombs places the cup within the aesthetic milieu of eighth-century Tang elites, and suggests a local production site. The depiction of women idling among stylized flora and fauna on the cup, as well as their shapely figures, the drapery of their garments, and their coiffures, further supports a Tang provenance. The cup's form, however, puts it in closer relation to Sogdian or Sasanian silverware. The eight-petal shape of the cup is further embellished with a ring of beads along the mouth and the base. This decorative flourish is also found on the handle, above which sits a triangular thumb rest with a design of a deer. A raised layer of eight lotus petals radiates up from the base of the cup, highlighting the exquisite repoussé and chasing technique of the craftsmen.[95] The eight-petal cup together with the other treasures of the Hejiacun hoard constituted a microcosm of the glorious Tang empire: a miscellany of materials, motifs, and techniques of ambiguous origins consolidated in a single site, a veritable melting pot, or three.

The artifacts of empire, as seen in the eight-petal cup or Shi Hedan's glass bowl, may not reveal specific details about their makers or even their owners. What can be gleaned from these objects is the profound space that aesthetic and technical exchanges occupied in the Tang empire. Desire for such luxury prompted innovations found across metalwork, ceramics, and especially silk textiles of the era.[96]

Cosmopolitanism as experienced in Chang'an, for the emperor and commoner alike, was mediated by material desires and sensory experiences of the body. Unlike the gilt motifs of palace women on the eight-petal cup, music and dance expanded the reach of sensory pleasures to a broader community living in, or traveling through, the capital. Images of musicians and dancers at imperial banquets and at the gatherings of Tang literati elites abound in the visual, material, and literary archive. Emperor Xuanzong's banquets at his Xingqing Palace were among the most decadent. At these extravagant festivities, which took place at Qinzheng Hall (Qinzheng Lou), Xuanzong treated foreign chiefs to performances by hundreds of palace women. Attired in embroidered, polychrome silks and adorned with pearls and kingfisher ornaments, these women emerged from behind the curtains and danced to tunes such as "Smashing the Ranks," "Great Peace," and "Superior Origin." The emperor would then call in the elephants or horses to perform for his guests. Qinzheng Hall was also where the emperor celebrated the Lantern Festival on the fifteenth day of the first month during his reign. Late at night, he sent the palace women to sing and dance in front of the Hall to entertain the city's residents.[97] Recollections of the Tang capital are peppered with descriptions of such sights and amusements, many associated with the reign of Xuanzong.

THE MATERIALS OF MEMORY

The checkerboard layout of Chang'an, with its clearly demarcated spaces and enclosed markets policed by street inspectors (*jieshi*) and patrol inspectors (*xunshi*), would suggest that the city was a place of limited amusement. Literary sources, culled from stories and poems about wine shops, gardens, and courtesans reveal a different kind of city. Shops and night markets within residential wards existed throughout the Tang dynasty, and warehouse inns and taverns (*didian*), as well as hostels and way stations, were distributed across in the city in multiple residential areas.[98] Other popular businesses that popped up outside of the two markets were wine shops and street stalls selling breads, including the highly sought-after *hubing* or foreign flatbread.

Wine shops, commonly run by Sogdians, proliferated in the southeast sector of the city, near Serpentine Pond. Of the Tang literati who frequented these establishments, Li Bai (701–762), extoled the pleasures of drinking wine served by beautiful girls of the Western Regions. In his poem "A Goblet of Wine," Li describes playing music, while enjoying his drink with a friend:

Playing a zither made from Longmen green paulownia,
As I strum the strings and grip the frets, I drink with you, my friend
Scarlet appears to be turning green, our faces begin to redden.
The *hu* girl, pretty as a flower
Standing by the brazier, she laughs like a spring breeze
Laughs like a spring breeze, dances in a luo-gauze dress
My friend, you are not drunk, how can you return home![99]

The scene portrayed in Li Bai's poem—warm wine served by a pretty foreign girl, who dances in a dress made from translucent silk, accompanied by the strumming of a zither—encapsulates the multiple forms of seductive and intoxicating enticements that could be found in Chang'an. Officials living in exile from the court, as in the case of the prolific Bai Juyi (772–846), longed for the sounds of the capital (*jingdu sheng*) strummed by a charming pipa player.[100] Nostalgia for the capital rhapsodized in poetic and epistolary exchanges between friends have survived as valuable stores of memory about the principal place of pleasure in Chang'an. Pleasure was a sensory experience, one that was produced by the aesthetic enjoyment of luxury things.

Like the beating of the drums that echoed the rhythms of the city, music and dance were essential to the sensory experience of the capital. Tang elites retained their own musicians to perform at their private estates. In 706, an imperial edict limited mid-ranking officials to no more than three female musicians (*nüyue*), while those with high-ranking positions were entitled to an entire troupe. Toward the end of Xuangzong's reign, the restriction was lifted and all officials, military commissioners, and prefects in the provinces were allowed to keep an unlimited number of musicians in their homes.[101] The government's regulation of musical entertainment extended into Chang'an's pleasure quarters, which in the ninth century found a home in Pingkang Ward, requiring the registration of all entertainers.[102] Their registration allowed officials, and newly minted degree-holders, to summon these women to perform at banquets. Also called the Northern Ward (Beili), Pingkang was a residential ward in the eastern sector of the city, adjacent to the market, and home to a large number of elites.[103] The courtesan households, clustered in three lanes in the northeast corner of the ward, occupied a critical position in the geographies of pleasure, commerce, and gendered relations that attracted scores of young examination candidates to Chang'an each year. The performance culture that emerged from this enclosure, jotted down in the ninth-century collection *Anecdotes from the Northern Ward* (Beili zhi) by Sun Qi (fl. 884), has been key to understanding the courtesan's role in the formation of a collective male literati identity.[104]

Within the palace, two separate bureaus planned the performance of music and dance: the Imperial Music Office (Taiyue Shu) was in charge of official banquets, state sacrifices, and other ceremonies; the Inner Court Entertainment Bureau (Nei Jiaofang), meanwhile, housed and trained palace musicians in more popular-style entertainment.[105] An avid lover of music and dance, Xuanzong expanded the palace music institutions and promoted new styles at court, especially tunes from the Western Regions.[106] In addition to dancing elephants and rhinoceroses, Xuanzong maintained a troupe of dancing horses. One year, the emperor decreed that four hundred horses be trained to dance. After the horses had been successfully taught, Xuanzong commanded that they be elegantly dressed (*yi yi wenxiu*); they were thus outfitted with saddles of gold and silver, their manes and forelocks adorned with pearls and jades (fig. 1.9). At every Thousand-Autumn Festival (Qianqiu Jie), Xuanzong ordered the horses to dance below Qinzheng Hall to the tune, "Music for the Upturned Cup" (Qingbei yue).[107] This famous anecdote, recorded in the ninth-century compilation, *Miscellaneous Records of Emperor Minghuang* (Minghuang zalu), became both a poetic trope in narratives about the excesses of Xuanzong's reign, and a prominent motif in art and crafts.

Surviving accounts of things seen, heard, and touched rested on the skillful deployment of both words and materials to render the ephemeral meaningful. One of the prized findings in the Hejiacun hoard was a silver flask, the form of which was adapted from the shape of leather bags commonly strapped to saddles (fig. 1.10). Each side of the flask displays a dancing horse holding a cup in his mouth, a reference to the "Tune of the Upturned Cup." This wine flask is an example of how materials mattered as chronicles of ephemera—such as the palace gossip about Xuanzong's troupe of nimble horses—that once cast, could be enjoyed again. Either documented on paper in the form of a poem or hammered in metal, memory itself was figured as material thing. The mutual constitution of person and of thing was central to fashion in Tang China, both in the term's root sense as "to make" or "to shape" and in its formulation here as aesthetic play.[108] Clothes, in particular, were enduring bearers of meaning and affect that worked upon the individual body-self, negotiated social relations, and transmitted historical information.

Luxury goods like the flask, and the many other splendid treasures found in Hejiacun, were objects that performed similar rhetorical and social functions.[109] Valued for the complexity of their production and the cost of materials, luxury items functioned as registers of aesthetic pleasures. The silver flask served as a mnemonic object that sparked musings about the once glorious reign of Emperor Xuanzong. Recollections of extravagant things—and the experiences they document—were central to narrating political and social change in Tang China.

The hit song of Xuanzong's reign was not "Tune of the Upturned Cup," but instead "Tune of Rainbow Skirts and Feather Robes" (Nishang yuyi qu), immortalized in two epic poems by Bai Juyi. The origins of the song and its accompanying dance became a central event in the romance between Xuanzong, who was credited for the composition, and Yang Guifei, who famously performed the dance.[110] In the first poem, "Song

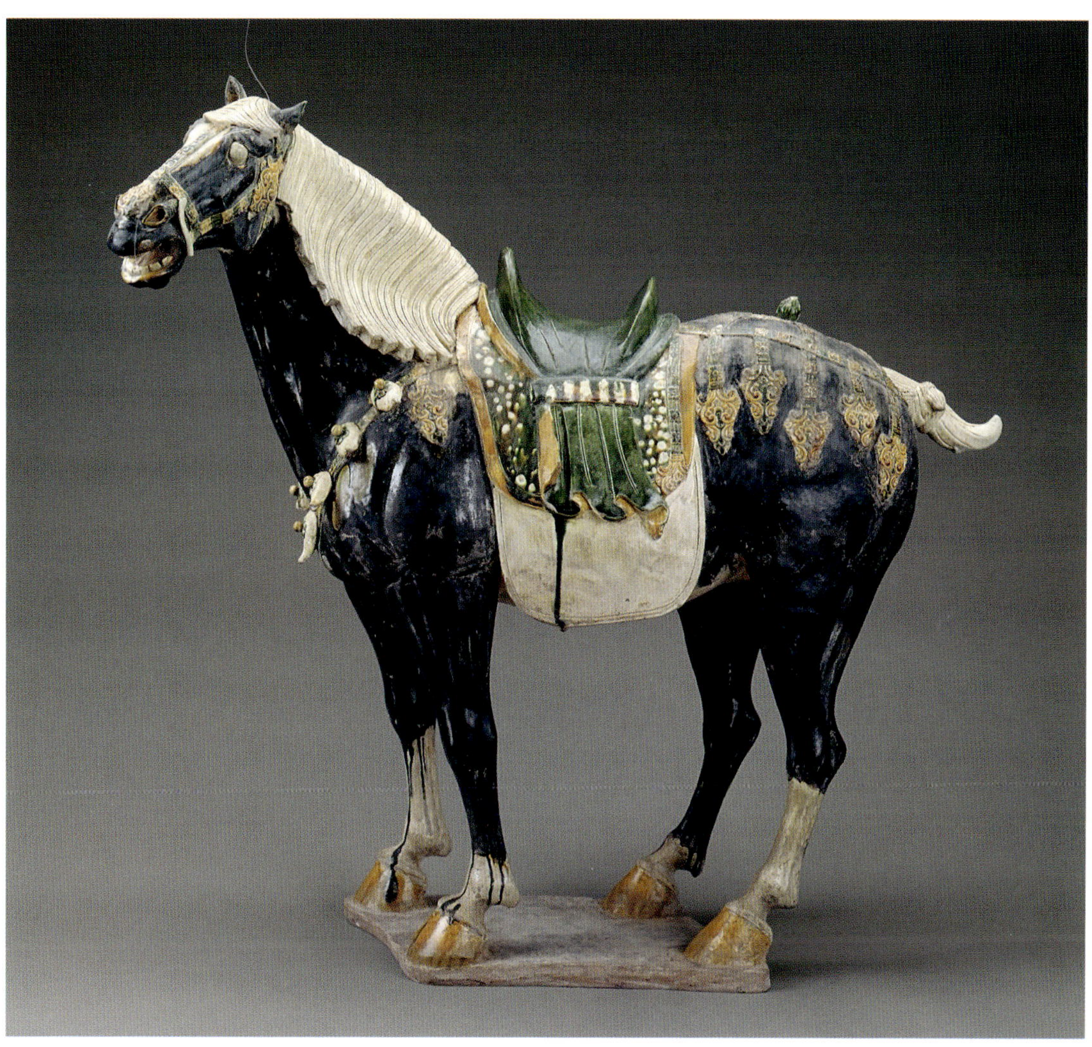

FIGURE 1.9. *Sancai*-glazed earthenware horse, early eighth century. This caparisoned black horse is outfitted in elaborate trappings and sports a green saddle, thus indicating its use in ceremonial parades. Black pottery horses are very rare. The most famous example sold at Sotheby's London in December 1989 for an astounding GBP 3.74 million. H. 73 cm. John Gardner Coolidge Collection, Photograph © 2019 Museum of Fine Arts, Boston.

of Everlasting Regret" (Changhen ge), Bai took Xuanzong's beloved Yang Guifei and enshrined her in the rainbow skirt and feather robe with the line, "From Yuyang, the beating of drums shook the earth / And smashed the tune of 'Rainbow Skirts, Feather Robes.'"[111] What had once brought the emperor so much satisfaction was also the source of his downfall. As the rebels stormed through the empire, the tune, and the woman who danced to it, came to a violent end.

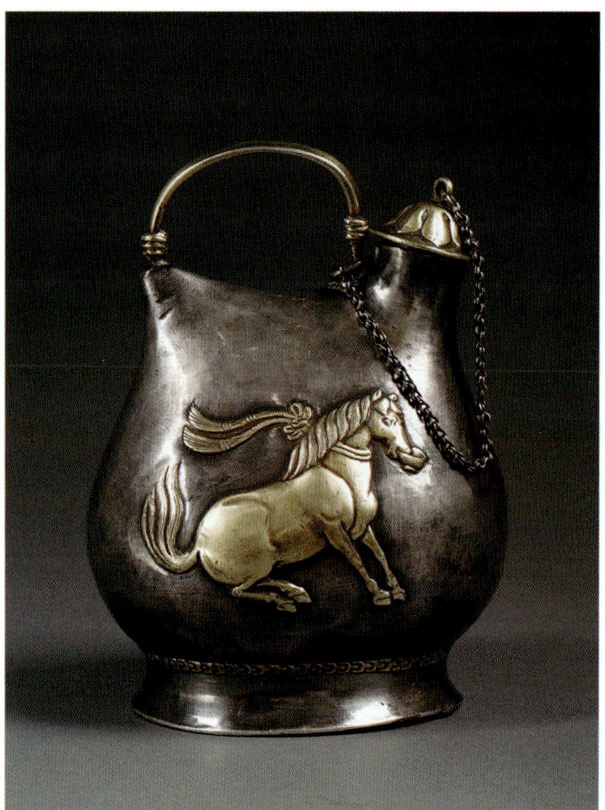

FIGURE 1.10. Flask, fashioned in the shape of a leather saddle bag, eighth century. Gilt silver; H. 18.5 cm. Excavated in 1970 in Hejiacun, south of Xi'an, Shaanxi Province. Courtesy of Shaanxi History Museum.

Bai Juyi penned the second poem, titled "Song of Rainbow Skirts and Feather Robes," upon receiving the score of the song from Yuan Zhen (779–831). Bai opened the poem by recalling the dance as one of his favorites to watch during his tenure in the court of Emperor Xianzong (r. 806–820). In his scrupulous reconstruction of the performance, we get a glimpse of the scene:

> In front of the table, dancers with jade-like countenance,
> Not dressed in the ordinary garb of common people.
> In rainbow skirts and misty shawls, their heads swaying as they walked,
> Gold ornaments jingling, jade pendants clinking.
> So delicate as if they cannot bear the weight of gauze and twill,
> Glancing back, hearing the suspended music, they walk and then stop.[112]

The extravagance of the dancers' costumes and their willowy figures no longer stirred up the tragedy of Xuanzong's and Yang Guifei's ill-fated love. Even before the dancers begin their dance, the banquet hall is filled with the sound of these women: the clinking and jingling of their ornaments and the swishing of their silk garments (fig. 1.11).

Bai's memory of the dance is brought to life by his longing for Chang'an and, more poignantly, to be in Xianzong's court again. The poem also alluded to the sustained enjoyment of music and dance. The "Tune of Rainbow Skirts and Feather Robes" and its accompanying dance may have cost Xuanzong the throne and Yang Guifei her life, but the music would continue to give pleasure to its listeners in Chang'an until the end of the dynasty.

CONCLUSION

The rebellion launched by An Lushan (ca. 703–757) took away Xuanzong's beloved horses too. After the emperor fled to Sichuan (Shu), the horses were dispersed. An Lushan had often watched the horses dance as a guest at Xuanzong's many banquets, and since he had always desired them, several of them were transported to his commandery, Fanyang. Following An's death, the horses fell into the hands of one his lieutenants, Tian Chengsi, who knew nothing of them. Thinking that they were battle horses, he moved them into the outer stables, where they died soon after.[113]

Xuanzong's nearly five-decade reign was the longest of all the Tang rulers. For the moralizing scholar-officials who documented his rule, Xuanzong's illustrious beginning as a capable sovereign was diminished by his hubris in later life. Gripped by his infatuation with Yang Guifei, he installed several of her kin, most disastrously Yang Guozhong (d. 756), in high-ranking positions. The last years of Xuanzong's reign was marked further by rapidly escalating expenditures and an overstrained administration. His negligence enabled An Lushan to set out from his Hebei base in the eleventh month of 755 and occupy Luoyang before the year's end. A couple of weeks after the emperor fled Chang'an in 756, his troops mutinied and demanded that he execute both Yang Guozhong and Yang Guifei. Xuanzong conceded and proceeded to Sichuan, but was soon forced to give up the throne. Stripped of his position by his heir, Emperor Suzong (r. 756–762), Xuanzong died in the imperial palace in 761. At the time of his death, the rebels had yet to be suppressed.

As for his paramour, Yang Guifei, her fleshy body and sumptuous trappings became her legacy. In Li Zhao's (fl. ninth century) compilation of miscellany from the Kaiyuan era through the Changqing era (821–824) of Emperor Muzong's reign, *Supplement to the History of the Tang* (Tang guoshi bu), he recorded an account of how an elderly woman at Mawei, the relay station where Yang Guifei was put to death, profited from the consort's tragic end. The elderly woman retrieved the consort's boot, made of woven polychrome (*jin*) silk, and charged visitors a fee of one hundred cash to fondle it. The profit she took in was so great that she made a fortune.[114] This association between things and

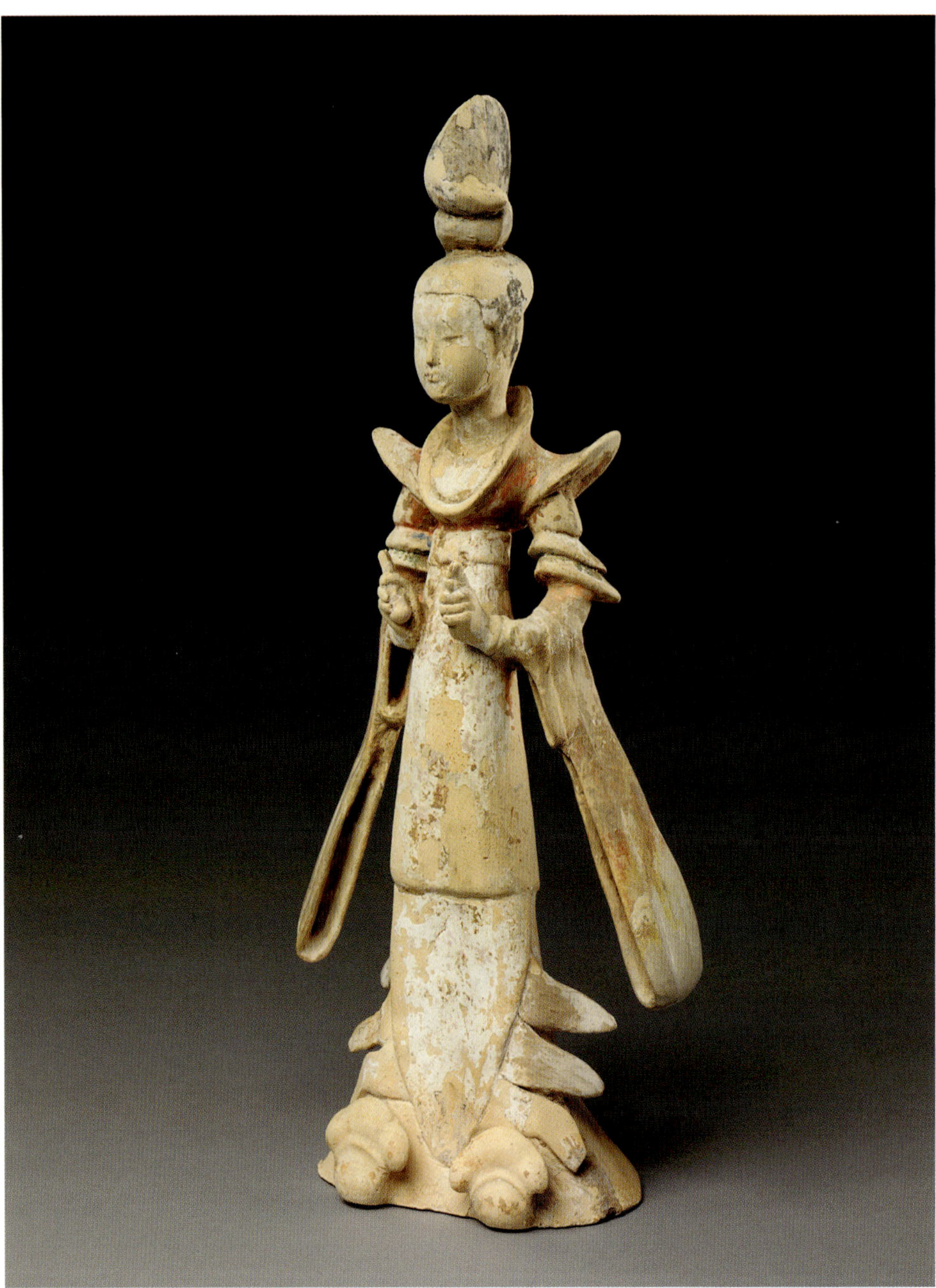

FIGURE 1.11. "Standing Court Lady," mid-seventh century. This figurine wears a costume that is commonly found on seventh- and eighth-century tomb figures depicting dancers. Bai Juyi's description of the dancers wearing rainbow skirts suggests that the title of "Tune of Rainbow Skirts and Feather Robes" may have referred to the costumes, but the absence of textual and pictorial sources has made it impossible to identify what they might have looked like. Earthenware with pigment; H. 38.4 cm. Anonymous gift, in memory of Louise G. Dillingham, 1978. The Metropolitan Museum of Art, New York.

memory—more broadly, objects and subjective experience—was fundamental to the aesthetic plays of Tang subjects and to the social fabrication of the empire.

For historians of the Tang dynasty, the period following the An Lushan Rebellion marked a tectonic shift in the course of Chinese history.[115] In the wake of the rebellion, the central government was forced to adopt wide variations in administration and abandon longstanding political and economic institutions, such as the equal-field system. By the early ninth century, the old pillars of government administration and social organization had nearly crumbled away, and were superseded by sweeping institutional, economic, and social changes. These structural changes fit into an overarching pattern of the state's loss of control over resources and subjects, which took place against the backdrop of rising commercialization. The decline of the old order was precipitated by the breakdown of long-established hierarchies, as the aristocracy was gradually displaced by professional elites recruited through an examination system. Although this narrative has undergone recent revisions, the periodization of Tang history according to the pre- and postrebellion model continues to hold sway.[116]

For the officials who lived through the rebellion and its turbulent aftermath, the events of Xuanzong's court and the policies of his administration constituted the main discursive frame for understanding political, social, and aesthetic change. In their retelling, not only had the cosmopolitan empire become a distant memory, it also ceased to be a desirable model for the dynasty. From their perspective, the desire for pleasure, most notably on the part of Xuanzong and Yang Guifei, had led to the empire's demise. Much to dismay of the moral Confucian scholar-officials, however, the rebellion did not curb the empire's appetite for sensuous indulgences. As the Tang court grappled with governing the consuming passions of the empire in the postrebellion era, concern about the dangers of excess and extravagance—signs of an immoderate empire—became entrenched in new laws regulating the hemlines of women's skirts.

CHAPTER 2

Discourse

FASHION AND SUMPTUARY REGULATION

IN AN EMPIRE WHERE SILK WAS THE DOMINANT MEASURE OF VALUE, IT WAS critical to the articulation of power by emperor and subject alike. As fabrics of political legitimacy, plain and decorated textiles manifested court privilege, local production structures, and social status. As material possessions, fine silks represented the powers of acquisition held by the owner. The production, exchange, and consumption of cloth thus constituted the material of both a political discourse and the fashion system.

Demand for sumptuous silks was an expression of the social logic of consumption, which also governed sartorial practices in Tang China. Eminently social and relational, consumption entailed the commissioning and manipulation of objects as status signifiers to mark one's affiliation with or aspiration to a particular rank (fig. 2.1). The value of silk, measured by the complexity of its design and by the brilliance of its color, was transferred to the wearer, who by trimming the edges of her garments—perhaps the sleeves, or the hem—differentiated the cloth on her body from the immeasurable quantities of plain textiles moving around the empire. Just as men and women looked to fabric to distinguish themselves from one another, Tang rulers sought to make and maintain subjects by regulating access to ornamented silks.

In keeping with classical models on ritual and propriety, the Tang court restricted access to the material trappings of status through the institution of an official dress code and the promulgation of sumptuary laws. Fine silk and costly adornments

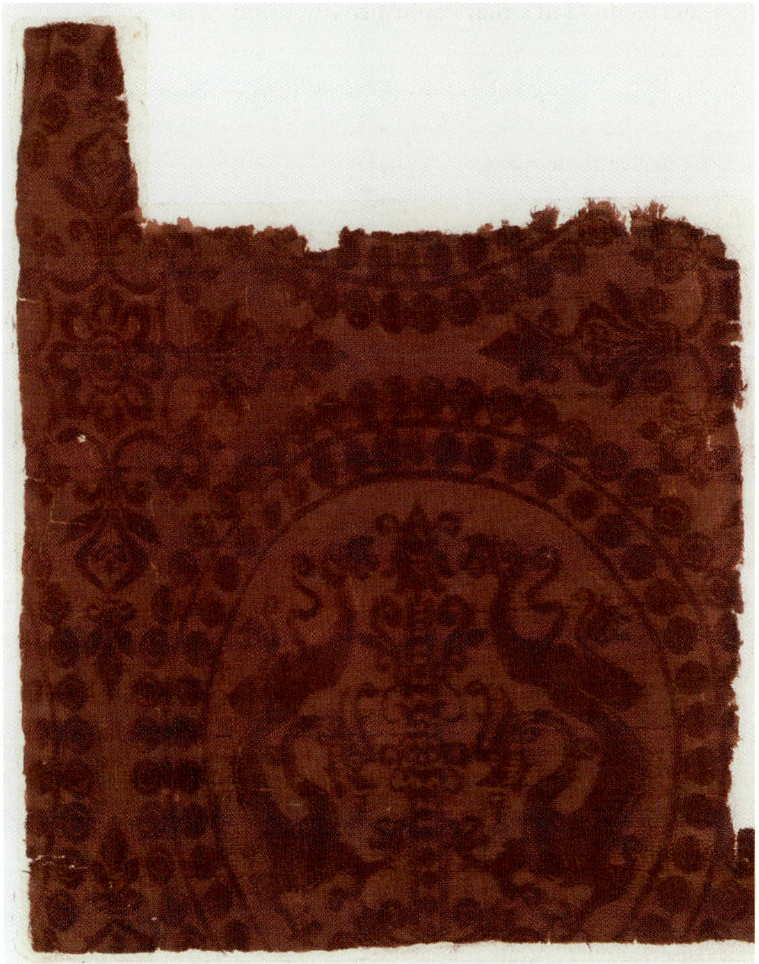

FIGURE 2.1. Textile fragment with confronted dragons enclosed in roundels. The Shōsō-in Treasures, Nara, Japan. Distinctions between social and official ranks were regulated according to the color of one's dress, silk weave, and pattern. Eighth-century sumptuary edicts repeatedly banned complex silk weaves featuring intricate patterns, like this fragment, from production. Monochrome tabby patterned in twill; L. 29.7 cm, W. 47 cm. Courtesy of the Imperial Household Agency.

distinguished between ranks, thereby linking the status of the wearer to the value of her wardrobe. In so doing, the Tang court established a hierarchy of fabrics that mapped onto social and political hierarchies, which in turn sanctioned dress and adornment as fundamental to the expression of status. To challenge the hierarchy of silk was to attack both the legitimacy of the Tang ruling house and its claim as fashion's elite.

Textile production was both the root of imperial power and the driving force of fashion. Recurrent efforts to prohibit the weaving and use of luxury silk only highlighted the limits of imperial power to dictate sartorial desires and regulate local markets. Such was the failure of sumptuary regulation that the language of the edicts began to reflect shifts in the organization of textile production and circulation, hinting at the increasing availability of luxury silks to those with the financial means to acquire them. While Tang laws and the discourses to which they were beholden maligned the practices of ornamentation (of silk and self), they confirmed the incontestable role of silk as the source of imperial authority and fashion.

Sumptuary regimes and fashion systems share similar processes of signification and social differentiation: objects are arranged as status values into a hierarchy, from which consumption practices derive their meaning. Whereas the former depends on imperial authority to regulate status claims and material possessions, the latter relies on powers of acquisition and on knowledge about goods independent of the court. In Tang China, fashion contested the idealized sartorial order by sustaining demand for extravagant silks and facilitating status competition among elites that eroded the traditional cultural work of dress in the reproduction of political and gender roles. Tang sumptuary laws thus reveal much about the social dynamics and economic changes that underpinned the fashion system.

HIERARCHIES OF SILK AND COLOR

The newly established dynasty inherited its concerns about social status and its appropriate display from the classic ritual text *Rituals of Zhou* (Zhouli), which first proposed an idealized ceremonial dress code for the emperor. The ritual prescriptions of dress articulated an ideal social hierarchy and underscored dress as an instrument of governance, subsequently serving as the model for the sumptuary codes of successive dynasties.[1] Edited during the first few centuries of the Han dynasty, *Rituals of Zhou* shares with all dynastic sumptuary regulations an assumption that the categories of rulers and subjects are absolute.[2] Everyday objects such as headdress and belts are then assigned to these immutable categories.

In 624, the imperial commission presented founding Emperor Gaozu with a new set of administrative statutes (*ling*) in thirty chapters, one of which outlined the official and ceremonial dress of the emperor and his court.[3] *Tang Code* (Tang lü) reinforced this static vision of society through the recognition of three social strata—privileged (imperial relatives and officials), free commoners, and base people (hereditary service households, personal retainers, bondsmen, and slaves).[4] Together with *Land Statues* and *Taxation Statues*, these texts served to accord legal force to the institutions of the Tang dynasty.

General sumptuary guidelines for each dynasty were compiled by the editors of the two official histories into the "Treatise on Carriages and Dress" (Yufu zhi) and constitute the principal body of textual evidence for what the emperor, his court, and his subjects were permitted to wear (and not wear). The editors of *Old Standard History of the Tang* and *New Standard History of the Tang*, completed in 945 and 1060 respectively, discursively linked the fall of the Tang to the court's failure to govern both the political and sartorial realms. The composition and editing of dynastic histories, completed after a dynasty had fallen, was a totalizing project aimed at consolidating a standard political narrative that affirmed the establishment of a new ruling house. The compilation of dress regulations and anecdotes of impropriety followed the didactic and diachronic principles of history writing, reinforcing the notion that dress like the organization of administrative units, complied with the temporal contours of the collapsed dynasty. In *Old Standard History of the Tang*, the treatise opens with the legend of the Yellow Emperor, who invented correct clothing and brought order to the realm. By invoking the origin myth of proper dress, the compilers, under the direction of Liu Xu (887–946), sought to underscore the enduring moral and political significance of dress and vehicles.[5] Ouyang Xiu (1007–1072) and Song Qi (998–1061), editors of *New Standard History of the Tang*, omitted the story of the Yellow Emperor, but maintained the emphasis on clothing as a government institution. The two versions of "Treatise on Carriages and Dress" thus offer a narrative of Tang dress practices from the view of a ritual-aesthetic model, in which proper regulation of status through status objects signified order in the cosmos and the state.

The narrative sequence of the treatises reinforced the discourse on hierarchy.[6] Divided into two sections—first vehicles, then dress—the treatises included entries on the individual ensembles and carriages that accorded with the social hierarchy, beginning with the emperor and concluding with the lowest rank of officialdom. The hierarchy of rulers and subjects was differentiated by imperial rank and gender: emperor, crown prince, officials and courtiers, empress, crown princess, and appointed women of the court (*mingfu*).[7] For the emperor, fourteen individual ensembles for state, ritual, and recreational activities were specified.[8] The crown prince was next in the vestimentary order with six, and the empress and crown princess were each allotted three ceremonial suits. The imperial family and officials were organized into one of the nine ranks (*pin*), which determined their status and privileges within the court.[9] Officials and their wives, royal princes and princesses, imperial concubines, and remaining members of the court were assigned robes and colors according to rank.

For officeholding elites, the "Treatise on Carriages and Dress" recorded further distinctions between court dress (*chaofu*), audience dress (*gongfu*), sacrificial ceremony dress (*jifu*), and everyday dress (*changfu*) at each rank.[10] A male official wore trousers and a jacket (*kuxi*), a vest, and a pair of boots for court. In everyday or ordinary dress, robe color and belt ornaments indicated the official's ranking and his affiliation with either the civil or military branch of officialdom. During the reign of Emperor Taizong, the official dress code was amended to clarify color regulations: civil and military officials of the first to third ranks wore purple, the fourth and fifth ranks wore red, the sixth and seventh ranks wore green, and the eighth and ninth ranks wore blue.[11] Officials without rank (*liuwaiguan*), commoners, retainers, slaves and servants were allowed to wear white and yellow garments made of plain, rough silks and bast-fiber fabrics with iron and copper ornaments.[12] In 674, Emperor Gaozong issued an edict reinforcing the sartorial order in response to officials without rank and commoners wearing red, purple, blue, and green colored tunics under their outer garments.[13] In 692, Wu Zetian, as emperor of the Zhou dynasty (690–705), bestowed upon the newly appointed commanders-in-chief and regional inspectors embroidered robes from the Imperial Treasury. Each robe was inscribed with palindromic text and embroidered with mountains. Two years later in 694, she presented embroidered robes to all civil and martial officials of the first to third ranks that featured animal motifs and eight-character palindromes: dragons and deer for the robes of princes, phoenix for grand councilors, a pair of geese for ministers, and a *qilin* (a mythical creature), tiger, leopard, eagle, or ox for the sixteen guards.[14] Animal motifs now served as additional symbols of official status—for which there is no extant material or pictorial evidence.

Women's dress, in contrast, fell under only two general categories of ceremonial (*lifu*) and ordinary (*bianfu*) garb. A woman's ensemble, for both ceremonial and everyday wear, would have included an unlined short robe (*shan*) or a short jacket (*ru*), a skirt (*qun*), and shawl (*pibo*). Emperor Gaozu's statutes of 624 dictated the exact color, silk weave, and individual items to be worn as formal attire on imperial and ritual occasions.[15] Ordinary attire referred to women's daily dress. In everyday dress, as in ceremonial attire, the colors and fabrics were assigned according to the ranking of her husband or son: "Kin ranking closest to those in the fifth rank and up [to the first rank], including mothers and wives, dress in purple robes, waist belts, and sleeve bands of embroidered silk. Mothers and wives of those in the ninth rank and up [to the sixth rank] wear cinnabar-colored robes. The officials outside of the nine ranks and the commoners do not dress in twill damask, silk gauze, crepe silk, nor do they wear green, yellow, red, white, or black woven boots or slippers."[16] Gaozu's clothing code permitted women to dress in the colors assigned to the lower ranks, but strictly prohibited them from dressing above their station.[17] This allowance served to undergird the connection between privilege and rank, and guaranteed the status of higher-ranking individuals. Like color and hue, silk weave was also subject to stringent regulations. The more complex, and therefore more luxurious, patterns and weaves were reserved for highest-ranked women of the court.

From the beginning, the Tang sartorial code with its hierarchy of silk and color was an ideal realized only on paper. Regulatory ordinances dictating cut, color, and fabric were rendered necessary because they were consistently transgressed. Such misconduct was generally imputed to women of the court. They opted to dress "according to their likes and taste," openly defying the silk hierarchy. Women's desire for aesthetic play—to participate in the fashion system—was the cause: "When not in court, their manners [women of high ranking] are extravagant and excessive, and they do not conform to regulations and dress in damasks, silk gauzes, *jin* silks, and embroidered silks according to their likes and tastes. Extending from court and reaching the commoners, the women all rush to imitate each other, and so the noble and the common people lack distinction."[18] Access to patterned silks, precious stones, and metals was a privilege reserved for court elites, reinforcing the symbolic function of luxury goods in maintaining the idealized regime of appearances. Records documenting the imprudence of women in court notably call attention to the flagrant wearing of proscribed sumptuous silks, highlighting the conspicuous role that dyed, embroidered, and decorated silks played in the fashion game. Here, the reference to the breakdown of distinction between elites and commoners shows that for fashion to exist, an audience attuned to changes in dress was necessary. Competition over sartorial savvy, fueled by the participation of this audience as both knowledgeable spectators and copycats, acted as a constant motive force of fashion spanning from pre- to post-rebellion-era Tang society.

In the case of Princess Anle's "hundred bird-feather skirt" (*bainiao qun*), this critique of faddish emulation was the centerpiece of the discourse on extravagance and waste. Commissioned by Princess Anle (ca. 685–710), the imperial workshop crafted a "hundred feather skirt," which "from the front looked like one color, from the side another color, in the light one color, and in the dark another color, so one could see the full form of the hundred birds."[19] Anle's skirt was so adored by her peers that "all of the wealthy elites tried to imitate it, so that the feathers and furs of the rare and precious birds and animals in Jiangnan and Lingwai have been plucked entirely." The sartorial record continually calls attention to this audience of imitators, composed of elite women and rich commoners alike, who competed to replicate the latest trend at court. This game of emulation, in which luxury fabrics and novel garments serve to mark both individual distinction and social adaptation, induces aesthetic play and is one of the key features of the Tang fashion system.

By imitating each other, women not only flouted sumptuary laws, but also the social hierarchy. As luxury materials serve to camouflage or reconstruct the social status of its wearer, they assume equal or greater symbolic power than the economic or social relations underlying their existence. Sumptuary laws contain an inherent contradiction: rather than maintaining social distinctions, the laws encouraged the usurping of status symbols since it was more affordable for elites and non-elites to compete over symbolic distinction.[20] The distillation of social prestige into a material good and a visibly recognizable symbol then adds incentive to the game of emulation and fosters the fashion impulse of those who can afford sumptuous silks, but are unable to attain other forms of state-sanctioned prestige. Since women were excluded from the political ranking system, social prominence depended more on their external trappings.

Although elite women dominated the textual record as conspicuous propagators and adherents of "new styles" (*xinyang*) of fashion, emperor and subject—men and women—were all susceptible to the lure of ornament. Subsequent amendments to the dress code targeted the extravagant expenditure of court elites and commoners by further restricting their access to luxury silks and precious ornaments. Behavior that did not cohere with a subject's social status was considered a criminal offense, such that the wearing of a color that did not correspond to one's rank was to be punished by forty blows with a light stick.[21] New provisions were promulgated as edicts or decrees that in addition to attacking commoners for usurping status displays, clarified or amended old regulations. Of the twenty-five major restrictions imposed on forms of wear over the course of the dynasty, five were issued in response to the appropriation of colors granted to the higher ranking court elites by unauthorized persons.[22] These regulations overlapped with additional efforts to codify official dress for members of the civil and military bureaucracy.[23] The remaining edicts promulgated by successive emperors sought to curb the wasteful sartorial practices of court elites and commoners that included wearing elaborately woven or embellished robes and footwear.

The central government aimed to maintain control over display in both the official and private realms. Gaozu's initial regulatory project tied display to a principle of *status performance*—one must perform the role conferred by a particular social or official status.[24] By targeting official dress, the laws articulated an idealized sumptuary regime that was bound to a male body.[25] Clothing was an instrument of governance that made social distinctions visible and ensured political order. The public body was a male official body, one that was mediated through vestimentary codes. Although a woman's wardrobe was linked to the male household to which she belonged, her garments were not subject to the insignia of the state, allowing her to subvert the sartorial code more easily than her male counterparts.[26] When women failed to dress according to their station, they were not in danger of compromising their social standing. On the contrary, they were increasing their prestige. Men who did not follow the sartorial code, however, were at risk of being dismissed from office and punished. Extravagant women's dress nonetheless prompted official scorn and regulation that exposed the government's growing anxiety about the stability of empire.

The sustained existence of sumptuary regulation has been taken to imply that the Tang dynasty lacked anything that resembled a fashion system, in which "taste" functioned as the consumption-regulating device.[27] Implicit in this framing of sumptuary regulation is a longstanding discourse that views laws proscribing luxury as artifacts of a precapitalist age and insists that fashion, powered by taste and individual choice, emerged alongside commercial capital and the modern self. In early modern Europe, these laws have been interpreted as tools of both social and fiscal regulation, initiated as a conservative defense of a hierarchical social order whose mode of existence and monopoly on power came to be threatened by the rise of merchant capital.[28] The notion that "clothes made the man" was gradually eroded by the commercialization of dress. Commerce thus severed the contiguous relationship between inner self and outer appearance, siphoning away power from early modern regimes to fashion subjects.[29] Most histories of sumptuary law in Europe, if not all, are histories of the failure of governments to resist the forces of capitalism and, ultimately, fashion.

In Tang China, however, the relationship between sumptuary legislation and fashion was not another case of commercialization's triumph over an aristocratic order and their last vestments of power. While increased commercial activity, particularly in the ninth century, distressed moralizing officials, the rise of merchant capital did not provoke sumptuary regulations to the same extent as it did in late medieval and early modern Europe. Not all Tang emperors issued edicts restricting access to luxury silks, nor did they all attempt to circumscribe production; and those who did instituted the laws with distinct aims. What tied the laws together was an abiding concern about the court's control over silk production.

The regulatory project inherited by successive emperors was indebted to two parallel discourses: one was a defense of a ritual-aesthetic model that emphasized a hierarchical social order made manifest through the display of exquisite objects and, most importantly, silk; the other advocated a political-economic model that cautioned against immoderate empire. Ornament and display through grand construction projects and a sumptuously attired court was fundamental to the emperor's expression of power, but such costly investment of imperial funds was also a potential source of his ruin. Tang emperors negotiated between these two modes of governance, resulting in the formulation of sumptuary regulations that proceeded from an anxiety about the proper display of status that affirmed the supreme power of the emperor and his government on the one hand, and consternation about the diversion of labor away from the production of plain cloth on the other.

A GENDERED ROOT

Concomitant with the government's concern about status display was a deepening concern about Tang imperial expansion, which stretched the frontiers of empire and extended long-distance markets. During the first century of Tang rule, the opening of borders brought skilled artisans and itinerant merchants, and their goods, to the empire, encouraging the operation of local and long-distance markets. Trade spurred innovations in crafts, especially in weaving, and drove material desires by introducing elites to new and imaginative designs. The complexity and variety attained in luxury silk production by the eighth and ninth centuries was owed largely to, and sustained by, imperial expansion and court patronage.

To pay for the extended frontier, the government poured vast amounts of tax and tribute cloth into every outpost, fueling the engine of imperial glory with silk and hemp. As military expenditures swelled during the eighth century, demand for plain cloth likewise soared. In response, sumptuary edicts banning the weaving of decorative silks were issued in an effort to increase the flow of plain silk and hemp cloth. As tax textiles became even more vital to the empire's survival, the Tang court turned to the classical discourse on extravagance as the underlying rationale for its regulatory policies.

Since the Han dynasty, moralizing officials have emphasized frugality as the model for a harmonious society, viewing the vicissitudes of dress and adornment as symptomatic of fermenting social disorder, brought about by frivolous desire, increased trade, and a decadent empire. This discourse against the production of commercial goods not intended for daily use and luxury spending was steeped in a tradition that valued agriculture as the foundation of the empire's wealth. Since sericulture belonged to the sphere of agricultural activity, it was critical to both the people's livelihood and government revenue. The production of nonessential textiles was regarded as superfluous work.[30] Concern about extravagant expenditure was not new in the Tang dynasty. Proclamations against wasteful consumption of nonessential goods frequently invoked *Debate on Salt and Iron* (Yantie lun), composed during the Later Han Dynasty (206 BCE–9 CE) as a critique of Emperor Wu's (r. 141–87 BCE) expansionist policies.[31]

Compiled by Huan Kuan (fl. 81–60 BCE), *Debate on Salt and Iron* reconstructed a major court debate over the creation of salt and iron monopolies under Emperor Wu that took place in 81 BCE. In the text, the Imperial Counselor (Yushi Daifu)—generally understood to refer to Emperor Wu's former advisor, Sang Hongyang (152–80 BCE)—is pitted against the Classical Scholars (Wenxue). Drawing on the metaphor of agriculture as *ben* ("root") and commerce as *mo* ("branch"), the rhetorical battle between the Imperial Counselor and the Classical Scholars unfolded as an ideological debate on the foundational relationship between state and wealth. The twin metaphors of "root" and "branch" emerged as moral metaphors that celebrated agriculture (farming and weaving) as the fundamental occupation (*benye*) and all other livelihoods as merely auxiliary.[32]

In one exchange, the Imperial Counselor argued that commerce was essential to the state's economy:

> Imperial Counselor: Guanzi said, "If palaces and houses are not decorated, the timber supply will be overabundant. If animals and fowls are not used in the kitchens, there will be no decrease in their numbers. Without profits from the branch [*moli*], the fundamental occupation [*benye*] will have no outlet. Without the embroidered ceremonial robes, the women will have no occupation." Therefore, artisans, merchants, carpenters and workmen are all for the use of the government and to provide tools and implements. They have existed from ancient times and are not a unique feature of the present age. . . . Farmers and merchants exchange their goods so that both the "root" and the "branch" may profit.[33]

Quoting *Guanzi*, a text ascribed to the philosopher Guan Zhong (ca. 720–645 BCE) of the Spring and Autumn Period (771–476 BCE), the Imperial Counselor cautioned against extreme frugality and staked the claim that commerce supported the satisfaction of universal needs (farmers and weavers) and maintained the proper balance of nature (trees and fowl). For him, the relationship between agriculture ("root") and commerce ("branch") was a codependent one that would enable the "effective circulation of goods." The Classical Scholars, drawing from Mencius, contended that wasteful expenditure of labor on the nonessential was a threat to the natural balance: "If the men folk abandon the fundamental in favor of the nonessential, carving and engraving in imitation of the forms of animals, exhausting the possibilities of manipulation of materials, then there will not be enough grain for consumption. If the women folk decorate the small things and work on the minute and form elaborate articles to the best of their skill and art, then there will not be enough silk and cloth for wear."[34] The argument is clear: ornamentation, synonymous with luxury and extravagance, leads to economic scarcity. By linking commerce to material insufficiency, the Classical Scholars directly challenged the Imperial Counselor's claim that "profits from the branch" (*moli*) in tandem with the "fundamental occupation" (*benye*) ensured order and wealth. Whereas the Imperial Counselor sought to recast the relationship between root and branch as a harmonious one that only required the intervention of the government, the Classical Scholars insisted on self-sufficient agrarianism as a moral value. Although they did not state it as such, "the root" was inherently gendered.

The doctrine that "men till, women weave" (*nangeng nüzhi*) underscored the belief that the growing of grain and the making of cloth were equally indispensable in ensuring the welfare of the people and the strength of the state. Weaving (*zhi*) as formulated in this classic axiom encompassed the entire process of cloth production from raising silkworms, or twisting ramie fibers, to weaving and sewing. The antithesis to this gendered model of morally productive labor was the parallel pairing of the ornamental carvings of craftsmen and the embroidered and patterned silks of women weavers. In contrast to carving and engraving, textile production occupied both "the root" and "the branch" of a productive society. The making of plain cloth—women's work (*nügong*)—was central to statecraft as a "fundamental occupation." Ornamented silks, products of craft (*gong*), were likewise central to the administration of empire. Silks intended for tribute, salary for officials, diplomatic gifts, and as materials for majestic dress were woven in workshops by artisans, who labored to produce all of the trappings of imperial power.[35] Like ornamental carvings or metalwork, weaving polychrome patterned silks required the specialization of skill and training into the craft, and did not depend on the gender of the artisan.[36] This fundamental difference between women's work and the work of silk artisans is obscured in Tang dynasty texts, which collapsed the distinction between the household and the workshop, and reified all products of the loom and shuttle as "women's work." So pervasive was the influence of this gendered division of labor that even when male weavers populated silk workshops, Tang writers would insist that seated at the loom was a toiling woman, tirelessly producing complex silks for the court (see chap. 5).

Tang administrative regulations and legal code reveal that while women dominated the discourse against ornamentation and extravagance as weavers and wearers, artisans were, in practice, held accountable by the state for violations against the sumptuary protocol. For example, artisans were subjected to harsher punishment than individual offenders of dress regulations. To prevent the unlawful manufacture and distribution of commodities, *Tang Code* stipulated that: "All cases of constructing or manufacturing such things as residences, carriages, clothing, utensils, goods, graves, or stone animals that are in violation of the statutes are punishable by one hundred blows with the heavy stick."[37] Subsequent sumptuary edicts instituted more severe penalties for the production of illicit goods. While the discourse of sumptuary laws targeted individual transgressions, the state was invested in regulating production through controlling supply to stamp the tide of fashion. That is to say, the state aimed to limit the circulation, accumulation, and display of silk by restricting the work of artisans.

This policy reached the frontier administrations too, as documented in *Regulations of the Board of Justice*, dated between 705 and 707, and transmitted as two fragments uncovered in Dunhuang.[38] The regulations stipulated that each person involved in the production of illicit silks, identified as *ling*-twill and *jin* silks with unsanctioned ornate patterns, was subject to a minimum of one hundred beatings. Further punishments were doled out according to the degree of participation, thus inadvertently revealing the various local agencies that propelled the motor of fashion empire-wide: for the principal in the crime (*zaoyi zhe* or *zaozhe*), who may have been the pattern designer, three years exile; for itinerant weavers and the master of the workshop, two and half-years exile; for the treadle operators and the village, ward, and village sector heads (who were in the know), eighty beatings. The pattern designer was held responsible as the primary offender, suggesting that the Tang court considered the dissemination of craft knowledge outside of official workshops a serious offense. Indeed, imperial control of specialized silks depended on the circumscription of skills, embodied in the artisan.

The fashion system threatened the government's claim on the social relations of production that underpinned its rule. Access to makers and materials was as critical as knowledge about what to wear in the fashion game. As implied in the case of Princess Anle's "hundred bird-feather skirt," the copycat women presumably had to first purchase the feathers and more crucially, find and employ artisans capable of reproducing the skirt's design. The power to consume was an explicit display of one's ability to procure specialized labor to produce goods prohibited by law, thus exposing the insufficiencies of the Tang legal code, of the empire's guiding moral ideology, and of the court's capacity to control artisan labor.

THE MORAL AND MILITARY IMPERATIVES OF SUMPTUARY LEGISLATION

Not all violators of sartorial propriety were women, nor were men the only critics of excess and extravagance. One of the documented voices against imperial excess belonged to Xu Hui (627–650), a consort of Emperor Taizong's inner court.[39] Celebrated by her biographers for her literary talent rather than her appearance (which earned no mention at all), Xu was gifted at writing poetry and prose from a young age. In 648 she submitted a petition to the emperor urging him to exercise restraint in his military campaigns and palace construction projects and to set a model of frugality in the face of endemic consumption of luxury silks at court. She pleaded: "Rare playthings and ingenious creations are the axes that destroy a kingdom; pearls and jades, *jin* silks and embroideries, are truly the poisons that confuse the mind . . . precious and unique textile tributes are like handiwork of the divine immortals. Pursuing the lavish silks of the latest season is truly to stray from the plain silk of the pure and honest ways."[40] As Xu saw it, desire for precious and novel things, such as fine silk tribute, was capable of corrupting minds (*xin*) and destroying kingdoms (*guo*). The contrast drawn between lavish (*hua*) silks of the current season (*jisu*) and the plain (*su*) silks of "pure and honest ways" (*chunfeng*) that circulated within the classical discourse stressed constancy over change. In the words of the Classical Scholars, to pursue the rare and precious was to promote the branch and undermine the root. Xu pushed further in her exhortations to the emperor, drawing an explicit connection between imperial excess and the destruction of empires, citing examples from antiquity. She was not alone in her reproach as Taizong's unsuccessful campaigns against Koguryŏ on the Korean Peninsula and his costly construction of the Daming Palace triggered staunch criticism from his officials. While the editors of the official histories likely transmitted the petition in Xu's biography because the content echoed their own moral and political convictions, her arguments about the relationship between court excess and imperial decline were certainly prescient.[41]

As the population grew and the borders of the empire extended farther west, the government required more cloth and grain revenues to finance the military, pay salaries of officials, and maintain tributes and diplomatic gifts. Beginning in the eighth century under the reign of Emperor Xuanzong, the discourse on root and branch was revived in the phrasing of his sumptuary decrees, which sought action either by closing workshops or by banning production empire-wide. When Xuanzong ascended the throne in 712, he inherited serious financial problems that included a chronic shortage of revenue. The government was determined to conserve resources. Inconsistent household registration had resulted in the omission of a large proportion of potential taxpayers. Court elites exacerbated the state's financial burden as taxes collected from wealthy households were reserved as income for the fiefs of maintenance (*shishifeng*) of the imperial family and families of officials who were granted noble titles.[42] During these early years, the emperor was eager to impose strict regulations on luxury and unnecessary expenditure in light of the empire's financial problems.

The influence of *Debate on Salt and Iron* and, particularly, its rhetorical use of "women's work" as a symbol of the suffering brought upon by imperial expansion and lavish consumption, is evident in the language of Tang dynasty sumptuary edicts and financial policies issued from the eighth century onward. In the seventh month of 714, Xuanzong issued three new sumptuary laws forbidding the production of *jin* and the wearing of embroidered clothes and pearl or jade ornaments. The first edict, "Prohibition on jade, pearl, *jin*, and embroidered articles," hearkened back to the Han dynasty discourse on ornamentation and material insufficiency: "I have heard that those jade and pearls cannot feed people when they are hungry, cannot clothe people when they are cold. Hence, Emperor Wen said: 'Carved ornaments and chiseled engravings are harmful to agriculture. *Jin* silks, embroidery, and vermillion silk ribbons are harmful to women's work. Injury to agriculture is the root of hunger; injury to women's work is the source of suffering from the cold.'"[43] With this introduction, paraphrased from an imperial edict issued by Han dynasty Emperor Jing (r. 157–141 BCE) in 142 BCE to promote agricultural output, Xuanzong situated the laws in a long-standing tradition that viewed the production of nonessential goods as detrimental to the state economy.[44] Unlike Emperor Jing's edict, Xuanzong's new regulations did not merely decree that the people eschew luxury and return to a more austere mode of living. Instead, he first demanded that all gold and silver ornaments found on dress and carriages be handed over to the officials to be melted down and cast into ingots to supply the armies. Xuanzong then ordered the burning of jade and pearl goods in front of the palace hall. Finally, he instructed the imperial consorts to wear old clothing and banned their use of kingfisher and pearl ornaments.

The other two edicts, "Prohibition on the use of extravagant dress" and "Decree forbidding *jin* silks, embroidered silks, jade, and pearls," added restrictions and stipulated harsher penalties.[45] No subject in the empire was allowed to own jade and pearls or carved ornaments and vessels. Owners of clothing made from embroidered or *jin* silks were required to dye them black, while those in possession of uncut bolts of silks were to sell them back to the government. The state manufactories for *jin* silks in Chang'an and Luoyang, which produced goods for the palace, were shut down. Artisans who produced embroidered, polychrome woven belts and sashes, as well as patterns of strange and mythical animal motifs woven in twill damasks and gauzes were to be punished by one hundred blows with a heavy stick. Hired workers and craftsmen would be downgraded one level. In 726, Xuanzong proclaimed another act against excess and extravagance.[46] Invoking the Han emperor's speech once again, the emperor reinforced his ban on clothing, carriages, and vessels embellished with precious materials. His persistent efforts at prohibiting valuable forms of ornamentation and banning the manufacture of such objects testify to the failure of these edicts to curb luxury production and consumption.

The discovery of the tomb of Li Chui (d. 736), a fifth-generation descendent of the founding Tang emperor, has shed light on how gold, pearls, and other rare stones were used to embellish dress during Xuanzong's reign (figs. 2.2, 2.3, and 2.4).[47] Gold and gilt ornaments were excavated in a multitude of forms: gold threads woven into her silk

FIGURE 2.2. (*Right*) Headdress. The amount of gold is striking, including a diadem, twelve large ornaments, and 251 blossoms. H. 39 cm (reconstruction). Tomb of Li Chui (d. 736), Xi'an, Shaanxi Province. Courtesy of Shaanxi Provincial Institute of Archaeology.

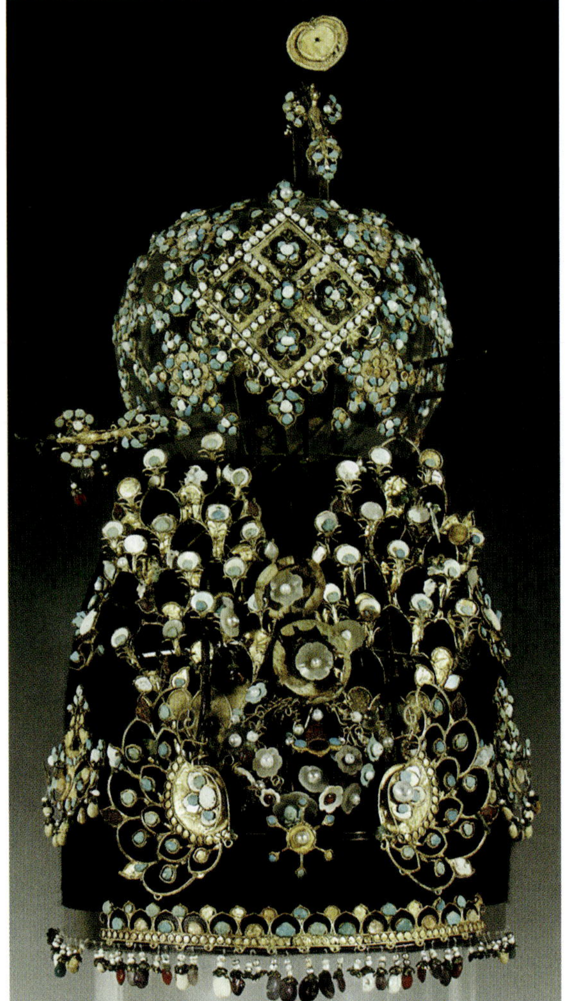

FIGURE 2.3. (*Below*) Waistband. The petals of the four-leaf gold blossoms were inlaid with turquoise, while the edges were trimmed with granules; each blossom contains a pearl in the center. H. 11.6 cm, W. 27.5 cm. Tomb of Li Chui, Xi'an, Shaanxi Province. Courtesy of Shaanxi Provincial Institute of Archaeology.

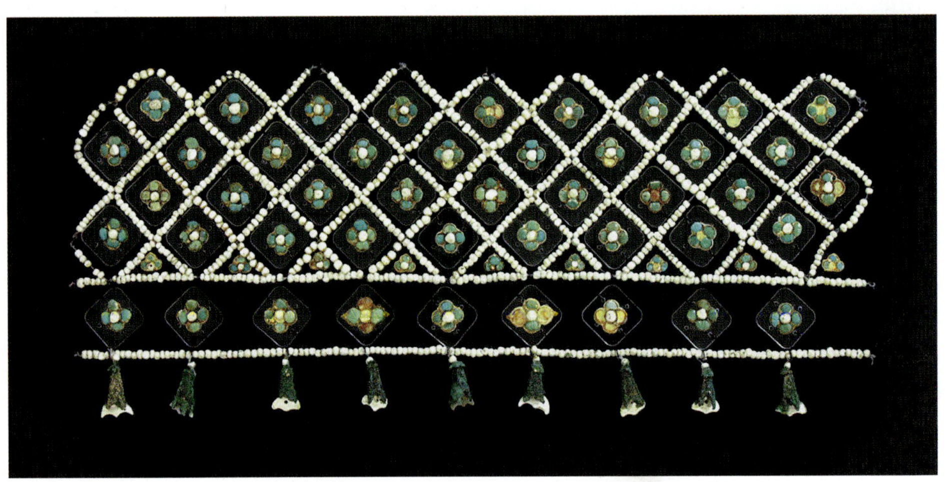

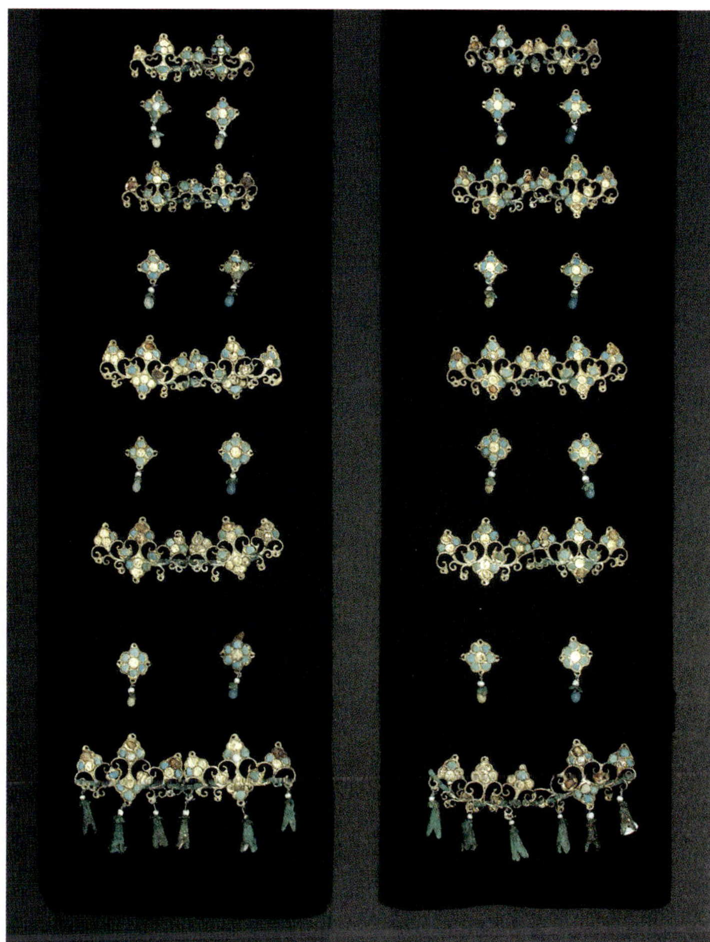

FIGURE 2.4. Ornaments for the lower body (*shuangpei*). Each group of ornaments features similar gold cell-work with turquoise inlay and granulation. The ornaments would have been sewn directly onto Li Chui's skirt, or stitched to two separate lengths of cloth before they were affixed to her skirt. Tomb of Li Chui, Xi'an, Shaanxi Province. Courtesy of Shaanxi Provincial Institute of Archaeology.

garments, gold blossoms made by cell-work technique, gilded bronze hairpins, and gold wires. Pearls, turquoise, mother-of-pearl, carnelian, amethysts, and glass beads were attached, inlaid, and fixed to the gold headdress. For the waist belt, miniature gold blossoms were interspersed within a net threaded with pearls. Archaeologists found additional gold blossoms with inlays of turquoise, pearls, and mother-of-pearl near Li Chui's lower body, suggesting that the ornaments formed a set of two bejeweled bands (*shuangpei*) and were attached vertically to opposite sides of her skirt.[48] The gold, silver, pearls, and other jewels would have been sourced from the newly conquered and reconquered territories in the southwest, as well as obtained through the tributary trade network.[49] Tang imperialism not only pushed silk into new territories, it also served to bring rare gems, stones, and metals into the fashionable lives of court elites.

Although Li Chui was a descendant of the royal family, she did not have a noble title and was married to a civil servant of the seventh rank. The luxurious goods found in her tomb may have reflected her status as a noble-born woman of the inner court, but not of her husband's rank in the civil bureaucracy. Such a discrepancy in her official rank and her private possessions brings to light the failure of the sumptuary protocol to dictate the sumptuous lives and afterlives of Tang elites.[50] Adorning one's lower body with a set of hanging pendants, for example, was a privilege granted to those of the fifth rank and above. Li Chui's tomb is remarkable, too, for what her epitaph reveals about the pervasive discourse on sartorial propriety and women's virtue. Having died at the young age of twenty-five, her epitaph was consequently brief. Apart from her patrimony, marriage, residence in Chang'an, and death, we learn that Li Chui possessed proficient textile skills, surrounded herself with luxurious silks, but did not shun faded fabrics.[51] Consistent with the gendering of textile production and fashion, her virtue was couched in terms of her relationship to silks as both maker and owner.[52] The declaration that she did not shy away from old silks harked back to Xuanzong's 714 edict that required imperial consorts to wear old clothing, demonstrating that while her gold and pearl adorned crown would suggest defiance of sumptuary protocol, on the textual level, Li Chui would be remembered as virtuous woman. The tomb is thus a microcosm of the Tang fashion system: discourse perpetuated gendered notions of fashion within discourse, which seldom cohered with practice.

By invoking the metaphors of root and branch in his edicts against extravagant ornamentation, Xuanzong endeavored to demonstrate that the state regulatory project was concerned about the moral economy and fiscal solvency of the empire. Examined in the context of the state's political problems and financial troubles, it becomes evident that the initial sumptuary laws of 714 were part and parcel of a larger campaign to reassert imperial authority and financial prerogatives. In attempt to restore efficiency to the central government, Xuanzong authorized a series of institutional reforms from 714 to 720 that were devised to promote a strong relationship between a powerful emperor and his court. Multiple organs of the central government were restructured, the selection process of officials refined, and uniform administrative laws were codified during this period. By the 730s, improved local administration, population growth, and stable agricultural production yielded unprecedented revenues.

Exceptional revenue growth, however, was matched by mounting military expenditures. Xuanzong's reign was marked by increased foreign expansion that resulted in a dramatic reorganization of the military. Beginning in 710, permanent military governors (*jiedu shi*) were appointed to command defense zones in lieu of regional commanders (*zongguan*) of expeditionary armies in an effort to establish a coordinated command structure. By the 720s, the northern and western frontiers had been grouped into a series of nine major command zones. In each of the nine commands, the military governor managed a large staff and sizeable defense army. Military governors also had absolute and complete jurisdiction in a specified number of border prefectures, with command over separate armies and garrisons. Provisioning commissioners (*zhidu shi*) were given the disposal of large central government funds to provide grain and supplies to the troops. A large proportion of the armies depended on local military colonies (*tuntian*), which were administered by the commissioners for state lands (*yingtian shi*) and farmed by the troops.[53]

The system of frontier commands evolved piecemeal until 737, when a fixed organization of armies, units, troops, and financial allocations for their support was established and the militia model was abandoned. That same year, the frontier forces were converted into professional armies composed of permanent troops. With the creation of a permanent professional army, the state required vast resources to provision and transport grain, clothing, and equipment to the frontier. During the Kaiyuan period (713–741), the cost of maintaining frontier troops had increased five-fold. Xuanzong's decree that the melted gold and silver be discharged to the troops in the first sumptuary edict of 714 was an early indication of the large-scale militarization that took place over the next century, depleting the state of its finances.[54]

A steady undersupply of coins turned cloth into an even more essential material for the empire. In the 730s, Xuanzong's government encouraged both plain and complex textiles as the preferred form of currency in a series of edicts. The first, issued in 732, permitted the use of *ling*-twill damasks, *luo*-gauzes, plain weave silk (*juan*), (hemp) cloth (*bu*), and miscellaneous goods. Collected as payment for *yong* and *diao* taxes, *ling*-twill damasks, *luo*-silk gauze, and plain weave silk (*juan*) circulated widely in the empire.[55] In 734, the government stipulated that all transactions involving the sale of property, slaves, and horses must be paid in plain weave silk, hemp cloth, *luo*-silk gauze, and silk thread or silk floss. Any other exchanges that exceeded one thousand coins must be paid for with cloth and goods. To champion this measure, the edict declared textiles as the root (*ben*) and coins (*qiandao*) as the branch (*mo*), and condemned the use of coins by proclaiming that, "To humble the root and esteem the branch is a serious offense."[56] By employing this classical idiom, the government transformed the use of textiles as money into a moral imperative. A few years later in 738, the government acted again, restricting all market transactions to silk.[57]

The growing number of troops stationed along the frontier also required an ever-increasing supply of cloth for uniforms and as currency to buy grain. Between 742 and 755, military expenditures escalated by a further 40 or 50 percent. By 755, the number of registered households increased to nearly nine million with a population of roughly fifty-three million.[58] This significant increase in taxable households and the accompanying rise in revenues supported the new professional army. In Du You's account of the state finances of the Tianbao era, he remarked that, "From the middle of the Kaiyuan into the Tianbao period, in opening up the border many honorific offices were established, so that every year the expense of supplying the troops increased day by day."[59] Approximately 3.6 million bolts of cloth were used to purchase grain and an additional 5.2 million bolts for clothing provisions were dispatched to the military commands. The permanent troops also began to push for lavish rewards for success on the field. Du You documented an additional two million bolts that were set aside for special payments.[60]

The Hexi military command, for example, consumed 1.8 million bolts of silk and hemp: one million to pay the soldier's salaries and eight hundred thousand to buy grain.[61] One of the documents recovered in the early 1900s from the caves in Dunhuang records the total grain and cloth expenses of the Doulu army in Hexi circuit (fig. 2.5).[62] Dated to 745, the document reported that twenty thousand bolts of cloth were authorized to be dispatched from Liangzhou to the army. The army, however, received 14,678 bolts in an assortment of silk textiles and wadding: 5,600 bolts of raw (undegummed) plain tabby woven on a wide loom (*da shengjuan*), 550 bolts of coarse, ribbed silk (*shi*) from Henan, 270 bolts of plain silk dyed scarlet red (*manfei*), 270 bolts of plain silk dyed green (*lüfei*), 1,927 hanks (*tun*) and ten *zhu* of silk floss (*da mian*), 1,700 bolts of wadding from Shaan Commandery, and over 4,361 bolts of degummed plain silk woven on a wide loom (*da lian*). The range of silks listed in this account, plain weave dyed red (*manfei*), wide-loom degummed plain silk (*da lian*), also appeared on the Turfan market register from 742, showing how tax silks from the interior province, sent to troops to tailor into uniforms and to purchase grain from local residents, then entered local markets to be sold again (fig. 2.6).

Xuanzong's government collected the bulk of its revenue in silk from the *yong* and *diao* taxes paid by prefectures in Henan and Hebei, where the population was greater than those of other silk-producing provinces.[63] During the last decades of Xuanzong's reign, of the twenty-seven million lengths and hanks of hemp, silk, and silk floss at the disposal of the Department of Public Revenue (Duzhi), thirteen million was disbursed as rewards for troops and as payment for the "harmonious purchase" (*hedi*) of grains.[64] The burgeoning demand for tax cloth for military provisions, as well as for trade and diplomatic gifts, resulted in the expansion of silk production across the empire. The government's growing need for money and provisions in an era of military expansion resulted in the widespread circulation of cloth, from the interior provinces to frontier—for example, the weft-ribbed silk (*shi*) from Henan, which was woven from silk yarn that had been reeled from local cocoons, collected as tax by prefectural officials, dispatched to the Department of Public Revenue, and finally disbursed to the Hexi military command. The heightened circulation of textiles, as subsequent sumptuary edicts reveal, also broadened the reach of textile technology and the fashion system.

FIGURE 2.5. (*Facing, top*) Account of textile sales and grain purchases of the Doulu army, dated 745. Roll of 25 sheets; H 27.3 cm, L. 808 cm. Pelliot chinois no. 3348, Department of Manuscripts, Bibliothèque Nationale de France.

FIGURE 2.6. (*Facing, bottom*) Clothing registry of the Doulu army, Tianbao era. Among the items listed are outer robes (*aozi*) made from ribbed silk (*shi*) from Henan. Roll of 20 sheets; H. 27.2–28 cm, L 666.6 cm. Pelliot chinois no. 3274, Department of Manuscripts, Bibliothèque Nationale de France.

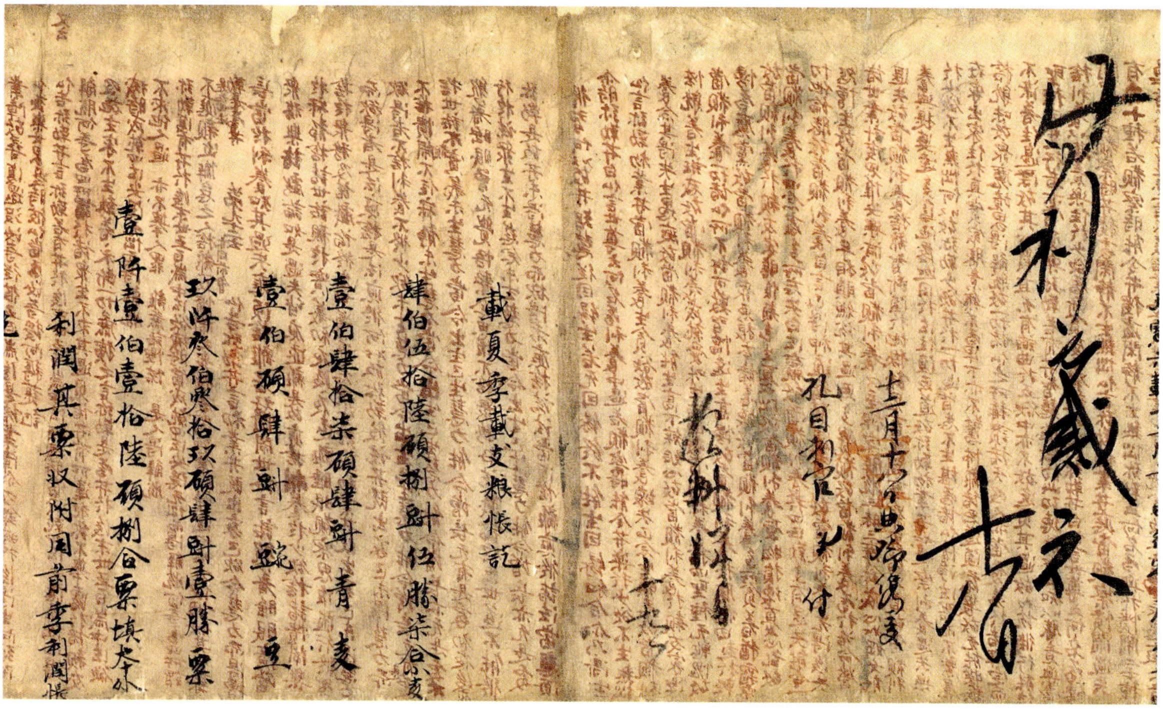

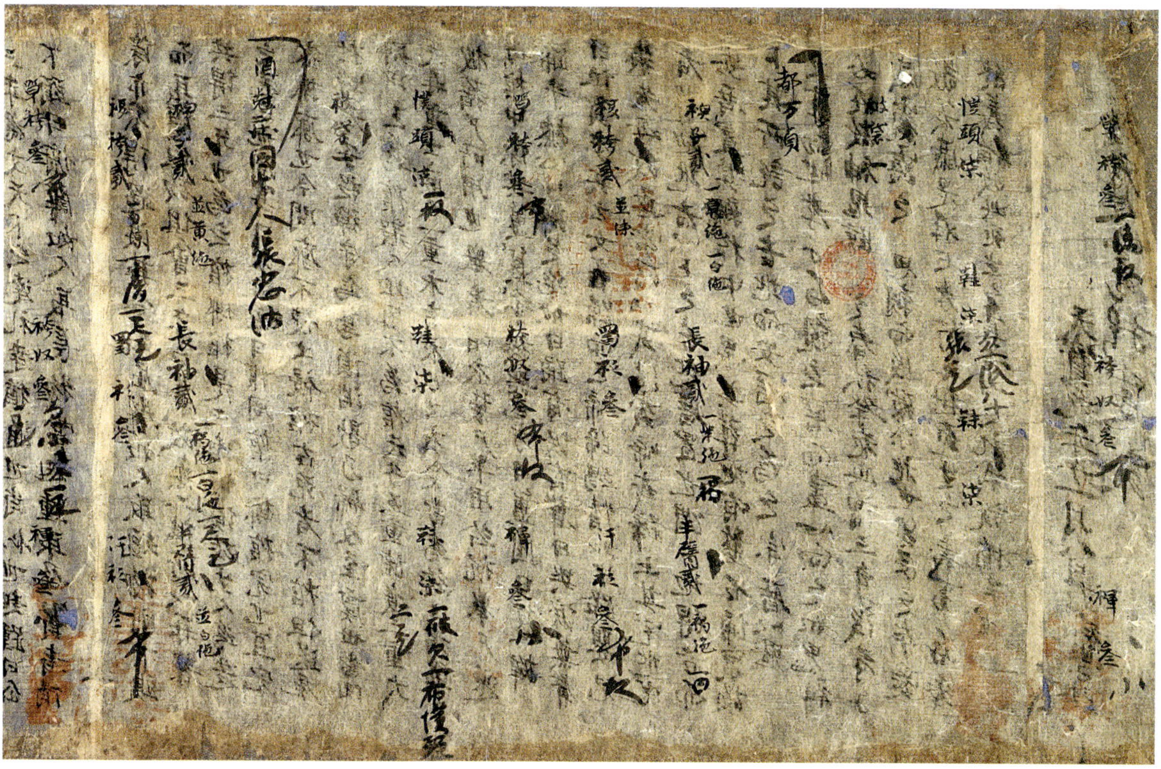

WOMEN'S WORK AND THE BURDENS OF PLAIN CLOTH

One major consequence of militarization during the reign of Xuanzong was the concentration of power in the hands of military governors occupying the northeast, laying the foundation for the rebellion of An Lushan and Shi Siming (703–761) in 755. In the winter of 755, An Lushan marched on the eastern capital of Luoyang, throwing the empire into chaos for over seven years. An Lushan was assassinated in early 757 and soon after the two capitals were recovered, but the war against remaining rebel forces lingered for another six years. When the insurrection finally came to an end in 763, the collapse of the state's financial structure, coupled with the rampant displacement of the population and the secession of Hebei and major portions of Henan, had thoroughly altered the geography of the empire. In the wake of the rebellion, militarization, border instability, and inefficient administration continued to characterize and affect state economic policies of the late eighth through early tenth centuries. The fashion system was affected by the rebellion as well. The loss of Hebei and Henan, home to the key silk producing centers, resulted in the relocation of production to south of the Yangzi River. The concentration of textile weaving in fewer prefectures increased the burden of weavers across the empire, amplifying the discourse on women's work as the making of plain cloth.

The Tang imperial court failed to recover absolute authority in the aftermath of the An Lushan Rebellion. The bulk of the state's inventory of silks had been destroyed during the insurgency. Decentralization of power impeded the state's repeated attempts to restore the dynasty to its former might and allowed for sweeping structural changes that radically altered the social and economic landscape. Militarization continued into the postrebellion era, with military officials wielding greater power over local government and gaining control of strategic locales. Regional separatism and provincial autonomy prompted the government to abandon universal forms of administration, including the entire body of codified law that regulated population registration, land, taxation, labor services, as well as civil and military officials.

To accommodate these changes, the central government had to accept variations in financial administration. With the loss of Hebei and parts of Henan to rebel provincial governors, the state could no longer collect taxes from its chief silk-producing regions.[65] Large-scale dislocation of the population, particularly the migration of people to the Huai and Yangzi river valleys, forced the state to finally dispense with the land allocation system. Unable to restrict landholdings, the government had to accept the widespread transfer of landed property into new private hands. The mass movement southward transformed the provinces of the Yangzi and Huai regions into the government's chief source of revenue. The disintegration of the empire's financial structure spurred the state to adopt new methods of raising revenue that culminated in the establishment of a monopoly tax to be administered by the Salt and Iron Commission. In spite of the commission's name, the tax was confined to salt and the inclusion of iron was done in deference to its Han dynasty precedent.[66]

Cloth such as plain weave silk (*juan*) played an even more critical role in the state's financial administration and in the general economy as the chief form of currency. The central government's loss of its stocks of revenue cloth during the rebellion, the subsequent secession of its chief silk-producing prefectures in Hebei and Henan, and the concurrent breakdown of the direct taxation system fueled the state's efforts to promote basic cloth production and stabilize its value. Beginning in 760, the government's stocks of silk were further depleted in purchasing horses from the Uyghurs. The Uyghurs charged forty bolts of silk per horse with the expectation that the Tang state would buy up to ten thousand per annum, but the postrebellion administration was unable to pay for the horses in full.[67] Combined with the empire's revenue troubles, the horse-silk trade only intensified the government's dependence on basic silk production, reinforcing the weaving of plain cloth as the foundation of the economy.[68] Production of luxury silks like patterned twill damasks and complex gauzes diverted valuable labor from the manufacture of revenue cloth, posing major problems for the government's continued attempts to control the economy according to the outmoded ideal of a traditional agrarian society. In 771, Emperor Daizong (r. 762–779) issued an edict forbidding the weaving of opulent and novel patterns on silks:

> Vermillion silk ribbons and embroidery certainly harm women's work. At present, the troops have yet to return from battle, the people have nothing. How can we allow extravagant customs to wreak havoc on our abiding traditions? The patterns woven on *ling* twills and *jin* silks including coiled dragons, paired phoenixes, *qilin*, lions, heavenly horses, *bixie*, peacocks, immortal cranes, auspicious *lingzhi* fungus patterns, *wanzi* [卍], interlocking shapes, double-sided designs, as well as *jin* patterned with hatching lines of six sections and above are all prohibited. The manufacture of lofty, Koryŏ [Gaoli] white *jin* silk, and *ling* twills and *jin* silks with small and large patterns may continue according to old regulations. Administrative offices in charge of such matters must clearly implement these instructions.[69]

The inventory of designs mentioned as examples of excess that impinge on women's work and "wreak havoc on abiding traditions" are remarkably elaborate, unlike the plainer twill damasks and *jin* silks with floral patterns permitted by the edict. Compared to the types of ornamentation prohibited by Xuanzong, the list of embroidered and woven motifs banned by Daizong is also striking in its scope and points to the innovations in silk technology made over the course of fifty years. Whereas the sumptuary regulations of the early eighth century focused on the production of *jin* silks, the edict of 771 highlights fine *ling*-twills as a popular weave. The recurrence of fine *ling*-twills in the records of local tribute points to the spread of more complex looms with mechanical shafts from imperial manufactories to private workshops.[70] Such technical innovations, driven by the government's promotion of cloth production for tax, tribute, and currency, ironically advanced the fashion system. Like the political regime, the fashion one was based on textiles. This enduring tension between the two regimes' competing claims on silk production intensified in the postrebellion era.

The rhetoric of Daizong's edict, similar to that of Xuanzong's statutes of 714, recited the classical critique of extravagance, conceived of as the wasting of resources that could be more usefully employed to clothe the empire. The targeting of embroidery, work that consumes substantial labor-time, suggests that the government's efforts to curb excess was tied to a concern about the squandering of productive labor on ostentatious silks.[71] One significant departure in Daizong's decree, however, is the detachment of embroidered silks from its traditional gendered pairing with ornamental carvings. Women's work, defined as the weaving of basic cloth, had eclipsed farming as the fundamental occupation. By stressing the misfortunes generated by complex silk patterns as the grounds for suppressing extravagant customs, Daizong hoped to redirect the expenditure of labor-time and raw materials toward the making of plain silks.[72] Bai Juyi's and Yuan Zhen's poems on women weavers (see chap. 5) portrayed government demand for plain silk to pay for the Uyghur horse trade and as supplies for the troops as equally damaging to women's work. Following Daizong's edict of 771, regulations targeting luxury silk production declined. Under his successor, Dezong (r. 779–805), the government focused its energy on overhauling the financial system.

MONEY, MARKETS, AND MOBILITY

Officials serving in the postrebellion government viewed the An Lushan Rebellion as a colossal rip in the social and moral fabric of empire. This sense of urgency stemmed from dramatic changes in the financial administration of empire that shifted the economy and society away from the root (agriculture) and toward the branch (commerce). Nowhere was this move more evident than in the institution of the twice-a-year tax system (*liangshui*) and the continuing growth of local and long-distance markets. The waning influence of the central government proceeded apace with the growing autonomy of provincial governors, who expanded their own fiscal administrations with the help of merchants. Provincial capitals flourished during the last century of Tang rule, attracting small- and large-scale merchants, artisans, and landless laborers. The investment of wealth and labor by this population, especially in the silk industry and other specialized crafts, stoked the engine of commerce.

The failure of the old tax system, which made farming a less desirable and sustainable livelihood, granted households greater autonomy to direct their labor into other trades. Lacking the prerebellion numbers of taxable individuals, as well as the administrative machinery necessary for the enforcement of the *zu-yong-diao* tax system, the state began to levy taxes on land and property. In the Dali period (766–779), the number of registered households fell to 1.3 million, with taxable households accounting for approximately 60 percent of the total, a slight fraction of the aggregate taxable households estimated in 755.[73] From 760 to 780, the state was only able to raise revenue through the land levy, an assortment of supplementary taxes, and the salt monopoly, which were all paid in either grain or copper cash. Provincial governors further extracted revenue through unauthorized and miscellaneous taxes.[74] Indirect taxation levied through the Salt and Iron Commission constituted the majority of revenues amassed by the government during this period. Owing to the severe loss of revenue, the state had to reevaluate its relationship with commerce and implemented a number of measures that relied on the agency of merchants to sustain a supply line of grain and cloth to the court.

In 780, Emperor Dezong finally abolished the *zu-yong-diao* taxes along with the provisional supplementary taxes enacted under Daizong, and replaced the old taxes with a twice-a-year tax system composed of a land levy (*dishui*) paid in grain and a household levy (*hushui*) assessed in coins.[75] Imposed in two installments, one in summer and one in autumn, the new system marked an important shift in state finance and provincial power. The two levies, based on an appraisal of the size and productive capacity of the taxpayer's property, were subsumed under a prefectural and provincial quota to be collected by provincial authorities. With the quota system, provincial governors were made responsible for sending the capital a fixed sum, but were largely free to dispose of the majority proportion of the revenue from the prefectures. The distribution of provincial quotas also varied so considerably that "the main sources of taxes and levies under heaven came from the Yangzi and Huai river valleys, where the life of the people was awfully difficult, but the collection of heavy taxes never ceased."[76]

Conceived as a way to bring revenue collection under the direct control of the central government, the two-tax system generated unbearable hardships for common taxpayers. Initial assessment of tax quotas according to money terms in 780 was completed during a period of high inflation, but with the expectation that taxes would also be paid in commodities—in particular, cloth—fixed at the same inflated prices. Beginning in 785, the economy experienced a long period of deflation with the market price of commodities falling progressively, which lasted until the reassessment of tax rates and quotas in commodity terms in 821.[77] The falling prices of commodities meant that an increasing quantity of goods had to be levied in order to fulfill the inflated cash quotas with silk cloth at deflated prices. Constant shortage of coins in circulation and limited copper resources compounded the state's inability to control price fluctuations. In 794, Lu Zhi (754–805) penned a memorial against the twice-a-year tax that estimated the tax quota paid in silk had doubled since its imposition in 780.[78] The government reacted to the deflation crisis and copper scarcity by reviving Xuanzong's initiatives that promoted the use of silk as an auxiliary form of currency to be combined with coins for payments in large amounts.[79]

For Lu Zhi, the twice-a-year tax signified a break with the state's traditional economic principles. Unlike the old taxation system, the new tax was based upon property and not the "adult male" (*dingshen*) or peasant-producer. He argued that the simple conversion of varying types of property that yielded different returns into a flat cash rate only contributed to significant inequalities in actual taxation. The system enabled those involved in commerce to prosper and vagrants to escape the burden of taxation while peasant-producers with fixed homes labored to meet ever-increasing quotas.[80] Given the extraordinary demands on peasant-producers, Lu Zhi's memorial articulated the longstanding fear among Confucian statesmen that the fundamental occupation (*benye*) would be gradually eschewed for other forms of livelihood. By the 780s, many officials were themselves "competing against the common people for profit" by investing their wealth in a variety of commercial and industrial ventures. By the end of Daizong's reign, a large number of official-owned stores (*si*) and warehouses (*di*) had sprouted up in Yangzhou. The government responded by unsuccessfully banning the enterprises.[81] Members of the imperial guard violated market regulations by setting up open stalls in the main streets of the capital.[82]

The social and economic landscape of the ninth century was characterized by a proliferation of markets in towns and cities and a concentration of the population in urban areas. The displacement of populations to the provinces, specifically the southern regions, powered the local economies and resulted in the expansion of tea, rice, and barley production.[83] Economic freedom from the capital allowed provincial revenues to be distributed locally, allowing regional trade and industry to flourish. Ongoing border conflicts with the Tibetan empire disrupted the trade routes and, in turn, transformed the demographic makeup of merchants. During the early Tang, Sogdians, Persians, and later Uyghurs formed the majority of large-scale traders and local shopkeepers. The political conflict along the shrinking northwest frontier resulted in the decline of foreign dominance of internal commerce, giving rise to local merchant capital.[84] These changes in the economic and political structure enabled the rise of local merchant elites, who became indispensable to the government—inciting outrage among scholar-officials.

The prosperity of merchants during the latter half of the Tang was precipitated in part by the dissolution of the enclosed market place.[85] In addition to the official markets in the two capitals of Chang'an and Luoyang, markets in multiple locations on the frontier were set up for "mutual trade" (*hushi*) with foreign merchants in the seventh and eighth centuries. A network of rural markets (*caoshi*), forbidden by the county and prefectural governments, existed alongside official markets in the provinces.[86] Beginning in the eighth century, rural markets outside of walled cities and at river crossings sprang up in multiple provinces.[87] While serving as the administrator of the revenue section (*sihu canjun*) in Hangzhou after the rebellion, Li Hua (715–766) witnessed "ten thousand merchants gather and the myriad of goods multiplying" in the city.[88] Situated at the southern terminus of the Grand Canal, Hangzhou became a thriving commercial center during the postrebellion era. As commercial activities increased, township markets (*zhenshi*) and rural markets became necessary venues for trade as the expansion of commerce called for more trading sites than were authorized by the state. In the late eighth and early ninth centuries, these markets popped up in large numbers across the empire, most notably in the Jiangnan region.[89]

By the mid-ninth century, the official market system had ceased to exist, but it remained legally in force until the end of the dynasty. In 851, the government endeavored to restore official control over trade by imposing the laws of the old official markets and outlawing the creation of markets in counties of less than three thousand households—with the exception of locales that served as important communication centers with established market facilities.[90] Two years later, the government abandoned the measure and made no further attempts to revive the controlled market system.[91] The disintegration of the government's restrictive market structure concurred with a relaxation of the laws and policies devised to maintain the inferior social status of merchants, including sumptuary regulations that circumscribed their dress, houses, and vehicles for transport. This shift in the court's attitude toward merchants and trade in the mid-eighth century suggests that the postrebellion government was less concerned with preserving direct control over commerce than with exploiting it as a source of revenue.

Prior to 755, the state derived little revenue from merchants under direct taxation, as merchants without landholdings were only expected to contribute labor services and special corvée duties (*seyi*). During the rebellion years, the government enforced a series of emergency measures to maximize revenues that openly targeted merchants and artisans. Grand families and wealthy merchants in the Huai and Yangzi river valleys were ordered to pay taxes on their property to the government; in 769 a new form of land tax designed to subsume merchants and artisans under direct taxation was instituted.[92] The government also began to tax commerce and participate in the production and monopoly sale of important commodities like salt, liquor, and tea. This new outlook on merchants was encapsulated in the recommendation by officials of Dezong's court to take (*kuo*) money from them: "Goods and profits are stored in the hands of wealthy merchants. We request that money be taken from them. [From among] those who can supply ten thousand strings of cash, we will borrow the rest [of their money] to supply the troops. We plan to borrow from no more than one or two thousand merchants in the realm, which should be sufficient for several years."[93] For the remainder of the dynasty, the government relied on the practice of "taking" (*kuoshang*), borrowing (*jie*), or taking loans from merchants (*daishang*) in times of crisis.

The growing population of small- and large-scale merchants, who came to dominate the urban areas and flourishing provincial regions, played a critical role in the fashion system through their participation in the silk industry. Small-scale merchants were composed primarily of petty commodity producers, including craftsmen and owners of minor workshops, and farmers who had abandoned agriculture to conduct trade. Large-scale merchants were involved in the manufacture and sale of basic and luxury commodities, including grain, silk, tea, and precious metals. Affluent merchants also offered high-interest loans, operated pawnshops, and during the currency crisis sought profit through currency speculation.[94]

How these merchants disposed of their accumulated capital has been recorded in anecdotes compiled in *Extensive Records from the Taiping Reign* (Taiping guangji), assorted jottings (*biji*), and tales (*chuanqi*). Merchants like Dou Yi, who lived during Dezong's reign, invested his capital in "Dou Family shops," reselling merchandise purchased with his wealth to maximize his profits.[95] Others hoarded their monetary wealth or squandered it on luxury goods. Yang Chongyi of the Kaiyuan era (713–741) spent his wealth on "things such as dress and ornaments, [and] he exceeded the [distinctions of] princes and nobles."[96] Similarly, Wang Yuanbao of the Tianbao era (742–756) "devoted his efforts to splendor and extravagance and in his ornaments and dress, he surpassed the princes and nobles."[97] Merchant capital was also turned into high-interest loans (both foreign and local merchants dabbled in usury) or was used to purchase land.

Finally, a small minority of merchants invested capital in handicraft production and, in particular, silk manufacture. He Mingyuan, a wealthy merchant of Dingzhou in Hebei, owned five hundred looms for the weaving of *ling*-twill damasks.[98] He likely paid hired laborers (*gugong* or *guyong*) to operate these looms.[99] Before the mid-eighth century, craftsmen were primarily employed by government-operated workshops as short-term corvée laborers. With the implementation of "monetary contributions in lieu of corvée service" (*nazi daiyi*) under Daizong in 773, the number of hired craftsmen working in the private handicraft industry increased as their labor was no longer controlled by the government.[100] Private investment in silk workshops fostered the growth of the luxury silk industry in the latter half of the dynasty. An increasing population of hired workers further boosted the number and productivity of these private workshops, which crafted a wide range of goods for the commercial markets.

By the mid-ninth century, the social landscape of the empire had experienced a sweeping transformation. The swelling population in the Jiangnan region of non-officeholding elites, made up of merchants, landowners, and families involved in regional industries, was evidence of the social and economic mobility afforded to nontraditional elites.[101] Wealthy merchants also pursued the established pathways of elite power by educating their sons in preparation for the imperial examinations. The government's dependence on merchant capital for revenue helped ease the restrictions on education and entry to examinations that had been imposed on the sons of merchants.[102] The intellectuals of the postrebellion era remained critical of trade, vocalizing their disapproval of the predatory merchant through poetry. The lingering reservations of the intellectual elite were not surprising since the development of commerce softened the social distinctions between wealthy merchants and officeholding elites.

THE FINAL ACT: A BAN ON NEW STYLES

The final sumptuary decree of the eighth century, enacted by Dezong in 791, amended the official dress of imperial commissioners and court officials. The emperor assigned new insignia to military and surveillance commissioners and ordered all officials who attended regular court audience to wear *ling*-twill damask robes with jade and gold ornamented belts.[103] This decree marked the final shift in Tang sumptuary practice, in which the proper display of imperially sanctioned status returned to the forefront of the emperor's concerns. At the beginning of the Zhenyuan era (785–805), Du You had submitted a memorial to the emperor, pressing him to return building works, the manufacture of textiles, and the provision of fuel to the responsibility of the regular offices.[104] By promulgating a new dress code for his officials, instead of directing his attention to matters of court-controlled silk manufacture, Dezong sought to assert his supreme authority through exercising his right as emperor to dress his officials. By the end of his reign, Dezong had failed to restore normal operations to many parts of his bureaucracy and govern his officials' sartorial behavior.

The next emperor to dedicate substantial attention to sumptuary regulation was Wenzong (r. 826–840), who soon after his ascension decreed that clothing, vehicles, and ornaments must correspond to one's rank in the official hierarchy in an effort to exhort officials to practice frugality and to uphold their status as state-sanctioned elites.[105] Two years later in 829, Wenzong issued a sumptuary statute targeting the invention of "new styles" (*xinyang*). He proclaimed, "Throughout the empire, new styles cannot be used to weave unique goods for tribute, and the looms for weaving fine and exquisite silks like patterned silk-hemp cloth and *liao ling*-twills are also forbidden. I order that in the first month of the New Year, all of the looms shall be burned and discarded."[106] Wenzong was not the first to resort to such coercive measures in order to ban the fabrication, circulation, and use of opulent silks, but he was the first to single out novelty as an object of regulation. In targeting "new styles," the emperor had called attention to the loss of government control over silk production in the provinces, where local officials had asserted supervisory power over the weaving households.

Wenzong's attack on new styles suggests that his court not only failed to seize control over silk weaving workshops, but also lost its privileged status as arbiter of what was new. The vague category of new styles points to the glaring fact that the court could no longer keep up with the latest designs and patterns. The driving forces of novelty may have been the silk artisans who migrated to provincial workshops following the rebellion, where they employed new styles to "weave unique goods." By calling for the destruction of looms, Wenzong's ban brought to the fore the inextricable relationship between textile technology, innovation, and demand. Desire for aesthetic play and demand for new styles were supported and propelled forward by the expanded technical infrastructure of the silk industry.

Undeterred by the court's tenuous grip on power and fashion, the emperor decided to take full action against the sartorial crimes of his subjects and dispatched Vice Director of the Left (You Pushe) Wang Ya (d. 835) to revise the sumptuary guidelines governing dress and vehicles in 832. Wenzong aimed to reinstitute a strict sumptuary regime similar to the set of regulations passed by the founding emperor Gaozu.[107] Wang Ya, after an extensive review of the extant codes, submitted a memorial to the emperor offering suggestions for reform.[108] His proposal was divided into six parts, the first on official dress, followed by sections on women, servants, and entertainers, robes (*pao'ao*), fabrics and cuts, makeup and adornment, and footwear. The colors and types of ornaments assigned to each rank of officials were reimposed: princes and officials of the first to third ranks were instructed to wear purple and jade; the fourth and fifth ranks were to wear red and gold; the sixth and seventh ranks were to wear green and silver; the eighth and ninth ranks were to wear blue and brass.[109] Persons not of official status and commoners were restricted to wearing yellow and copper and iron ornaments.[110]

By the first half of the ninth century, the epic proportions of fashionable dress led the emperor to sanction Wang Ya's proposal for regulations on the lengths and widths of robes, skirts, and sleeves. The trains of men's robes were not to exceed six centimeters and sleeves could not be wider than thirty-nine centimeters.[111] Women's skirts were not to exceed five *fu* or roughly 2.65 meters, the trains of skirts were limited to ten centimeters long, and sleeves were restricted to approximately fifty centimeters wide.[112] The initiative also sought to curtail popular styles of adornment such as elaborately tall coiffures, shaved eyebrows, exposed foreheads, and the wasteful expenditure incurred on account of this vanity. One of the reforms instituted a ban on the manufacture of novel products that targeted the production of woven straw sandals (*gaotou caolü*) from Wu-Yue in Zhejiang.[113] The woven straw slippers (*gaotou caolü*) from Wu-Yue, described as "fine and delicate like twill and crepe silks," were an innovation of the ninth century ("the previous dynasty did not have [them]"). Since making these slippers was "time-consuming and harmful to productivity," as well as a "rather profligate use of skill[ed labor]," Wang Ya recommended that they be promptly banned.

Wang's memorial merely rearticulated the idealized sartorial regime that had been prescribed by the Ministry of Rites (Libu) with suggestions tailored to ninth century sartorial tends. Following the promulgation of the new dress codes, the people complained; thus, Wang Ya's recommended restrictions on dress and vehicles were never carried out.[114] Wenzong, however, remained committed to his regulatory project. A few years later, in 839 on the night of the Lantern Festival, Princess Yan'an entered Weitai Hall to watch the lantern-lighting ceremony alongside Emperor Wenzong, the three grand empress dowagers, and her fellow princesses. Draped in billowy folds of silk, Yan'an was dressed according to the reigning silhouette of the ninth century—capacious sleeves and a long, trailing skirt. Enraged by the sight of her extravagant dress, Wenzong rebuked the young princess and sent her home immediately. As punishment for the offense, her husband, Dou Huan, suffered the loss of two months' salary.[115] That same year, Li Deyu (787–850), serving as commissioner of Huainan, sent a memorial to the throne requesting to limit the lengths and widths of women's garments.[116] Although the emperor approved the measure, there is no evidence of enforcement.[117] Wenzong, like Xuanzong and Daizong before him, struggled to regulate the immense quantities of cloth that coursed through the empire as money, gifts, and materials for aesthetic play.

CONCLUSION

Elites in Tang China availed themselves of a wide range of materials to fashion a body/self to be looked at, scrutinized, and remembered: silk for dress, paper for letters and manuscripts, and stone for tomb epitaphs.[118] However, none received more regulatory attention than the possession and display of sumptuous silks. A ubiquitous store of value, textiles played a central role in social, economic, and literary exchange. As money, silk—together with hemp cloth—was the dominant form of payment used in the handling of large and small transactions. As gifts, silk mediated diplomatic relations between rulers, maintained tributary relations between emperor and subject, and confirmed affective bonds between friends. As garments, silk conveyed the status of the wearer. As metaphor, silk signified the excesses of empire. Most importantly, silk, and more broadly, cloth, served to materialize social roles, gendered relations, and political hierarchies. Cloth constituted the fabric of society, weaving together emperor and empire to the labor of his gendered subjects. Such an invaluable resource (and metaphor) was accordingly subject to stringent control by the government.

The sumptuary regime, however, aimed to restrict all subjects, including the emperor himself, from the pleasures of aesthetic play. Appeals to the people's frugality and sense of propriety were undermined by the extravagance that Tang emperors themselves exhibited in their construction of palaces, in their enthusiasm for lavish banquets with dancing horses, and especially in their desire for painstakingly woven silks. During his brief reign, Emperor Jingzong (r. 824–826) commissioned one thousand bolts of *liao*-twill damasks (*liaoling*) from the workshops in Yuezhou (located in today's Zhejiang). Jingzong's decree was a clear exercise of his prerogative as emperor.[119] Upon receiving this order, however, Li Deyu, as the surveillance commissioner of Zhexi, implored the emperor to abandon the mandate by stressing the exorbitant nature of the order, "Black swans and heavenly horses, forest leopards and spiral braids, the patterns and colors are rare and extraordinary, but are only for Your Majesty's enjoyment. Currently the cost of weaving one thousand bolts would be extreme. I humbly beg Your Majesty to abandon the imperial order of silks."[120] Li concluded by pleading, "so that the common people everywhere can benefit from the Emperor's frugality." Neither the emperor, nor his subjects, could resist the allure of sumptuous silks in their pursuit of aesthetic play.

PART TWO

Surfaces

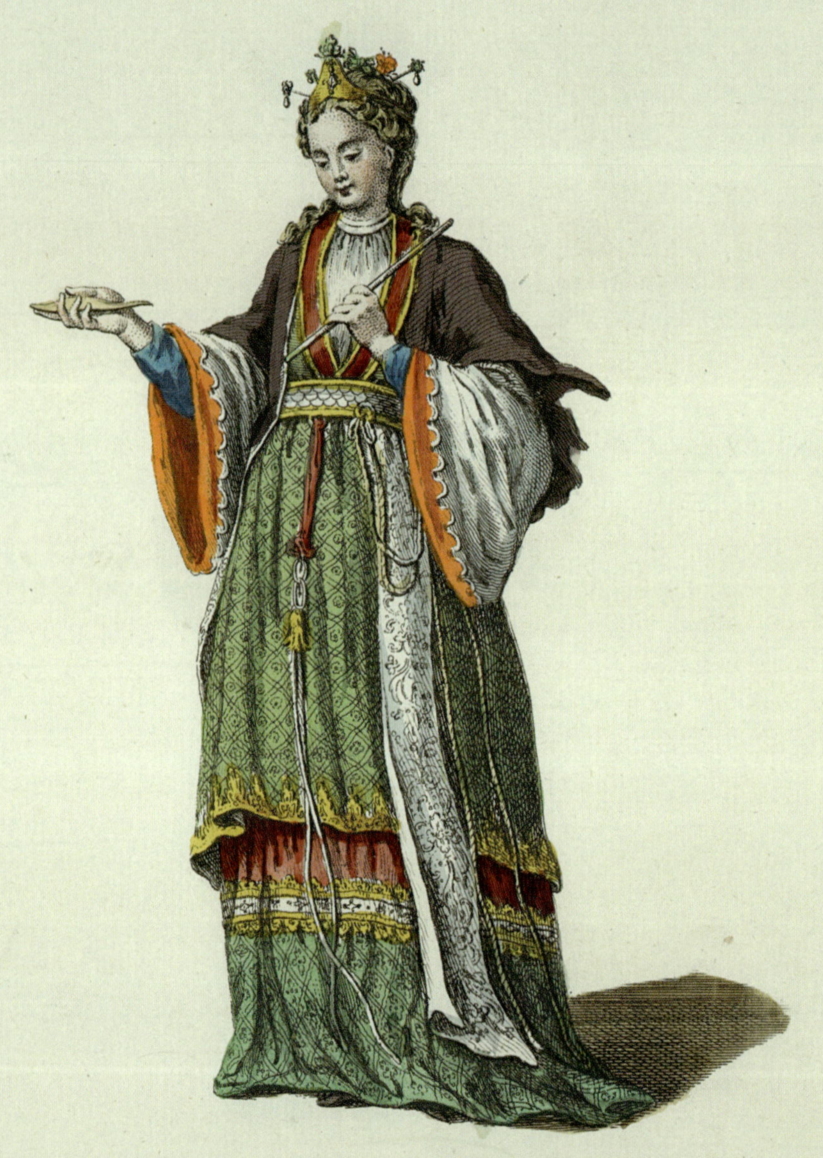

Habit of a Lady of China, in 1700

Dame Chinoise

CHAPTER 3

Style

FASHIONING THE TANG BEAUTY

FASHION IN CHINA, AS ELSEWHERE, IS INDEXED BY CHANGES IN STYLES of dress. In an article titled "The Fashions Change in China Just as They Do Here," published in the *New York Times* over a century ago, the writer proclaimed that new modish styles were "springing up in China, phoenix-like, with startling rapidity."[1] Photographs of women in the "old style" were contrasted with the "new style" and the "latest thing": shortened coats, high collars, cotton gloves, and skirts of varied shades, with wider hems. The writer located the spirit of fashion in the penetrating influence of foreign dress and mentality on Shanghai women's sartorial desires, declaring, "in China, there are fashions, dazzling shop windows full of new ideas in women's clothing, seasonable departures from the garments of yesterday that prove to the Chinese feminine as all-absorbing as the fleeting fashions of her sisters of the West." In one sweep, the writer captured the longstanding assumptions that have shaped histories of fashion: we know fashion occurs, at home and in distant lands, when yesterday's dress looks different from that of today. By the turn of the twentieth

FIGURE 3.1. Jean-Baptiste du Halde (1674–1743), "Habit of a lady of China in 1700. Autre Dame Chinoise." Hand-colored engraving, H. 34 cm. The Miriam and Ira D. Wallach Division of Art, Prints and Photographs: Art and Architecture Collection, New York Public Library. The New York Public Library Digital Collections.

century, this understanding of fashion as a predilection for change in dress styles, one with a Western root, had become a powerful, universal truth.

European writers have long opined the lack of fashion in China. Already by the eighteenth century, the French Jesuit historian Jean-Baptiste du Halde (1674–1743) had identified dress as a key site of difference between China and Europe: "As for what is here called Fashion, it has nothing at all in it like what we call so in Europe, where the manner of Dress is subject to many Changes."[2] To illustrate his point, he included engravings of Chinese dress to augment his descriptions of their customary nature. The pairing of images with exhaustive descriptions of Chinese customs, culled from eyewitness sources, served to strengthen du Halde's claims about veracity. Du Halde had never traveled to the empire, but rather relied on the accounts of Jesuit missionaries to compose his four lavishly illustrated folios. He emphasized the exactness of the illustrations, asserting that he had supplied the artist Antoine Humblot (ca. 1700–1758) with Chinese pictorial sources (fig. 3.1).[3] The draping of fabric on "Dame Chinoise," along with the shape and cut of her garments, is unlike the seventeenth- or eighteenth-century representations of women found in Qing dynasty court paintings, such as the contemporaneous screen of *Twelve Beauties*, made for Emperor Yongzheng (r. 1723–1735) when he was a young prince (fig. 3.2).

Instead, Humblot's drawings of Chinese subjects stand in closer relation to the engravings of Athanasius Kircher's *China Illustrata* (1667) or Cesare Vecellio's *De gli habiti antichi et moderni di diversi parti del mondo* (1590), and the later work of William Alexander (1797). Du Halde's account, nonetheless, circulated alongside these illustrated texts on China that helped to lock an image of the enrobed, fashionless Chinese figure in the European imagination (fig. 3.3). What made the engraving of the "Dame Chinoise" compelling to a European audience, whose primary contact with dressed Chinese bodies was mediated by comparable texts and images, was its coherence with the pictorial style and form that had preceded and followed the publication of du Halde's tome. When Fernand Braudel echoed du Halde's observation that China lacked fashion two centuries later, he offered up as proof the uniformity found in their pictorial depictions, remarking that "the silk costume with golden embroidery drawn by Father de Las Cortes in 1626 was the same shown in so many eighteenth-century engravings."[4] For Braudel, and du Halde before him, continuity in Chinese dress and culture was sufficiently validated by individual perception of the visual evidence. Pictorial style gave change a visual and material form, making novelty recognizable to the viewer through modifications in the formal-aesthetic qualities of representation. Fashion's existence rested on its historical documentation through images, such that an American reader of the *New York Times* can flip through photographs of Shanghai women and agree with the writer that the new style of skirts was indeed different from the old. This reliance on stylistic change as the marker of fashion gave rise to a long-lasting conflation of dress with style and in turn with fashion.

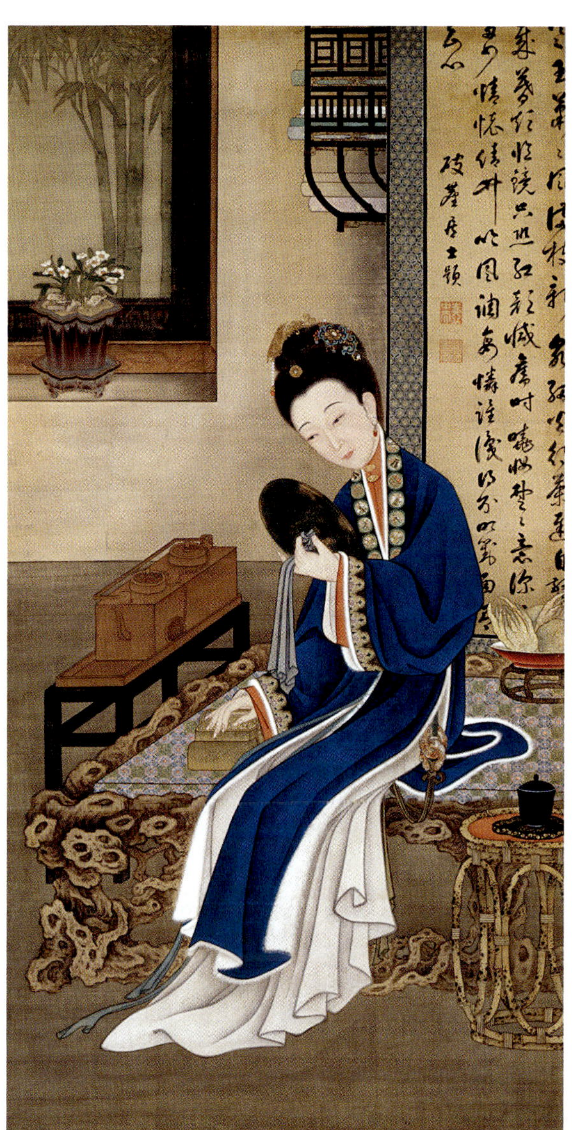

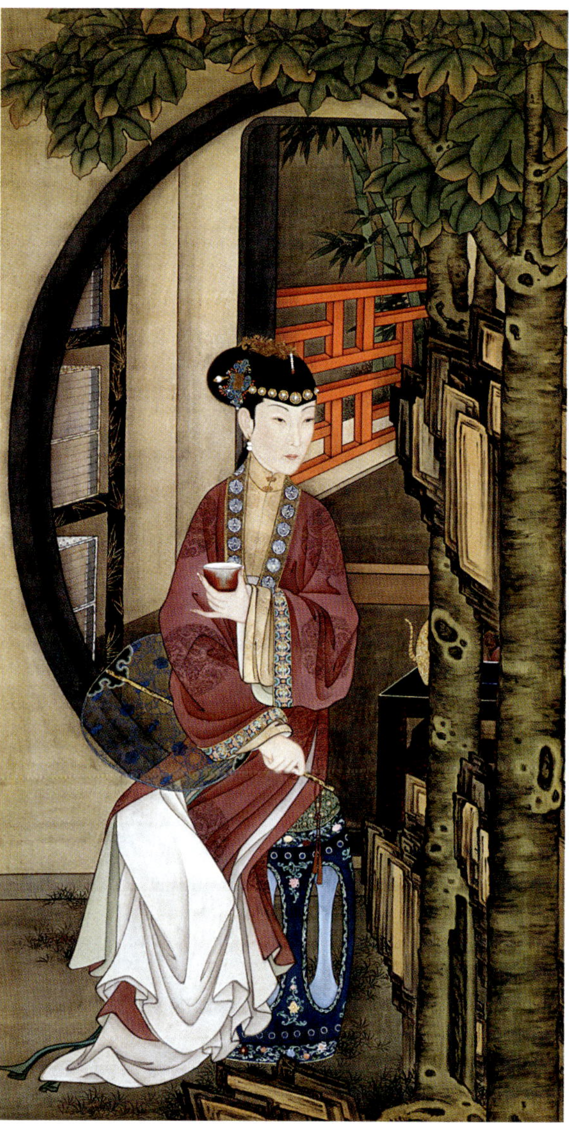

FIGURE 3.2. Unidentified court artists, Qing dynasty, eighteenth century. *Twelve Beauties at Leisure Painted for Prince Yinzhen* (the future Emperor Yongzheng), two of a set of twelve. The paintings of twelve beauties, each dressed in Han Chinese women's attire, decorated a screen in the prince's study at the Summer Palace (Yuanmingyuan). Each woman wears a high-collar, short robe, and long skirt underneath an overgarment (*pifeng*). With the exception of the skirt, the silk garments are differentiated by color, pattern, and decorative trim. Hanging scroll, ink and color on silk; H. 184 cm, W. 98 cm. Photo provided by the Palace Museum, Beijing.

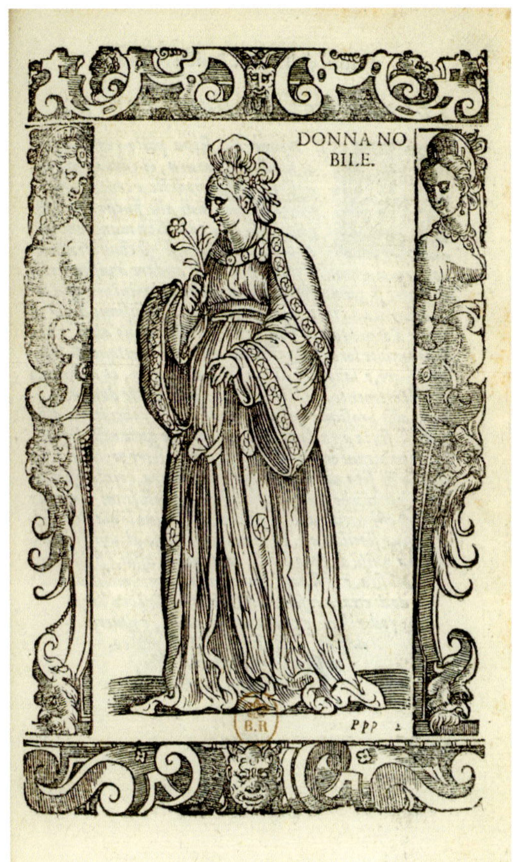

FIGURE 3.3. Cesare Vecellio (1521–1601), *De gli habiti antichi, e moderni di diverse parti del mondo libri due*, "Donna nobile della China," 1590. The wide sleeves, trimmed with a decorative band, and full skirt are consistent with the "Dame Chinoise." Woodcut; H. 16.7 cm, W. 12.5 cm, D. 5.2 cm (overall). Département Estampes et Photographie, Bibliothèque Nationale de France.

In the twentieth century, fashion became synonymous with change and belonged exclusively to the domain of clothing—and more specifically, women's clothing. Such a narrow understanding of fashion is supported by the reliance of fashion scholars on the evolution of garments and accessories, as registered in print and image, to identify the development of individual taste and social competition. The writing of fashion history then entails what art historian Alexander Nagel has described as "the endless quotation of past styles [that] relies on a continual raiding of the visual record."[5] Shifting hemlines and waistlines become markers of fashionable change, while stagnant silhouettes indicate the absence of a desire for change—which by definition signifies the absence of fashion. Missing from this approach is an examination of the historical relationship between pictorial style and dress style, and in turn, between pictorial style and fashion.[6]

Changes in pictorial style—a cohesive visual form pegged to a particular time and locale—did not merely document dress styles, but also facilitated the spread of fashion in Tang China.[7] Awareness of pictorial style bespoke a temporal-spatial consciousness that was critical to how men and women in the Tang fashioned themselves. Across the

Tang empire, variations in shape, silhouette, and pattern across time were rendered to the viewer through its visual representation in paintings, decorative objects, funerary goods, and sculpture. Anticipating du Halde, the ninth-century scholar Zhang Yanyuan stated in his preeminent text on painting that one's knowledge of the vicissitudes of clothing was conducted primarily through encounters with older representations found in works of art. In discovering temporal and geographical difference in older works, people in the Tang empire could not escape the sense of living and belonging to a new and different world. This historical consciousness about dress and its representation was made sensuous in the creation of the voluptuous Tang Beauty at the beginning of the eighth century, whose iconic form and trailing skirt came to signify a host of ideas about female sensuality, luxury, and empire. So pervasive was this image that representations of the plump beauty came to stand for the Tang empire itself. In becoming aware of the temporally sensitive bodies, swathed in silks, with high coiffures, people also came to a new understanding of the historicity of pictorial representation. Works of art, through their presence and by presenting a *presence*, intervened in the fashion system.

The formats and mediums of tomb figurines, murals, and hand-scroll paintings reveal how painters and artisans depicted the relationship between clothes and the female body through the principle of fashion as aesthetic play.[8] Excavated murals and figurines from elite tombs provide the largest archive of visual evidence documenting the clothing culture of the Tang dynasty.[9] Conceived of as a residence for the spirit of deceased, the tomb was constructed accordingly as a ritual space and an enacted space, inhabited by the cosmic and the mundane alike.[10] As a space to be lived in and thus, enacted by the spirit, tomb walls and niches were populated by servants, musicians, dancers, grooms, and horses.[11] Whereas male guards, attendants, and musicians were depicted in near homogeneous forms, Tang dynasty painters and artisans approached the clothed female figure as a surface to be *fashioned*. A painted, sculpted, or dressed figure was rendered individual and distinct through her bodily adornment, and the style of the figure's depiction tied her to a specific time. Changes in style were made possible by both transformations in wardrobes and innovations in aesthetic forms. Analysis of the formal properties that governed the representation of the clothed image is key to uncovering how artist-image makers participated in a process of fashioning.

Image-making shared a deep-rooted affinity with fashioning as both practices were supremely semiotic. In pictorial representation, Tang painters and artisans replicated the process of seeing and acquiring information to arrange visual material in an intelligible manner for the beholder. Artist-image makers treated the face and the clothed body as sites to be differentiated through forms of adornment that they pulled from the material world; in so doing, they were engaged in the same aesthetic play that they sought to represent. Like an artisan drawing from a repertoire of patterns, shapes, and bodily poses to build a likeness of a court attendant, a woman in the court presumably pulled out garments from a "wardrobe" to fashion a look with the aim of communicating her status—social, temporal, and geographic—to the spectator. In tandem with the silk industry, this reciprocal process of image-making and fashioning, guided by aesthetic play, was the motor driving fashion forward.

STYLING THE WOMAN'S WARDROBE

In order to see how pictorial style and dress style were rendered and made accessible to Tang dynasty viewers, we must first undo our modern notions of fashion as hemline history. Pictorial representation constituted a parallel discourse to sumptuary legislation, in that the locus of difference was placed in the ornamentation and fabrication of garments. The pictorial program of tombs drew from the visual codes of popular dress and adornment to situate the clothed body in a social, ritual, and historical context.

A survey of this archive confirms that the staples of a Tang woman's wardrobe included an unlined short robe or top (*shan*) or a short jacket (*ru*), a skirt (*qun*), and shawl (*pibo*). These basics could be combined with a coat (*ao*), a cloak (*pao*), or the *banbi*, a cropped, short-sleeved jacket. Skirts, classified by color and pattern, were commonly high-waisted and worn belted underneath the bust. Each ensemble began with the short robe (*shan*), made from a single cut of silk fabric, or the jacket (*ru*) as the foundation on which the artist-imager maker layered more pieces (fig. 3.4). The versatility of these pieces allowed the artist-image maker to devise multiple looks. The shawl, in particular, provided a flat piece that could be draped across the shoulders, coiled around the arms, inserted under skirts, or loosely wrapped around the chest.

The inventory of painted, sculpted, and molded figures depicting officials, attendants, foreigners, and entertainers demonstrate how clothes were thought to look on a body. Painters and potters presented variations in dress practices that also denoted the physical properties of textiles, highlighting the way clothes shaped a body. Wall paintings depicting female attendants, private eunuchs, and officials constituted a significant portion of the decorated surfaces of Tang elite burial spaces. Unlike Buddhist murals intended for the living audience, artists working underground did not follow the same process for decorating temple walls, which included the use of preparatory sketches, pounces, followed by a combination of underdrawing (*baihua*), color painting, and finally, overdrawing or outlining.[12] In seventh-century murals, clothing was first outlined in moist black ink and then painted with an even application of opaque color. Following the application of color, artisans further augmented the details of the garments by overdrawing or with additional brushwork.[13] The ubiquitous A-line striped skirt of seventh-century tomb murals brings to mind the engineering of skirts, which were constructed from alternating panels of colored fabric sewn together.[14] Steady, continuous black ink lines in these early murals put on view the constructive instinct of

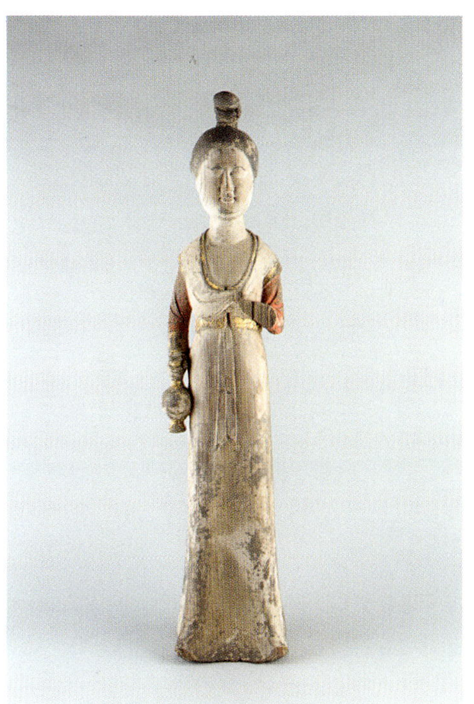
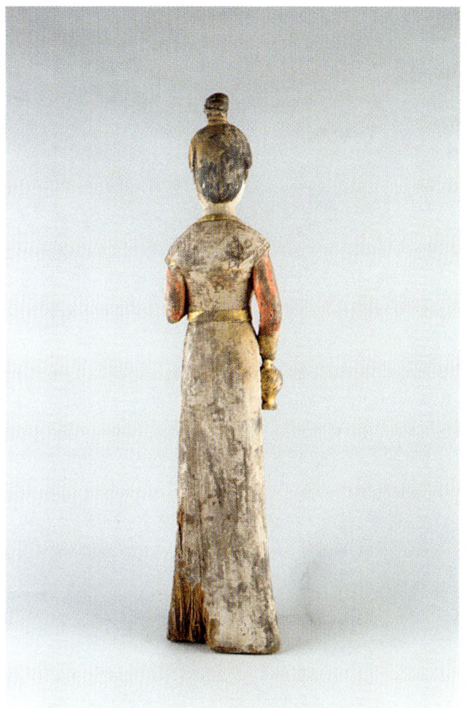

FIGURE 3.4. Standing female attendant, late seventh or early eighth century. The figure is clothed in the basic ensemble: a slim-fitting, long-sleeved robe with a low neckline; a high-waisted skirt; a *banbi*, which features a gold-painted trim; and a shawl. Wood with pigments; H. 49.5 cm. Gift of Enid A. Haupt, 1997, Metropolitan Museum of Art, New York.

the mural painter (fig. 3.5). The monochrome skirts feature even, contouring lines that run from the top of the skirt to the hem and delineate the skirt's structural form. Sleeve cuffs painted on the upper arms of the women show that they are wearing *banbi* over the long-sleeved top and tucked under the skirt. Shawls, wrapped around the figures' shoulders or wound around the arms, are executed in the same style of controlled brushwork that prioritized form over drapery. Each figure was adorned differently, a feat that the mural painter achieved through illustrating the countless possibilities of draping that was provided by the shawl.

By the first decade of the eighth century, monochrome skirts in hues of red, ochre, and mauve had displaced the striped skirt drawn in unvarying black lines. Murals of female figures found in the imperial tombs of Princess Yongtai and Crown Prince Yide exhibited a new direction in brushwork that was characterized by decorative restraint (fig. 3.6). Completed in 706 under the orders of Emperor Zhongzong, mural painters assigned to the three tombs used modulating lines to suggest shape and emphasize

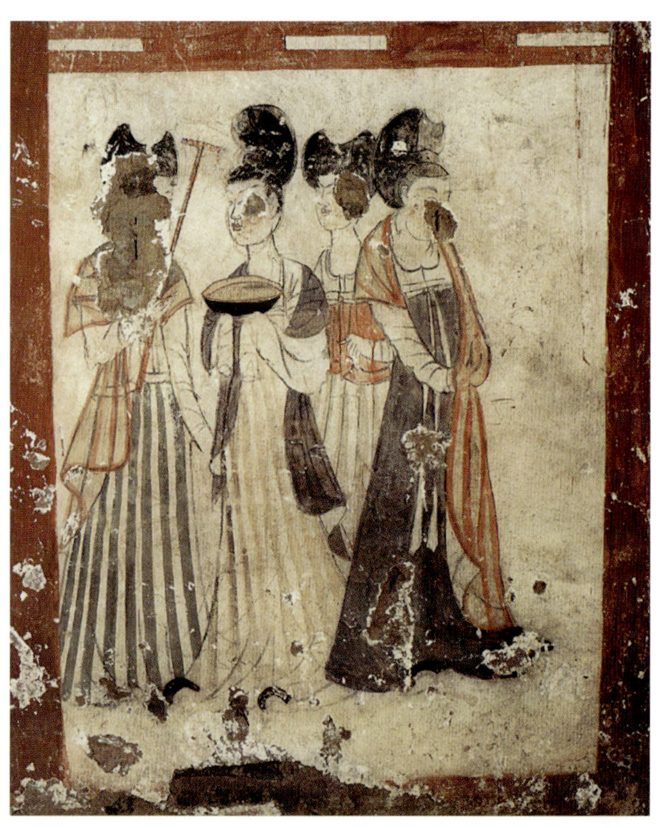

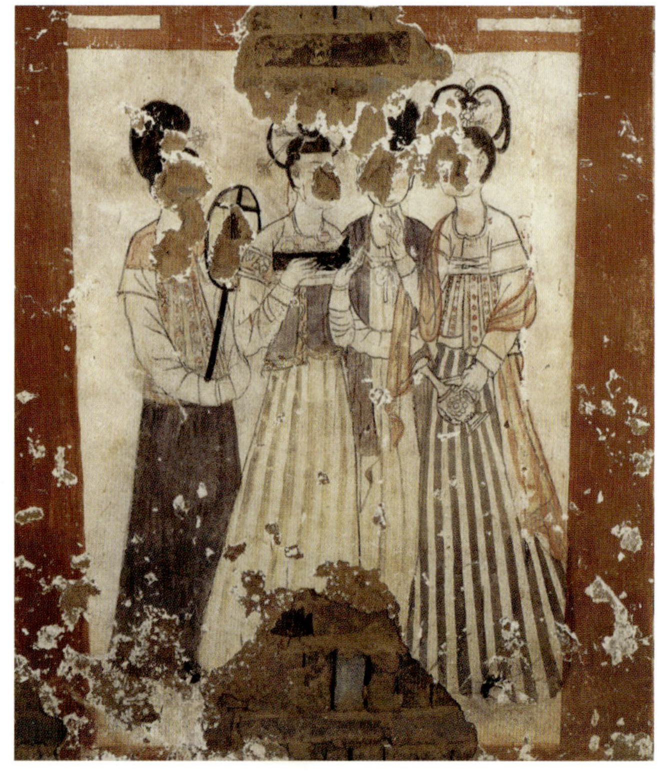

FIGURE 3.5. Female attendants. Groups of four female attendants carrying ritual and everyday objects are distributed between pillars. In each group, three of the women are shown wearing striped skirts and one is in monochrome. For the painters, the *banbi* and the shawl, in contrast to hairstyles and poses, were the key sites of differentiating the women. The painters worked to capture the translucency of the shawls, thus allowing the patterned bands of the *banbi* to peek through. H. 185 cm. East wall of the main tomb chamber, Tomb of Princess Xincheng, dated 663. Zhou Tianyou, ed., *Xincheng, Fangling, Yongtai gongzhu mu bihua* (Beijing: Wenwu chubanshe, 2002), 34–35.

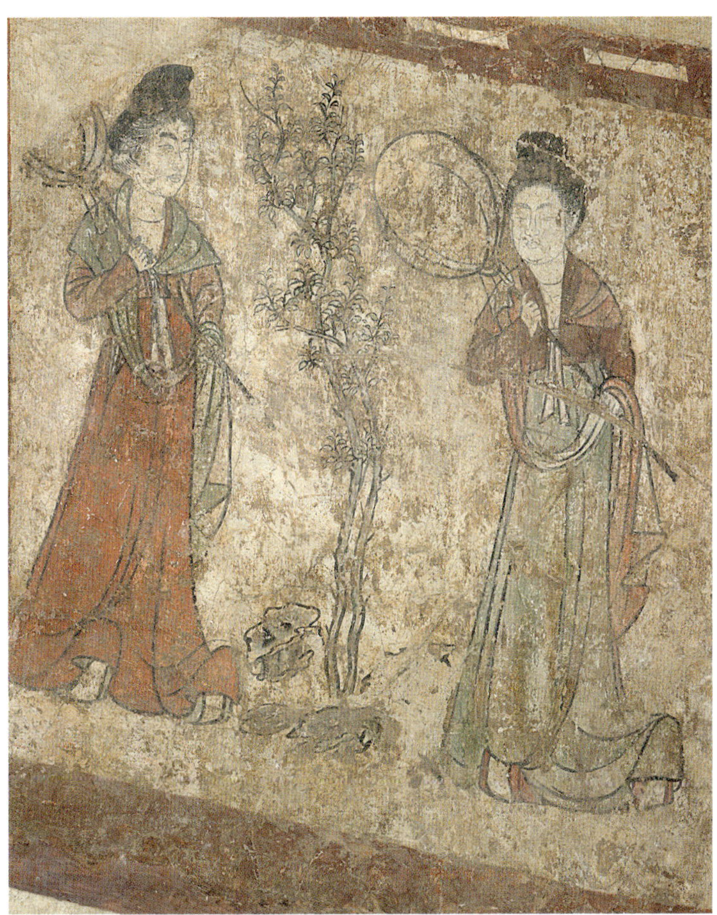

FIGURE 3.6. Female attendants. In contrast to Xincheng's tomb murals, color, rather than pattern, distinguishes the dress of the two figures. H. 166 cm. Mural on west wall of third corridor, Tomb of Crown Prince Yide, dated 706. Courtesy of Shaanxi History Museum.

drapery. Rather than relying on even-width lines to give garments structure and form, the artisans drew from an expanding repertoire of contouring and tapering brush lines of varying lengths and thickness to underscore loose folds around the figures' elbows and feet. Accompanying the new techniques in brushwork was an attention to the effects of light and dark shading. Mural painters increasingly played with light and shadow as a tool to highlight the surfaces of garments. Compared to seventh-century images of women, the early eighth-century figure's dress was simplified, sketched in sparse lines, and lightly color washed. The basic articles of the court woman's wardrobe also show modifications in cut and shape. Palace women are presented in long-sleeved short robes (*ru*) paired with the *banbi* over flowing skirts, accentuated by soft drapery folds. Wide shawls envelop the women's shoulders with one end tucked behind the jacket and the other looped around the arms. The open-front jackets are left unfastened, leaving a slight cleavage visible on many of the depicted women. Waistlines have dropped to further below the bust.

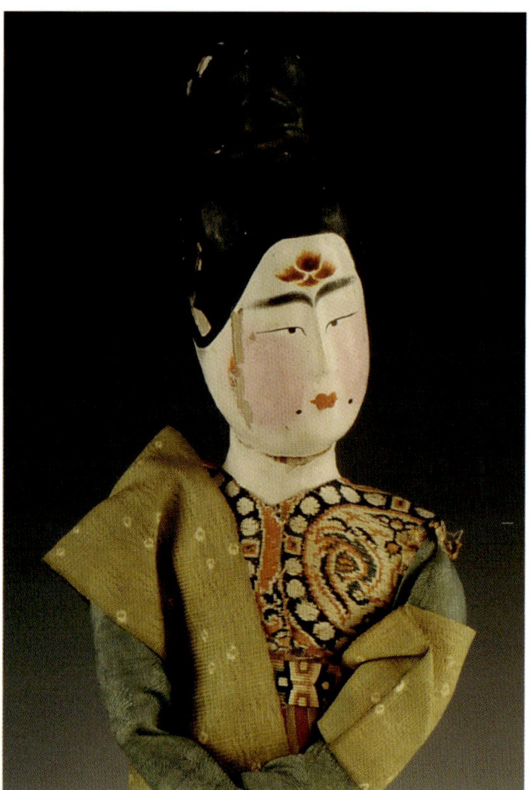

FIGURE 3.7. Female dancer (detail). Tomb of Zhang Xiong and Lady Qu, dated 688. Courtesy of Xinjiang Uyghur Autonomous Region Museum.

The three-dimensional form of tomb figurines allowed artisans to reproduce the tactility and drapery of garments through a range of visual strategies. Tomb figurines were maintained as representations of social and ritual bodies in the afterlife of the deceased, serving as markers of the deceased's status unto eternity.[15] Aided by technological advancements in low-fired ceramic production and glazes, the manufacture of pottery figurines reached its height in the Tang dynasty.[16] The head and the body were first modeled separately and then joined together. The surfaces of the body and face were carefully decorated by hand before the artisan glazed or painted the figurine.[17] In this way, artisans layered distinctive features onto the homogenous mass of bodies and heads to produce an assemblage of differentiated individual figures.

In the case of the wooden figurines clad in miniature replications of late seventh-century dress, which were found in the joint tomb of Lady Qu and Zhang Xiong, the artisans had to put the clothed bodies together in stages (fig. 3.7). Lady Qu's dancer, for example, was composed of four separate parts: the head molded from clay and painted white, the body made from a wooden frame, the paper arms, and her outfit. The wooden body was likely first clothed in the blouse, followed by the *banbi* that was tucked into the skirt. Then came the fastening of the belt, and, finally, the shawl was

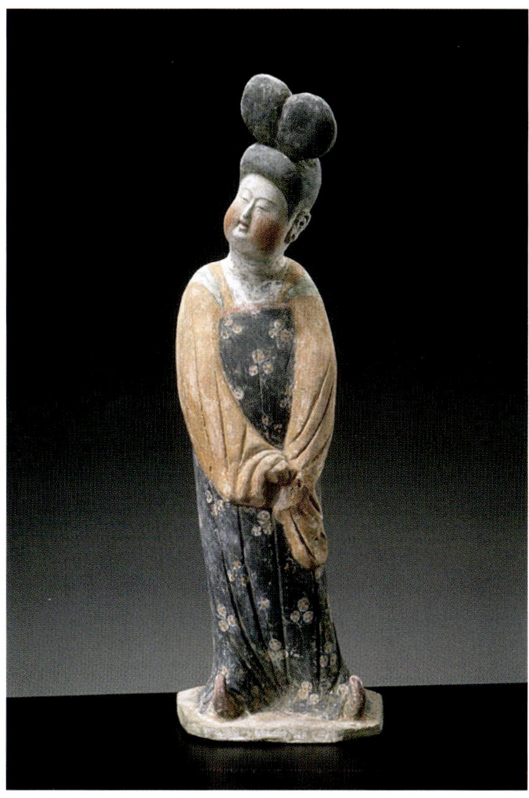

FIGURE 3.8. Lady with chignon, mid-eighth century. The figure wears a printed blue skirt fastened just over the bust and covering a loose robe with capacious sleeves. Her heavily rouged cheeks puts her in close relation to the female figures depicted in the screen paintings excavated from Astana Tomb 187 (fig. 3.29). Glazed earthenware with pigments; H. 54 cm. bpk/RMN-Grand Palais/Roger Asselberghs (70231762), Musée national des arts asiatiques–Guimet.

wrapped around the shoulders—replicating the stages of dressing.[18] Dressed in a sleeveless jacket secured with a belt made of silk tapestry, with a shawl of figured silk, and an A-line skirt assembled from alternating panels of patterned silk, the female figure is covered in seventh-century luxury silks. The jacket made of *jin* silk is decorated with a motif of two medallions, in which a pair of confronted birds is enclosed within a pearl roundel in each medallion. The shawl's repeated circle pattern is an example of the resist-dyeing technique that was also employed to decorate the modeled clothing of glazed figurines.

With earthenware figurines, Tang artisans deployed a host of techniques that included painting with pigments and applying lead-based glazes. Hand-painting the modeled body allowed artisans to replicate the repeated floral designs that were suggestive of advances made in silk weaving and dyeing. Patterned trimming on sleeve bands, collars, or along the front opening was the most common way to embellish a monochrome robe or jacket. Prominently displayed on the embellished robes, belts, and shawls of the figurines, the painted motifs refer to textile patterns that were in circulation during the period (fig. 3.8).[19] Decorative techniques applied to the surfaces of clay figurines occasionally overlapped with approaches to silk decoration. One popular

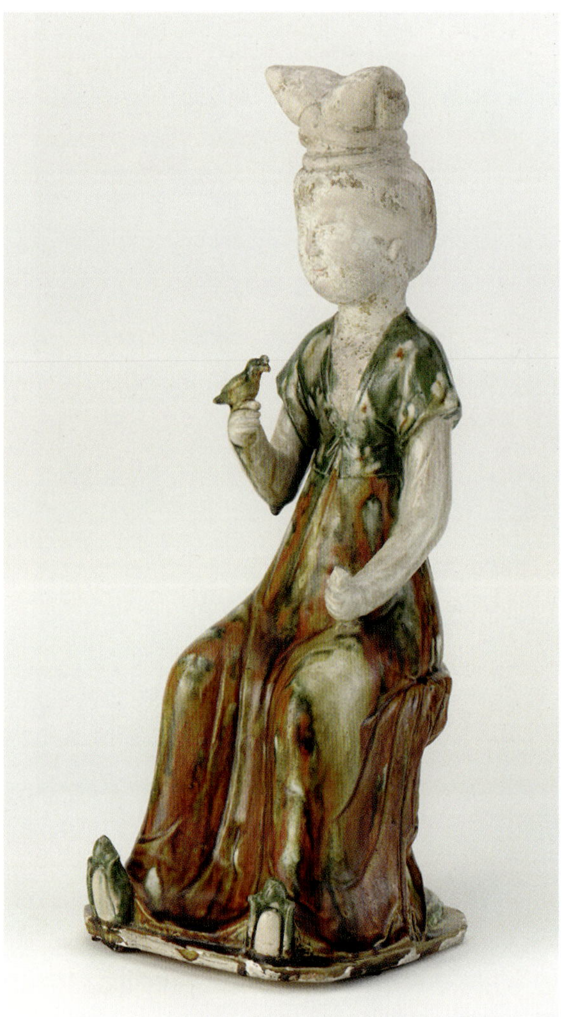

FIGURE 3.9. Tomb figure of a seated woman holding a bird, first half of eighth century. The floral motif on the figure's *banbi* mimics woven or resist-dyed patterns found on silks. Earthenware with *sancai* (three-color) lead-silicate glaze; H. 40.6 cm, W. 17.9 cm, D. 15.6 cm. Freer Gallery of Art and Arthur M. Sackler Gallery, Smithsonian Institution, Washington, DC: Purchase—funds provided by the Friends of the Freer and Sackler Galleries, F2001.8a-d.

method was the use of a resist substance, such as hot wax, to embellish the surfaces of both textiles and tomb figurines.[20] The finished pottery figurine would feature spots or floret patterning, closely resembling the polychrome woven, dyed, or printed silks of the period.[21] Such an effect can be seen in the "three-color" (*sancai*) glazed tomb figurines of the Tang dynasty, for which the artisan controlled the flow of the glaze with the use of a resistant substance to achieve repeating patterns (fig. 3.9).[22]

Artisans also incorporated molded appliqués as a technique for adding decorative texture to modeled garments (fig. 3.10). Used to create the floral ornaments on the seated figurine's paneled skirt, this technique aimed to imitate the popular persimmon calyx motif that would have been printed on or woven in a wide variety of silk weaves (fig. 3.11). The green silk tabby skirt excavated from Tomb 187 in Astana, Xinjiang, bears

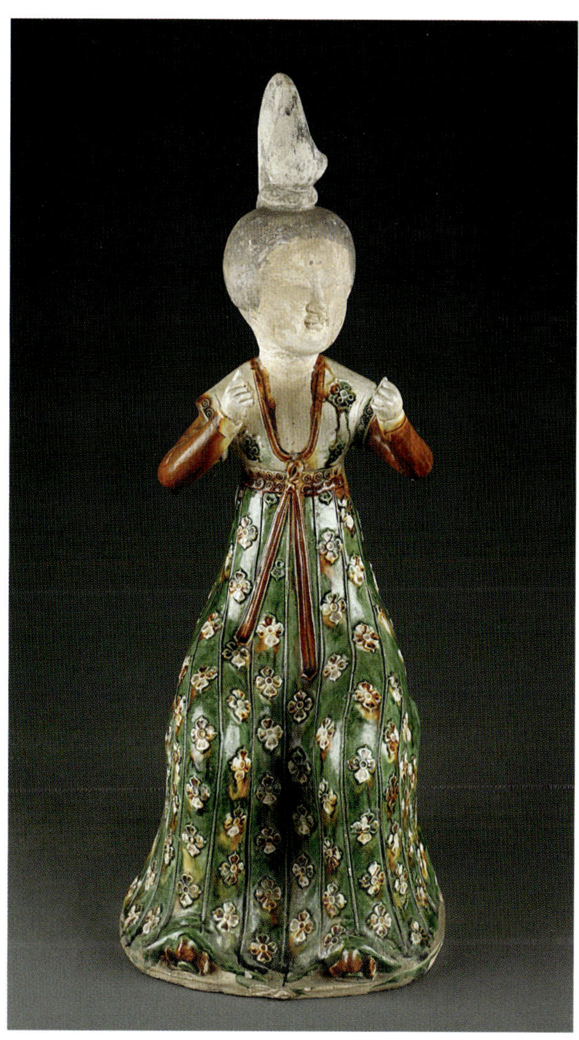

FIGURE 3.10. (*Left*) Seated female attendant. The figure wears a slim-fitting, low-cut blouse underneath a *banbi* and a high-waisted skirt. Earthenware with *sancai* (three-color) lead-silicate glaze; H. 47.3 cm. Wangjiafencun Tomb 90, dated early eighth century. Courtesy of Shaanxi History Museum.

FIGURE 3.11. (*Below*) Printed, plain-weave silk (*juan*) skirt. Composite flower and persimmon calyx patterns printed on green ground; L. 25 cm, W. 41 cm (hem). Tomb 187, Astana, Turfan, eighth century. Courtesy of Xinjiang Uyghur Autonomous Region Museum.

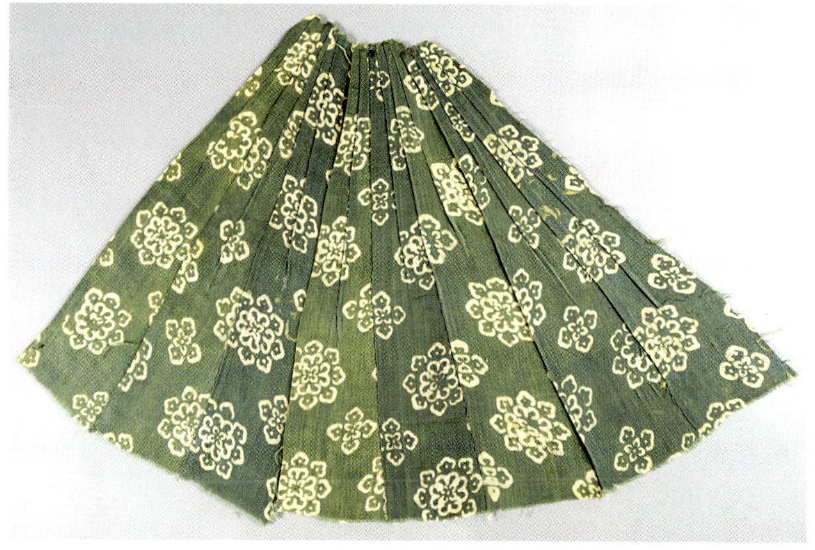

a striking resemblance to the figurine's high-waisted green skirt. The large composite flower interspersed with the persimmon calyx pattern on the skirt was executed with a similar resist technique to the one used on *sancai* ceramics. For the skirt, the artisan stenciled the design in wax and then dyed the textile green. Where the motifs are slightly misaligned, it is clear that the skirt was assembled from strips of cloth sewn together. The artisan who crafted the tomb figurine incised parallel lines, running from the top of skirt to the hem, to mark the strips of silk that would have been used to make a Tang skirt. Allusions to the real construction of garments, like this figurine's skirt, suggest that artisans worked to mimic the visual and tactile effect of clothing.

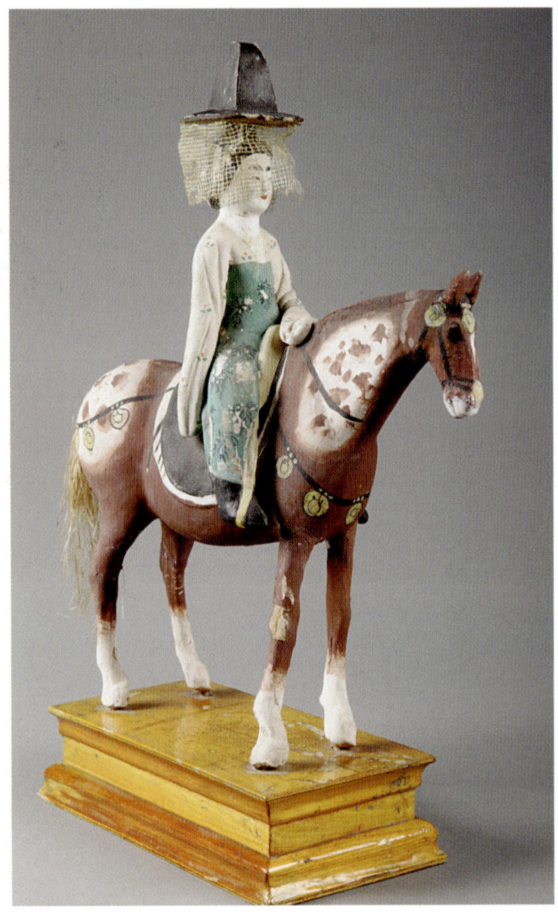

FIGURE 3.12. Female rider and horse. The figure wears a *weimao*, a wide-brimmed hat with an attached veil. Modeled clay figure with pigments, silk, and linen; H. 39 cm. Tomb 187, Astana, Turfan, eighth century. Courtesy of Xinjiang Uyghur Autonomous Region Museum.

Supplementing the basic skirt, top, and shawl ensemble was an assortment of kaftan-like robes, cuffed trousers, riding boots, and elaborate hats that had filtered into the empire from the west via the Silk Road. Classified as *hufu* ("barbarian dress") to mark its foreign origins, foreign dress first entered the empire around the third century and gained widespread popularity during the Northern and Southern dynasties (420–589). Foreign attire, unlike luxury silk and precious ornaments, did not mark social status in the traditional hierarchy of dress and was not subject to sumptuary regulations.[23]

The semantics of *hu* was adopted to refer to non-Han Chinese populations, including the Eastern Turkic peoples (Tujue), Uyghurs (Huihe or Huihu), Tibetans (Tufan), and Khitans (Qidan), living in the regions to the north and west of the empire. When attached to attire (*hufu*), objects or dance, *hu* functioned as both a marker of the thing's exotic appeal and a critique of the thing's foreignness.[24] During the early Tang dynasty, the *hu* sartorial influence can be best described as a pastiche of Turkic, Uyghur, Sogdian, and by extension Sasanid Persian (*bosi*) dress.[25] The styles associated with this

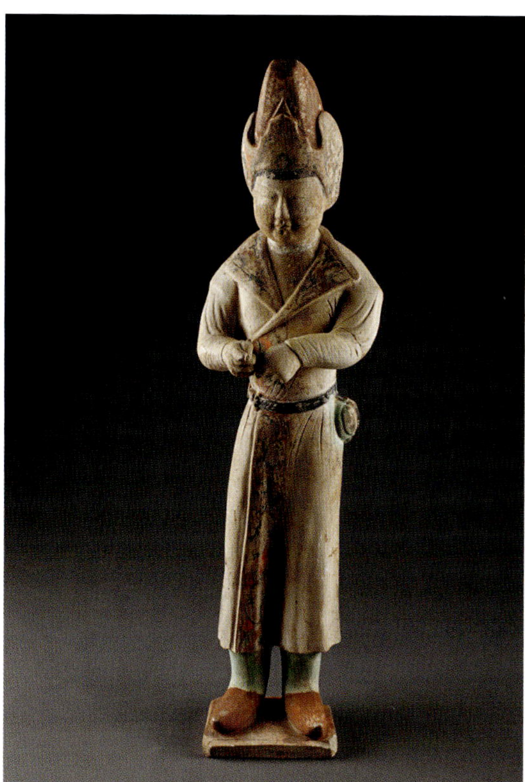

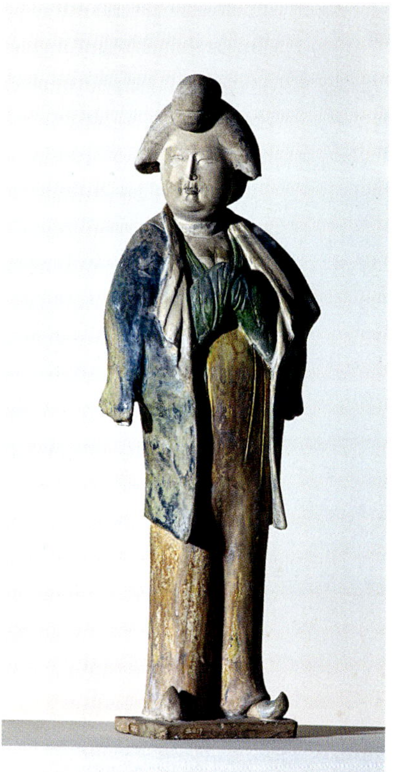

FIGURE 3.13. (*Left*) Female figure. The figure wears a *kuapao* that has patterned lapels and is belted at the waist. Modeled clay figure, painted; H. 52 cm. Tomb of Yang Jianchen, dated 714. Courtesy of Shaanxi History Museum.

FIGURE 3.14. (*Right*) Female figure. The *kuapao* is presented here as an overgarment. Earthenware with *sancai* (three-color) lead-silicate glaze; H. 46 cm. Tomb of Xianyu Tinghui, dated 723. Courtesy of National Museum of China, Beijing.

period included the open-front jacket with narrow-fitting sleeves; striped, tapered trousers; woven boots; and the *weimao*, a wide-brimmed hat with an attached gauze veil (fig. 3.12). Another modish robe popularized in the seventh and eighth centuries was the *kuapao*, a kaftan-like robe with a front opening, tight-fitting sleeves, and double overturned lapels (fig. 3.13). Similar to the round-collared robe, the *kuapao* could be enriched with floral trimmings along the front opening, at the cuffs, and on the lapels. Eighth-century figurines show the *kuapao* as a versatile piece of clothing that can be worn as the main garment by a cross-dressing attendant or draped across the shoulders of a female-attired figure like a cloak (fig. 3.14). The general clothed appearance of these figures shared an iconographic form, which varied little in shape and design over the first half of the dynasty.[26]

Fascination with foreign dress was linked to the popularity of equestrian outings and sports, as well as foreign music, dance, and goods that were all readily consumed by the Tang court. Anecdotes of the court's love of all things *hu*, incorporated into the "Treatise on Carriages and Dress" by the editors of the dynastic histories, served as evidence of an empire ruined by its desire for the foreign. This discourse on the decline of empire brought upon by openness to foreign influence was already present in Han dynasty debates about imperial expansion. The interpretation of strange sartorial behavior (*fuyao*) as omens of dynastic collapse was a trope that spanned genres, from dynastic histories to "records of the strange" (*zhiguai*). In the fourth century text, *Records of Searching for the Supernatural* (Soushenji), the wearing of felt was branded as a harbinger of "decline in the Central Kingdom."[27]

Although the influence of nomadic dress culture can be dated to the preceding centuries, the editors of *Old Standard History of the Tang* situated the height of *hufu*'s popularity in the court of Emperor Xuanzong. Written in the aftermath of the An Lushan Rebellion, the association of *hufu* with the reign of Xuanzong is a product of a revisionist trend that condemned the consumption of foreign things as an omen of the empire's demise at the hands of the Sogdian-Turkic general. Nowhere was this revisionism more explicit than in the account of how Xuanzong's female attendants spread the *hu* trend.

> At the beginning of the Kaiyuan period [713–741], the emperor's female horse-riding attendants all wore *hu* hats, with beautifully made up faces that were exposed. They did not conceal their faces again. The elites and commoners, as a result of this, again imitated the palace attendants. The custom of wearing the *weimao* was never used again while on the road. After a short time, the women started to expose their hair, which was tied in topknots, when they rode horses; there were also those who dressed in men's robes, boots, and shirts. The noble and the common, the women inside and outside of the palace all partook without any distinction.[28]

Hu hats were not perceived by the editors as threatening in themselves, but when viewed in relation to more unsettling developments, such as the blurring of social and gender distinctions, they became signs of disorder. The editors further insisted that "men and women all dressed in *hu* robes, and so there was the rebellion of Fanyang by the Jie barbarians, an omen of favoring the far-away."[29] The "Jie barbarians" of Fanyang referred to no other than An Lushan and his followers.[30] Ouyang Xiu and his fellow compilers of *New Standard History of the Tang* maintained this polemic that following the An Lushan Rebellion, people across the empire took the rebellion as proof that the wearing of *hufu* was indeed an inauspicious omen (*fuyao*).[31]

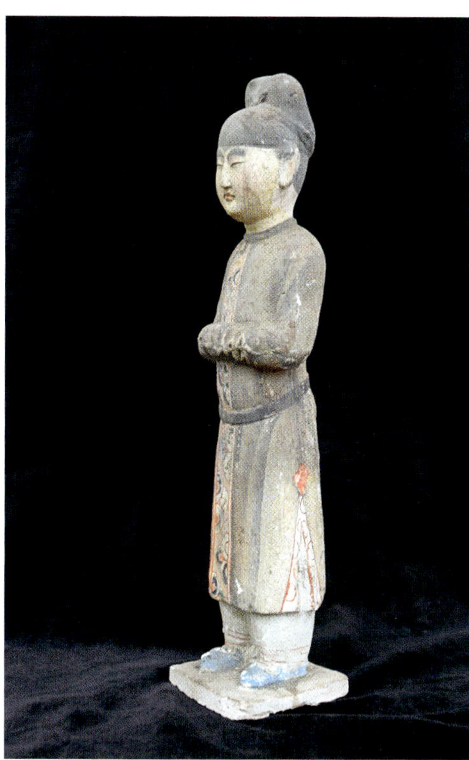

FIGURE 3.15. Female attendant. The attendant's robe is belted just over the hips and worn over red-bordered trousers. Her facial features are nearly identical to another figurine of a female attendant, dressed in women's attire, from the same tomb. Glazed earthenware with pigments; H. 31 cm. Tomb of Zheng Rentai, dated 664. Courtesy of Zhaoling Museum.

This revisionist history of *hufu* propagated by the conservative Confucian scholar-officials is belied by the visual archive, which contains a vast inventory of murals showing female attendants wearing knee-length robes, belted at the waist and worn over striped pants, dating to the mid-seventh century (fig. 3.15). One such figurine was excavated alongside 465 painted and glazed pottery figures from the lavish tomb of Zheng Rentai (601–663), a prominent frontier commander who prospered during the reigns of emperors Taizong and Gaozong. The female attendant is dressed in a round-collared, slim robe trimmed with a band featuring a floral motif that runs from just below the collar to the hem, belted below the waist, and over a pair of cuffed pale trousers. Her hair is swept up and concealed by a black headscarf or *putou*, completing the menswear look.[32] Depictions of *hufu*-attired figures have been excavated in large numbers from the seventh-century imperial tombs of princesses Changle (buried 643) and Xincheng (buried 663) and the early eighth-century tombs of crown princes Zhanghuai (buried 706), Yide (buried 706), Jiemin (buried 710) and Princess Yongtai (buried 706), which confirms that the popularity of this mode of adornment predated Emperor Xuanzong's reign (fig. 3.16).[33] They appear in a myriad of scenes: as hunters on horseback, as entertainers, and as attendants alongside other female attendants (fig. 3.17). Similarly, representations of court women in men's attire do not disappear from the visual record following the end of the An Lushan Rebellion.

Modern historians have interpreted the prevalence of female figures attired in foreign dress and accoutrements as the example par excellence of both Tang cosmopolitanism and fashion, focusing attention on the court's fondness for collecting the exotic during the peak of dynastic power.[34] Foreign dress alone did not make Tang women and, by extension, the Tang empire fashionable. The popularity of such gender- and

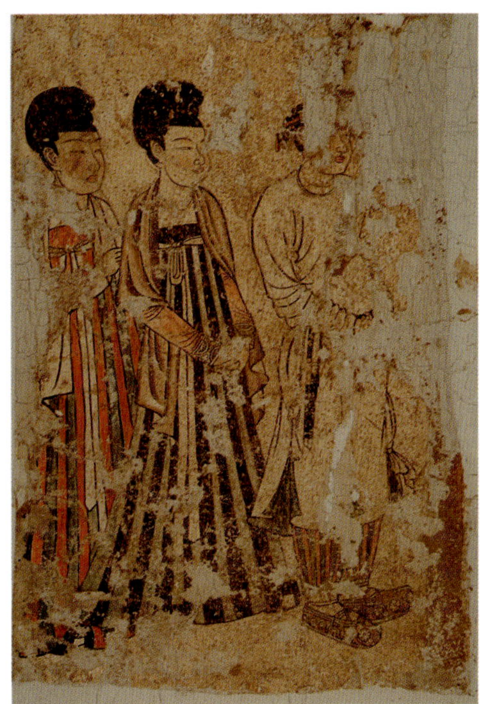

FIGURE 3.16. Female attendants. The attendant on the right is wearing a round-collared robe, belted above the hips, over striped trousers. H. 195 cm, W. 108 cm. Mural on the eastern wall of the fifth niche, Tomb of Duan Jianbi, dated 651. Courtesy of Zhaoling Museum.

culture-bending dress practices had a deeper root: it signaled the rise of a playful conception of clothing as a technique tied to the visual presentation of the body. In donning *hufu*, Tang women, "noble and common" and "inside and outside of the palace," exploited the fact that their clothing did not correspond to any intrinsic identity. Participation in the *hufu* craze displayed women's privileged knowledge of the latest trends, their means to replicate such trends, and communicated a connection, real or desired, to the court. Through an assemblage of boots, men's robes, and topknots, women outside of the palace put together a fashionable self that spoke to their immediate context.

What distressed moralizing Confucian scholar-officials writing after the rebellion was not simply the visual resemblance between palace women and foreigners, elite and common, or male and female, but rather the behavioral emulation that obscured social, cultural, and gender distinction. Cross-dressing bespoke a negotiation of the gendered body, social relations, and the cultural Other that allowed for the construction of composite selves, as opposed to the uniform and stable identities that ritual and sumptuary protocol aimed to preserve. The women were guilty of aesthetic play: putting on appearances that did not cohere with their status as Han Chinese subjects of the Tang empire, but that reflected their engagement with the material context of the cosmopolitan empire. Thus fashion's link to the instability of selves, shifting regimes of value, and the march of time turned it into a contemptible practice in the eyes of those intent on protecting the hermetically sealed universe of court power. Through

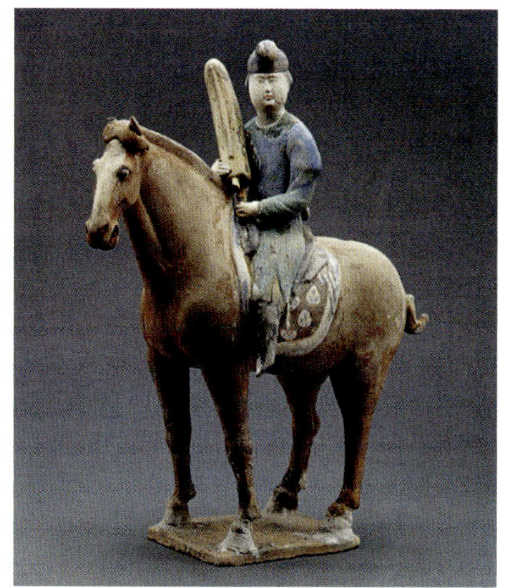
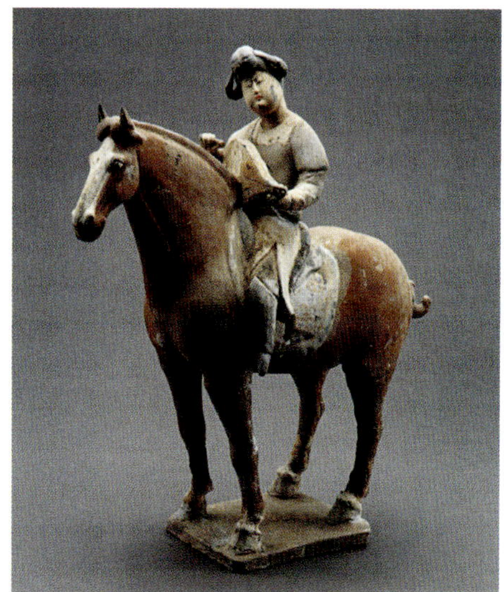
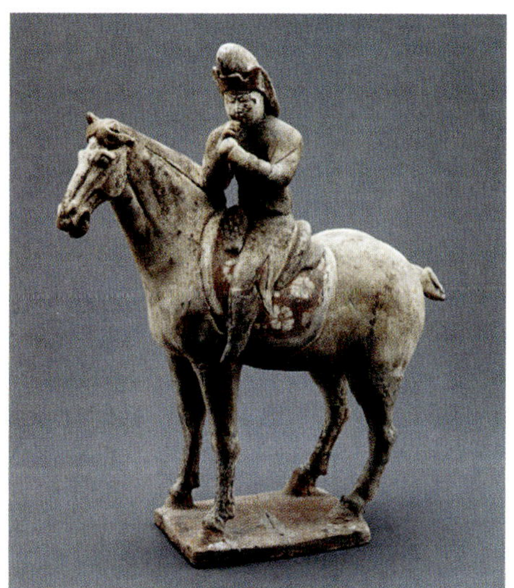
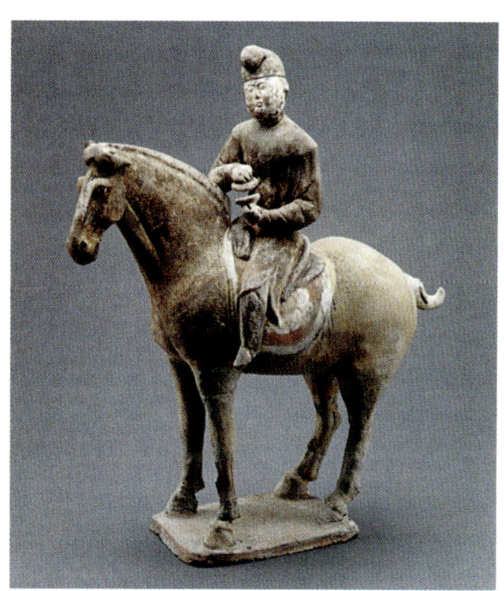
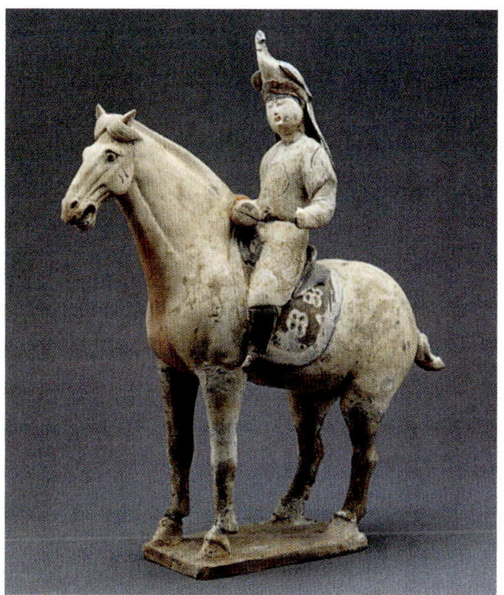

FIGURE 3.17. Female musicians on horseback. Each figure and horse is dressed differently: the women's robes, hats, and instruments are distinct, as are the saddle covers of their horses. Painted earthenware; H. 35.5–37.5 cm. Tomb of District Princess Jinxiang, 724. Courtesy of Xi'an Museum.

employing visual strategies to know and enact a world, whose social coherence was not structured according to proper and correct dress, Tang dynasty women and artist-image makers turned fashion into a distinct mode of knowledge. Dressing oneself and dressing a body constituted the key mode through which the body and the self were made legible to a knowing audience.

A TEMPLATE IS BORN

Clothing was both meaningful and functional as it communicated something about a person, a place, and a time. In painting, the clothed image belonged to the artist's repertoire of visual categories that when combined with landscape or architectural forms produced a scene. The viewer drew from her perceptual experience of world, such as an awareness of physiognomic features, regional customs, and dress styles, to bring narrative coherence to the overall composition. According to Zhang Yanyuan (fl. ninth century), such active viewing was the only way to look at a painting.[35] In his monumental *Record of Famous Painters of Successive Dynasties* (Lidai minghua ji, preface dated 847), the first comprehensive history of painting and calligraphy, Zhang advised: "If one is to discuss dress and vehicles, local customs and paintings of personages, all are different according to the period, and there are the distinctions between North and South [traditions of painting], so that the proper way to look at paintings consists of close observation."[36] Paintings, as registers of things found in the lived world, were viewed as products of a historical moment and place. By citing examples such as "when Wu Daozi painted Zhongyou, he showed him wearing a wooden sword, and when Yan Liben painted Lady Zhao, he showed her already wearing a curtain hat, entirely ignorant of the fact that the wooden sword dates only from the Qin dynasty and that the curtain hat [*weimao*] arose during the present dynasty," Zhang sought to emphasize these anachronistic representations as "one of the weaknesses of painting."[37] Arguing for the necessity of historical verisimilitude in figure painting, he pushed further, advising that:

> The nomadic clothes, boots, and shirts [worn today] should on no account be suddenly used in representations of Antiquity, nor are the long robes, the caps, and braided pendant-strings [of Antiquity] suitable any longer to represent people today. Straw sandals are not suited to [regions] north of the pass, and oxcarts are not found south of the ranges. If one carefully distinguishes between things of today and those of Antiquity, discussing and comparing the usages of local custom, one may verify the period (to which a painting belongs) by the subject represented and the objects rendered in it.[38]

Zhang's attention to historical time and regional variation as epitomized by clothing and accoutrements, paired with his insistence on their accurate depiction in painting, suggests an awareness of adornment as a practice bound by a particular time and space.[39] Historical consciousness was fundamental to the faithful representation of the past. For Zhang, the ability to achieve likeness in form further depended on the perceptual experience of the painter. Members of the Northern tradition of painting who had never laid eyes on the mountains and streams of the Yangzi Delta were limited by their knowledge, not by skill. Paintings were thus semiotic and epistemic objects that imparted cultural meanings and practices, as well as established links between the experience it represented and the beliefs held by the viewer.

Throughout *Record of Famous Painters of Successive Dynasties*, Zhang's judgment on the significance of verisimilitude in painting, however, was inconsistent. In the preceding section on the "Six Elements of Painting," Zhang declared, "the representation of things necessarily consists in formal resemblance, but this likeness of form requires to be supplemented with *guqi* [lit., bone energy]."[40] Mastery over representation depended on the deft use of the brush and not the correct reproduction of form. In an unexpected turn, he then followed with the conclusion "that the appearances of the things (themselves) were quite different (in those days)."[41] His oscillation between the primacy of formal likeness over brush method and vice versa, reflected in his concern that one must be able "to verify the period (to which a painting belongs) by the subject represented and the objects rendered in it," was an attempt to reconcile pictorial style with historical change. At the same time, this tension in Zhang's historical schema of painting suggests ambivalence toward the notion that, like the things themselves, the perception and representation of things in paintings were socially and historically conditioned.

Zhang Yanyuan lived at the end of the Tang dynasty, when the voluptuous Tang Beauty was the prevailing style of portraying the palace woman, and leading him to boldly remark that "the palace ladies of olden times (really) were dainty of finger and small of bosom." Looking at the emperor's attendants in Yan Liben's (ca. 600–673) *Emperor Taizong Receiving the Tibetan Envoy*, it would be hard to disagree with him (fig. 3.18). The great expanse and the staid poses of the female figures in the painting *Court Ladies Pinning their Hair with Flowers* represented the archetypal Tang dynasty court woman in Zhang's lifetime (fig. 3.19). When Zhang and his contemporaries compared Yan Liben's painting to a more recent composition, such as one of Zhou Fang's representations of palace women, they would have further reason to reflect on the phenomenon of changing pictorial style alongside changing fashions.

The surface treatment of these women and their dress—in other words, the style of their depiction—became key to their narrative coherence. Although the sensuous court woman at leisure was a subject matter that came to dominate eighth-century painting, she served multiple rhetorical aims. Simply put, not all plump women were rendered the same. Close observation, as Zhang stressed, enables us to see how differences in pictorial style—together with the differences in approaches to dress—came to index both the time of production and the skills of the artist. For artist-image makers, the

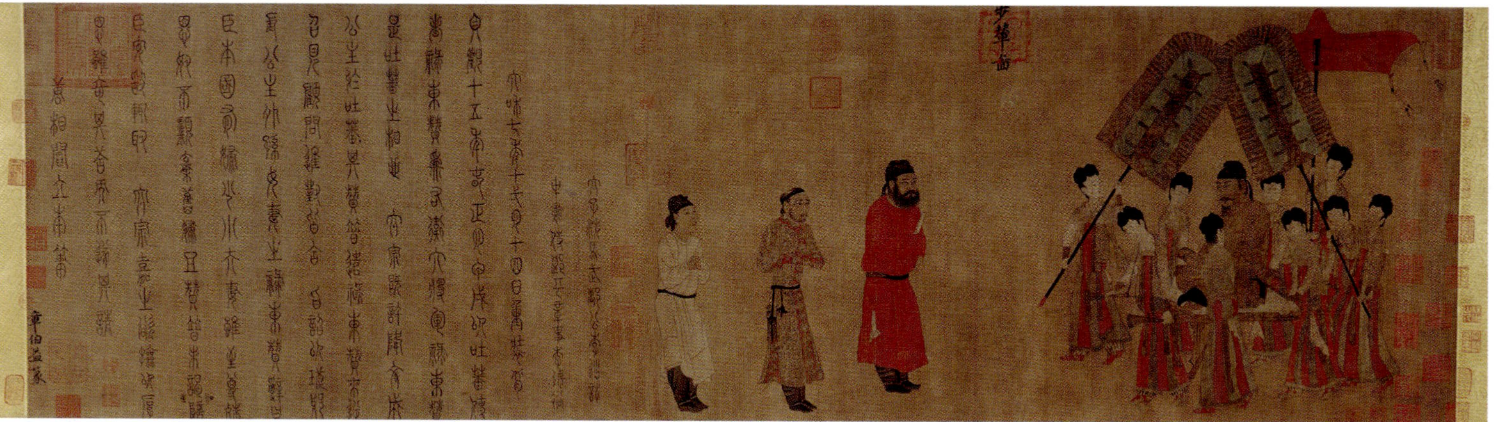

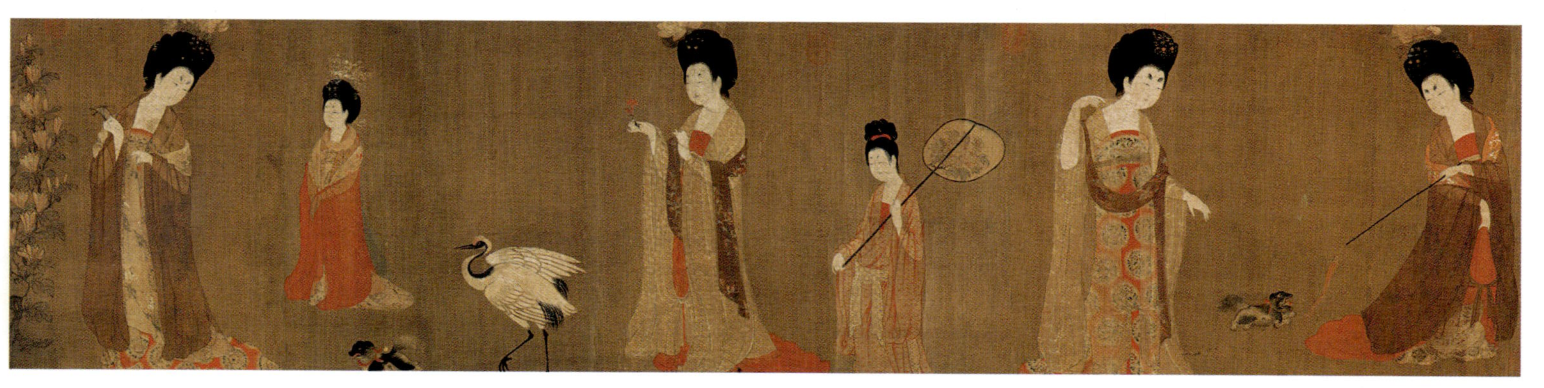

FIGURE 3.18. (*Top*) Traditionally attributed to Yan Liben (ca. 600–673), *Emperor Taizong Receiving the Tibetan Envoy*, Song dynasty copy. The nine women surrounding the emperor are uniformly depicted, their slender bodies dressed in striped gowns, gathered and tied around the hips with a sash, revealing striped trousers underneath. Handscroll, ink and colors on silk; H. 38.5 cm, L. 129 cm. Photo provided by the Palace Museum, Beijing.

FIGURE 3.19. (*Bottom*) Traditionally attributed to Zhou Fang (ca. 730–800), *Court Ladies Pinning Their Hair with Flowers*. Each of the five palace women are presented as variants of the central theme: woman as a flower. Handscroll, ink and colors on silk; H. 46 cm, L. 180 cm. Courtesy of Liaoning Provincial Museum.

Tang Beauty was the ultimate object of aesthetic play, and of fashion, as she provided them with a form with which to contemplate matters of style and to elaborate upon the sensuous world. As a template to be *styled*, the Tang Beauty made explicit the purpose of representation as a mode of knowing the world and as a vehicle for commentary. The style of the image, not the content, tied the painting to a historical moment.

In the seventh and eighth centuries, the transmission of copy sketches from the capital to frontier, and from region to region, gave rise to a common stock of figural forms and motifs. The template of the Tang Beauty likewise traveled along open roads, contributing to a vernacular convention of figure painting from Turfan to Nara Japan. Such wide dissemination granted painters freedom for adaptation. Dress and its ornamentation were opened up to painters as flexible semiotic spaces, rather than as sites of decorum, where appropriateness of expression and character was dictated by custom—and costume. The template challenged the spatial conception of custom as costume, splitting the perceived bond between the body's cultural identity and its appearance. Clothing remained meaningful and functional as it continued to convey information about a place and about a time, but in the Tang Beauty, it more purposefully communicated the aesthetic play of the painter. The ability to discern the time of production no longer hinged on the things registered in the painting; instead, it also depended on knowledge of the painter's style. Thus, dress became a more vital space to be fashioned by the painter.

Perceptions about painting were facilitated by perceptions about the material world. The notion that styles of painting changed just as styles of dress changed did not break epistemic ground. What the template postulated was a synchronic view of style and of things, such that changes in the way the world was presented could be viewed as embodied visions of the world that did not progress in a linear fashion. Surviving works from the eighth through tenth centuries show that devotion to custom and verisimilitude continued to be practiced by artists. The coexistence of contrasting approaches to the Tang Beauty and her dress encouraged the synchronic view of aesthetic practice. In so doing, the template reinforced the relationship between pictorial style and fashion.

PLAYING WITH BEAUTY

Later scholars attributed the development in the iconography of the Tang Beauty to the shapely consort of Emperor Xuanzong, Yang Guifei.[42] Like the *hufu* craze, the new paradigm of female sensuality embodied by the representations of soft corpulent bodies swathed in silk can be found in tombs dated to the early eighth century. It thus preceded the rise of Yang Guifei at court. An early incarnation of the iconic plump palace lady can also be traced to the more corpulent bodies decorating Crown Prince Li Xian's (654–684) tomb chamber (fig. 3.20). The sixth son of Emperor Gaozong and the second son of Empress Wu Zetian, Li Xian was made heir apparent until he was exiled for treason in 680. Following his death in 684, he was buried in a common tomb.

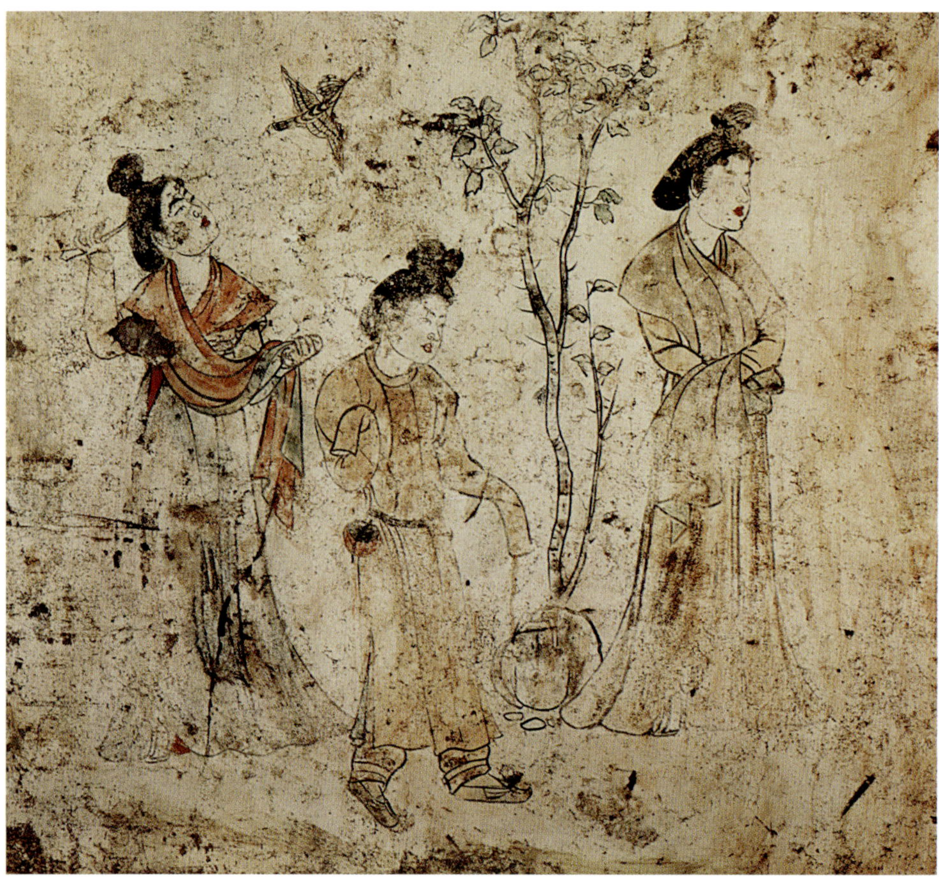

FIGURE 3.20. Female attendants. The attendant in the foreground is attired in *hufu*, while the two other attendants are wearing the basic skirt, short robe, and shawl ensemble. The garments are drawn in bold outlines and color has been applied uniformly. H. 175 cm, W. 180 cm. Mural on west wall, south section of the front chamber, tomb of Crown Prince Zhanghuai (Li Xian), 711. Zhou Tianyou, ed., *Zhanghuai taizi mu bihua* (Beijing: Wenwu chubanshe, 2002), 64.

Along with Crown Prince Yide and Princess Yongtai, Li Xian was reburied in one of the attendant tombs of the Qianling burial complex, the final resting place of Gaozong and Wu Zetian, in 706. Li Xian's tomb was renovated in 711 when his consort, Lady Fang, was interred in the rear chamber.[43] That same year, he was given the posthumous name of Zhanghuai. The images of women posing between trees and rocks in the front and rear corridors, as well as the murals in the antechamber and rear chamber, were all repainted for Lady Fang's burial.[44]

The understated treatment of sartorial details introduced a new iconography of the clothed female form that came to dominate mid-eighth century tomb murals (712–765), as well as pottery figurines, around the capital.[45] The sparse but emphatic brushwork

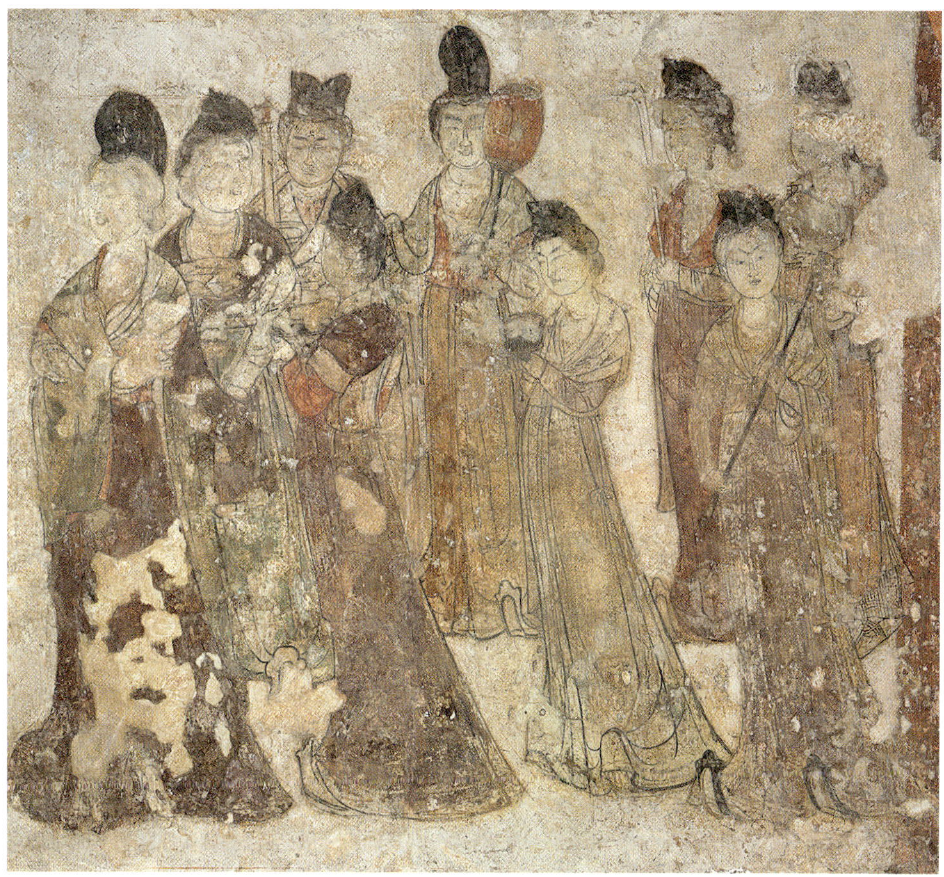

FIGURE 3.21. Group of attendants. Like the female figures of the tombs of Yide and Zhanghuai, the women here are executed in strong brushstrokes and color wash. The mural painters of the early eighth century did not spend time on decorative details, such as patterned sleeve cuffs. H. 176 cm, W. 196.5 cm. Mural on the southern section of east wall of the antechamber, Tomb of Princess Yongtai, dated 706. Courtesy of Shaanxi History Museum.

found on these murals expresses a significant divergence in the decorative treatment of human figures and their dress when compared with the earlier paintings of officials and foreign envoys that commemorate the prince's court life. Stripped of meticulous details, the ink lines primarily sketch the structure of the individual figures and garments.

Closer scrutiny of early eighth-century tomb murals, however, shows that in place of decorative textures to draw the gaze were contouring lines that emphasized the body's mass (fig. 3.21).[46] Underpinning this movement toward clean lines was a shift in the artist's approach to three-dimensionality as evidenced by the move away from bold ink lines aimed at delineating the contours of the body toward fluid, more stylized strokes directed at illuminating the body's engagement with private spaces. Wall painters of

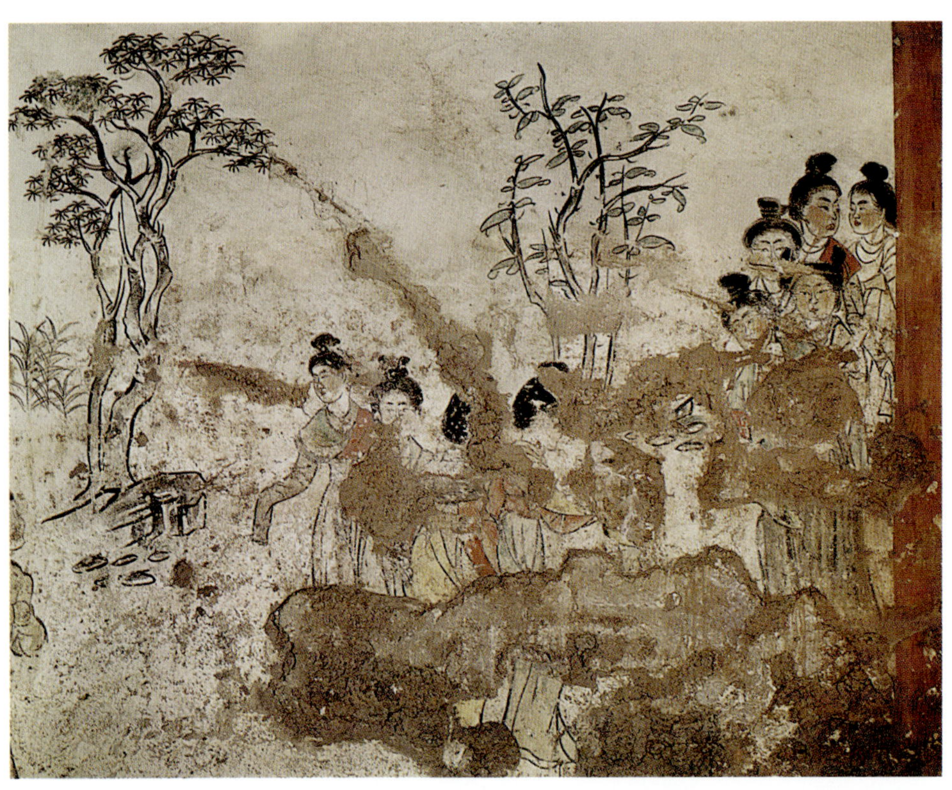

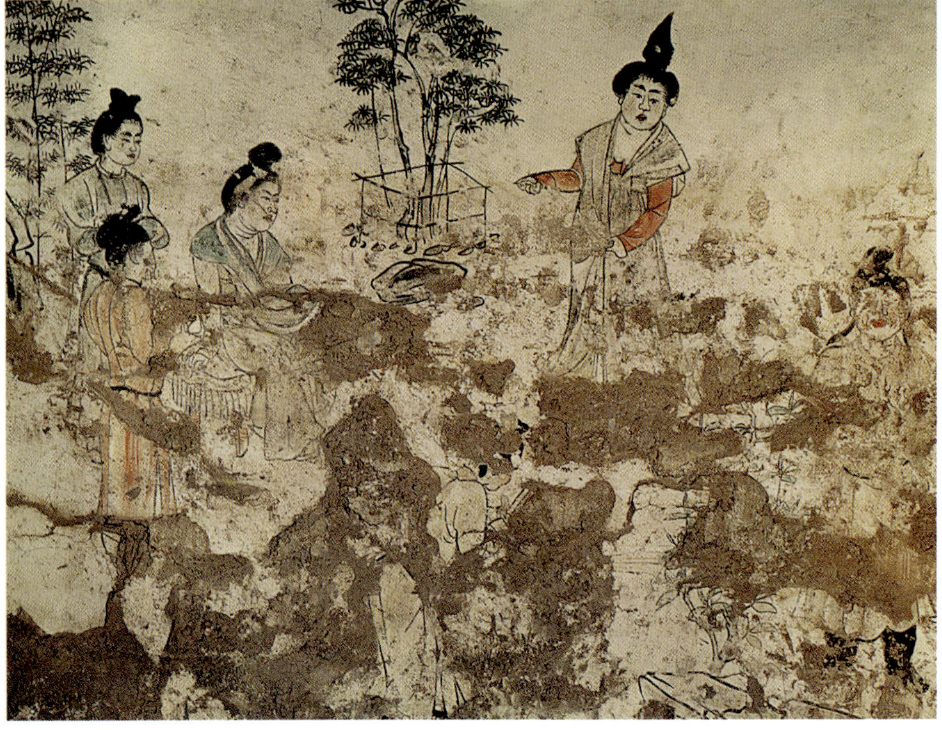

the early eighth century transferred emphasis from the figure's social and ritual role, as demarcated by her dress and static pose, to the figure's existence in natural spaces. The popularity of connotative brushwork in eighth-century tomb murals was symptomatic of developments in painting practice as well.[47]

Scenes of women seated in courtyards resting below trees or watching birds first appear in the tomb of Zhanghuai, marking the beginning of a pictorial program that increasingly favored images of private life over representations of court pomp (figs. 3.22 and 3.23). The staging of full-bodied women in loose robes, formed by repeated drapery folds, standing or seated under trees, idling, or playing music, was the most popular subject matter of eighth-century painting.[48] By interpolating the template of the Tang Beauty into a landscape, artist-image makers established an analogic relationship between women and their surroundings. Coherence and legibility of the image was constructed relationally through recursive links between surface and form, supporting the rhetorical use of pictorial style.

Variations on the "ladies under trees" theme have been discovered in Chang'an, Turfan, and Nara Japan in a variety of formats. The lavish stone sarcophagus of Wu Huifei (d. 737), Xuanzong's favorite consort prior to Yang Guifei, featured ten panels of court women and their attendants along the inner walls (fig. 3.24). Framed by rocks, butterflies, and assorted flora and fauna, nearly all of the twenty-one women of the stone sarcophagus are presented in similarly floral-patterned robes. Like the women in *Court Ladies Pinning Their Hair with Flowers*, the carved figures of Wu Huifei resonated with their environment.

Continuity of subject matter found in surviving works from eighth-century tombs reveals a wide range of stylistic possibilities and rhetorical strategies. In the Wei family tomb dating to the mid-eighth century, six contiguous screens enclosing female figures positioned under trees were found painted on a wall (fig. 3.25).[49] The figures, like the trees, were executed in sparse and modulated brushwork, finished with dabs of color to add hue and texture. In Nara Japan, a contemporaneous set of six folding screens, known as *Folding Screen of Standing Women with Bird Feathers* (Torige ritsuyo no byōbu), has survived in the collection of the Shōsō-in (fig. 3.26). Dated to 752, the women in the screens bear a close resemblance to Wu Huifei's figures. The manner of their illustration, ink applied with a dry brush with limited use of color and feathers to adorn the women's robes, distinguish the women from their Chang'an counterparts.

FIGURE 3.22. (*Facing, top*) Women touring the garden. Mural on the northern section of east wall of rear chamber, Tomb of Crown Prince Zhanghuai, 711. Zhou Tianyou, ed., *Zhanghuai taizi mu bihua* (Beijing: Wenwu chubanshe, 2002), 76.

FIGURE 3.23. (*Facing, bottom*) Women resting in the garden. Mural on the southern section of east wall of rear chamber, Tomb of Crown Prince Zhanghuai, 711. Zhou Tianyou, ed., *Zhanghuai taizi mu bihua* (Beijing: Wenwu chubanshe, 2002), 78.

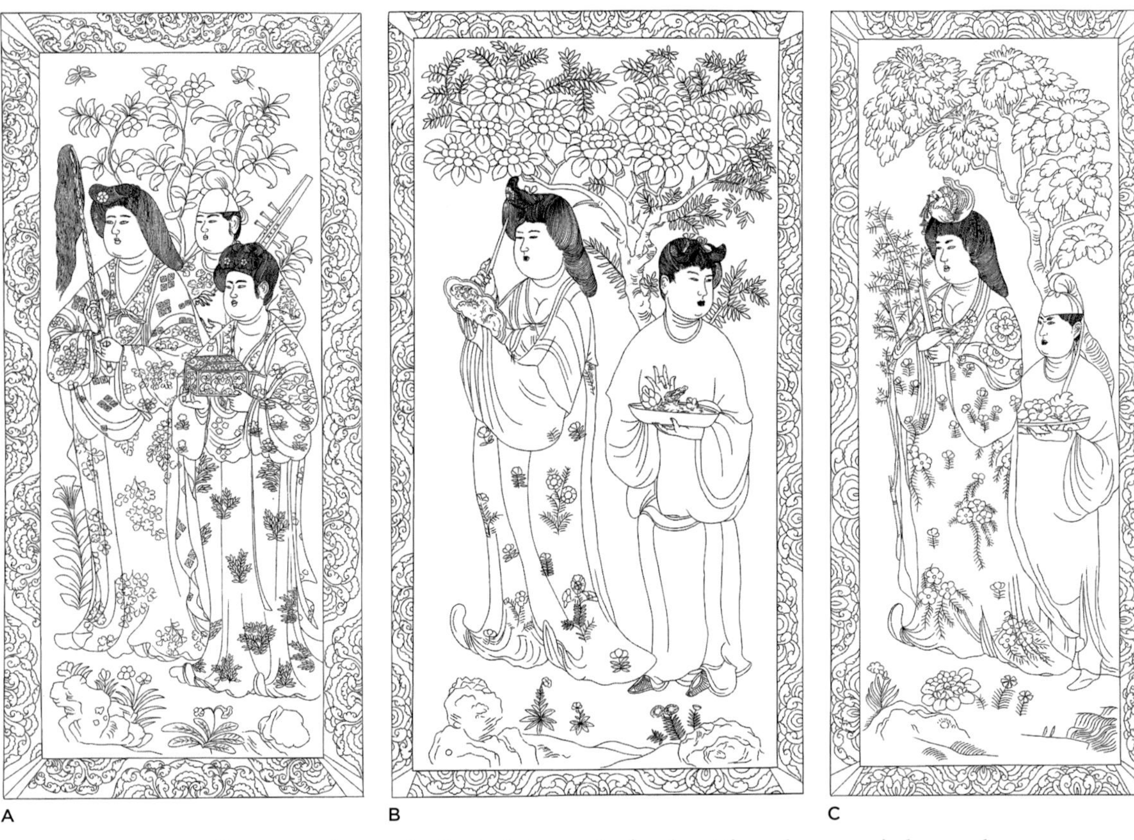

FIGURE 3.24. Stone sarcophagus. Continuity between the floral motifs on the women's dress and the floral surroundings creates an immersive environment, in which the women are conflated with the landscape. (A) Panel B1b, H. 165 cm, W. 77 cm; (B) Panel B7b, H. 165 cm, W. 88 cm; (C) Panel B10b, H. 165 cm, W. 70 cm. Tomb of Consort Wu Huifei, posthumous title, Empress Zhenshun, d. 737. After Cheng Xu et al., "The Stone Guo-sarcophagus of Empress Zhenshun in the Jingling Mausoleum of the Tang Dynasty," *Wenwu*, no. 5 (2012): 74–97.

In Turfan, two separate works were uncovered from the Astana graveyard. The first, *Lady under a Tree*, was brought to Japan by the Otani expedition and originally formed a pair with the painting of *Man under a Tree* that is currently stored at the Tokyo National Museum (figs. 3.27 and 3.28). The other examples, found in Astana Tomb 187 and dated to the Tianbao era, exist as fragments of a set of screen paintings (fig. 3.29). In the original composition, the standing women may have been positioned as spectators watching a game of go (*weiqi*). The two works differ substantially in the painters' treatment of the women's dress. In the former, both the court woman and her attendant are shown in monochrome robes. Only the painter's use of undulating ink lines for the drapery, stressing the great expanse of the figures' robes, catches the eye. The other is a luxurious display of color and pattern. Painted on silk, the figures are executed

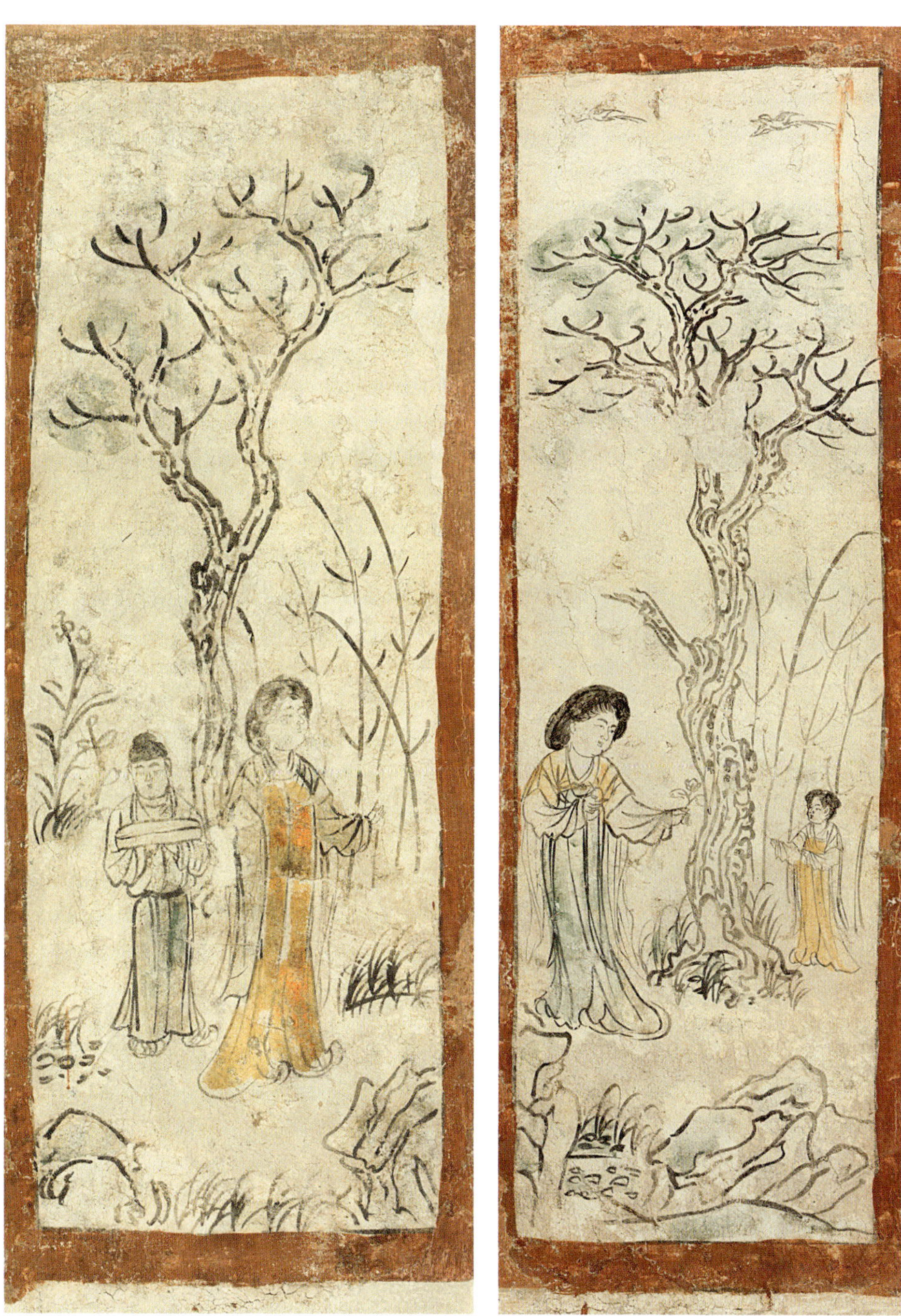

FIGURE 3.25. "Ladies under Trees," two of six screens. Paint on plaster; each screen H. 1.44 m, W. 45–50 cm. Wei family tombs, mid-eighth century. Nanliwang Village, Chang'an County, Courtesy of Shaanxi History Museum.

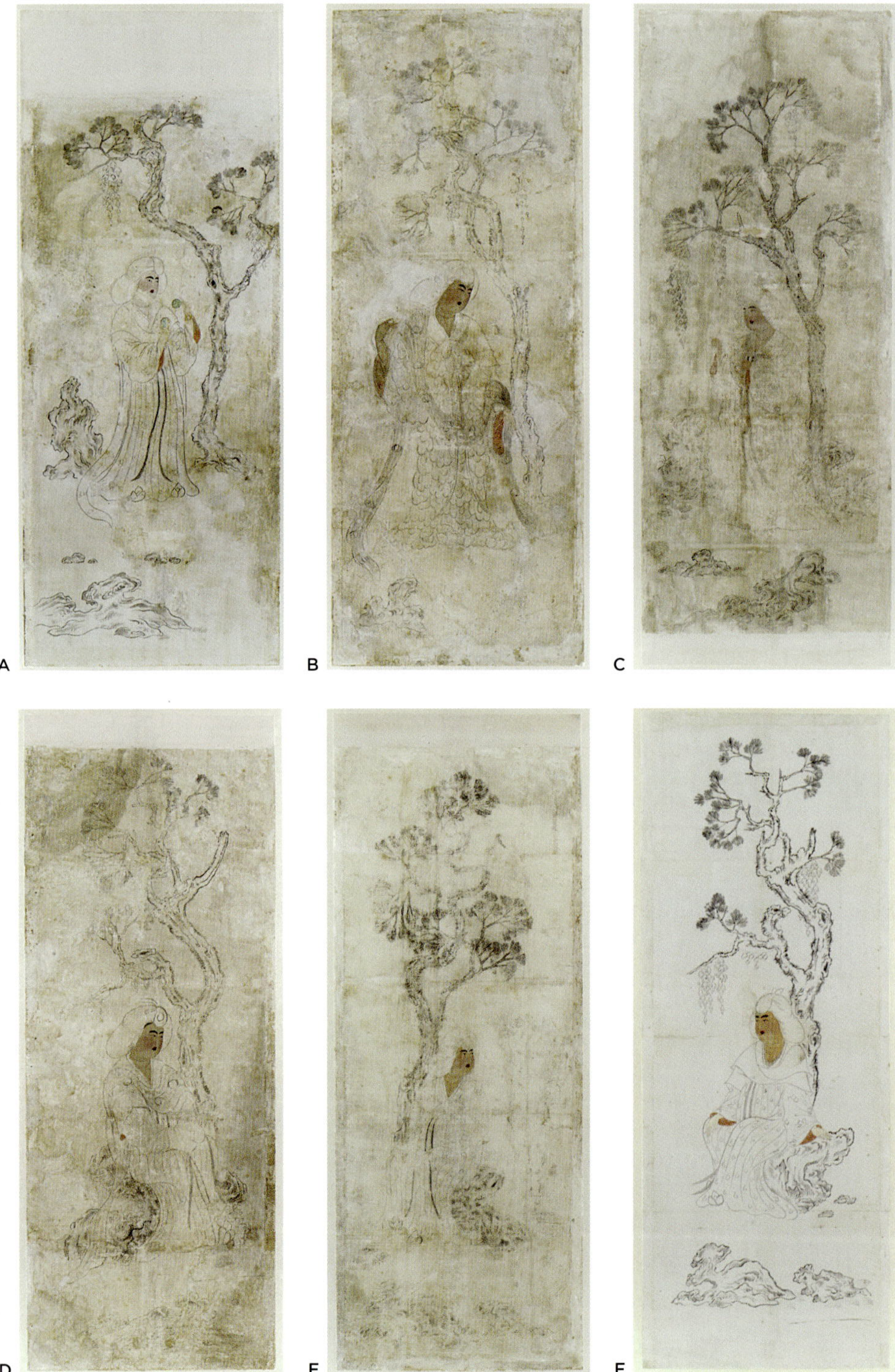

FIGURE 3.26. *Folding Screen of Standing Women with Bird Feathers* (Torige ritsuyo no byōbu), ca. 752–56. The Shōsō-in Treasures, Nara, Japan. Paper, color on white with traces of feathers of copper pheasant. From left to right: (A) H. 135.9 cm, W. 56.2 cm; (B) H. 36.2 cm, W. 56.2 cm; (C) H. 135.8 cm, W. 56 cm; (D) H. 136.2 cm, W. 56.2 cm; (E) H. 136.2 cm, W. 56.5 cm; (F) H. 136.1 cm, W. 56.4 cm. Courtesy of the Imperial Household Agency.

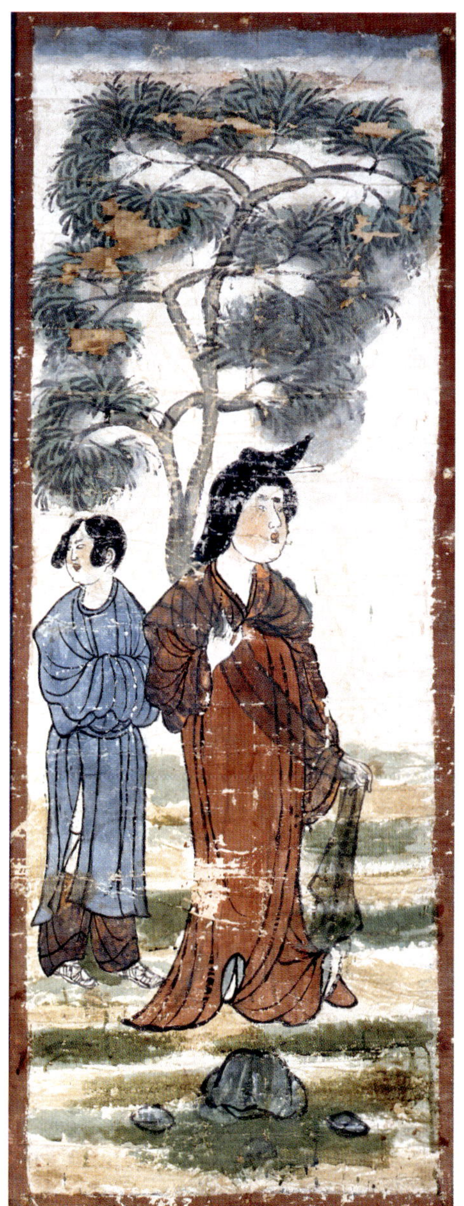

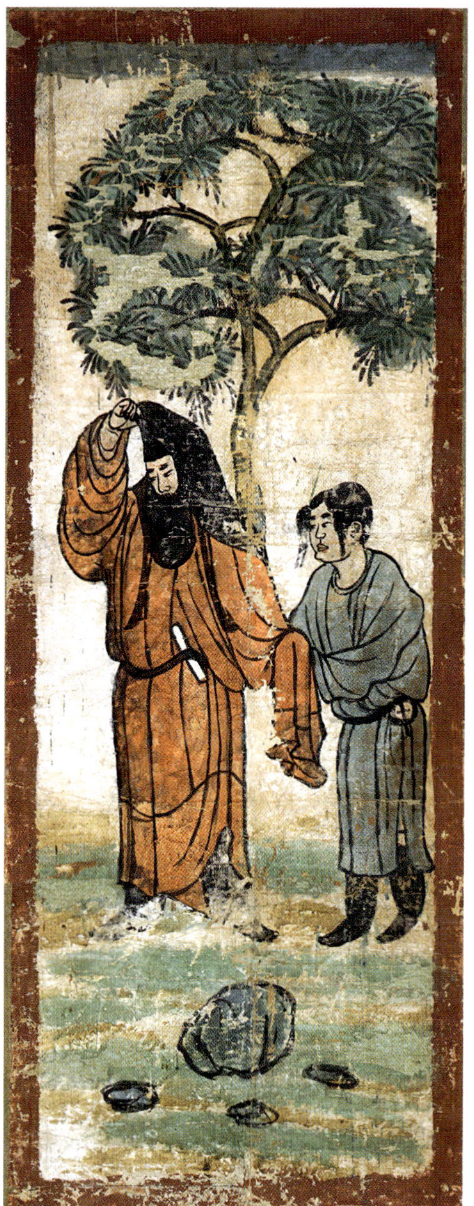

FIGURE 3.27. (*Left*) *Lady under a Tree*, eighth century. Ink and color on paper; H. 139.1 cm, W. 53.3 cm. Astana, Turfan. MOA Museum of Art, Shizuoka.

FIGURE 3.28. (*Right*) *Man under a Tree*, eighth century. Ink and color on paper; H. 138.6 cm, W. 53.2 cm. Astana, Turfan. Tokyo National Museum. Photo courtesy of TNM Image Archives.

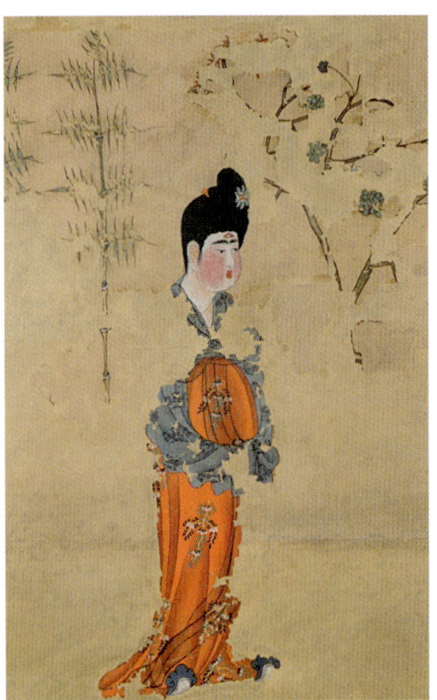
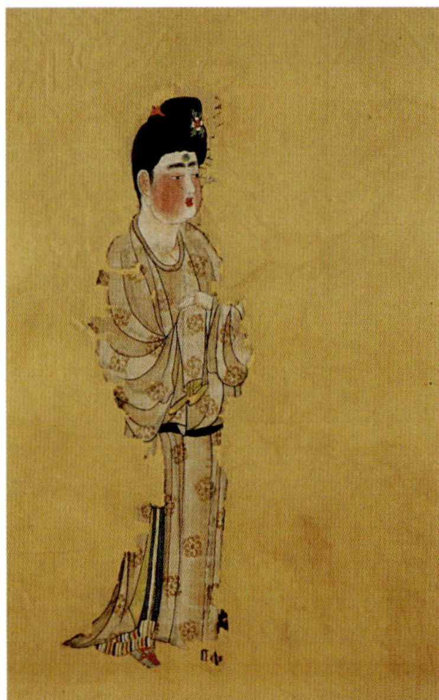
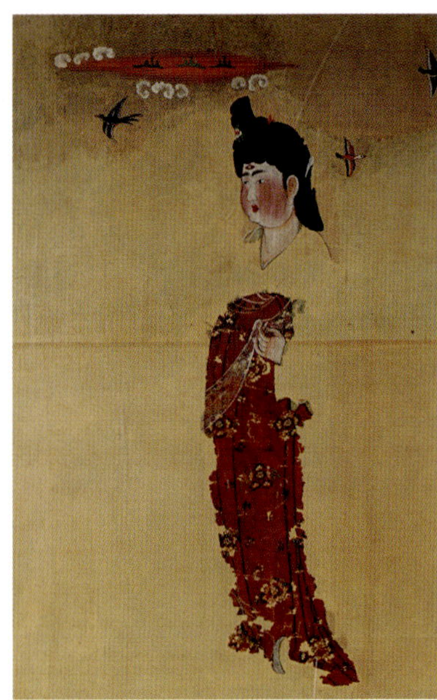

FIGURE 3.29. Restored screen paintings from Astana Tomb 187. Eleven images of women and children have survived. A seated woman playing a game of go was depicted on the central screen, surrounded by female attendants, elite women, and children. From left to right: H.89.8 cm, W. 74.4 cm; H. 83.4 cm, W. 69 cm; H. 67.3 cm, W. 71.5 cm. Astana Tomb 187, dated to mid-eighth century. Courtesy of Xinjiang Uyghur Autonomous Region Museum.

in sinuous black ink lines. Their round faces are powdered white and accentuated by bright splashes of crimson on the cheeks.

Unlike the painter of *Lady under a Tree*, the range of patterning found on the women's dress in these screen paintings suggests that the artist paid scrupulous attention to color and pattern. Two out of the three skirts feature stylized floral designs on a red ground that evoke the opulence of *jin* silks, while the figure on the far left wears a spacious blue blouse layered with patterns outlined in a darker hue suggestive of silk damask. The figure in the center sports a version of the popular eighth century *hufu* ensemble, which has been modified according to the new template for female beauty. Her round-collared tunic of voluminous proportions falls to her feet, a side slit exposes trousers with a wide striped cuff. The cascading sleeves, trailing skirts, and the transparent gauze shawls highlighted in white demonstrate an embrace of lush and richly ornamented surfaces.

The most sumptuous example of this style has survived in the form of a handscroll painting titled *Court Ladies Pinning Their Hair with Flowers*, which displays five sumptuously attired women and their attendant among dogs, a crane, and a flowering plant (figs. 3.19 and 3.30).[50] The attire of these elaborately adorned female figures would

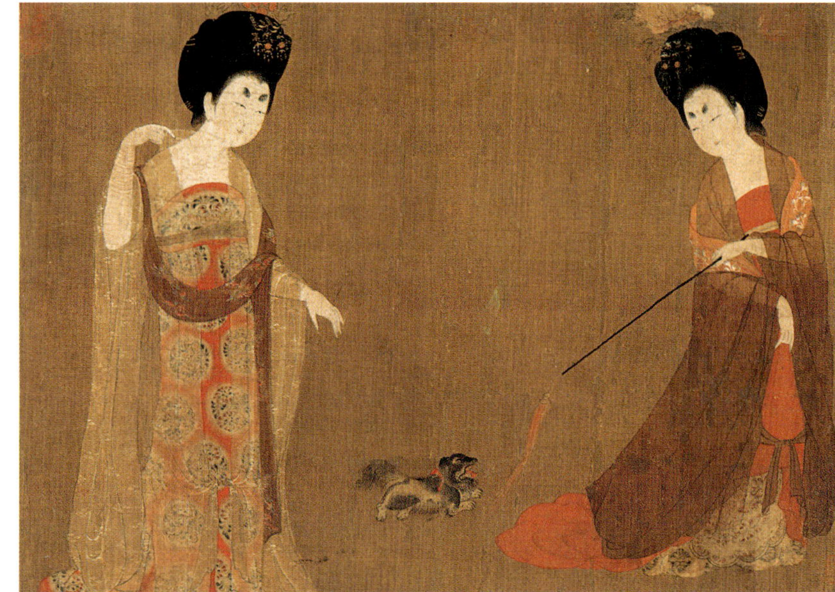

FIGURE 3.30. Traditionally attributed to Zhou Fang (ca. 730–800), *Court Ladies Pinning their Hair with Flowers*, detail. Handscroll, ink and colors on silk. Courtesy of Liaoning Provincial Museum.

suggest that cloaks and shawls made from silk-netted sheer gauze were de rigueur at the time of the painting's production. Each assemblage is composed of a sleeveless, billowy gown worn under an open robe with wide sleeves, accessorized with a shawl. Three of the six female figures are fashioned with two skirts. The women to the far right and far left of the painting, as well as the attendant, wear overskirts that have shorter hems allowing the underskirts to peek out from below. Only the attendant, situated in the foreground and depicted smaller than the other figures, is attired differently. Her gossamer cloak is wrapped around her frame and belted around her hips. Nearly each garment featured on the women is elaborately patterned. The gauzes showcase woven motifs of lozenges and faintly dyed florets, adding decorative texture to their bare shoulders.

Commonly attributed to Zhou Fang (ca. 730–800), who was described by Zhang Yanyuan in his *Record of Famous Painters* as having "reached the utmost in stylish appearance, devoting his whole art to the robes and caps,"[51] the painting is likely to be the composition of tenth-century artists working in the Zhou style.[52] On Zhou's style, Zhang claimed, "his robes were powerful and simple, his use of color soft and bright." Such a description of Zhou's work is inconsistent with the style of *Court Ladies Pinning Their Hair with Flowers*, but does conform to the brushwork in another attributed Zhou painting, entitled *Palace Ladies Tuning the Lute* (fig. 3.31).[53] The extant work, now in the Nelson-Atkins Museum, is likely a twelfth-century copy of the original.

Here, three seated court women and two standing attendants are integrated into a stark landscape scene. The women's garments were made tangible and tactile through

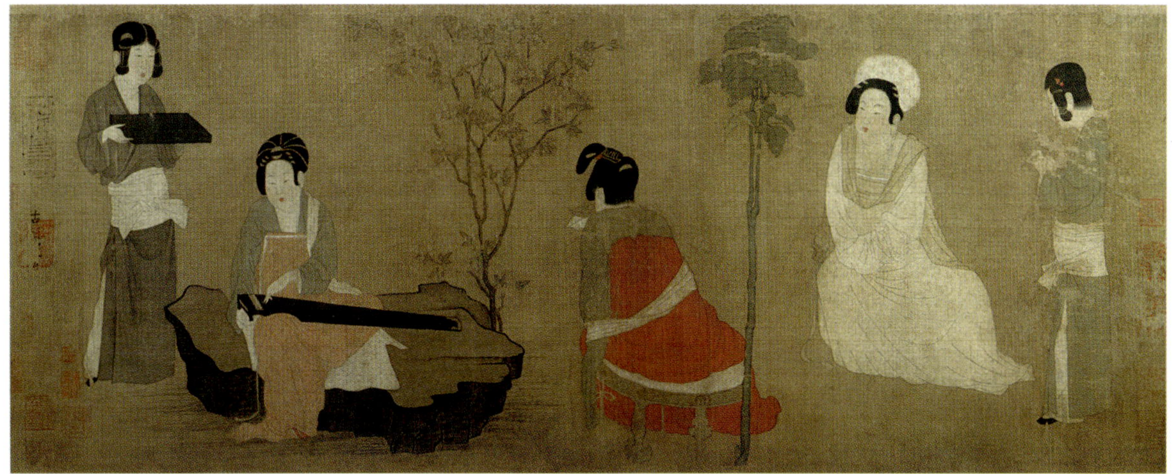

FIGURE 3.31. Copy after Zhou Fang, *Palace Ladies Tuning the Lute*, Song dynasty, twelfth century. The fine brushwork is enhanced by the application of subtle and subdued color washes. The two attendants to the far right and far left of the painting, along with the landscape elements, frame the space in which the three palace women are seated. Handscroll, ink and color on silk; H. 28 cm, W. 75.3 cm. The Nelson-Atkins Museum of Art, Kansas City, Missouri. Purchase: William Rockhill Nelson Trust, 32-159/1. Photo: John Lamberton.

the application of clean ink lines and a sparing use of color wash. In contrast to the opulently patterned robes of the women with flowers adorning their hair, the women of *Tuning the Lute* represent what Jonathan Hay has identified as a "rhetorical distance" from the decadence of Xuanzong's court.[54] Whereas the exquisitely adorned surfaces of *Court Ladies Pinning Their Hair with Flowers* celebrated the sensuality of the female forms, the restraint seen in Zhou's surface treatment signified a moral commentary on the excesses of the age and embodied in the corpulent Tang Beauty. Style was the distinguishing mark.

Beginning in the eighth century, the plump Tang Beauty was gradually distilled into a template, a form recognizable to the beholder as a trace of a decadent, flourishing era, but subject to artistic fashioning (fig. 3.32). She can be found in Dunhuang portraits of donors, as in the late ninth-century wall hanging *Bodhisattva as Guide of Souls* (fig. 3.33).[55] In *Bodhisattva as Guide of Souls*, the painter illustrated a human figure guided by a bodhisattva into the Western Paradise. The female figure positioned in the lower right of the banner, following the path of the splendidly adorned bodhisattva, wears a comparable ensemble to the court ladies with flower headdresses. Instead of diaphanous gauze, the woman wears a red outer robe with voluminous sleeves, the cuffs of which are painted in an orange hue, over a gown of light green.

The shawl, which is wrapped around the figure's back and tucked behind her sleeves, is the only patterned item on her body. Her tall coiffure and painted moth eyebrows,

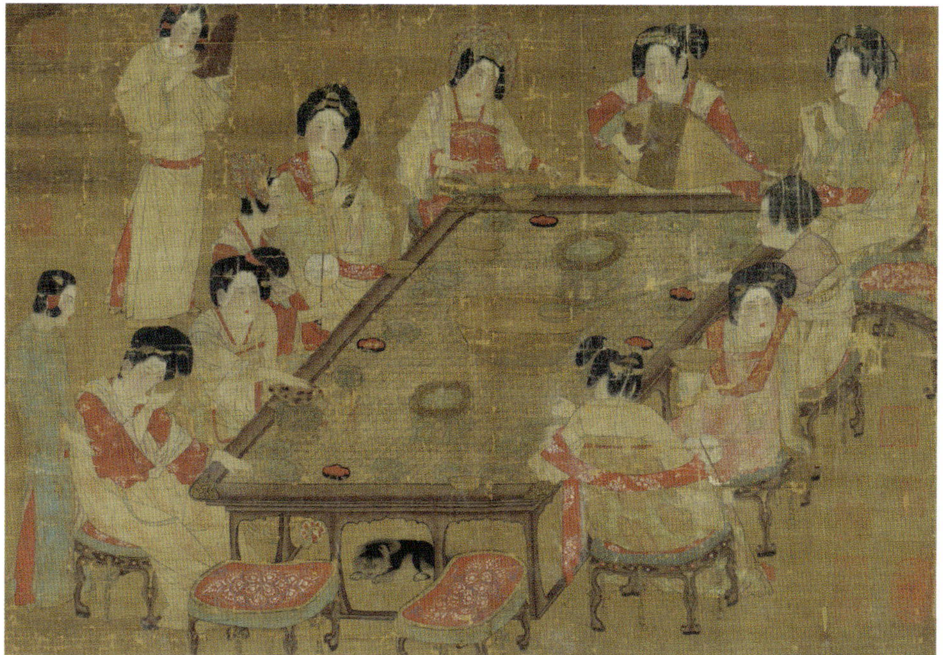

FIGURE 3.32. Anonymous, *A Palace Concert*, Tang dynasty. Not only is each female figure attired differently, but the painter has carefully rendered them in distinct poses, such that each figure's body creates an individual shape within the surface of the painting. Together with the furniture, the women's bodies produce a virtual surface. Hanging scroll, ink and colors on silk; H. 48.7 cm, L. 69.5 cm. The Collection of National Palace Museum, Taipei.

identical to the court ladies, suggests a shared iconography. In contemporaneous portraits of donors and ancestors found in the Mogao Caves near Dunhuang, connections between the rich, material world of the patron and the ritual space of Buddhist devotion were also rendered through layers of decorated silks (fig. 3.34). Cave 231, completed around the mid-ninth century, features two female figures attired in decorated silks who stand in glaring contrast to the two male figures dressed in monochrome robes. The figures of the kneeling woman, a portrait of the patron's mother, and her standing servant are draped in colorful and patterned silks—evoking the wealth and status of the family.[56] The juxtaposition of the sumptuous female figures and the somber male figures foregrounds the unfailing association of women with the sensuous world, found in secular paintings and in the social commentary of Tang writers. In this way, the Tang Beauty served aesthetic and polemical needs.

The template remained popular in the tenth-century tomb of the military governor, Wang Chuzhi (d. 923). Draped on the female figures were loose-fitting blouses, tucked under long full skirts, concealed by either a curved or lobed bib, and fixed in place by a sash. Hues of red and occasionally indigo were used in contrast with white

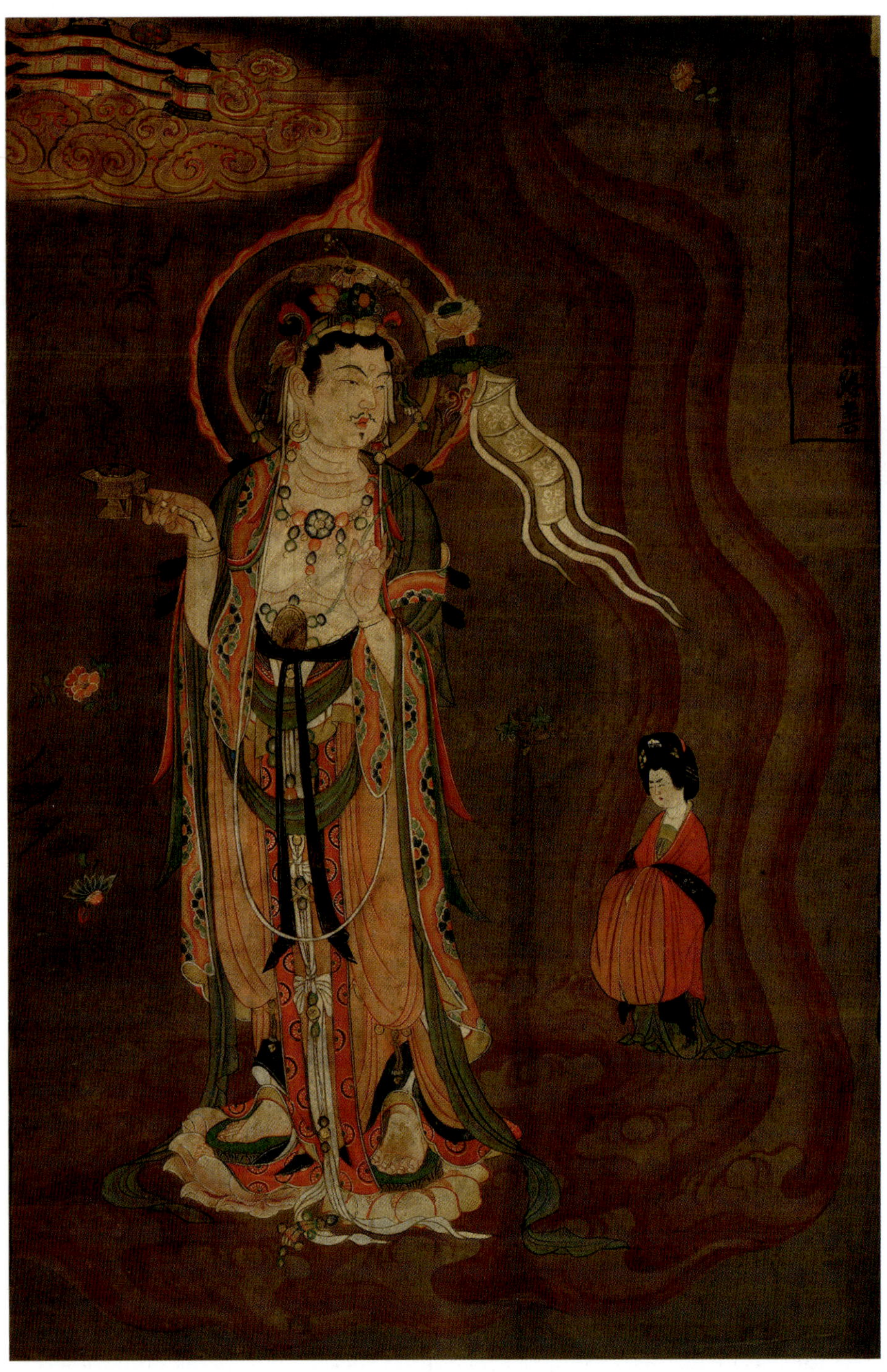

FIGURE 3.33. *Bodhisattva as Guide of Souls*, late ninth century. Hanging scroll, ink and color on silk; H. 80.5 cm, W. 53.8 cm. Excavated from Cave 17 of the Mogao Grottoes. © Trustees of the British Museum.

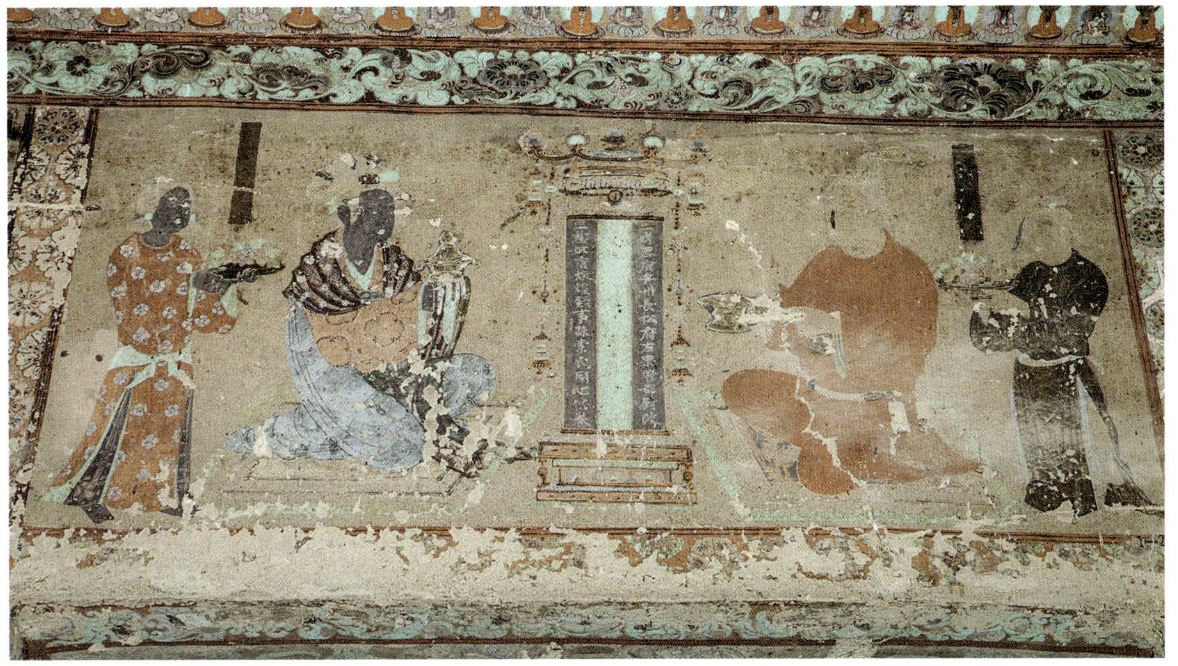

FIGURE 3.34. Ancestor portraits, ca. 839. Two columns of inscriptions separate the male and female donors. The inscription on the right identifies the male figure as the deceased father, Yin Bolun; the line on the left identifies the woman as the deceased mother, born into the Suo family. Patron: Yin Jiazheng. H. 76 cm, W. 100 cm. Mogao Cave 231. Courtesy of Dunhuang Research Academy.

to differentiate the separate articles of dress, which were outlined in black. The black brush lines, highlighting the creases in the fabric, gave softness and motion to the garments. Stone reliefs depicting a group of female attendants and a group of female musicians also populated the tomb. These monumental female figures with large heads framed by heaps of hair, like their early eighth-century counterparts, served to elicit pleasures associated with court life—conjuring up nostalgic images of the prerebellion era. Tenth-century depictions can be viewed as the tiger's leap into the past.[57]

The continuity of the plump Tang Beauty between the early eighth and tenth centuries has been interpreted as constituting a single pictorial style. A closer examination of the range of clothed, full-figured images, however, reveals a broad range of visual styles. As a template and a theme, the Tang Beauty could be fashioned to convey a yearning for more decadent times, or could be lightly color washed to articulate a moral commentary on the era. These images were designed to turn pictorial experience into the primary object, to engage close reading and interpretation. Indeed, visual representation during the postrebellion era may have drawn from prerebellion forms, but the style of their depiction insisted on their temporal-spatial configuration—on their historicity.[58]

This recognition detached visual experience from material existence, enabling the viewer to understand the layering of forms, styles, and historical relationships that underpinned painting. Women's bodies and their dress, the palace lady genre, played a critical role in this development. As aestheticized surfaces, women's dress, hair, and make-up provided painters with the freedom for artistic fashioning. Dress style was thus linked to pictorial style through aesthetic play, and both relied on fashion as a mode of knowing the world.

CONCLUSION

For fashion to exist as a way of knowing and actualizing the world through aesthetic plays—image-making and fashioning—a conception of style as historical was necessary. Historical consciousness about painting and style was spurred by changes in painting practice and conditioned by transformations in the social and political landscape. In fact, it was Zhang Yanyuan's anxiety about the violence of historical change that led him to pen *Record of Famous Painters*. The text is brimming with angst about loss: works locked up in the Inner Storehouse that would never be seen again, others lost during war and rebellion. He lamented, "Now gold comes from the mountains, and pearls are produced in the waters and men gather these things without ceasing for all under Heaven to use. But paintings with the passage of the months and years are destroyed and scattered until almost none are left. And since the famous men and ingenious scholars [who created them] can never live again, can one refrain from grief?"[59]

Like his contemporaries, Zhang could not shake the feeling of living in a degenerate age. For him, to look at paintings of the former masters was to be transported to a more ideal time. Zhang's sense of loss is most acutely felt in his condemnation of "modern painters," who only "defile their painting silks." He goes on to bemoan how painting practice had been debased in more recent times: "From ancient times those who have excelled in painting have all been men robed and capped and of noble descent, rare scholars and lofty-minded men who awakened the wonder of their own time and left behind them a fragrance that shall last a thousand years. This is not a thing that humble rustics from village lanes could ever do."[60] These "humble rustics" were the mass artisans who became painters during his lifetime. They, alongside those "who do not know how to value and enjoy" works of art, were corrupting and destroying the practice. His anxiety betrayed a sense of urgency about historical change that was echoed by scholar-poets, like Bai Juyi and Yuan Zhen, who similarly felt that the desire for material things eclipsed all else. For them, the metaphor of profligate palace woman and the poor weaving girl encapsulated the troubling relations of the postrebellion era.

By brokering engagement between the social and material worlds, the practice of aesthetic play became constitutive of subject and subjective experience. Visual representations of dress—the delineated structural forms and embellished surfaces—were products of a process of image-making, in which Tang painters and artisans paralleled the fashioning practices of Tang elites. As such, they mediated ideas about sartorial change as related to historical change. The pictorial and sculptural images of Tang women illuminate how the fixed assemblage could be manipulated to form a myriad of styles, and also provided Tang artist-image makers a template with which to develop an individual pictorial style. Decorated silk textiles, too, were products of aesthetic play that encouraged and shaped the desires of fashionable elites.

CHAPTER 4

Design

SILK AND THE LOGICS OF FASHION

THE SPECTACLE OF THE TANG BEAUTY'S BODY, ITS CORPOREALITY AND tangibility, was achieved through surface embellishments that materialized the connections between ornament, drapery, and flesh. Tang artist-image makers employed drapery to define the contours of her body, mass, and presence. The thick folds of silk that gathered at her feet, firmly planting her to the ground, made her a tangible presence—one that was fleshy and material. Decorated silks added pattern, texture, and luster to her corpulent frame, playing a fundamental part in the creation of a sumptuous image-body. For the viewer, the color and pattern of represented fabrics served an additional purpose as temporal and cultural markers that together approximated a real dressed body. The multiple and varied combinations of silk gauze cloaks, decorated robes, striped trousers, and shawls found on the Tang Beauty belonged to the artist-image maker's continual process of rendering visual and palpable the possibilities afforded by forms of adornment. In the real world of fashion, silks maintained the same function of making the clothed body tactile and current.

Such was the power of ornament that led the ninth-century poet Zheng Gu (ca. 851–910) to remark, "When the cloth is plain, grand families will certainly not even look at it / Without decorative patterns, it is hard to keep up with the times [*rushi*]."[1] From Zheng's perspective, to be au courant—or to inhabit time (*rushi*)—was to possess patterned silks. "Time" (*shi*) here is the object of the transitive verb "to enter" (*ru*),

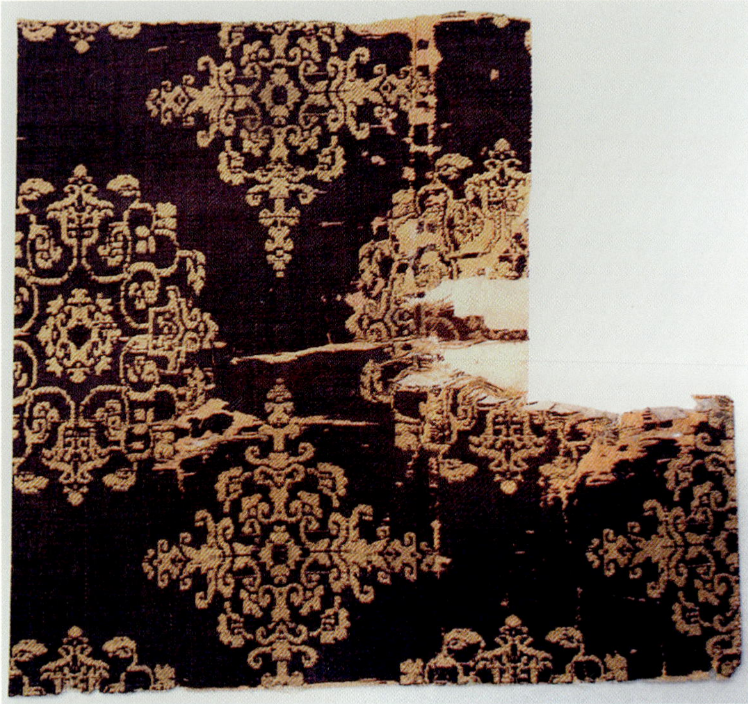

FIGURE 4.1. Textile with floral medallion, eighth century. This fragment is identical to one preserved in the Shōsō-in Treasures, Nara, Japan. The purple dye used for the ground may have been obtained from cochineal. Weft-faced compound twill; H. 18.4 cm, W. 19.7 cm. Seymour Fund, 1965. The Metropolitan Museum of Art, New York.

suggesting that the time of *fashion* was a virtual space that could be accessed bodily. In Zheng's poem, patterned silks were affective surfaces, capable of transporting the body-self into the time-space of fashion. As cloth and, more specifically, forms of adornment became a central trope for depicting material transience, the notion of change itself became reified as a visual and material act. Through its association with silk and ornament, the progress of time became a condition that could be observed, scrutinized, and lyricized. In the Tang fashion system, as discerned by Zheng Gu, perception of change was accelerated by an experience of change in one's possession of silk textiles.

The aesthetic plays of fashion were thus intimately tied to an awareness of one's relationship to their historical context and of one's social belonging. The negotiation of time, space, body, and social relations allowed for the construction of a fluid and composite (nonmodern) self, rather than a fixed, uniform (modern) self. In this way, fashion in Tang China was a materialization of the inconstancy inherent in the making of selves, first during an age of imperial expansion and then, in an era of political upheaval. Silk was the means by which self-fashioning was actualized, as it offered artist-image makers and Tang elites alike the materials to fabricate a gendered body, in dialogue with a specific time and locale, and presented in relation to a social group. This body-self was made legible through its ornamentation and in the act of aesthetic play.

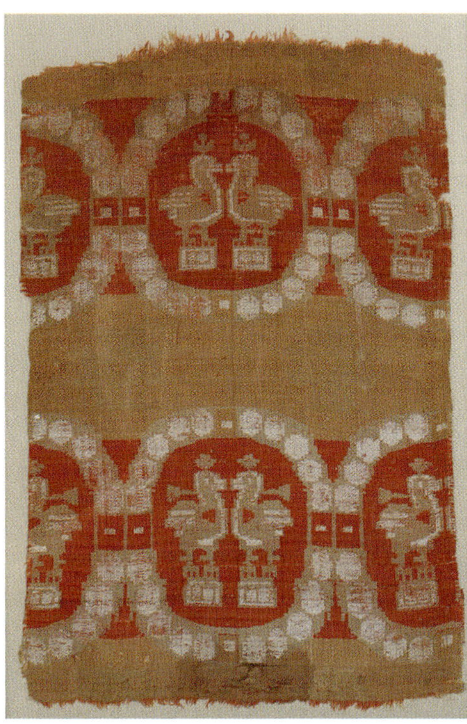

FIGURE 4.2. Facing birds in pearl roundel, dated ca. 662. Warp-faced compound twill; H. 26 cm, W. 17 cm. Excavated from Astana Tomb 134. Courtesy of Xinjiang Uyghur Autonomous Museum.

Taking another look at Lady Qu's dancer (see fig.1.1), we can see how the combination of silks worked to link the body to the imperial court and to the broader empire. The dancer's striped skirt and resist-dyed shawl, two staple patterning techniques found on both representations of Tang palace women and excavated silk artifacts, situated her among her seventh-century contemporaries in the capital, Chang'an. Her belt, the earliest example of *kesi* (lit., "carved silk") or silk tapestry weave, and her *banbi* featuring two pearl roundels enclosing confronted birds call attention to her cosmopolitan status. *Kesi* was an innovation in silk weaving that was adapted from wool tapestry techniques local to west and central Asia, and likely emerged from exchanges between textile artisans on the northwestern frontier.[2] The roundel pattern, assumed to have originated in Sasanian Iran (ca. 224–642 CE), became a dominant motif in textile design across the territories of the Silk Road during the seventh and eighth centuries, stretching from Nara Japan to Byzantium (fig. 4.2).[3] Viewed together, the dancer's ensemble established her as a subject of an increasingly interconnected world, in which Tang court style combined with colors, textures, and motifs imported and adapted from multiple locales. The artist-image maker's grouping of textiles that featured motifs of different scales—compare, for example, the large medallions of her *banbi* with the small florets of her shawl—is an example of the type of aesthetic play that the expanding silk industry, and the skill of the weaver, afforded Tang elites.

Whereas the fundamental articles of men's and women's dress changed with slight modifications to sleeve widths, hemlines, and waistlines, the surface and form of silk textiles were subject to constant alterations through design. The transfer, adoption, and formation of skills, techniques, and equipment enabled textile artisans to produce designs that captivated buyers near and far. As the dynastic sumptuary laws made clear, and as echoed by Zheng Gu, the purveyors of "new styles" (*xinyang*) were first and foremost silk artisans—designers and weavers—and not tailors. Silk design and technology was the innovative force underpinning the Tang fashion system.

Design conveyed symbolic content and, like pictorial style, stood in oblique relation to time and locale. Through contact with objects of the past that bore the stamp of local characteristics, makers and users also came to distinguish between the *jin* silks of Shu (modern Sichuan) and those made in the ninth-century weaving center of Yuezhou (in Zhejiang). Knowledge about design, surface, and form was inextricably linked to a consciousness of change, and was made indispensable to aesthetic play. In a society where textiles deeply penetrated into all aspects of life, it is not surprising that they became registers of time-space, both embodied and historical. Patterned silks became essential to differentiate oneself, and one's body, from the monochrome mass. Innovations in silk design and changes in production show how it was primarily the material, rather than the shape and silhouette of garments, that equipped Tang elites with the means to "keep up with the times."

SILK AND POWER

In Tang China, silk production was foundational to the exercise of imperial power. Collected as tax and used as a form of money, plain weave silks were ubiquitous throughout the empire. Delivered as tribute, regional silk textiles guaranteed the link between court and periphery. Offered as gifts in political exchanges, plain and decorated silks were instrumental in brokering alliances and demonstrating the empire's wealth. As the materials for imperial and official regalia, silk functioned to distinguish the emperor from his subjects and elites from non-elites.

During the first century of Tang rule, an extensive system of workshops was established to facilitate the production of complex silk textiles for imperial use. The court's and local administration's continued investment in silk production, along with increased trade and continued demand for textiles, broadened the geographical scope of silk production and fostered major innovations in technique and design. Thus, the imperial tax and tribute system, an institution that was key to the survival of Tang rule, also provided the framework for advancements in silk production that nurtured the fashion system. The tributary system was a complex network that reinforced the political, ritual, and material nature of the relations between center and periphery. The system operated on the principle of local difference as it required local governments

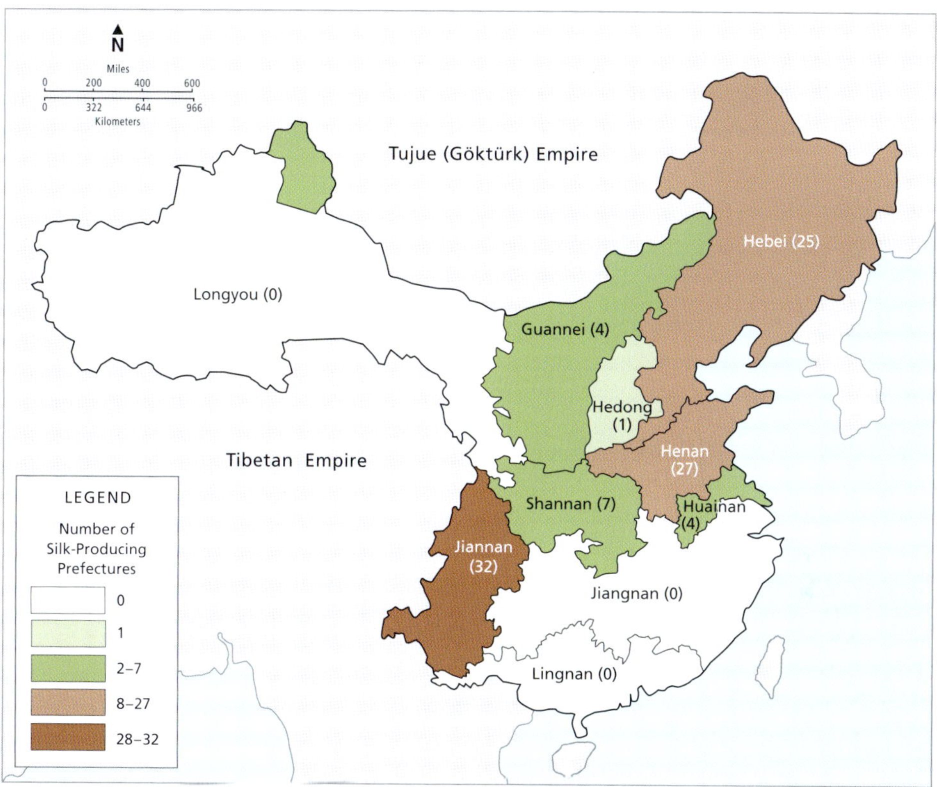

MAP 4.1. Tax-silk-producing regions, based on estimates from the Kaiyuan era (713–741). Drawn by Jennifer Shontz.

to submit agricultural and craft products specific to the region and was consequently a counter to the universal taxation model. By prizing difference, the tributary system encouraged innovation in weaving through specialization at the local level and provided the lexical categories for the regional products that circulated empire-wide.

By the Kaiyuan era (713–741) of Emperor Xuanzong's reign, an enormous variety of silks were produced in the empire, as tax payment, money, and gifts, including *ling*-twill damasks with patterns of celestial beings and clusters of flowers, and complex *luo*-gauzes that were light as gossamer. The circulation of *ling*-twill damasks and *luo*-gauzes had become so abundant that in the 730s the court permitted their use as forms of payment. The bulk of production, however, remained centered on plain or simple-patterned silks woven for tax payment, distributed across three regions—the lower reaches of the Yellow River (Hebei and Henan circuits), the Ba-Shu region (modern Sichuan) encompassing Jiannan circuit and the western section of Shannan circuit, and later, the area south of the lower reaches of the Yangzi River (Jiangnan circuit). Prior to the An Lushan Rebellion in 755, Hebei and Henan formed the chief silk-producing region for both tax and luxury silks for the court (table 4.1).[4] All twenty-five prefectures of Hebei and twenty-seven prefectures of Henan wove the best quality silk plain weave or tabby (*juan*), the most basic weave with one warp thread (threads running parallel to the length of the loom) passing over one weft (drawn perpendicular to the warp and across the width of the loom) and under the next weft thread, creating a crisscross pattern. Several of the prefectures in Hebei and Henan turned out *ling*-twill damasks, plain *sha*-gauzes, and complex *luo*-gauzes. The Ba-Shu region consistently supplied the court with the coveted polychrome compound weave *jin* silks and *luo*-gauzes.

Throughout the dynasty, textile production took place in four main types of establishment: (1) rural households; (2) official workshops; (3) private urban workshops; and (4) weaving households. Even after the government abolished the *zu-yong-diao* system in 780 and introduced the twice-a-year tax that aimed to fix local cash rates for each province, cloth produced in rural households remained a sizeable portion of the state's total revenue. Tax cloth varied according to locale and could be paid in plain *ling*-twill damasks, or silk woven with additional weft threads (*shi*), in lieu of the typical plain weave (*juan*) or hemp cloth.[5] In the Tianbao era, approximately 7.4 million bolts of tabby and over 1.85 million hanks of silk floss were levied upon a population of 3.7 million taxable individuals. An average household in a silk-producing region would have planted one hundred mulberry trees in a field about the acreage of ten *mu* (roughly one-sixth of an acre). Textile historian Zhao Feng has estimated that such a field would have yielded enough silk to produce about five bolts of plain weave, of which two bolts (a total of 40 percent of the household's annual silk production) would have been collected by the state as tax.[6]

Since woven textiles circulated in the economy as forms of payment, the government imposed procedures to standardize the names, production, and processing of woven textiles. These actions aimed to guarantee consistent quality in silks produced across the empire and, in so doing, affixed a universal system of value to textiles in circulation. All silk cloths were woven to measure one *chi* and eight *cun* in width (approximately 54 centimeters) and four *zhang* in length (twelve meters).[7] A standard bolt or roll (*pi*) of silk measured four *zhang*, while the unit of measurement for bast-fiber fabrics, such as hemp, was *duan* and equaled five *zhang*.[8] In excavated documents from Dunhuang and Turfan, complex weave silks like *jin* were identified by *zhang* (sheet).[9] Production of cloth that did not adhere to the standard measurements was a crime.[10] Variations in raw materials and processing of fibers affected the quality of the weave, which the government also sought to regulate. The Court of the Treasury, responsible for evaluating tax silk and hemp cloth, issued a grade between one and eight—grade one for the finest quality and grade eight for the coarsest—to each circuit.[11] Taxation of textiles was then adjusted according to the resources of each locale. Hebei and Henan circuits consistently secured the highest grades, while silks from Jiannan circuit earned grades in the

TABLE 4.1. Distribution of tax-silk-producing areas (Kaiyuan era, pre-733)

CIRCUIT (*dao*)	NUMBER OF PREFECTURES (*zhou*)	NUMBER OF SILK-PRODUCING PREFECTURES
Guannei (northern Shaanxi, central Inner Mongolia, Ningxia, Gansu)	22	4
Henan (Henan, Shandong, northern Jiangsu, northern Anhui)	28	27
Hedong (Shanxi)	19	1
Hebei (Beijing, Tianjin, Hebei, northern Shandong, northern Henan, western Liaoning)	25	25
Shannan (southern Shaanxi, eastern Sichuan, Chongqing, southern Henan, Hubei)	33	7
Longyou (Gansu)	21	0
Huainan (central Jiangsu, central Anhui, northeastern Hubei)	14	4
Jiangnan (Jiangxi, Hunan, southern Anhui, southern Hubei, southern Jiangsu, Zhejiang, Fujian, Shanghai)	51	0
Jiannan (central Sichuan, central Yunnan)	33	32
Lingnan (Guangdong, eastern Guangxi)	70	0

lower range. Only a few prefectures in the Jiangnan region, which had yet to emerge as a major revenue silk-producing region, were ranked and barely made the lowest grade.

Standardization of silk names served the government's project of establishing universal values of silk. For such an enterprise to succeed, however, local officials would require textile expertise. The excavation of a tax silk fragment from Astana Tomb 226 bearing the designation "fine *ling*-twill" (*xiling*)—when the weave is, in fact, damask on plain weave (*qi*)—demonstrates how easily misclassification could occur.[12] The fragment is instructive on two counts: first, the mistake perpetrated by the tax official suggests that his textile knowledge did not extend to weave structures, but was restricted to the surface appearance of silks; and second, it shows the limitations of textile nomenclature to account for technical variations and modifications found in archaeological silks. The latter holds true especially for the complex silks that have been excavated along the Silk Road and dated to the Tang dynasty.

Specialized silk production took place in official workshops, private urban workshops, and weaving households. Under Emperor Yangdi (r. 604–618) of the Sui dynasty (581–618), the Directorate of Imperial Workshops (Shaofu Jian) was formed as the principal agency of the central government responsible for supervising the manufacture of goods for palace use.[13] The Tang court kept the principal agency and established smaller official workshops in the capital and the provinces, all under the directorate's jurisdiction. Headed by a director (*jian*), the agency was further organized into a Central Service Office (Zhongshang Shu), Left Service Office (Zuoshang Shu), Right Service Office (Youshang Shu), Weaving and Dyeing Office (Zhiran Shu), as well as a Foundry Office (Zhangye Shu) that managed the Directorates of Casting, Coinage, and Tributary Trade. Charged with the production of robes for the emperor, heir apparent, and officials, the Office of Weaving and Dyeing also included twenty-five workshops dedicated to the manufacture of textiles for court use: ten workshops for weaving (*zhiren*), five for sash-making (*zushou*), four for spinning and twisting silk yarn (*chouxian*), and six for dyeing (*lianran*). Each workshop specialized in a particular weave, yarn, and color dye. Eight of the ten workshops of the weaving section was dedicated to one type of weave: plain weave silk, weft-ribbed plain weave (*shi*), open-weave *sha*-gauze, *ling*-twill damask, complex *luo*-gauze, polychrome compound weave silks (*jin*), twill-patterned tabby weave (*qi*), and polychrome compound weave silks patterned with stripes (*jian*). The two remaining workshops specialized in bast-fibers (*bu*) and animal fibers (*he*).[14] A group of eighty-three unofficial craftspeople worked in the inner workshop (*neizuo*) for the weaving of twill silks (*ling*) while a supplementary workshop of 365 craftspeople dedicated to twill and *jin* silks (*lingjin fang*), separate from the twenty-five workshops, were also housed in the palace, under the command of the directorate.[15] Palace women, supervised by the Office of Inner Court Services (Yiting Ju), an office of the Palace Domestic Service (Neishi Sheng), also participated in the production of silks for court use. The Office of Inner Court Services, for example, managed 150 *ling*-twill damasks weavers.[16] In total, the directorate employed over five thousand short-term and permanent artisans in the workshops. Aside from the Inner Court Services, the distribution of men and women textile workers in the palace workshops, as well as the gendered division of labor maintained in the processing of cloth, is unknown.

Outside the palace, official workshops producing *jin* silks were established in the two capitals, Chang'an and Luoyang, and in Yizhou (Jiannan circuit), Mianzhou (Jiannan), Yangzhou (Huainan), and Zhaozhou (Hebei).[17] Private workshops also existed alongside imperial manufactories. Whereas court-controlled workshops received raw materials and equipment from the state, private workshops were responsible for producing their own raw materials and acquiring tools. The largest privately owned workshop recorded in historical sources was run in Dingzhou by He Mingyuan, who owned five hundred looms for the making of *ling*-twill damasks.[18] Weaving households (*zhizao hu*), located throughout the main silk-producing regions, manufactured specialized silks for the imperial court and a large percentage of tribute silk on behalf of the local government. These workshops maintained a direct connection to the court and fell under the supervision of local prefectural administrations, but were not strictly official workshops. The prefectural administration requisitioned the materials from local stocks and determined the type of complex weave, such as *jin* or *ling*-twill, that each weaving household produced for tribute to the court. *Ling*-twill damasks, for example, were produced in multiple workshops located in Hebei (Dingzhou and Youzhou), Henan (Xianzhou and Yuzhou), Jiannan (Zizhou), and in the Jiangnan region (Runzhou and Yuezhou).[19]

The value of tribute silks was tied to the geography of their production, such that the names of silks often derived from the place of production. The tribute system mapped onto imperial geography a taxonomy of local skills and expertise, and served to reproduce the hierarchical relationship between center and periphery. Promotion of regional production through the tributary order also furthered the cosmopolitan vision of empire, in which the possession of rare tribute goods reaffirmed the emperor as ruler of a vast and diverse polity. As Emperor Jingzong's request for *liao*-twill from Yuezhou illustrated, unique silk tribute was highly desired.[20] In this spatially ordered hierarchy of goods, local place names underscored the singularity of the tribute and added to its value.

Throughout the first half of the eighth century, Yizhou (renamed Shu Commandery in 757) and Dingzhou were most renowned for producing high volumes of exquisite silks for the imperial court (table 4.2).[21] Although celebrated for its *jin* silks, which were known throughout the empire as Shu *jin* (Shu was an ancient name for Sichuan), Yizhou also supplied the court with highly regarded complex gauzes, including the light, airy weave known as "single-thread gauze" (*dansi luo*).[22] Jiangnan circuit did not supply the court with regular tax payments in plain weave silk, but the vast area in the lower reaches of the Yangzi Delta did produce an array of complex silk weaves including *ling*-twills and *jin* silks for tribute by the early decades of the eighth century. When Wei Jian was appointed as land and water transport commissioner in 743, he constructed a new canal parallel to the Wei River for tax and tribute boats traveling to

TABLE 4.2. Distribution of tax and tribute silks during the Kaiyuan era

CIRCUIT	TAX	TRIBUTE
Guannei	1. Plain weave (*juan*) 2. Silk floss (*mian*)	—
Henan	1. Plain weave (*juan*) 2. Weft-ribbed plain weave (*shi*) 3. Silk floss (*mian*)	1. Patterned twill (*wenling*) 2. Cloth woven from a silk-kudzu vine blend (*sige*) 3. Twills patterned with squares (*fangwen ling*), mandarin ducks (*xichi ling*), clusters of flowers (*jinghua ling*), and celestial patterns (*xianwen ling*) 4. Twill woven from two sets of silk yarn or double-silk twill damask (*shuangsi ling*)
Hedong	—	1. White thin plain weave or crêpe silk (*baihu*) 2. Fan made from twill and plain weave silks (*lingjuan shan*)
Hebei	1. Plain weave (*juan*) 2. Silk floss (*mian*) 3. Silk yarn (*si*)	1. Complex gauze (*luo*) 2. Twill (*ling*) 3. Coarse plain weave (*pingchou*) 4. Cloth woven from a silk-bast fiber blend (*sibu*) 5. Spun silk, coarse plain weave (*mianchou*) 6. Thick silk gauze with meshes (*chunluo*) 7. Silk gauze patterned with peacocks (*kongque luo*) 8. Tabby with two medallions patterned in twill (*liangke xiling*) 9. Open-weave gauze (*sha*) 10. "Fanyang" twill (*fanyang ling*) 11. Tabby with pattern in twill (*xiling*) 12. Twill with auspicious patterns (*ruiling*) 13. Twill with a single large medallion (*da duke ling*) 14. Open-weave gauze in tabby (*pingsha*)
Shannan	1. Plain weave (*juan*) 2. Weft-ribbed plain weave (*shi*) 3. Coarse, plain weave (*chou*)	1. White crêpe silk (*baihu*) 2. Twill (*ling*) 3. Cross-shot crêpe, a thin and loosely woven tabby weave (*jiaosuo hu*) 4. Crêpe silk patterned with small squares (*zifang hu*) 5. Patterned twill (*wenling*) 6. Twill produced from a special cocoon, local to northeastern Sichuan (*chonglian ling*) 7. White silk kerchief (*bai guanjin*)
Longyou	—	1. White twill (*bailing*)
Huainan	1. Plain weave (*juan*) 2. Weft-ribbed plain weave (*shi*) 3. Silk floss (*mian*)	1. Cross-shot weave (*jiaosuo*) 2. Mixed silk-bast fiber cloth (*sibu*) 3. Patterned open-weave gauze (*huasha*) 4. Central Asian–style *jin*, polychrome compound weave, robe (*fanke jinpao*) 5. *Jin* shawl (*jinbei*) 6. *Jin banbi*, or half-sleeved short jacket (*banbi jin*) 7. *Jin* robe (*xinjia jinpao*) 8. Plain weave with single medallion patterned in twill (*duke xiling*)

TABLE 4.2. Distribution of tax and tribute silks during the Kaiyuan era (*cont.*)

CIRCUIT	TAX	TRIBUTE
Jiangnan	—	1. Open-weave gauze (*sha*) 2. Twill (*ling*) 3. White-braided twill (*baibian ling*) 4. Cross-shot twill (*jiaosuo ling*) 5. Wu twill (*Wu ling*) 6. Twills patterned with wave designs (*shuibo ling*) and chessboard design (*fangqi ling*) 7. *Jin* 8. Kerchief in purple (*zi guanjin*) and red silk (*hong guanjin*)
Jiannan	1. Plain weave (*juan*) 2. Silk floss (*mian*)	1. Complex gauze (*luo*) 2. Twill (*ling*) 3. Cross-shot weave (*jiaosuo*) 4. Single thread gauze (*dansi luo*) 5. Spun silk, coarse plain weave (*mianchou*) 6. Twill patterned with almond-shaped designs, similar to the shape of a weaving shuttle (*shupu ling*) 7. Mixed silk-bast fiber cloth (*sibu*)
Lingnan	—	—

the capital.[23] Boats from Kuaiji Commandery (also known as Huiji; today's Shaoxing, Zhejiang) carried *Wu ling*, a twill damask named after the Wu region in which it was woven. From Jinling Commandery (today's Changzhou, southern Jiangsu), auspicious *ling*-twill damasks were also shipped to the court. Although Dingzhou held onto its status as the unrivalled center of *ling*-twill weaving, presenting the court with over 1,500 bolts of patterned twills in the early years of Tianbao, the court also desired silks sent out from weaving households in parts of Jiangnan circuit.[24]

The court instituted this complex and expansive network of manufacture with the intention of exerting control over the most important store of value, textiles. The establishment of workshops within the palace and in locales with a tradition of silk weaving was critical to the empire's imperial ambitions, but also contributed to the expansion of the industry outside the purview of court control. By the end of the dynasty, silk-producing centers, dispersed across the empire, were no longer solely dependent on court patronage. As late eighth- and ninth-century sumptuary measures lay bare, the postrebellion court exercised negligible power over regional weaving households, where "new styles" were used to weave silk textiles for imperial tribute and local markets. The flourishing of complex silk production depended foremost on the skilled weavers who labored across the empire to satisfy the desires and demands of the court and the market.

WEAVERS AS BOOTY

One of the most significant developments in the silk industry was the emergence of Jiangnan as the economic heart of the empire. Large-scale migration to the lands south of the Yangzi River in the eighth century had begun to shift economic productivity from the northeastern provinces. The ninth-century scholar-official Du Mu (803–852), described the sweeping transformation of the Jiangnan area, "Weaving and farming have elevated these seven prefectures; from their levy of silk cocoons and salt for preserving food, there is enough to clothe and feed the empire."[25]

The dislocation of silk production from the north to the Jiangnan region has been attributed to the loss of critical tax-silk prefectures in Hebei and Henan circuits following the An Lushan Rebellion in 755. When Hebei and northern Henan circuits, which had contributed approximately two-thirds of the central government's revenue in silk during the early empire, became autonomous in the wake of the rebellion, the capital was cut off from its main supply of silk cloth. By the early ninth century, Hebei had ceased to produce anything for the capital. Southern and central Henan, which remained part of the empire in principle, were only able to contribute tax payments at irregular intervals. The Tang court, forced to cede control over its chief silk-producing territories in the northeast, began to levy heavy taxes and tribute quotas on Sichuan and Jiangnan. Beginning in the ninth century, several prefectures in Jiangnan sent more plain silk to the capital than any other region in the empire. Economic historian Lu Huayu has estimated that the area produced an average of thirty-four million bolts of plain weave silk each year for the government, more than four times the average amount of tax silk collected during the Tianbao era.[26] Du Mu, in a letter to the chief minister petitioning for the prefectship of Hangzhou, wrote again in 849, "Now all under heaven regard the Yangzi and Huai valleys as the lifeblood of the nation."[27] The lower reaches of the Yangzi Valley would also become the leading supplier of "new styles" in the ninth century.

Tax and tribute records from the Kaiyuan and Tianbao reign eras reveal, in contrast to the literary record, that advancements in silk weaving began in Jiangnan circuit prior to the rebellion (table 4.2). What shifted in the wake of the rebellion was the quantity and range of silks produced in the region, and the government's control over the centers of production (table 4.3).[28] Yuezhou, famous for originating the labor-intensive and complex *liao*-twill damask desired by Jingzong and lauded in Bai Juyi's aptly named poem "*Liaoling*" (translated in chap. 5), was one of the key silk-manufacturing centers to spring up in Jiangnan during the postrebellion era. In the ninth century, Yuezhou presented the court with treasure-flower patterned (*baoxiang huawen*), *luo*-gauzes, and radiant *ling*-twills as tribute. According to the official records, Yuezhou, which lacked a tradition of handicrafts, quickly developed into one of the superlative silk production centers of the empire before it was gradually overtaken by Hangzhou and Suzhou

TABLE 4.3. Silks produced for tribute in Jiangnan circuit in the ninth century

PREFECTURE	YUANHE ERA (806–820)	CHANGQING ERA (821–824)
Runzhou	—	1. Complex gauze robes (*luoshan*) 2. Twills (*ling*) patterned with water waves (*shuiwen*), squares (*fangwen*), "fish mouths" (*yukou*), embroidered leaves (*xiuye*), and floral motifs (*huawen*)
Changzhou	—	1. Coarse, plain weave (*chou*) 2. Plain weave (*juan*) 3. Silk wadding (*mianbu*) 4. Tightly woven open-weave gauze (*jinsha*)
Huzhou	1. Plain cloth (*bu*)	1. Imperial robes (*yufu*) 2. Twills patterned with bird eyes (*niaoyan*) 3. Plain weave silk cloth (*choubu*)
Suzhou	1. Cloth woven from a silk-kudzu vine blend (*sige*)	1. Cloth woven from a silk-kudzu vine blend (*sige*) 2. Silk floss (*simian*) 3. Silk yarn reeled from eight cocoons (*bacan si*) 4. Red twill (*feiling*)
Hangzhou	1. White braided twill (*baibian ling*)	1. White braided twill (*baibian ling*)
Yuezhou (starting in the Zhenyuan reign era, 785–805)	1. Wu twill (*Wu ling*) 2. Patterned open-weave gauze (*huagu xiesha*) 3. Wu open-weave gauze in red (*Wu zhusha*)	1. Treasure-flower motif (*baohua*) and other patterned complex gauzes (*luo*) 2. White-braided (*baibian*), cross-shot (*jiaosuo*), and persimmon-calyx motif twills (*shiyang huawen ling*) 3. Light, unfigured gauze with square holes (*qingrong sha*) or fine open-weave (*qingrong*) 4. Crêpe made from raw silk yarn (*shenghu*) 5. Patterned open-weave gauze (*huasha*) 6. Wu plain weave (*Wu juan*)
Mingzhou	—	1. Wu twill (*Wu ling*) 2. Cross-shot twill (*jiaosuo ling*)

toward the end of the dynasty.[29] Xue Jianxun, military commissioner of the eastern Jiangnan circuit under the reign of Emperor Daizong (r. 762–779), is credited with the launch of the silk weaving industry in Yue: "At first, the people of Yue were not skilled at the loom and shuttle. When Xue Jianxun became commissioner of Jiangdong [the area east of the Yangzi], he recruited soldiers who had not yet settled into a marriage to go north and marry weaving women, generously rewarding the men with money. Over a few years' time, they obtained several hundred women. This led to a significant transformation in the customs of Yue; the people competed to create new patterns and their twill damasks and gauzes were praised as the most exquisite left of the Yangzi."[30] The story begins by remarking on the absence of skilled weavers to emphasize that the transformation of Yuezhou necessarily depended on the movement of weaving women into the region. The displacement of women weavers from their northern homeland led the poet Shi Jianwu (780–861) to bemoan, "Pity the girls from north of the Yangzi, only singing songs of the south Yangzi."[31] Such stress on weaving and more generally, crafts as embodied, suggests that technical skills and knowledge were perceived as innate to a person or embedded in a group of people. The transfer of these embodied skills then depended on movement of laboring bodies, rather than the looting of technology.[32] The government was well aware of the invaluable role of skilled artisans in the dissemination of weaving knowledge, such that a pattern designer (the *zaoyi zhe* of the crime; literally, "to create the intention") faced three years of exile, and his weavers two and a half years, if caught producing illicit silks.[33] By meting out punishment according to skill and role, the Tang government codified a hierarchy of craft production that positioned the pattern designer at the top.

Accounts of craftspeople and young women captured as booty during violent incursions and rebellions comprised one of the recurrent themes of Tang literary and historical sources.[34] In 829, the Tang court suffered a devastating loss of skilled labor and resources when troops dispatched by the Nanzhao Kingdom (situated in modern Yunnan) sacked Chengdu (formerly Yizhou), the seat of the Shu Commandery.[35]After ten days of fighting, the Nanzhao army retreated to the south, taking with them an estimated ten thousand young women, craftspeople, and laborers.[36] Following their invasion of Shu, the Nanzhao, who previously lacked the skills and labor necessary for producing complex silks, were able to "weave twill damasks and silk gauzes" that were "on par with those woven in the empire."[37] The sudden sophistication of the Nanzhao silk industry suggests that among the thousands of captives, textile artisans were included in the total figures of those captured. [38] Writing a few decades later in 855, Lu Qiu, a Tang scholar-official, claimed that half of the artisans in Chengdu and the neighboring areas were taken and half of the population had been wiped out during the invasion.[39] Lu certainly exaggerated the devastation, as weaving households in Shu recovered from the attack and in the next year provided several thousand bolts of *ling*-twill damask, *luo*-gauze, and *jin* silks for its annual tribute.[40]

In a society where work and status were inextricably linked, it was common sense for Li Zhao, and Lu Qiu after him, to conceive of skills as residing in the body of the maker. The rapid development of local textile industries in Jiangnan and Nanzhao required the presence of the weaver herself. The conviction that talent, skill, and capability were inalienable might have appealed to Tang dynasty intellectuals, particularly those living in the ninth century, for other reasons (see chap. 5). But how weavers and designers created the "new styles" (*xinyang*) that charmed Tang elites, and which sumptuary laws could not keep up with, is a mystery that still remains.

Examination of silk textiles excavated from along Silk Road allows us to explore the circumstances surrounding the exchange of weaving skills that led to an expanded repertoire of textile motifs and improvements in patterning techniques. Silks excavated from oasis cities along the Silk Road and elite tombs in the inner empire show a dazzling array of patterns that highlight the ingenuity of the weaver. From the sixth to eighth century, trade along the Silk Road and Tang expansion into Central Asia filtered new goods, technology, and people into the frontier towns and interior cities of the empire. The dynamism of this trade yielded a profound impact on the production of luxury silks by introducing Tang artisans to a new stock of patterns, colors, and weaves from visual and material cultures west of the empire. These weavers and their embodied skills, then, rank with the tax and tribute system as equally critical to the Tang fashion system.

ORNAMENT AND EXPERIENCE

Of the corpus of silk artifacts dated to the Tang dynasty, polychrome silks with a design consisting of a central pattern, such as animals or hunters encircled in a roundel border, and combined with floral composite motifs in the interstices were the most innovative and fashionable, and thus have commanded the most attention from textile historians. One example of this complex design structure is the banner featuring four lion hunters mounted on winged horses, arranged symmetrically along a central axis (fig. 4.3). Now preserved at the Hōryūji Temple in Nara, Japan, the textile is believed to have been woven in Tang China and sent to Nara in the early eighth century.[41]

Depicted in two tiers, each of the four horsemen are presented aiming a bow at a pouncing lion. In the upper tier, the horses are yellow-green and bear the character *shan* (mountain) on their hindquarters. The horses in the lower tier are indigo and feature the character *ji* (auspicious). A flowering tree stands at the center of the medallion, the outer band of which is composed of twenty white pearls divided into four sections by a nested square positioned at the four cardinal points. Dispersed in between the rows of medallions are quatrefoil motifs combined with small pearl roundels enclosing a lotus flower woven in the center. The artifact is remarkable for both pattern design and weaving technique, which place the textile in close relation to Sasanian ornament and excavated silks from Antinoë, Egypt.[42]

Beginning in the sixth century, the medallion style, classified as a series of repeated round-bordered pattern units that frame an animal or human figure, spread across the territories linked together by the Silk Road. We see, in the attributed Yan Liben painting *Emperor Taizong Receiving the Tibetan Envoy*, the envoy Mgar Ston Rstan

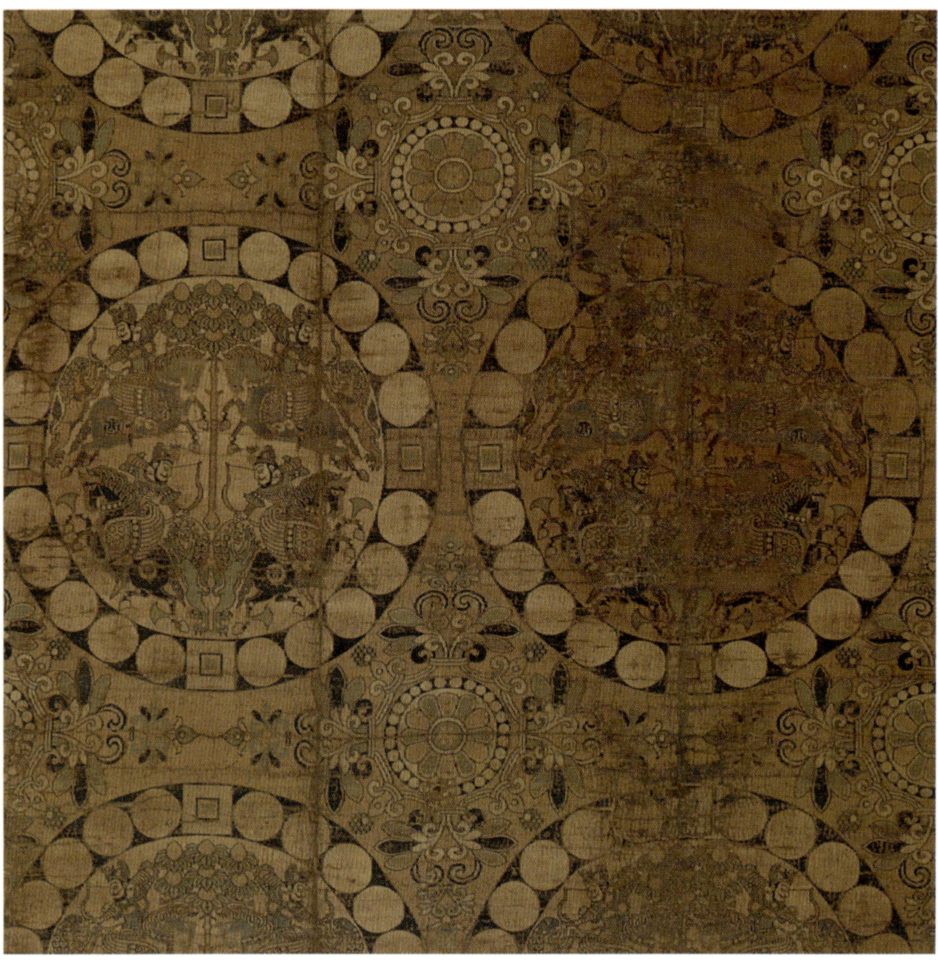

FIGURE 4.3. Horsemen hunting lions with Chinese characters *shan* (mountain) and *ji* (auspicious), eighth century. The hunters are mirrored in the horizontal direction of the weft. The two upper horses are yellow-green, while the horses below are indigo. Weft-faced compound twill; L. 250 cm, W. 130 cm. Treasure of the Hōryūji Temple, Nara, Japan. Image courtesy of TNM Image Archives.

(Ludongzan) portrayed in a *jin* robe patterned with rows of medallions (see fig. 3.18).[43] A coat with a similar cut and decorated with rows of confronted birds standing on pedestals in pearl roundels is preserved in the Abegg-Stiftung (fig. 4.4). The sheer quantity of similarly designed silks, made with identical techniques, has made it challenging to discern unequivocally which fragments were woven by Tang artisans, or by Sogdians, or even by artisans from further west of the empire. Such was the immense appeal of the medallion style that one scholar of the late Roman empire and Sasanian Iran has described the fluid cultural borrowing of motifs between the third and eighth centuries as a phenomenon of "global aristocratic ornament."[44]

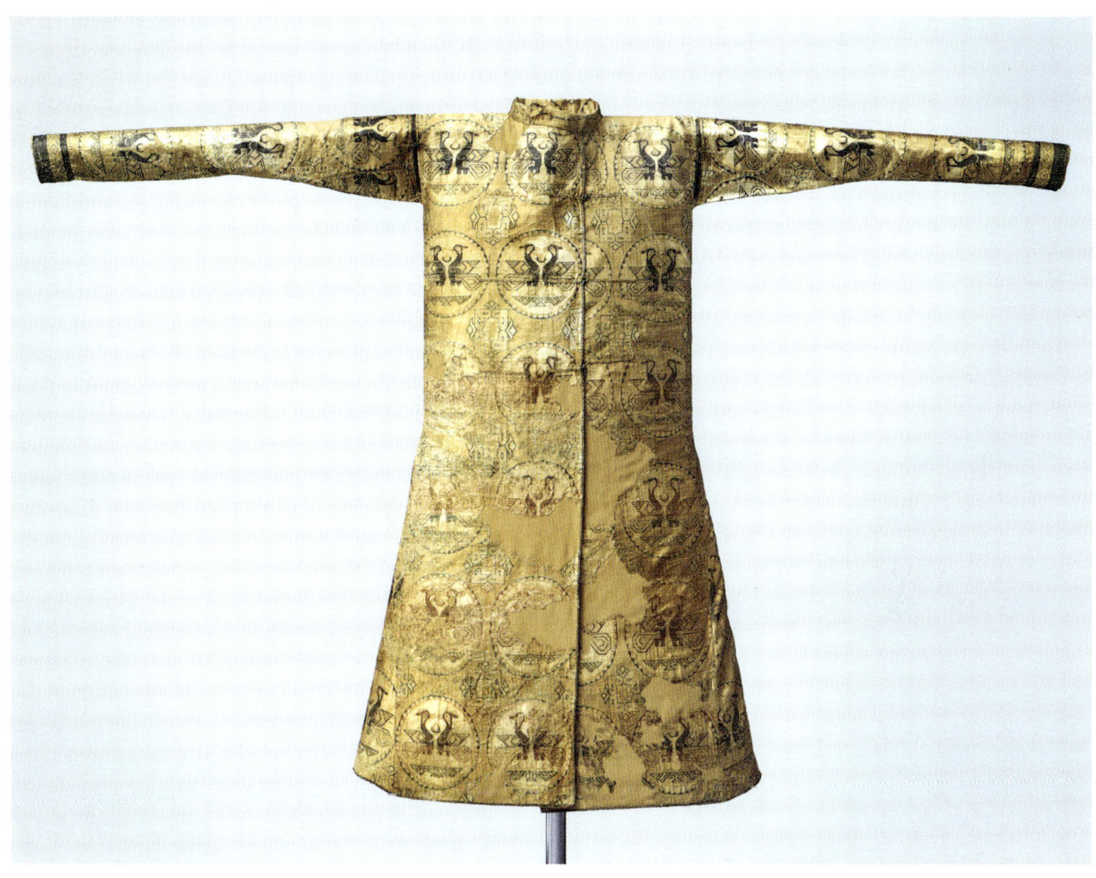

FIGURE 4.4. Coat with facing ducks in pearl roundels, ninth or tenth century. Weft-faced compound twill (samite). Central Asia. ©Abegg-Stiftung, CH-3132 Riggisberg, 2011; photo: Christoph von Viràg.

The woven medallion design, similar to the Tang Beauty, was a template adopted, adapted, and transformed by designers and weavers across the empire. The medallion style offered a versatile framing, occasionally linking, structure that could be customized in a myriad of ways (see fig. 4.1). In the eighth century, weavers used composite flowers, rosettes, or scrolling plants to compose the border in a style known as treasure-flower medallion pattern (*baoxiang huawen*). This pattern can be found on several surviving garments dated to the eighth century including the *ling*-twill damask robe in the China National Silk Museum, a fragment of a *banbi* (*hanpi*) in the Shōsō-in, and the prince's jacket and pants in the Cleveland Museum of Art (figs. 4.5, 4.6, and 4.7). Both the coat and pants in the Cleveland Museum were lined with a *ling*-twill damask patterned with a large-scale floral medallion, made up of a central rosette framed by two floral wreaths. Preserved in Tibet, the garments illustrate the flexibility of ornament

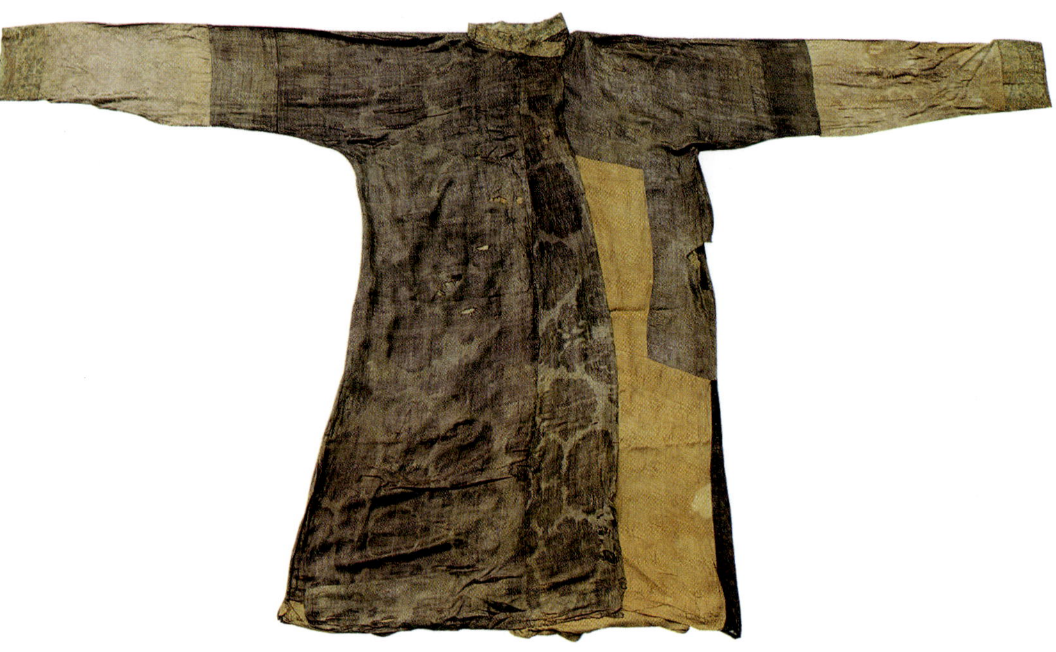

FIGURE 4.5. Robe with treasure-flower medallion pattern, Tang dynasty. Each medallion pattern unit has a diameter of 44 cm and consists of three layers: a flower with eight petals in the center, an enclosing eight-bud scrolling cloud pattern, and an outer eight-petal lotus pattern. *Ling*-twill damask with a border of *jin* silk; L. 138 cm, W. 248 cm (across sleeves). Courtesy of China National Silk Museum, Hangzhou.

FIGURE 4.6. Surviving fragment of *banbi* with treasure-flower medallion pattern, dated eighth century. The Shōsō-in Treasures, Nara, Japan. Sewn from two different bolts, one with a red ground and the other with a green ground. Silk, *jin*. L. 61 cm. Courtesy of the Imperial Household Agency.

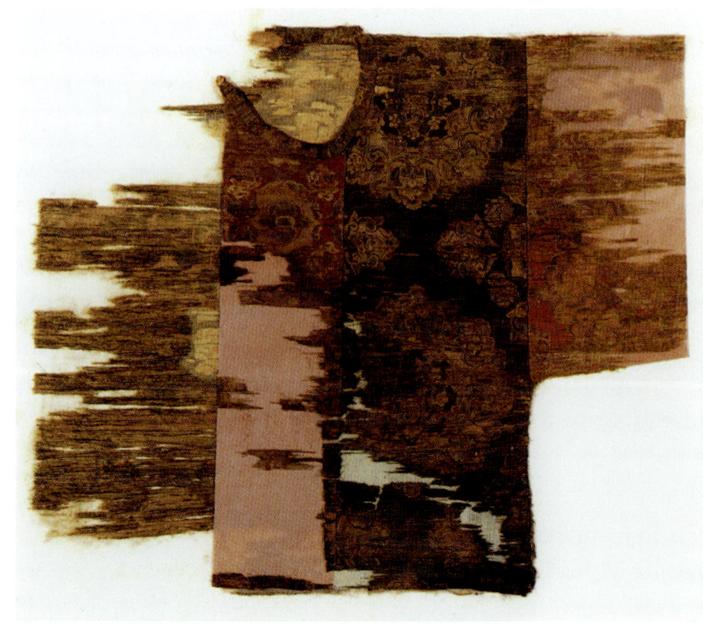

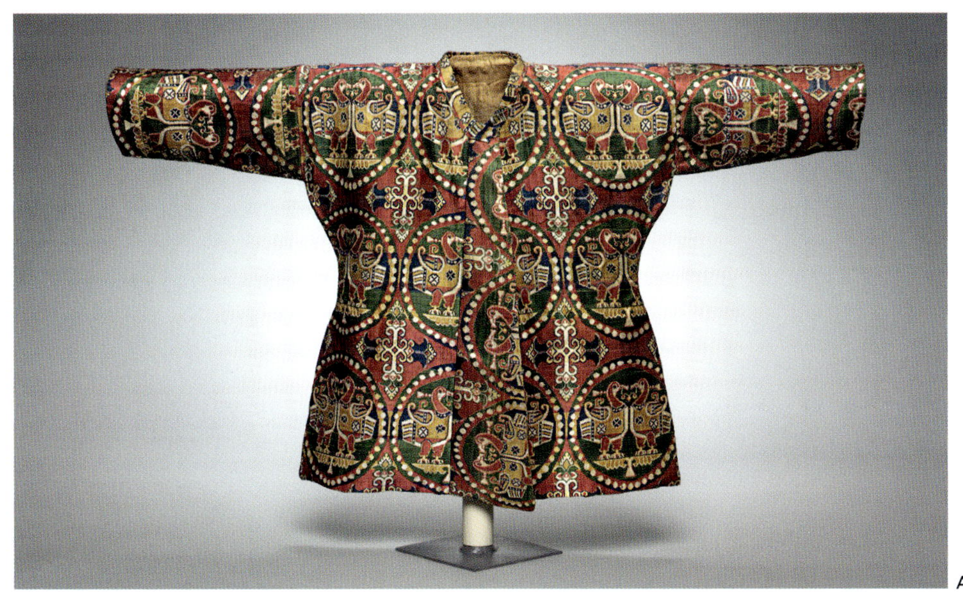

A

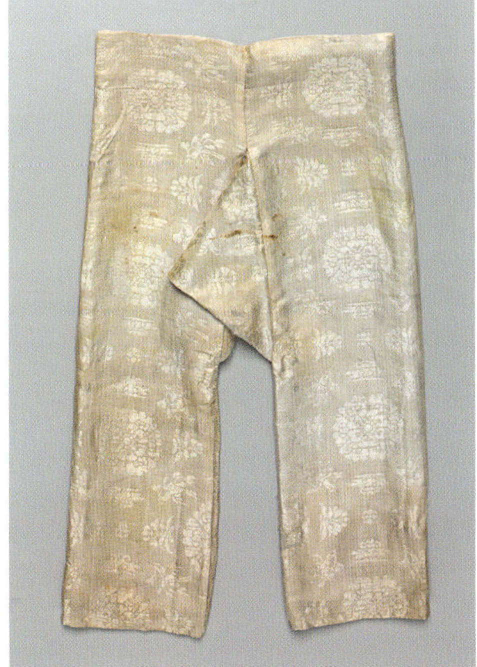

B

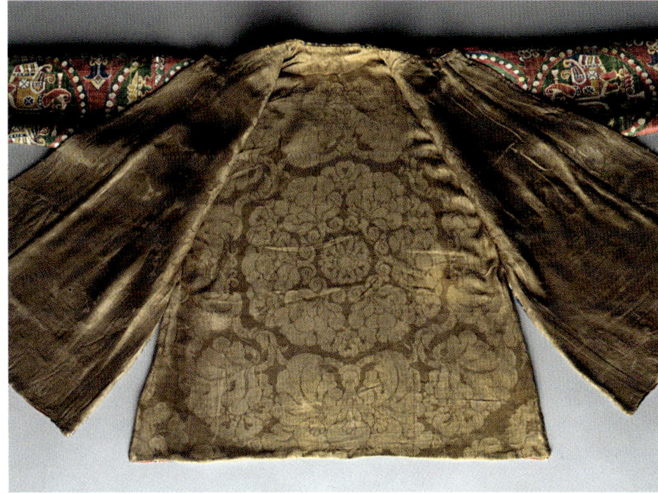

C

FIGURE 4.7. (A) Child's Coat with Ducks in Pearl Medallions, eighth century. Probably Uzbekistan. Samite (weft-faced compound twill): silk. Lining: twill damask (*ling*), silk; L. 48, W. 82.5 cm. The Cleveland Museum of Art, purchase from the J. H. Wade Fund 1996.2.1. (B) Prince's trousers and (C) lining, dated eighth century. The large-scale treasure-flower medallion pattern composed of a central rosette encircled by two layers of scrolling flowers is similar in concept to the motif found on the damask robe in the China National Silk Museum (fig. 4.5). China, Tang dynasty. Trousers: twill damask (*ling*), white silk; L. 52 cm, W. 28 cm; Lining: twill damask (*ling*), brown silk. The Cleveland Museum of Art, Purchase from the J. H. Wade Fund 1996.2.2.

and more significantly, the portability of silk textiles, design, and technique during this era. The hybrid form and decoration of the coat and pants have suggested that the items may have been produced within the Tibetan empire, which extended into parts of Sichuan, Gansu, and Turfan in the late eighth century.[45]

Imperial expansion would have brought Tibetan elites in closer contact with goods made by Sogdian and Tang artisans living in the newly conquered territories. A combination of stylistic, iconographic, and technical features have led specialists to conclude that the outer fabric of the coat with a design of paired ducks in pearl roundels and palmettes in the interspaces is of Sogdian origin. The pants and lining are believed to have been made by Chinese weavers.[46] The evidence, however, is largely circumstantial. In any case, that the coat, pants, and lining came to be fabricated from this combination of silks is in itself suggestive of the pathways that transported motifs, patterning techniques, and even artisans in a fashion system that was dispersed geographically across vast distances.

The ubiquity of the medallion attests to the central role ornament played in exchanges between empires and their subjects and, also, in the aesthetic play of fashion. Within the context of imperial and elite display, ornament defined court culture and conveyed prestige and power. As surface decoration and a principle of style, ornament could also intervene in the user's relationship to the object, and with respect to the user's own social place and time. In seizing the ornament of a distant cultural sphere and integrating it into the local visual sphere of ornament, patrons of luxury silks continually generated and enacted new images of themselves—and of the world. The visual and sculptural program of elite Tang dynasty tombs, for example, re-created such a world for the deceased to experience in the afterlife. This practice of meaning-making, performed through an encounter with the visual and material cultures of one's contemporary moment, was precisely the type of aesthetic play that underpinned the Tang fashion system. In other words, ornament was a medium of cultural and social experience that opened up a world of symbolic, visual, and material possibilities that other modes of address could not. Tang painters exploited the visual field of dress to serve semantic functions for the same reason. As such, ornament and its design was far from superficial, and in fact fundamental to the aesthetic plays of fashion.

DESIGN AS INTENTION

How weavers in Sui and Tang China came to produce designs that bear a striking likeness to decorative patterns found on the rock carvings and metalwork of Sasanian Iran remains largely unknown. One longstanding theory about the introduction of foreign textile design techniques focuses on the specific role of He Chou (540–620), a Sogdian official of the Sui court, whose talents in engineering and manufacturing earned him a place in the dynastic histories.[47] A third-generation migrant, He Chou was appointed to the Imperial Wardrobe (Yufu Jian) and the Imperial Treasury (Taifu Cheng) at the beginning of the Sui dynasty.[48] When the emperor tasked him with copying the marvelous *jin* robes woven with gilt thread that were regularly presented by Persian emissaries, he created ones that surpassed the originals. He did not merely replicate the golden *jin* robes, but constructed something even more beautiful.

From Zhang Yanyuan's *Record of Famous Painters*, we learn that another designer of silks, Dou Shilun, enfeoffed as Duke of Lingyang under Emperor Taizong, introduced designs on *jin* silks that featured pairs of confronted pheasants, fighting rams, and soaring phoenixes.[49] During his service as the minister of public works in Yizhou, Dou created (*zao*) these patterns on *jin*-polychrome silks and *ling*-twill damasks, which were described by Zhang as "rare and magnificent." The arrangement of confronted animals and mythical creatures, likely within a medallion or roundel border as found on the *banbi* of Lady Qu's dancer, came to be remembered by the people of Shu as the "Duke of Lingyang design."[50] Discoveries of *jin* silks and *ling*-twill damasks featuring twin ducks, flying phoenixes, dragons, and running *qilin*, contained within a composite roundel border made of scrolling leaf, lotus, or leaf-and-grape patterns, attest to the popularity of such designs during the seventh and eighth centuries, but they bear no direct connection to Dou Shilun (fig. 4.8).

By including Dou in his discussion of historical *painters*, Zhang drew a parallel between painting style and pattern design: both the painter and the textile designer manipulated form and surface to create an object of visual pleasure. Decorated silks, like the Tang Beauty, enticed the eye and mind. Intricacy of design and composition further communicated the skill and labor required to enhance the beholder's experience of pleasure. Textiles, however, go further than paintings to engage the full sensory experience of the body. Texture, determined by the quality of the fibers and the smoothness of the weave, was an important consideration for the uses of textiles. In Tang China, as now, palette, decoration, and feel of fabric were paramount in matters of dress and in the presentation of the body. Silk design was the innovative force bolstering up the Tang fashion system.

Like He Chou before him, the case of Dou Shilun, who was "deft beyond compare," demonstrates how innovations in design were ascribed to the unparalleled genius of individual figures. Since the accounts of He and Dou concentrate on motif, rather than the weaving process, it is unclear if either men were involved in the making of textiles. The lack of textual records prevents any reconstruction of the relationship between textile design and production as it took place in Tang dynasty workshops. The association of novel patterns on silk textiles with the two men is still suggestive of how designer-type figures were perceived to have participated in the Tang fashion system.

The role of He Chou and Dou Shilun as designers and makers implies that changes in the appearance of things or the arrival of new ornamental styles were interpreted as acts of innovation, carried out by talented individuals, and then as widely disseminated

FIGURE 4.8. Confronted dragons in a doubled pearl roundel, dated ca. 710. Monochrome tabby patterned in twill; H. 21 cm, W. 25.1 cm. Shuangling county (Sichuan); excavated from Astana Tomb 221. Courtesy of Xinjiang Uyghur Autonomous Museum.

practice. The biographies of He and Dou emphasize their creations as products of a design process that began with intentionality, in the form of a sketch or a plan, and then were executed by a weaving workshop. He Chou reproduced and surpassed the gilt robes that the emperor received from Sasanian Iran, while Dou Shilun created (*zao*) "rare and magnificent" patterns for court use. Dou's creations even earned him the brand "Duke of Lingyang designs." By virtue of possessing certain ideas or "designs," they become the agents of innovation—and fashionable change. Novelty was distinguished from the old and familiar first by surface appearance; it derived value from the level of skill deployed by its makers. Luxury silk textiles made explicit the connection between value and labor. When produced in the service of the emperor, these novel objects of pleasure affirmed the supreme privileges of his court and his dominance over skilled labor within the tributary and fashion systems. The palace women who popularized men's riding coats, or Princess Anle's hundred-feather skirt, in contrast, were not celebrated by their biographers as innovators, but derided as transgressors. By associating women with illicit adoption of extravagant garments or foreign modes of adornment, compilers of the Tang dynastic annals—like the painters of the Tang Beauty—promoted a feminization of fashion that anticipated nineteenth-century discourses in Europe, in which a propensity for sartorial matters was likewise located in women's natures.[51]

Such a distinction between the ingenuity of the maker and the desire for, and the acquisition of, fashionable things might account for why the court's relationship to novel creations in silk teemed with contradictions. New styles, so long as they served the court, were treasured. If produced illicitly, pattern designers were subject to the harshest penalty. When Emperor Wenzong reformed official dress in 832, he stipulated patterns for robes and coats that were as ornately designed as the silks he prohibited a few years earlier, such as *ling*-twill damasks with wild geese holding auspicious plants in their beaks and paired peacocks for the highest ranks.[52] He also proscribed the use of *liao*-twill damask for clothing, though the ban did not extend to himself. Wenzong summed up his concerns when he remarked in conversation with his grand minister, Li Shi: "I have heard that there exists two *jin* silk robes with patterns of gold birds in the imperial palace. In the past when Xuanzong visited the hot springs, he and Yang Guifei each wore one. These days, the rich often have them."[53] The emperor's grievance captured the paradoxical relationship between the court and silk production, and, in turn, its fashionable subjects. The court, through its continued investment in silk and attendant desire for ornament, was the culprit that made complex, ornamented silks key to the expression of wealth, status, and fashion consciousness.

Dou Shilun and He Chou may have designed exquisite objects for the imperial court and generated desire for complex silks, but increased production of luxury silks depended on a design process of an entirely different nature. Creativity and intention, performed by designers like Dou and He, are insufficient to explain how the broader population of weavers adopted new patterning techniques to make "new styles" that then became more widely available to "the rich." The ingenuity of designer-types like Dou Shilun may account for the pairing of motifs, such as the confronted dragons enclosed in a pearl roundel, found in extant Tang dynasty silks, but such marvelous designs could not have taken place without the skill of the weaver and the availability of technical equipment.[54]

DESIGN AS MAKING

The locus of change in silk design, and in the fashion system, was the patterning process that entailed either the development of new weaving techniques or the introduction of printing and dyeing techniques. Since weavers—unlike the creative officials, He and Dou—were not persons of interest to the compilers of Tang records, the history of weaving has been excluded from textual documentation. Changes in silk technology and weaving practice can only be reconstructed from the material artifact. Two innovations, weft-faced patterning and clamp-resist dyeing, illustrate the critical relationship between skill, technology, and design as the key driving force of fashion. In short, the expanding range and quantity of decorated silks produced for the court and the larger empire were made possible by changes in how textile artisans wove and patterned. Modifications in weaving in particular, although imperceptible to the user, were critical to the sheer abundance of complex silks with symmetrical designs that have survived from Tang China.

As alluded to in the record of He Chou, the shared vocabulary of the medallion style was most likely sustained by frequent interactions through trade, diplomacy, and war, and was mediated by mobile populations living in the interstices. Sogdian merchants and craftsmen, who had settled in oasis towns along the Silk Road, would have played a pivotal role in facilitating trade and in commissioning textile production between Sui-Tang China and the Sasanian empire.[55] Sogdian merchants assisted in the transmission of skills by financing the weaving of new patterns.[56] Home to one of the largest colonies of Sogdians, Turfan has been a key archaeological site for documenting innovations in silk weaving.

Silk textiles excavated from the region dated to the sixth through eighth centuries reveal one of the major shifts in weaving technique: the adoption of weft-faced patterning technique, in which supplementary sets of weft threads inserted across the warp were used to produce a design (fig. 4.9). Up until roughly the sixth century, complex silks were exclusively warp-faced (see fig. 4.10). Textile historians remain divided on the origins of weft-faced weaving and the motivations for its adoption.[57] Weft-faced compound tabbies and the more complex, weft-faced compound twills woven with silk threads began to appear around the sixth century (figs. 4.11 and 4.12). Since the warp threads must be stretched under high tension during the warp-faced patterning process, the threads must be coarser, resulting in a product of greater tensile strength. In weft-faced patterning, a weaver could use finer silk yarns, as weft threads do not need to be stretched across the loom, yielding more lustrous and delicate silks. Such a shift in the feel of silks would have been registered by the users as novel, but the underlying cause for the change may not have been interpreted as one of technique. As tax and tribute records confirm, variations in silk textiles were documented by pattern and by place of production. By the turn of the eighth century, weft-faced compound twill weaves had entered the official workshops, as evidenced by the Hōryūji silk with the four hunters. Weave structures changed again around the mid-eighth century. Weft threads now appeared on both the front and back of the finished textile (fig. 4.13).[58] The development of weft-faced compound weaves and the subsequent Liao-style depended on advances in loom technology that enabled the weaver to manage multiple sets of warp and weft threads, and in a more controlled manner.[59] Innovations in weave structures

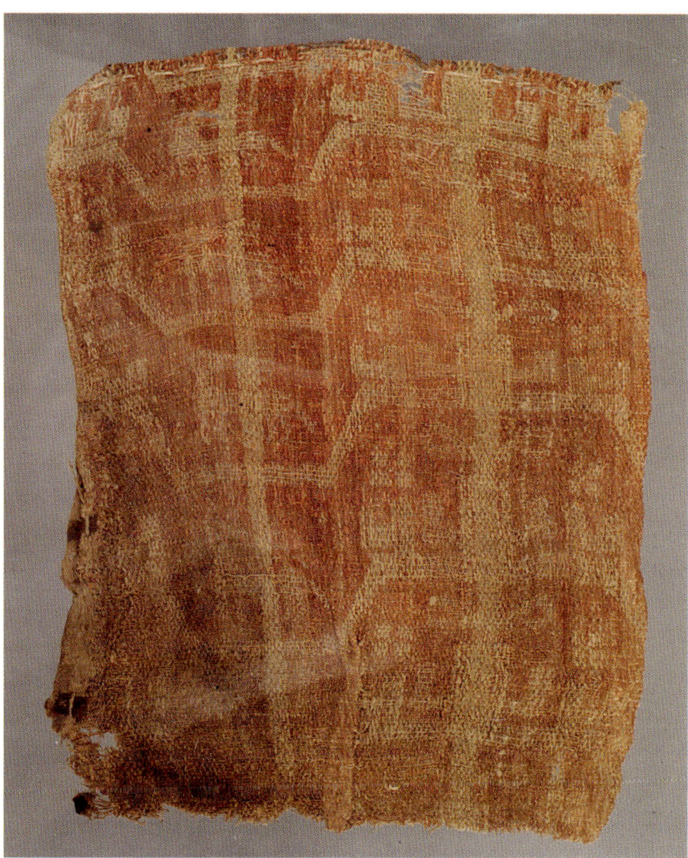

FIGURE 4.9. Stylized cloud band and auspicious creatures, dated ca. 548. This is one of the earliest textiles showing a pattern repeat in the weft direction. Weft-faced compound tabby (taqueté); L. 15 cm, W. 20.5 cm. Excavated from Astana Tomb 313. Courtesy of Xinjiang Uyghur Autonomous Museum.

were largely dictated by the technical possibilities of the loom, such as the addition of multiple heddle shafts for depressing and lifting warp threads in the drawloom.[60] With a drawloom, a weaver can raise and lower any combination of warp threads in a predetermined sequence, easing the process for repeating large-scale motifs.

The invention of the drawloom was critical to the production of compound weave structures as it allowed the weaver to repeat the pattern unit in both warp and weft directions.[61] A warp-faced compound twill with rosettes enclosed in small pearl roundels excavated from one of the Astana tombs dated to 653 is one of the earliest known textiles with pattern repeats in both warp and weft directions (fig. 4.14). The existence of this textile indicates that a drawloom must have been developed by the seventh century to enable the weaver to repeat the rosette in both directions.[62] In 2013, archaeologists discovered four pattern loom models in a Han dynasty burial site in Laoguanshan, Chengdu.[63] Dated to the second half of the second century BCE, the find confirms that Han weavers in the Sichuan region used a complex loom with multiple pattern shafts for producing the polychrome, warp-faced compound tabby silks that were celebrated

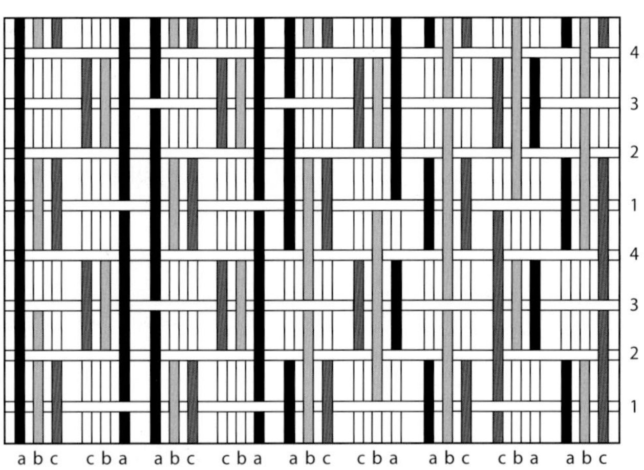

FIGURE 4.10. Warp-faced compound tabby. A warp-patterned weave consists of complementary warps of two or more series (the warp ends are marked *abc*), and one weft (weft threads or "picks" run horizontally and are marked *1234*). Drawn by Jennifer Shontz.

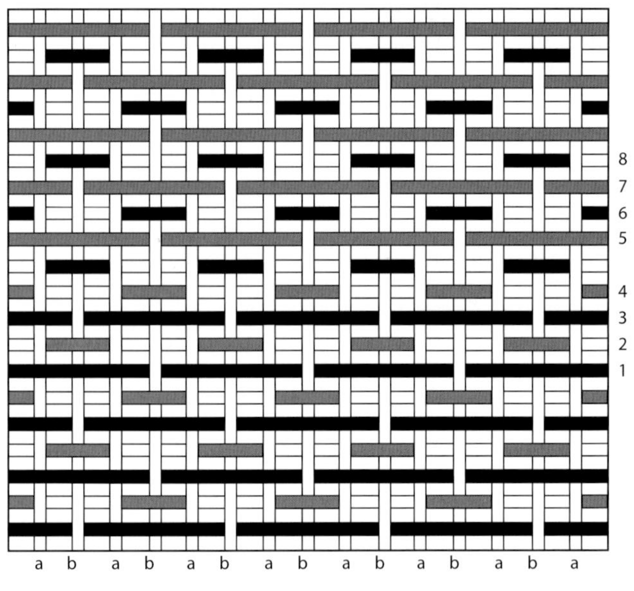

FIGURE 4.11. Weft-faced compound tabby. A weft-faced pattern weave is formed by complementary wefts in two or more series (*1234* and *5678*), and a main warp (*a*) and a binding warp (*b*). The surface of the weave is covered by weft threads that conceal main warp ends. Drawn by Jennifer Shontz.

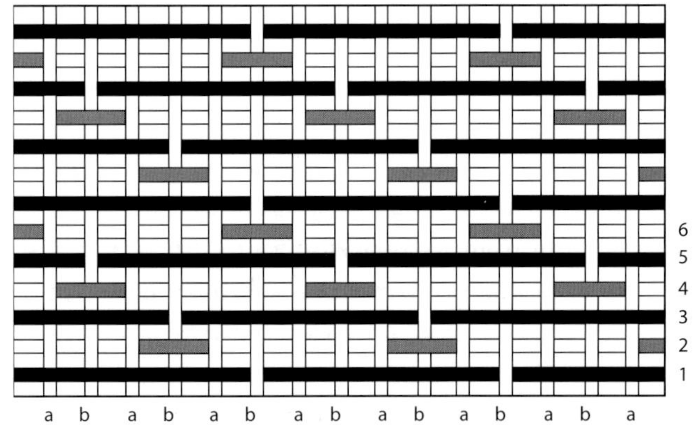

FIGURE 4.12. Weft-faced compound twill. Binding warps (*b*) bind the weft in twill. See the appendix for a diagram of basic binding units. Drawn by Jennifer Shontz.

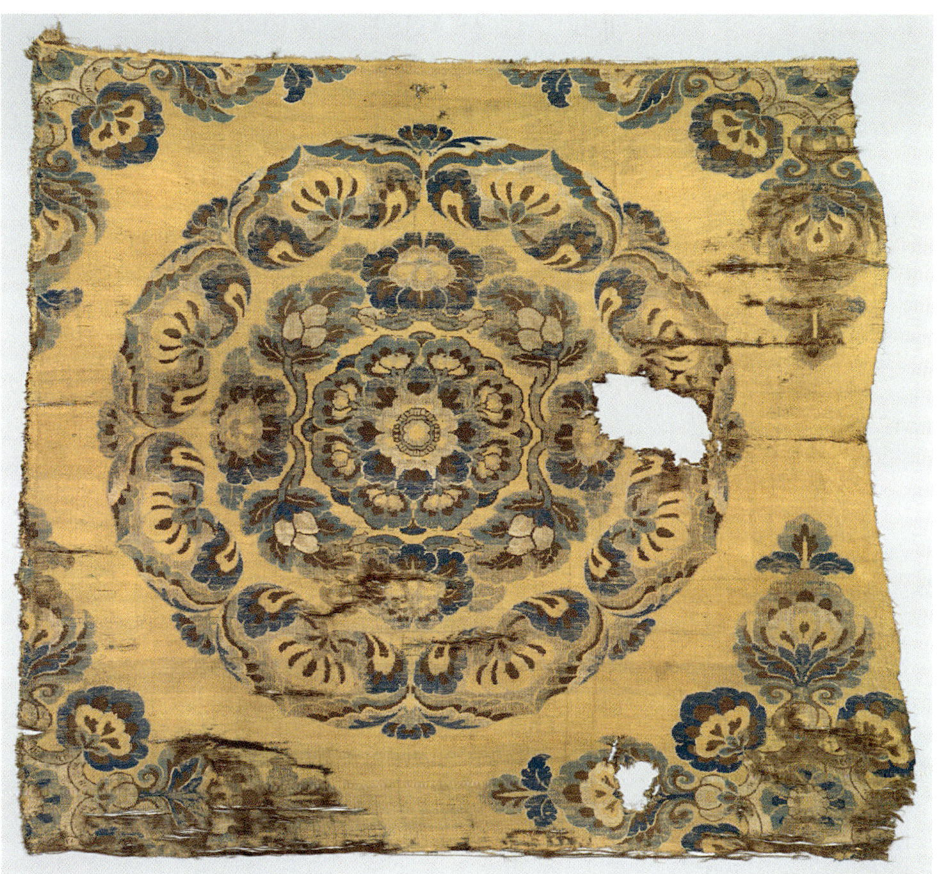

FIGURE 4.13. Treasure-flower medallion (*baoxiang huawen*) with quatrefoils, eighth or ninth century. Weft-faced compound twill; H. 61 cm, W. 71.1 cm. Purchase, Joseph Pulitzer Bequest, 1996. The Metropolitan Museum of Art, New York.

as *Shu jin*. The drawloom employed in Tang dynasty workshops may have been derived from these early models.

The absence of textual sources about looms in the Tang makes it difficult to determine whether the shift to weft-patterning techniques was spurred by mechanical invention; nor can we establish conclusively the reasons for the widespread adoption of weft-faced patterning. What the sources do show is that the expansion of production coincided with the shift from warp-faced to weft-faced weaving, suggesting that weft-faced patterning was a skill that weavers in both imperial and provincial workshops were able to learn quickly. One motivation for the transition to weft-faced patterning may be that it eased the design-making process, since dressing the loom required less time. Changes in design were not inspired by aesthetic concerns alone, but also by labor-saving interests.

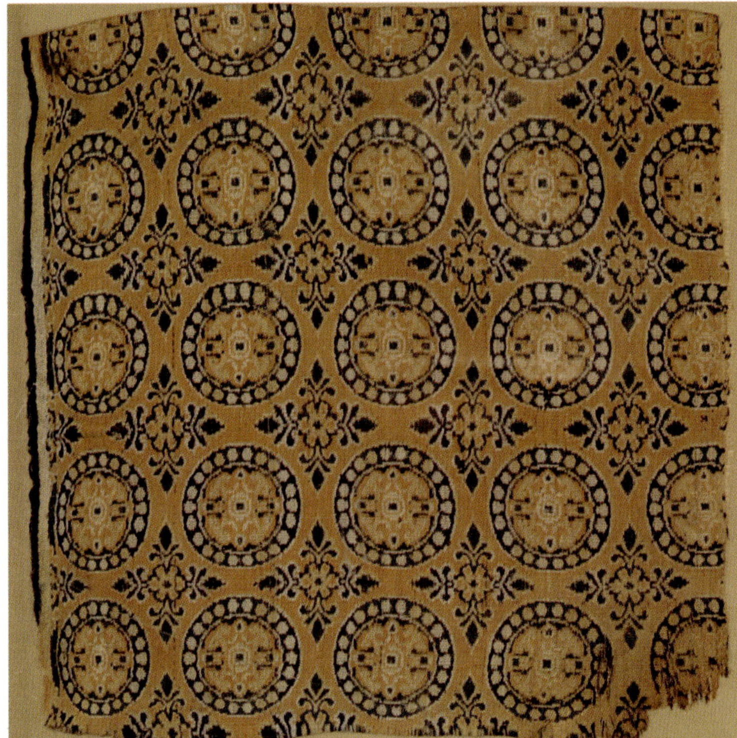

FIGURE 4.14. Pearl roundels and rosettes, dated ca. 653. The pattern unit is small, allowing for six to eight repeats within the width of the loom; the rosettes repeat in the warp and the weft directions. Warp-faced compound twill; H. 19 cm, W. 19 cm. Excavated from Astana Tomb 211. Courtesy of Xinjiang Uyghur Autonomous Museum.

This major change in weaving practice must have occurred alongside the invention of shafts, for the lifting of warp threads to allow for the insertion of the wefts. The abundant references to *ling*-twills suggest the spread of weaving technology from imperial to private workshops.[64] The dissemination of skills was as significant as that of weaving technology.

Court demand and elite taste alone were insufficient to drive innovation in textile design, which depended on the capabilities of the loom and the knowledge of the weaver. Ornament, as in the case of the medallion style, came about through sustained interaction between pattern and technique. Intentionality and functionality were equally important considerations for the designer-maker, who created the repeating, symmetrical patterns of varying scales and complexity in an era of technological innovation. New techniques were employed to create old patterns in new structures, such as the skirt fragment of a *ling*-twill woven with a series of eight colored warp threads to produce alternating stripes now in the Xinjiang Uyghur Autonomous Museum (fig. 4.15).[65] A similarly designed silk has alternating rows of six-petal flowers against a background of stripes in a double-layer compound weave *jin* (*shuangceng jin* or *shuangmian jin*), in which two sets of warp ends were used to interlace with its own weft to produce two layers (fig. 4.16). A square fragment of bicolor *ling*-twill damask showing a standing

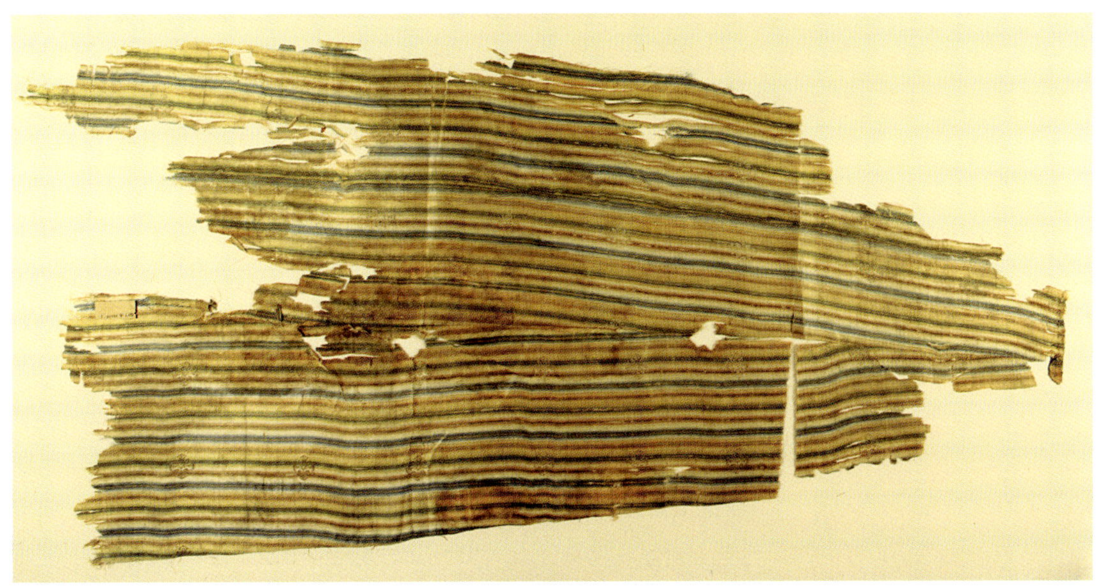

FIGURE 4.15. Stripe-patterned *jin* silk with interspersed persimmon calyx, Tang dynasty. The striped pattern is produced by warp threads lined up in gradations of color. Twill-patterned; L. 95 cm, W. 47 cm. Excavated from Astana Tomb 105. Courtesy of Xinjiang Uyghur Autonomous Museum.

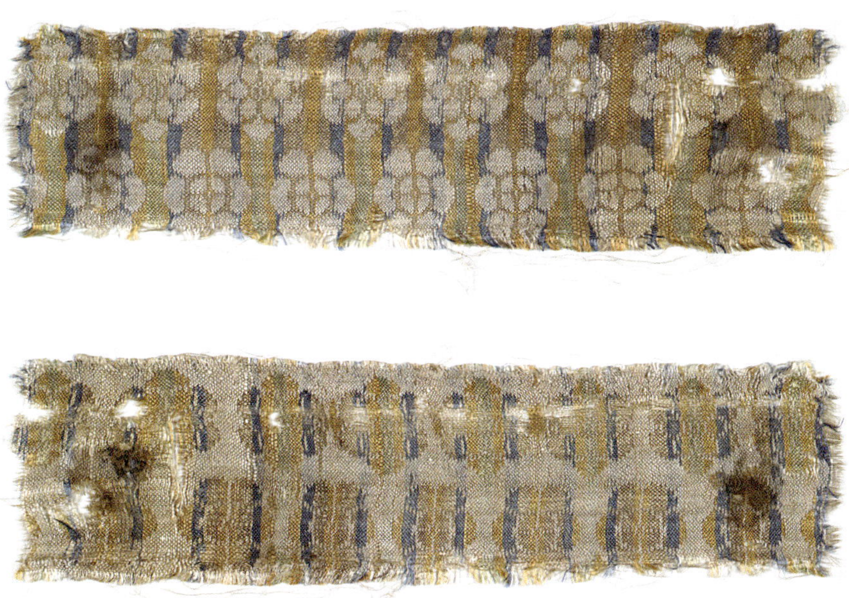

FIGURE 4.16. Stripes and flowers, late seventh or early eighth century. (*Top*) Front; (*Bottom*) verso. Two sets of warp and weft threads were used. Double-weave *jin* (plain weave); L 22.5 cm, W. 5.5 cm. Excavated from Cave 17 of the Mogao Grottoes. © Trustees of the British Museum.

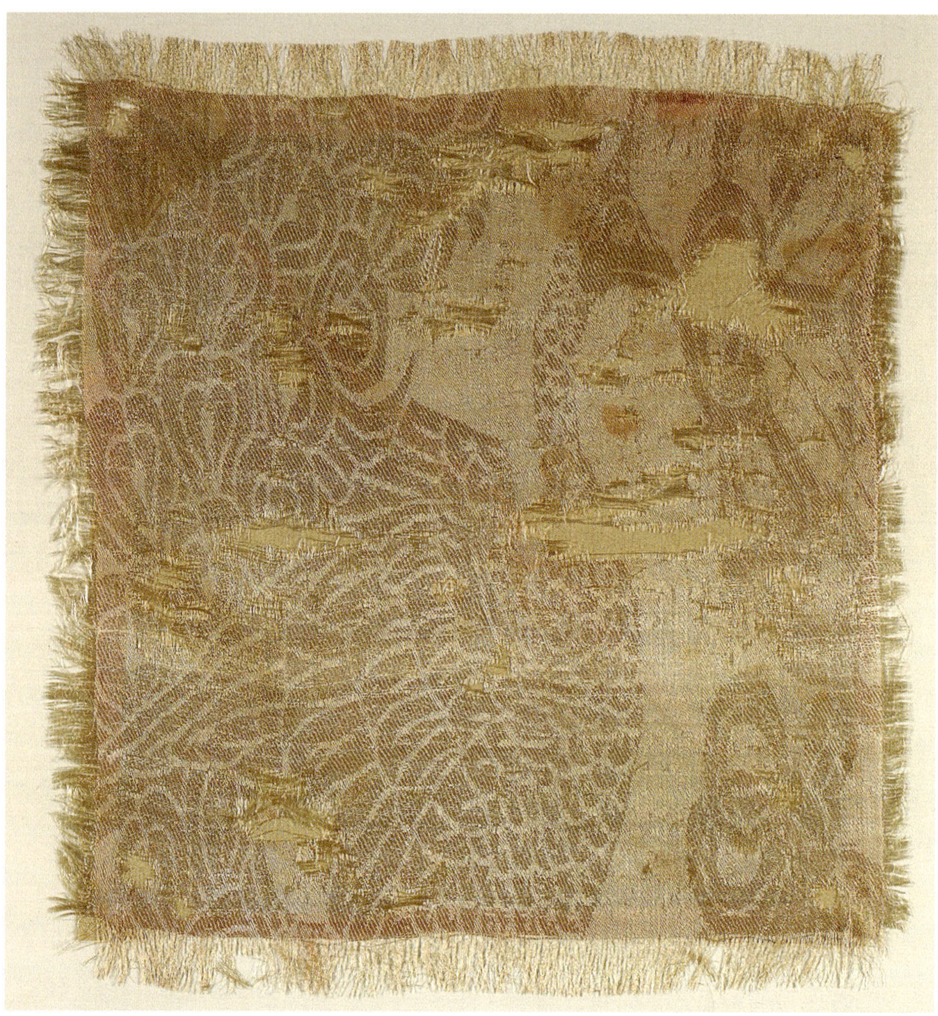

FIGURE 4.17. Standing peacock with ribbon in its beak, late eighth or early ninth century. Bicolor *ling*-twill damask: the ground is a warp-faced twill and the design is a weft-faced twill. L. 27 cm, W. 25.4 cm. Excavated from Cave 17 of the Mogao Grottoes. © Trustees of the British Museum.

peacock holding a knot of a ribbon in its beak may have been part of a larger pattern unit that included a facing peacock within a single medallion (fig. 4.17). Bicolor *ling*-twill damasks were woven with warp and weft threads of different colors to create a gradation of hues in the finished design. Though banned by Xuanzong at the beginning of his reign in 714, the emperor was recorded bestowing upon An Lushan eight pieces of bicolor *ling*-twill coverlets in addition to four red robes made from "auspicious *jin*" (*ruijin*) silks.[66]

In the latter half of the eighth century, a new method for producing rosettes and floral medallions, interlocked roundels, and pearl roundels enclosing confronted animals entered the repertoire of textile artisans (fig. 4.18).[67] Clamp-resist dyeing (*jiaxie*) entailed carving concave wooden blocks, which were then dipped in a dyebath. The textile was likely folded in half lengthways before it was clamped so that convex parts of the blocks resisted the dye, while the concave parts allowed the dye to penetrate the textile.[68] The earliest examples of clamp-resist dyeing date to 751 CE and were excavated from Tomb 38 and Tomb 216 at Astana, Turfan. By the end of the dynasty, this patterning technique had become a widespread decorative technique (fig. 4.19). An inscribed inventory of silks presented to the Famen Temple, dated to 874, listed several clamp-resist dyed items.[69]

Little is known about the development of clamp-resist dyeing. An anecdote recorded in the Song dynasty (960–1279) anthology of stories *A Forest of Sayings from the Tang Dynasty* (Tang yulin), claims that the method of using two symmetrically carved concave blocks to print patterns on textiles was invented by the younger sister of an imperial consort during the reign of Emperor Xuanzong:

> Emperor Xuanzong held Consort Liu of the third rank in high esteem for her talent and learning. Consort Liu had a younger sister in the Zhao clan who was clever and skilled by nature. She ordered a craftsman to carve a pattern into a wooden board and use it to make a press [for dyeing.] On the occasion of Consort Liu's birthday, the younger sister presented a dyed bolt of silk to Empress Wang. The emperor saw it, and regarded it so highly that he ordered all the other palace ladies to follow her model. At the time it was kept secret within the palace, but slowly it became known, then spread throughout the empire. And now it has been cheapened to make clothing.[70]

The archaeological evidence indeed confirms that clamp-resist dyeing did not exist before Xuanzong's reign.[71] The story situates Xuanzong as the champion of clamp-resist silks and his court as the key disseminator of the technique. Like the *jin* robes that he and his beloved Yang Guifei wore to the hot springs, clamp-resist dyed textiles were desired and possessed by elites beyond the court. The final observation, that the once-concealed method was employed to make fabrics for clothing, neatly encapsulates how textile design was key to the aesthetic play of Tang elites. Textiles remained the key material through which elites encountered novelty; when placed on the body, they became an indispensable technique of the self.

The weaving and dyeing methods developed in the inner empire and on the frontier constituted a dynamic phase of technological development in the history of Chinese silk (fig. 4.20). Along with weaving and dyeing techniques, there were also major

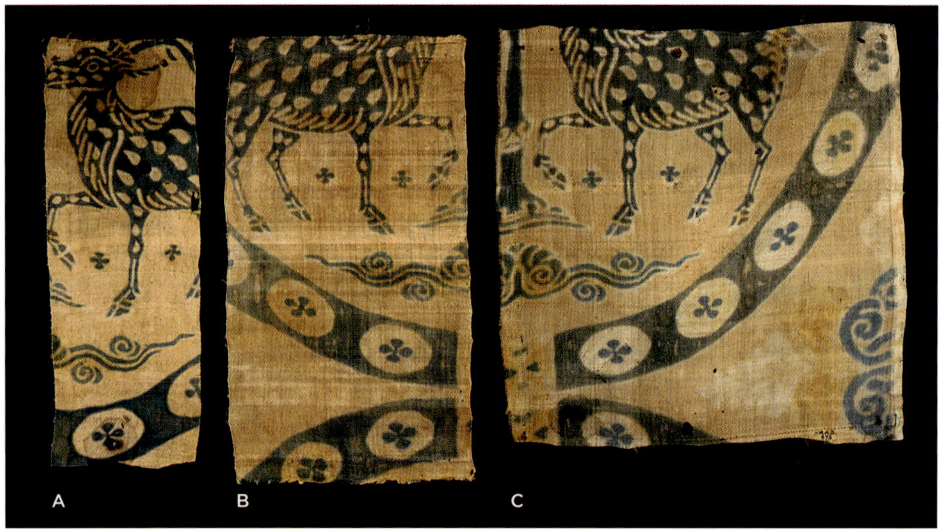

FIGURE 4.18. Roundel enclosing a pair of deer with a flowering tree, ninth century. These pieces were dyed with two colors (reddish orange for the ground, blue for the pattern) and two sets of blocks. Clamp-resist dyed plain weave; from left to right: (A) L. 28.7 cm, W. 10.9 cm; (B) 30.2 cm, W. 16.5 cm; (C) L. 28 cm, W. 28 cm. Excavated from Cave 17 of the Mogao Grottoes. © Trustees of the British Museum.

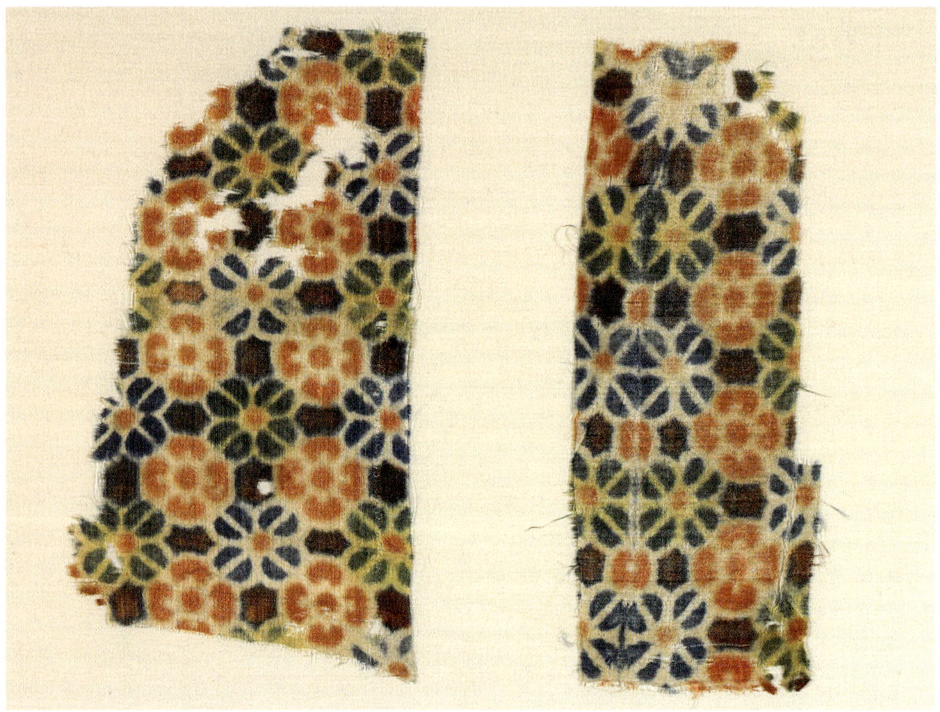

FIGURE 4.19. Interlocking rosettes and leaves, late eighth or early ninth century. The textile was folded before it was dyed, and some areas appear to have been dyed twice. Clamp-resist dyed plain weave; left: L. 16.5 cm, W. 9.2 cm; right: L. 16.5 cm, W. 6 cm. Excavated from Cave 17 of the Mogao Grottoes. © Trustees of the British Museum.

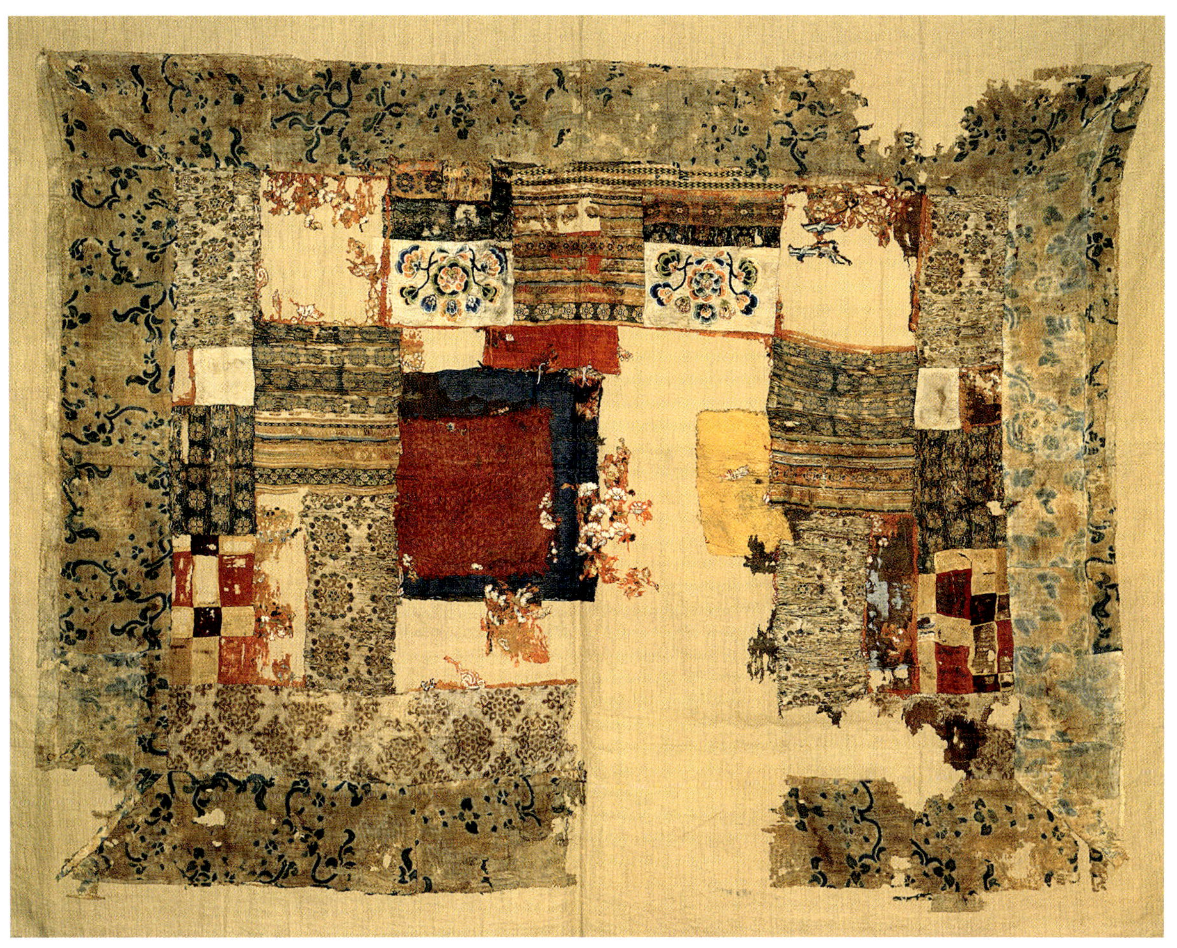

FIGURE 4.20. Patchwork of silk. This piece has been assembled from over twenty pieces of silk textiles, including *ling*-twill damask, *jin* silk, clamp-resist dyed plain weave, plain woven silk, damask on plain weave, and embroideries. The individual fragments date to different periods of the Tang, but the patchwork was likely completed in the late eighth or early ninth century given the presence of clamp-resist dyed pieces. H. 108 cm, W. 147 cm. Excavated from Cave 17 of the Mogao Grottoes. © Trustees of the British Museum.

innovations in printing, painting, and embroidery. Excavated silks from Turfan, Dunhuang, and the underground crypt of the Famen Temple exhibit patterns that were painted with gold and silver appliqués and printed in gold.[72] Such innovations in the design and production process constituted the material and technological basis of fashion in Tang China. Although the designer-makers who created these sumptuous silks were not recognized as innovators in the textual record, like Dou Shilun and He Chou, their contributions abound in the material archive.

CONCLUSION

In Fernand Braudel's grand narrative of structural change, fashion in Europe was launched by the "sudden shortening" of the tunic around 1350.[73] Over the course of the Tang dynasty, the line and shape of garments changed as sleeves expanded to epic proportions and the skirts of gowns ballooned out into long, trailing expanses of fabric. But silk design was the primary catalyst, and the most vivid manifestation, of change. Ornament was an inextricable part of visual, social, and cultural experience. For patrons of fancy textiles, color, pattern, and texture played a fundamental role in how they negotiated their relationship to social status and historical context. Innovations in design, like pictorial style, put historical change in open view. It is possible that the prevalence of billowy gowns in eighth-century pictorial depiction was related to the shift to weft-faced weaving that produced decorated silks of lighter weight, as represented in *Court Ladies Pinning Their Hair with Flowers*, in which two of the voluptuous beauties wear gowns with patterns of repeating medallions.

As captured in Zheng Gu's poem, the increased flow of an expanding range of "new styles" was met with delight by some Tang elites, but it also produced a deep-seated anxiety among others. For the intellectuals writing during the political instability of the late eighth and ninth centuries, the demand for sensuous silks promoted the renewal and obsolescence of things and people alike. In an anecdote collected in *Extensive Records of the Taiping Era*, the son of the prominent Lu clan overhears a man reciting a Bai Juyi poem on weaving:

> I learned to weave *liao* twills, a lot of work for nothing,
> Recklessly I threw the shuttle of the loom back and forth.
> I did not want the government weavers to see,
> For they would surely mock my patterns.
> These days, nobody cares about patterns on silk,
> And boasting of one's weaving skills is meaningless.

Stunned, young Lu initiates a conversation with the man, who tells him:

> My family name is Li. For my entire life, I have been a twill damask and *jin* weaver. Before the rebellion, I was an artisan in the official workshop weaving *jin* for the palace in the eastern capital. After the fall, I came with my modest skills seeking to return to my trade. But they all say, "The patterns of today are different from the ones before." They no longer talk about skill; those who court buyers with intricate colors and patterns are no longer valued in this world, and so I will return east.[74]

Li's lament is a tale of the changing tides and fashions of postrebellion life. Although trained in the production of *jin* silks and twill damasks, his weaving skills are now obsolete. His life's account describes the experience of being passed over by a society in flux that parallels the basic mechanism of fashion, which continually discards outmoded patterns in favor of the new ones. What weaver Li and the narrator had in common was a stirring awareness that one's relevance to both society and history was constituted by objects in the material world. Silk textiles were no longer merely symbolic of change; desire imbued them with the potential to enact change.

The story of weaver Li belonged to a discourse that drew on forms of adornment and the age-old trope of the poor woman weaver to express concerns about social and political change. For intellectuals writing in the ninth century, the conviction that "skill"—literary and otherwise—was no longer desired was a formidable one. As the concerns of these writers turned dress and ornament into a powerful trope for thinking about historical change, fashion took root at the level of language.

CHAPTER 5

Desire

MEN OF STYLE AND THE METRICS OF FASHION

NEW DESIGNS AND FORMS OF ADORNMENT, FOR NINTH-CENTURY OBSERVers like Bai Juyi, bespoke a new, less-stable form of social and political organization in the postrebellion era. At the turn of the ninth century, Bai declared, "With currents of the times, there is neither near nor far."[1] This line, from one of his didactic ballads on the social ills witnessed by his generation, "Adornment of the Times" (Shishizhuang), bemoaned the prevailing forms of self-fashioning that had swept across the empire. These "currents" or "trends" (*liuxing*) refer to the so-called barbarian modes of hair and makeup that had transformed the appearances of Tang women. Bai's use of women's penchant for foreign looks as a cipher for moral decay and the degeneration of "Chinese custom" belonged to a longstanding tradition, in which the literary trope of vestimentary change brought to the fore questions about the mutability of the material world and, in turn, social relations. Through their association with historical time, dress and adornment furnished intellectuals with convincing imagery to explore the experience of material transience and to indulge in their nostalgia for the halcyon days of empire.

Fashion, as alluded to by Bai, trumped "Chinese custom" and introduced a pattern of change, eclipsing the old value system. In the postrebellion era, poets, weavers, and frivolous women alike had to contend to be current, or of the times, in order to stay

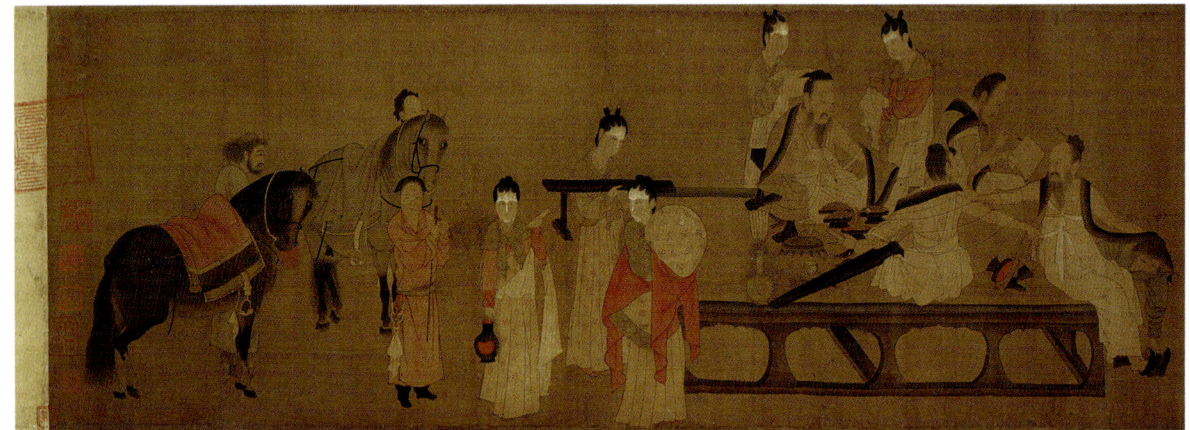

FIGURE 5.1. (*Above*) Traditionally attributed to Yan Liben (ca. 600–673), *Northern Qi Scholars Collating Classic Texts* (detail), Northern Song dynasty, eleventh century. (*Right*) Detail of three attendants. The female attendants are sporting the popular *sanbai* (lit., "three whites") look, where the forehead, nasal ridge, and chin are heavily powdered white. This technique can be found on female figures in paintings spanning the Tang to Ming dynasties, including the famous hanging scroll, *Court Ladies of the Former Shu* (Wang Shu gongji tu) by Tang Yin (1470–1524). The manner in which the women's faces were painted white varied significantly—compare, for example, the angular application of white and red on the women's faces in *A Palace Concert* (fig. 3.32). Handscroll, ink and color on silk; overall: H. 28.5 cm, W. 731.2 cm; image: H. 27.5 cm, W. 114 cm. Denman Waldo Ross Collection. Photograph © 2019 Museum of Fine Arts, Boston.

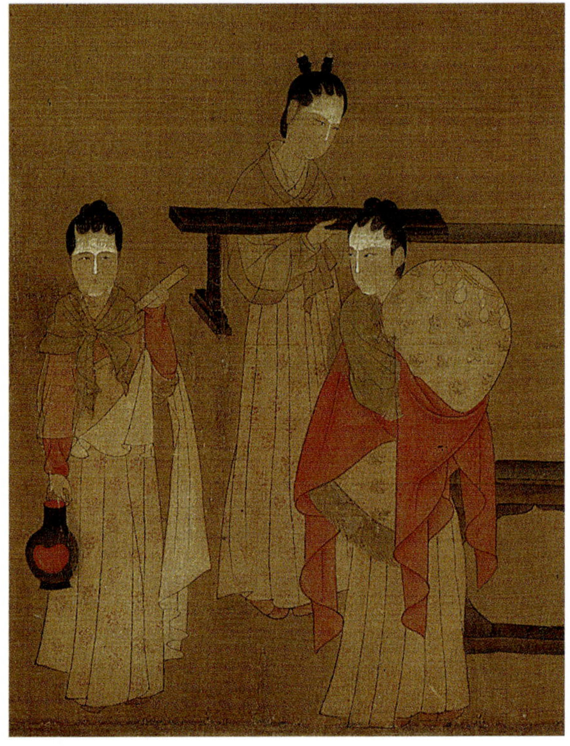

relevant. In Weaver Li's recounting of his plight following the rebellion, he speaks about the displacement of the court by "buyers" (*shanzhe*) as the drivers of new styles. Just as his trade as a weaver was no longer secured by the imperial center, the appointment of postrebellion intellectuals to positions of power ceased to be guaranteed by their education and birthright alone. The critique is taken further in the story of poor Weaver Li: change had usurped skill as a value. More troubling was that the buyers' desire for novelty rendered artisans like Li, whose talents in weaving *jin* silks were no longer wanted, obsolete. For Bai Juyi and his contemporaries, the opposition between men of skill and talent and their less qualified rivals was a real one.

For postrebellion intellectuals, success continued to be linked to an appointment to the central bureaucracy in the capital. Having obtained the "presented scholar" (*jinshi*) degree in 800, Bai Juyi began his official career holding several positions in the central and local bureaucracy of a government still reeling from the An Lushan Rebellion.[2] Over the course of the late eighth and ninth centuries, military commissioners vying for provincial autonomy forced the court to adopt and accept wide regional variations in administration. This institutional change was marked by a decline in the political power of court officials and the rise of sinecure appointments to failing organs of the central bureaucracy. Under the consecutive reigns of Dezong (r. 779–805) and Xianzong (r. 806–820), the government's attempts to consolidate power over a shrinking empire were repeatedly contested by brutal rebellions in the northeast and court factionalism.

A brief renewal of imperial power through a series of military and administrative measures that weakened provincial authority under Emperor Xianzong offered hope to Bai's generation, who sought to both change the world and attain recognition through literary practice. Evoking the spirit of ninth-century intellectual change, Bai Juyi announced, "Once poetry reached the Yuanhe period, the genre turned new."[3] His insistence on the newness of poetry in the early ninth century evinces the inventive exuberance of his generation—intellectuals who made a name for themselves on the fringes of literary conventions and social norms. Efforts to restore the supreme authority of the emperor and his officials, however, ultimately proved to be ephemeral. The hope that Bai Juyi's generation experienced during the early years of Dezong's and Xianzong's respective reigns was quickly shattered by the failures of the imperial court to overcome military governors, powerful eunuchs, and provincial autonomy.[4] Against the backdrop of a demoralized empire, postrebellion Tang intellectuals maintained an acute sense of urgency about the political crisis and their place within it.

Late eighth- and ninth-century Tang intellectuals articulated the desire to be contemporaneous with change as both the action of "keeping up with the times" (*rushi*) and the state of being "of the age" (*shishi*). The abstraction of time as a space to be inhabited or as a condition to be embodied reflected the new value system of the postrebellion world.[5] In so doing, they contributed to the chronology of the Tang empire that remains familiar to modern historians: the An Lushan Rebellion was a watershed event, a rupture that altered the course of history. As evidence of the tectonic shift, they offered up the weaver's lament. Indeed, the most salient feature of the Tang fashion system was the conspicuous space occupied by women, who were repeatedly bound to the sensuous world through their (perceived) labor as weavers and their (constructed) desires as consumers. Bai, along with a select group of his contemporaries, employed the twin tropes of fashion and the toiling woman weaver in their narratives of social and political decline.[6] In their exploration of fashion as a trope that denoted elite desire for material pleasures, these writers found a means to represent the new modes of power at work in postrebellion society. The poetry, through which the newly current language of fashion circulated, embedded that language in a powerful social critique. The richly attired woman and her disheveled, laboring woman weaver came to signify the corrupted moral and social order that privileged style over substance, change over custom. At work in these poems was not an uncomplicated male desire for the female object, but rather a desire for public recognition that was social, political, and shared within the male community (fig. 5.1).[7] This desire was likewise structured by the temporal logics of Tang fashion.

THE POLITICS OF STYLE

Bai Juyi and his colleagues were not so different from the novelty-seeking elites they derided. In their elevation of style as the true measure of a man, evident in their adoption of style-as-political, intellectuals of the postrebellion era pursued individual distinction through inserting themselves into the changing social and political landscape. The plural poetic forms and expanding lexicon through which late eighth- and ninth-century writers drew from to rail against social and political change re-created the same stylistic variability that was the subject of their critique. In embracing style and contemporaneity, these men were also active participants in the Tang fashion system. Instead of decorated silk, cosmetics, and other fineries, paper was their medium for aesthetic play. Bai Juyi emerged as the most prolific and popular chronicler of desires in the late Tang world—in representing the fashionable women of his lifetime, he too gained relevance.

Intellectuals living during the Yuanhe reign of Emperor Xianzong (r. 806–820), an era of great literary production ignited by the promise of political renewal, sought to distinguish themselves through a wide range of literary means.[8] These men—including two of the most vocal, Bai and his lifelong friend Yuan Zhen (779–831)—were hopeful that literary practice (*wen*) could restore order to the empire, but diverged in their approaches. The diverse styles and genres spawned in this era, nonetheless, were shored up by the belief that the literary tradition offered the best guide for reforming the present. Though these writers devised literary acts that were often championed in opposition to each other, they all reinvented the forms and practices of the past (*fugu*) as a wellspring for literary and political renewal. Above all, they held onto the conviction that literary writing (*wenzhang*) harbored the potential to enact change.

The Yuanhe reign era marked a regeneration in literary production, but the men associated with the era—Bai, Yuan, Han Yu (768–824), and Meng Jiao (751–814)—were active beyond its temporal boundaries. Already in the ninth century, the label "Yuanhe style" (*Yuanhe ti*), was in circulation as a description of the works produced in the style of these men. One of the first attempts to identify coherence in the writings of the era was undertaken by Li Zhao, compiler of *Supplement to the History of the Tang*, during the reign of Xianzong's successor, Muzong (r. 820–824):

> Since the Yuanhe era, those engaged in prose writing have learned eccentricity from Han Yu and bitterness from Fan Zongshi; those composing ballads [*gexing*] have learned the flowing style from Zhang Ji; those composing poems have learned the pressing style from Meng Jiao, the readable style from Bai Juyi, and the meticulous style from Yuan Zhen. All of these were called Yuanhe style. Generally speaking, the mode of the Tianbao era favored the straightforward, that of the Dali era the plain, that of the Zhenguan era the vast, and that of the Yuanhe era the strange [*guai*].[9]

Yuanhe style functioned as a temporal marker, rather than a designation of a unified stylistic tendency of this period's literary culture. Li Zhao contrasted works of the Yuanhe era with those of the previous reign periods to emphasize their "strangeness" (*guai*), betraying his deprecatory view of these men. As he saw it, men of the Yuanhe era only sought to be unusual or strange and did so by emulating the most extreme writers of the time.[10] Li's use of Yuanhe style referred to the imitators, not the creators. Through competition over style and content, these writers vied for status and patronage. In this way, literary practice came close to fashion practice—distinction was propelled by a desire for individual differentiation and achieved through imitation. Distinction was, undeniably, a concern of Yuan Zhen, who complained about young upstarts from the provinces writing second-rate verse in imitation of his and Bai Juyi's poetry. These imitators claimed to be working in the "Yuanhe poetic style" (Yuanhe shiti).[11] Postrebellion intellectuals were participants in their own fashion game, in which the desire for fame and prestige was as pressing as their desire to rehabilitate society.[12]

Despite the absence of generic unity, this community of writers shared a deep concern about contemporary political and social issues. Their dedication to literature as a vehicle for social commentary and didactic teaching is perhaps the hallmark feature of ninth-century literary culture.[13] Nostalgia for the glory of the prerebellion political order, coupled with a persistent angst about moral decay, incited this generation to look to the past for solutions. In the end, they arrived at the conclusion that the "ancient" (*gu*) should serve as a model for the present. Nowhere was this commitment to the emulation of ancient, venerable forms and practices more evident than in the "ancient-style prose" (*guwen*) movement led by Han Yu.[14] How to represent the world mattered precisely because literary practice enabled and enacted challenges to existing political structures—an ideal that was grounded in classical texts and of which postrebellion writers availed themselves.

For Bai Juyi and Yuan Zhen, the pursuit of a well-governed society required a revitalization of the age-old tradition of using poetry to communicate social and political concerns to the emperor, represented by *Classic of Poetry* (Shijing) and the Former Han institution the Music Bureau (Yuefu).[15] The construction of a direct, lyrical style in their "New Music Bureau" (Xin Yuefu) ballads was a political act. Composed during the early years of the Yuanhe period, Bai Juyi authored fifty poems under the title of "New Music Bureau," while Yuan Zhen produced a collection of twelve poems. Bai outlined, in a famous letter to Yuan dated to 815, following his demotion and exile, how he discovered literature's and poetry's true purpose while serving as the Reminder of the Left (Zuoshiyi).

> After I passed the imperial examinations, even though I had devoted myself to examination subjects, I did not abandon poetry. By the time I became an Editor, I had written more than three or four hundred poems. When they were shown to you and friends, after looking at them, you all said they were good work; but I, in fact, had not yet discovered the realm of the writer. By the time I was promoted to a post at court, I was older and had experienced more and more things. Whenever I spoke to people, I always asked them about current affairs; whenever I read books and histories, I always sought out the principles underlying good government. It was then that I realized that *literature should be written for its time*; poetry should be created for the sake of real affairs [emphasis mine].[16]

Motivating Bai's intellectual shift was a growing concern with good government and social welfare following his entry into official service: a realization that literary composition must serve the present and that poetry, in particular, must be used to influence "real affairs." His political consciousness now stirred, he was also awakened to the importance of literature as written "for its time." Bai then proceeded to narrate how this new sense of purpose motivated him to compose his collection of "New Music Bureau" ballads:

> A new emperor had recently ascended the throne; there were upright men in the offices of the chief ministry. Time and again His Majesty sent imperial letters inquiring about the urgent needs and sufferings of the people . . . when there were cases where I thought I could relieve people of their suffering, or remedy current policies, but I found it difficult to broach the matter directly, I would write a song about it, hoping that it would be passed on from person to person and finally reach His Majesty's ear. I wanted to broaden the emperor's hearing range and assist His Majesty in his worries and diligence to the people; and secondly, I wanted to repay His Majesty's kindness and encouragement, while fulfilling my duty to speak out. And also, to realize my life's aim. Yet before I could fulfill my aim, things that caused me regret had already occurred, and before my words were heeded, slander against me had already formed![17]

Bai's turn to poetry as his chosen medium through which to make "real affairs" known to the emperor and to realize his "life's aim" reveals how poetic practice was central to his political ambitions and self-cultivation. Through the dissemination of his writings, he aimed, rather than merely hoped, to secure advancement within Xianzong's court. Unfortunately for Bai, he suffered a series of promotions and demotions that frequently displaced him from the capital until he retired from official life in 842.

In his early work, Bai's preoccupation with contemporary themes bespoke a sense of urgency in the present and moral seriousness that largely characterized the Yuanhe era. He identified his "New Music Bureau" collection as part of his "poems of remonstrance" (*fengyu shi*), which he described to Yuan as possessing "stimulating thoughts and plain speech."[18] The poems were arranged chronologically with the first four about events before Xuanzong's reign, followed by five situated during Xuanzong's reign, eleven situated during Dezong's reign, and the remaining twenty-eight situated during Xianzong's reign.[19] The final two poems served as the conclusion. Bai provided each with two titles: the first was a statement of the subject; the second imparted words of admonition. Eleven of the fifty poems concerned women.[20] Other recurrent themes include foreign cultural influence, greedy officials, and the common grievances of the toiling masses. In Bai's general preface to the "New Music Bureau" collection, he declared his responsibility in upholding the moral efficacy of poetic practice:

> Preface: A total of 9,252 words, divided into fifty poems. Each poem is without a fixed number of lines, each line without a fixed number of words, they are connected by content, not by pattern. The first line conveys the topic, the final stanza makes clear the intent—such was the meaning of *Classic of Poetry*. The words are plain and direct, because I wished that those who look at them would be easily instructed. The language is straightforward and to the point, because I wished that those who heard them would be easily warned. The matters are honest and real, so that compilers can transmit the truth. The form is flowing and rhythmic, so that it can be spread through music and lyrics. Finally, this was written for rulers, for ministers, for the people, for things, for affairs, and not done for literary culture.[21]

By invoking *Classic of Poetry* in his preface, Bai Juyi situated himself within a tradition of poetry that prioritized meaning and message over style and form. In describing his method of expression as "plain" and "direct," "straightforward" and "to the point," and "honest" and "real," he wrote in defense of his commitment to composing poetry for the people and not for the practice of *wen* or literary culture.[22] The distinction drawn is one between the frivolous pursuit of artistry and the serious potential of verse to transform the world. Bai believed that the *Classic of Poetry* performed necessary political work, and sought to revive the practice of reporting social and political matters to the ruler through his collection of the people's grievances. By titling their work

"New Music Bureau," Bai and Yuan claimed filiation to the age-old tradition, while emphasizing their update to the genre by focusing attention on contemporary problems or "real affairs."[23]

How to represent real affairs absolutely mattered because demonstration of literary skill would bolster Yuan Zhen's and Bai Juyi's claims on bureaucratic success and imperial recognition. Bai's promotion of a direct narrative and argumentative style targeted at a wide audience represented his youthful conviction that literature must serve society and, more expressly, that he can serve society. As he made clear, the "flowing and rhythmic" form of his ballads were to enable their circulation "through music and lyrics." Bai's insistence on a plain style also conveyed his opposition to literary adornment and rhetoric, which he considered to distract from the didactic purpose of writing.[24] His attack on what he described as "empty beauty" in literary practice mirrored his disdain of fashion—both detracted from real affairs—as he made evident in his critique of fashion in two "New Music Bureau" poems, "The White-Haired Lady of Shangyang Palace" (Shangyang baifa ren) and "Adornment of the Times" (Shishizhuang).

A TIME FOR FASHION

The sumptuously attired court woman and her opposite, the unkempt, laboring woman weaver were longstanding poetic topoi, but their new function as tropes of historical change in the ninth-century was conditional on the poets' experiences of the postrebellion world. In Bai Juyi's "New Music Bureau" poems, the imagery of dress and textiles served as commentary on corrupt officials, profligate elites, and the suffering masses. His scrupulous attention to female adornment in "The White-Haired Lady of Shangyang Palace" and "Adornment of the Times," on the other hand, revealed an enhanced awareness of the relationship between historical change and the material world. The fit of sleeves, painted eyebrows, and hairstyles served as metaphors of specific reign eras that prompted historical reflection. A historical vision surfaced in the recognition that styles of ornament and modes of adornment possessed an origin. Such a historicist understanding of style, which had been central to literary practice, was also taken up by postrebellion artists, who in updating older compositions and themes, provided contemporary viewers access to earlier visual and pictorial modes.[25] Thus, people living in the postrebellion era were given ample opportunities to reflect on historical change, as it inhered in the visual, material, and literary practices of their time. It is in this context of heightened consciousness about history and appearances as fundamentally correlated that Bai authored and circulated his poems.

In "The White-Haired Lady of Shangyang Palace," Bai Juyi used the dated style of the protagonist's dress and makeup to emphasize her aging body and wasted life.[26] Subtitled "Pitying the Spinster" (Minyuan kuang ye), this poem takes as its subject the poor imperial consorts who spent their lives trapped in the palace.[27]

Lady of Shangyang Palace, Lady of Shangyang Palace
Unnoticed, her rouged face grows old, but the white hairs are new.
A green-robed attendant guards the palace gate,
How many springs since Shangyang Palace closed?
Selected for the palace during Xuanzong's final years,
At sixteen entered, sixty now.
More than a hundred chosen at the same time,
They fell away as the years passed, only this body remains.
Remembering long ago swallowing her sorrow when she took leave of her family,
Helped into the carriage, not allowing herself to cry.
They all said, once in the palace she will surely receive favor.
A face pretty like a lotus flower, a bosom smooth like jade.
But before it was allowed that the ruler could see her face,
He had already been seduced by the distant glances of Consort Yang.
Jealously ordered secret banishment to Shangyang Palace,
To spend a lifetime sleeping alone in an empty room.
Living in a barren room, autumn nights are long,
Long sleepless nights, the sky will not brighten.
Fading lamps casting a flickering shadow by the wall,
The splashing sound of dark rain beating against the window.
Spring days pass slowly,
Long days spent sitting alone, dusk slowly approaches.
A hundred chirps of palace orioles, she grows tired of listening.
A pair of swallows nesting in the beams—old, she no longer envies them.
Orioles fly home, the swallows depart, her sorrow continues to linger,
Spring ends, autumn arrives, but she can't recall the years.
From deep inside the palace, she gazes at the bright moon,
Moving from east to west, she has watched its cycle four or five hundred times.
Now she is the oldest in the palace,
From far away the ruler bestows the title of "Matron."
Slippers like pointed peaks, in a tight-fitting gown,
With dark pigment, she dots her brows, so they become slender and long
People outside don't see; if they saw, they would have to laugh,
Adorned in the fashions of the late Tianbao era.
Lady of Shangyang Palace, she has suffered the most.
Suffered in her youth, suffering in old age.
Sorrowful youth, sorrowful old age, do you know what she has endured?
In the past, the emperor did not read Lu Xiang's *fu* on "Beautiful Women,"
Even now, he does not read this ballad on the white-haired Lady of Shangyang Palace.

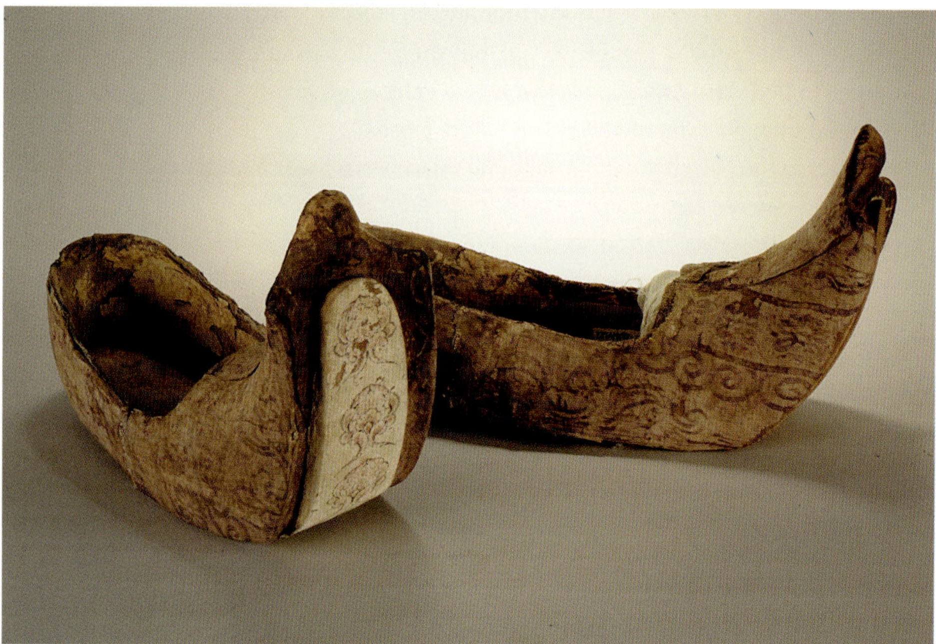

FIGURE 5.2. Slippers with upturned toes. Damask on plain weave (*qi*); L. 30 cm, W. 9.5 cm. Excavated from Astana Tomb 187, dated to the mid-eighth century. Courtesy of Xinjiang Uyghur Autonomous Region Museum.

When she was selected to serve the emperor at the age of sixteen, the Lady of Shangyang Palace had a "face pretty like a lotus flower" and a "bosom smooth like jade." Now, her "rouged face" ages imperceptibly as "new white hairs" continue to sprout. The sharp contrast in the maid's physical appearance is intensified in Bai's lament, "Slippers like pointed peaks, with a tight-fitting gown / With dark pigment, she dots her brows, so they become slender and long / People outside don't see; if they saw, they would have to laugh / Adorned in the fashions of the late Tianbao era." Bai's sartorial description of this hopelessly out-of-date figure relies on dress as a literary device (fig. 5.2).

In 809, during his term as Left Reminder, Bai submitted a memorial to Xianzong petitioning the emperor to send home more women from the inner palace, claiming: "I am concerned that there are more women than necessary for the services of Your Majesty. The court continuously has to provide food and clothing for them and bear the burden of having to supply funds for their sustenance. The women have been separated from their families and clan, suffer from loneliness, and are denied a married life." In the poem, the lady's attire assumes a metonymic role for her aging body, illuminating the power of dress in situating the body in or behind the times. Laughably "adorned in the fashions" (*shishizhuang*) of a bygone era, Bai tells us that the old woman has been sequestered away as a relic of the past. His description of the palace woman as outmoded suggests that his ninth-century audience would have related to the "people outside," who in looking at their own dress would view themselves as current. Historical representation in Bai's poem depended as much on his details of late Tianbao dress as his audience's self-awareness as subjects fashioned by a new era.

In Tang China, the language of fashion had as much to do with space as it did with historical time. Time (*shi*) was attached to world (*shi*), or alternatively generation, to emphasize the temporality and reach of adornment (*zhuang*). In the translation provided here, *shishi* is rendered as a temporal marker to indicate "of the times" or "of the day"; when combined with *zhuang*, the title reads "adornment of the times." Underlying the joining of these three terms was an understanding that fashion was both "current" and "common."[28] Bai Juyi best captured this logic in one of his last "New Music Bureau" poems titled "Adornment of the Times" (Shishizhuang).[29]

Written as a critique of the empire's widespread adoption of *hu* or "barbarian" dress and bodily ornamentation, "adornment of the times" (*shishizhuang*) here exclusively refers to popular beauty practices in the Yuanhe reign.[30] By focusing on hair and makeup, Bai suggests that the desire to be current was tied to the desire to *look* different.

> Adornment of the times, adornment of the times,
> Departing from the capital, it spreads across the empire.
> With currents of the times, there is neither near nor far,
> Cheeks free of rouge, faces powderless.
> Lips painted raven black, making them muddy,
> Eyebrows drawn slanted, drooping like the character *ba* 八.
> Beautiful and ugly, dark and fair, the original is lost,
> Makeup completed, they look as if they are crying tears of sorrow.
> Hair combed into two coiled knots without sidelocks, in the style of
> barbarian topknots.
> They do not apply rouge, instead they use ruddy face powder.
> In the past, I heard of disheveled hair along the Yi River,
> If you are unfortunate enough to see it, know that there are barbarians in
> the land.
> Later rulers, remember the styles and adornment of the Yuanhe period,
> Topknots and faces painted ruddy are not Chinese customs!

Bai opens the poem by stressing the "commonness" of the trend, maintaining that "there is neither near nor far" (*wu yuanjin*) when it comes to this new look. The pervasive desire for "currents of the times" enabled an obliteration of both cultural and geographical space as women across the empire piled their hair into two tall loops (*yuanhuan*) and painted their lips black like the "barbarians," which in the early ninth century likely referred to Tibetan and Uyghur forms of female adornment. One example

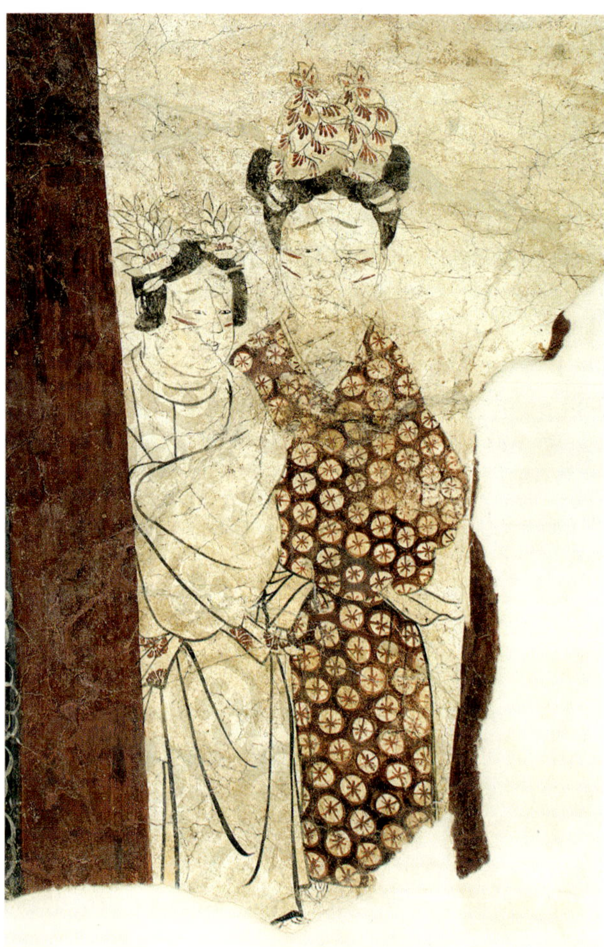

FIGURE 5.3. Two young female attendants with makeup in the style described by Bai Juyi in "Adornment of the Times." Eastern wall, Tomb of Zhao Yigong, 829. Collection of Anyang Municipal Institute of Cultural Relics and Archaeology.

of how this might have looked comes from the tomb of Zhao Yigong (d. 829), excavated in the city of Anyang in northern Henan province (fig. 5.3). The two female attendants are depicted with eyebrows in the shape of the character *ba* 八, with slashes of rouge across their faces.

The discovery of the tomb in Henan, several hundred kilometers away from where Chang'an once stood, lends support to Bai's claim that "there is neither near nor far" when it comes to fashion. The "currents of the times," as he described in the poem, moved across space, collapsing physical ("across the empire") and cultural ("in the style of barbarian") boundaries, and forged temporal coherence ("Yuanhe period"). Anxiety about fashion's power to obscure bodies, cultures, and borders is underscored in the final line of Bai's poem, "Later rulers, remember the styles and adornment of the Yuanhe period / Topknots and faces painted ruddy are not Chinese!" For Bai, the fashionable impulse to look foreign was symptomatic of a weak society and a failing empire.

His emphasis on "Chinese custom" in the final line of the poem contrasts directly with "adornment of the times," highlighting his alarm at the moral and cultural degeneration in postrebellion society that compelled one to value time over customary practice. In situating the practices of these women within a specific reign period, however, Bai makes a point that these "currents" are temporally bounded, having a beginning and an end. The expression, "currents of the times" conjures up images of movement, of ebbs and flows, giving an impression of motion and fluctuation. Bai's exhortation to future rulers to "remember the styles and adornment of the Yuanhe period," gives away his view that with time, or in the next reign era, a new look will sweep across the empire.

Writing against the backdrop of an unstable empire struggling to retain its political and geographical unity in the face of constant domestic and foreign military threats, Bai intended his condemnation of *hu* fashion in the "music bureau" (*yuefu*) form to raise awareness of the greater political implications that such aesthetic plays occluded. Transitory modes of dress and adornment eclipsed more threatening political and social developments like "barbarians in the land." The women's styling choices demonstrate no concern for the threat of barbarians; instead, their engagement with the cultural Other calls attention to dress and adornment as the ultimate forms of play. The spatially unobstructed nature of "current of the times" not only enables barbarian topknots to be adopted simultaneously, but also grants force to fashion itself. The phenomenon of fashion, in this sense, provoked deep-seated anxieties about the relationship between desire, material life, and historical change. Art historian Craig Clunas has made an argument for fashion in the Ming dynasty, proposing that significant institutional and economic transformations over the course of the sixteenth and early seventeenth centuries led to a "less uniform sense of spatiality, in which local specificity coexisted with the regular administrative grid of prefectures and counties, came together with a new, less stable and much more troubling form of temporality . . . through the idea of fashion, the 'mode of the times' [*shiyang*]."[31] This "less stable and much more troubling form of temporality" was already in circulation in the ninth century through the idea of fashion as "adornment of the times." As Bai saw it, temporal coherence imposed through fashion collapsed spatial difference. In other words, it was the uniformity across space that brought to light the instability of time.

The myriad terms used to describe current forms of dress and adornment in the late eighth and ninth centuries conveyed Bai Juyi's deep sensitivity toward temporal change and relayed a new ideology of time (*shi*). Absent in the semantics of "adornment of the times" and "keeping with the times" (*rushi*)—from Zheng Gu's poem on elite taste for polychrome silks—is a notion of time as concrete, linear, or cyclical, seasonal change. Instead, time (*shi*) is abstracted as a state of being current that was repeatedly tied to appearance and bound to the Tang woman. In the poem "A Lesson" (You suojiao), Yuan Zhen addressed the ninth-century Tang woman directly, imploring her to draw short eyebrows and to apply rouge.

Don't paint long brows, paint short ones,
Rouge is better applied upright than languidly.
Everyone knows how to contend for the trend of the times,
But each must look for what suits her own self best.[32]

Yuan employed an alternate pairing of characters for *shishi*, "of the times," to express the state of being "current." The second character *shi* (world or generation) is swapped out for one of its homonyms, which can mean "propensity," "situation," "impulse," or "trend." When combined with time (*shi*), the resulting compound can denote both "state of the times" and "current trend." Whereas Bai's choice of *shi* (world) denotes "common" or "worldly," Yuan's use of *shi* (trend) implies the "power" rooted in being "of the times." In Yuan's lesson about appropriate makeup, he disparages the "trend of the times" as commonplace—what "everyone knows how to contend for." To find what best suits oneself becomes the mark of distinction. Here, Yuan is asserting a tension between the fashionable self and the self a priori. In contrast to Bai, Yuan does not appeal to Chinese custom. His critique shows that the fundamental service performed by fashion is social cohesion. Fashion drives uniformity in appearances at the cost of personal style. His critique further calls to mind the contemporaneous debates over literary style, in which Yuan worked to distinguish himself from his peers and imitators.

The language of fashion that took shape in the poetry of the postrebellion world was undeniably one of critique, in which the desire for novelty was construed as a force for disorder. Adornment was perceived as a reliable marker of body and self that facilitated the reading of people as objects of a fashionable present (the women of Bai's "Adornment of the Times") or as relics of the recent past ("The White-Haired Lady of Shangyang Palace"). Elite women occupied one role in this critique of fashion, exposing not only the pervasive desire to be "current," but also the profligate waste of resources essential to fashion's continued existence. The poor girl and the weaving woman, juxtaposed against the palace woman, became another popular trope of the ninth century that was embedded in social and political discourse. As a counterpart to the vanity of wealthy elites, the labor of the poor weaver came to stand in for those discarded and left behind by fashion. Bai Juyi and like-minded ninth-century poets exploited this tension to signal the consequences of a value system based on desire.

WOMEN'S WORK AND THE FASHION SYSTEM

By foregrounding their heightened awareness of historical change as structured by desire and as manifested through adornment practices, ninth-century intellectuals voiced their angst about their own precarious position in society. The experience of postrebellion life, as observed in material life, made them acutely aware of how a desire for change and novelty could turn anyone into the "white-haired lady," wasting away on the margins of imperial power. The weaving woman, toiling away in the provinces to produce both plain textiles for tax and tribute and fancy silks for elite buyers, came to embody the physical and emotional damages wrought by increasing demands on her labor.

In choosing the trope of the woman weaver, ninth-century poets inserted themselves into a general discourse on women's work and luxury that had been circulating in Tang sumptuary regulations. Beginning with Xuanzong, successive edicts prohibiting the production of elaborate designs on *jin* silks and *ling*-twills cited the dangers posed to proper women's textile work (*nügong*) as the motivation.[33] Daizong's decree of 771 drew on the classical critique formulated in Han dynasty texts, which viewed extravagance as a moral and economic threat to the agrarian ideal. In danger was women's work, narrowly conceived as the weaving of plain cloth for tax and tribute. Poets writing in the ninth century pushed the critique further, viewing the young weaving girl as a victim of both the fashion and tax systems.

In late eighth- and ninth-century poetry, the laboring girl was eulogized through two overlapping but distinct figures as the "poor girl" (*pinnü*) and the "weaving woman" (*zhifu*). The most common figure was that of the "poor girl" (*pinnü*), who was often characterized by her "hairpin of thorn and skirt of plain-weave cloth" (*jingchai buqun*). Qin Taoyu's (fl. late ninth century) famous poem "A Poor Girl" (Pinnü) is the most representative of this trope of the undesired girl of meager means.

> Under a thatched roof, never knowing the fragrance of twill-patterned
> tabby and complex gauze silks,
> She longs for a marriage to be arranged, but she pities herself all the more.
> Who could love her natural beauty and high character,
> When everybody is enamored of girls dolled up in the look of the times.
> Her fingers can embroider beyond compare,
> But she does not paint her two brows longer.
> Year after year she bitterly makes couching with gold thread,
> To make wedding gowns for other girls.[34]

Qin's poor girl has never known the fragrance of twill-patterned plain weave (*qi*) and gauze (*luo*) silks, but year after year she has embroidered sumptuous bridal robes with gold thread for other girls. Li Shanfu (fl. ninth century), a contemporary of Qin's, also opens his poem "A Poor Girl" with a similar line, "She has not known embroidered robes her entire life."

In both poems, the poor girl's unadorned face and simple dress are presented as the essential point of difference between her and her fashionable counterparts.

Never in her life has she known embroidered robes,
As she listlessly grabs her thorny hairpin, she pities herself.
In the mirror, she is greeted by a familiar unadorned face,
But in the world, people put trust in red faces.
In those years, not yet married, she worried that she was getting old,
All day, she beseeched a matchmaker until she talked crazy.
When she is finally engaged, she knows there is nothing to negotiate,
Beads of tears trickle down her face, making the silkworm basket wet.[35]

Unlike the girls of marriageable backgrounds, the poor girls of Qin's and Li's poems are pitiable for not being made up in accordance with the times.[36] In Qin's poem, the girl's skill and talent at embroidery is meaningless without painted eyebrows.[37] The poor girl's suffering is further amplified by the tragic irony of her embroidering wedding robes for other girls. This contrast between the fashionable rich girl and plain poor girl was best captured by Bai Juyi, when he remarked, "The poor girl is abandoned by the times, while the rich one is pursued by it."[38] In this sense, her longing can also be read as a desire to overcome her neglected status to become current and, therefore, valued.

With this trope, Qin and Li found a voice to express their individual frustrations over occupying peripheral positions in the court. For the generation of ninth-century writers who had traveled to the capital to take the examinations in pursuit of political success, attaining a position in the official hierarchy remained the supreme goal. Social advancement depended on the support of influential patrons. Li Shanfu, who had failed the examinations, sought service in the courts of independent warlords in Hebei.[39] His exasperation over his failure is personified in his "poor girl," who is "growing old" and "talking crazy" waiting to find a match. Qin Taoyu succeeded in earning the presented scholar (*jinshi*) degree only through the support of eunuch protectors.[40] The poor girl's lament—her wish for a match—served as metaphor for the hapless scholar, eagerly waiting for social and official recognition.[41] Like the poor girl, these scholars feared being abandoned by the times.

In contrast to "poor girl" poems, those concerning the "weaving woman" (*zhifu*) were often composed in the music bureau form and belonged to the poems of political critique. Frequently depicted as an unwed, older woman, this figure was central to the critique of the imperial court's excesses in its struggle to retain authority in the aftermath of the rebellion. Wang Jian's (ca. 767–830) ballad, "Song of a *Jin* Weaver" (Zhijin qu), presents the bitter life of a weaving woman who exhausts her body to create the coveted *jin* silks for court tribute.

Eldest daughter, born in a *jin* weaving household,
Her name appears on the county's list of artisans who produce tribute.

The head of the workshop has drafted the patterns, sent to the supervisor to be inspected,
I hear the one for the official's family is bitterly difficult:
Turning flowers beside leaves and separated from human figures,
Fear that on this autumn day, the silk threads will be too dry.
The red yarn is rich and delicate, the purple smooth and soft,
As if a butterfly is whirling around flower blossoms.
The sound of the shuttle being thrown, again and again,
Her silk gauze sleeves rolled up, her jade wrists not stopping.
Sitting by the window, late into the night, longing for sleep, her chignon aslant,
Her hairpin falls, hanging off her shoulder.
Long after Orion has disappeared, she falls asleep, fully dressed,
The light is extinguished, only to be lit again before the rooster crows.
One *pi* is worth a thousand in gold, but will not be sold in the market,
The palace will send reprimand if it is not finished in time.
As the waters of the Jin River start to dry up, more tribute is delivered,
Everyone in the palace is still wearing single-thread silk gauze.
Do not say the task of amassing silk will never be finished,
A hundred *chi* building is worth a verse of song.[42]

The weaving woman in Wang's poem belongs to an official *jin* silk workshop in Shu that produces bolts of silk for palace use. In a similar manner as the template of the Tang Beauty, the figure of the weaving woman was subject to stylization: silk netted-gauze sleeves rolled up, hair disheveled, and desperate for sleep, she works all night to weave the elaborate patterns commissioned by the court official. Even before the season demands it as "everyone in the palace is still wearing single-thread silk gauze," the woman must slave away to weave the heavier, *jin* silks. Wang Jian's condemnation of the court is made explicit in the final couplet, "Do not say the task of amassing silk will never be finished / A hundred *chi* building is worth a verse of song."

Like the *jin* weaver of Wang's poem, the women of agrarian households also labored to produce silk for tribute and tax collection. In one of Yuan Zhen's "New Music Bureau" poems, "Song of a Weaving Woman" (Zhifu ci), he attributes blame for the weaving woman's arduous life to the government's military campaigns.

How busy is life of the weaving woman,
Silkworms will soon stop spinning cocoons after their third sleep.
The silkworm goddess produces the silk yarn early,
Early too comes this year's collection of the silk tax.
The early order is not the evildoing of the officials,
Last year's war affairs demand it.

Frontier soldiers, suffering from battle, bandage their sword wounds,
The commanding general, his merits high, needs to change his silk gauze
tent.
She continues her efforts to reel silk threads to weave plain silk,
After the threads are spun, she works hard at the loom, weaving.
In a house to the east, there are two daughters with hair already white,
Since they are adept at making patterns, they will never be married off.
Before the eaves, the gossamer threads floats up,
A spider working deftly, moves back and forth
She envies those creatures who understand heaven's way,
They can weave a gossamer web out of thin air.[43]

Yuan makes explicit the cause of the weaving woman's suffering: "last year's war affairs." Following the rebellion, the imperial court relied on expanding the army of professional soldiers to secure the frontiers and to subdue repeated rebellions. The government dispatched increasing numbers of soldiers to the frontier and the troubled provinces to suppress outbreaks of violence and to prevent powerful regional commanders from leading future rebellions. Payment to the military was facilitated through heavy grain and silk taxation levied on the laboring peasants, like the female weavers of Yuan Zhen's poems.

Striking a parallel between the woman striving to meet the tax quota and the two daughters deprived of marriage because of their skills in weaving complex silks ("adept at making patterns"), Yuan's poem suggests that while the causes of the women's suffering are varied, the plight of all weaving women is one and the same. Consistently presented as a slave to the profligate elites or as a victim of unfair tax policies set forth by an inefficient government, the figure of the poor weaver can be interpreted as a figuration of the intellectuals' unease about a world turned upside down. The denial of marriage recurs in these poems to underscore the inversion of the gendered order of society, in which all women must fulfill their womanly roles as wives and mothers. Lingering beneath the surface of Yuan's critique was the classical discourse on women's work that asserted the primacy of the traditional marriage-based household economy, promoted, for example, in *Classic of Poetry* and *Debate on Salt and Iron*.[44] In "Song of the Weaving Woman," he cites the poor daughters who will never be married off, precluding them from realizing their proper roles in biological and social reproduction, to teach the disastrous effects of war and of poor governance.

Yuan's condemnation of the burden imposed on weavers was most clearly articulated in his poem "Yinshan Circuit" (Yinshan dao), on the court's horse and silk trade with the Uyghurs. In "Yinshan Circuit," the Uyghurs, court officials, and provincial governors are all complicit in the persistence of this costly trade at the expense of the people.

Year after year, horses are purchased at Yinshan Circuit,
Horses die at Yinshan and silk is wasted for nothing.
The Son of Heaven of the Yuanhe era thought about the women weavers,
Paid with gold and silver from the treasury in place of silk.
Your subject has a word to present at the risk of death,
Life or death I am willing to repay your favor.
Squandering money for horses that do not live,
There are other robbers who waste silk and hurt laborers.
Your subject heard that in peaceful times, there were seven hundred thousand horses,
They were left neglected in the central plains and their cries could be heard.
Forty-eight supervisors selected Longmei Stable,
To pay tribute to the imperial court.
Now there is not even one out of ten in the outer field,
They are all in the Flying Dragons Stable brutally stepping on each other.
Ten thousand bales of hay and grass is provided day and night,
A thousand *zhong* of beans and millets constantly transported along the canal.
Armies stationed in over a hundred counties and towns,
Jian silk and *xiang* silk are offered annually, the weavers labor through spring and winter.
Taxable households flee and the quota is imposed on the rest,
When officials convert the taxes into goods, they are greedy and corrupt.
Weaving patterns by interchanging threads, efforts are doubled,
Abandoning the old and adopting the new is what people like.
To weave one bolt of Yue silk crepe and *liaoling*-twill,
Even the work of making ten *pi* of plain *jian* silk is not enough.
Grand families and rich merchants transgress the standard regulations,
Honorable clans and their kind lack elegant character.
Favored servants accompanying outings are seen in silk robes,
Soldiers with falcons on their arms carry sheaths of cloud-patterned *jin*.
A multitude of officials seek personal profit and willfully commit transgressions,
The Son of Heaven's deep concern becomes empty compassion.
Standing upright on the flowering bricks, the phoenix moves,
When can I repay your favor that resembles rain and dew?[45]

Yuan opens with a forceful statement about the deaths of imported horses each year, the result of the strenuous migration, to demonstrate that the silk was traded in vain. With the loss of Hebei province, the empire surrendered control over its main tax silk-producing region and horse-pastures to autonomous military commands. This defeat, along with the court's debt to the Uyghurs for their assistance in suppressing the rebellion, pushed the court into a trade imbalance.[46] The Uyghur empire negotiated a large-scale trade agreement, offering horses for forty bolts of silk per sale. When Emperor Daizong settled on the purchase of six thousand horses, the total payment amounted to 240,000 bolts. With the price set at pieces of silk, the government's spending on the horse trade was also subject to problems of inflation. Officials at the court contested the demand for these horses, arguing that the expense was unnecessary and the burden to meet payments too heavy.[47] In 807, Emperor Xianzong issued an edict ordering the imperial treasury to pay for the horses with gold and silver, which Yuan mentions in the second couplet. He proceeds to show, however, that the officials did not abide by the emperor's orders.

In couplet four, the narrative shifts direction as Yuan goes on to identify the other thieves who waste silk and hurt laborers: officials, grand families, affluent merchants, and the military. His account of the horse-silk trade says very little about the squandering of government funds to acquire horses. Instead, Yuan's criticism is a lament about postrebellion society expressed through the labor of weavers, which he describes in detail. The hundreds of armies (*tunjun*) stationed in the counties and towns demand *jian* (densely woven) and *xiang* (lightly yellow-colored) silks, exhausting the weavers throughout the year. The people, having developed a desire to discard the old to make way for the new, order the weavers to increase their efforts to come up with more and more intricate patterns. To weave a single piece (*duan*) of silk crêpe (*hu*) and *liao*-twill damask from the region of Yue would require more labor than what is necessary to produce ten bolts of plain *jian* silk. Attendants accompanying wealthy elites on outings and beloved servants are dressed in silk robes. Even soldiers carry sheaths made from *jin* silk. Grand families and rich merchants alike openly transgress sumptuary regulations to participate in the spectacle of lavish spending. By associating the desire for and possession of patterned silks with a broad range of social groups, and not just the court-sanctioned elites, Yuan is responding to how desire for novel goods confused the social hierarchy as "honorable clans and their kind lack elegant character." At the heart of his attack is the idea that such desire forged a new kind of social coherence, in which novelty functioned as a shared value and silk remained the preferred expression of status.

Yuan's ballad "Yinshan Circuit" offers additional commentary on the reckless waste of resources by the court, officials, and elites. The court's abuse of the people's labor to produce silks for trade is matched and exceeded by the exploitation of weavers to satiate the sumptuous desires of these "robbers who waste silk and hurt laborers." The aspiration to "keep up with the times" was realized, as pointed out by Zheng Gu, through the consumption of extravagantly patterned silks. And waste was an inevitable consequence of the pursuit of novelty. The target of Yuan's critique was the fashion system.

Like his friend, Bai Juyi was staunchly critical of the waste generated by the court's taste for new and alluring silks. Composed about the same *liao*-twill damask that appears in couplet twelve of Yuan's "Yinshan Circuit," Bai wrote "*Liao* Twill" (Liaoling) to "commemorate the labor of the weaving woman" (*nian nügong zhilao ye*). He begins the poem by asking, "*Liao*-twill, *liao*-twill, what are you like?" to focus attention on the elusive quality of this weave. He follows with a comparison of *liao*-twill damask to other types of luxury silk to establish the unique features of this coveted material produced in the silk workshops of Yuezhou. Owing to the limited textual and material documentation of this particular twill weave, scholars of Tang dynasty textiles have relied on Bai's description, which suggests that *liao*-twill damask might have featured elaborate motifs first woven and then dyed.[48]

> *Liao*-twill, *liao*-twill, what are you like?
> Not like simple gauzes or plain twills.
> It is like, on the top of Mount Tiantai, before the moonlight,
> The forty-five-*chi* waterfall.
> The patterns formed are marvelous,
> On a ground of white haze, flowers like clusters of snow.
> Who is the weaver? Who wears the robe?
> A poor woman from the valley of Yue, and a lady in the palace in
>   Chang'an.
> Last year, messengers delivered the imperial decree,
> Heaven's designs to be woven by human hands.
> Woven patterns of autumn geese soaring above the clouds,
> And dyed with the color of spring streams south of the Yangzi.
> Made wide for cutting the robe's sleeves and long for the skirt,
> Irons to smooth the creases, sharp scissors to trim the seams.
> Rare colors, strange designs that fade and shine,
> The patterns constantly changing when viewed from different angles.
> For the dancing girls of Zhaoyang, an expression of imperial favor,
> A set of spring robes, worth a thousand pieces of gold.
> To be soaked by sweat and stained by makeup, never to be worn again,
> Dragged on the earth, trampled in mud, without care.
> Weaving *liao* silk requires skill and toil,
> Not to be compared with the common *zeng* and *bo*.
> Fine threads endlessly twisted, until the weaver's hands ache,
> The loom sounds a thousand times, not even a foot is finished.
> Singers and dancers of Zhaoyang Palace,
> If you could see her weaving, then you too would pity her![49]

In the fourth couplet, Bai asks, "Who is the weaver? Who is the wearer?" To which, he answers, "a poor woman from the valley of Yue, and a lady in the palace in Chang'an." Commissioned by the emperor ("messengers delivered the imperial decree"), these robes cut from *liao*-twill require "skill and toil" (*gongji*) and are worth "a thousand pieces of gold." Bai dedicates as much space to describing the exquisite patterns as he does to detailing the labor invested in the making of the silks—"made wide for cutting the robe's sleeves," "irons to smooth the creases," and "fine threads endlessly twisted." But the weavers labor in vain, as the robes are "soaked by sweat and stained by makeup, never to be worn again" by the dancing girls of the court. Bai concludes the poem with a direct plea to the entertainers of the palace, exclaiming, "If you could see her weaving, then you too would pity her!"

CONCLUSION

While the An Lushan Rebellion provided ninth-century intellectuals with an event around which to organize historical change and to frame their literary response, the unabated desire for novel silks and barbarian hairstyles offered them a comprehensible trope for representing imperial decline and social disorder. Postrebellion scholars idealized the reign of Taizong and the early years of Xuanzong's court as the golden age of the dynasty, when the emperor with the guidance of his ministers secured the empire's boundaries and the needs of the people. For the great majority of intellectuals living in the late eighth and ninth centuries, the late Tianbao era marked the decline of good governance, as alluded to in Bai's poem "The White-Haired Lady of Shangyang Palace." Xuanzong, led astray by his desire for Yang Guifei, set into motion a series of catastrophic events that culminated in the fragmented, highly competitive political landscape of the ninth century. Change across the social, political, and material realms were connected to this timeline of the rebellion and its aftermath, and continued to dominate how future generations periodized the Tang dynasty.

Fashion was no exception. Its unstoppable dominance in the ninth century also mirrored the chronology of the empire's decline. Implicit in this chronology was a critique that perceived desire as a yearning for pleasure that was so powerful it toppled the glorious Tang empire. This troping of desire and novelty may account for why Yang Guifei's biographers insisted that her plump figure was the reason for her appeal. The association of Yang Guifei with the shift to more voluptuous female beauty was a product of the postrebellion discourse that repeatedly linked rupture and change to the femme fatale. The plump body of the Tang Beauty was a synecdoche for the Tang empire: an empire plump with desire. Fashion and its seemingly arbitrary pursuit of novel pleasure was a distressing manifestation of all that was wrong with the world.

Bai Juyi, Yuan Zhen, Wang Jian, and others all sang the laments of the poor weaver, who occupied a conspicuous role in their representation of society's turn to fashion in the postrebellion era. For this generation of ninth-century writers, anxiety about waste was entwined with impressions of fashion as a source of excess and obsolescence. What troubled them above all was how the desire for novelty accelerated the rate and scale of change in the material world, and with grave social consequences. As the political condition worsened alongside rampant moral corruption, women weavers suffered even greater demands on their labor. The trope of women's work circulated as part of the critique of a growing economy of waste that had obscured the value of resources and labor and, in turn, the traditional values of society, government, and hierarchy. Fashion was not a shadow play that concealed real change, but became a force of change itself. The criticism of fashion as wasteful and superficial only served as evidence of the continued relevance of fashion in the postrebellion Tang world, even as its designs, patterns, and meanings changed to conform to the new realities of the times.

Epilogue

Over a century after the devastation of the An Lushan rebellion, another insurgent leader, Huang Chao (d. 884), took advantage of the weakened empire. By the end of 881, he had marched his troops across the Yangzi River, captured Luoyang, and occupied Chang'an. The reigning Tang emperor fled to Shu, like Xuanzong before him, while Chang'an's inhabitants suffered through two years of plunder and desolation. The event was enshrined in verse by the ninth-century poet Wei Zhuang (836–910), who narrated the sack of Chang'an through the lament of a woman in the music bureau (*yuefu*) style. Wei opens "Lament of Lady Qin" (Qinfu yin) with his chance meeting with the eponymous lady on the side of the road:

> Her hairpins, shaped like phoenixes, were thrust in crooked,
>   her sidelocks twisted awry;
> Rouge was blotched, mascara streaked
>   and her eyebrows wrinkled in pain.

Like the women of Bai Juyi's and Yuan Zhen's "New Music Bureau" collections, Lady Qin's disheveled visage served as evidence of the fallen empire. Throughout the poem, female dress and adornment dramatize the destruction of the capital and the dynasty. When the lady describes the violence of the rebels through the plight of her four female neighbors, she introduces each of them as beautifully made-up, in contrast with their miserable and messy fates:

> My neighbor to the west had a daughter lovely as a goddess . . .
> Some thugs leapt up her golden staircase,

Ripped her dress to bare her shoulder,
    about to shame her.
But, dragged by her clothes,
    she refused to go through the vermilion gate.
So with rouge powder and perfumed cream on her face,
She was stabbed to death.

All of the women in the poem, with their painted eyebrows smudged, their virtue threatened, and dragged away by their silk robes, symbolize the doom met by their fathers and husbands. Lady Qin herself fell into the rebels' hands:

Though I lay behind mandarin-duck curtains,
    how could I know pleasure?
Though I had many jewels, much finery,
    they were not what I longed for.
Their hair disheveled, faces filthy,
    even their eyebrows daubed with red:
Often I turned my eyes toward them
    and as often I couldn't stand the sight;
Their clothes untidy, slovenly,
    their speech barbaric . . .
They even try to stick ornate pins into their shaven hair![1]

Just as the women's fine robes and dressed-up hair stand for the civilized Tang empire, the rebels' filthy, unkempt bodies are testament to their barbarism. Their barbaric bodies made them fundamentally unfit to rule, even as they "try to stick ornate pins into their shaven hair." Such savagery had displaced all hope for pleasure, as the lady, sitting behind silk curtains and surrounded by jewels, was made to endure the rebels' attempts at playing emperor and officials. Although the Tang emperor and his imperial defenses managed to recapture the throne in 884, the dynasty lived on only in name. Following the dethronement of the final Tang emperor in 907, what remained of the empire split apart into competing polities. Neither the Tang cosmopolitan model of empire nor Chang'an survived the collapse, but the "Lament of Lady Qin" would survive as one of the most popular poems of the dynasty, bringing its author a measure of fame that carried his name, and the image of fallen and bedraggled Tang women, across time.

What the "Lament of Lady Qin" illustrates is that appearances were an essential part of the Tang historical narrative. In Tang China, fashion was repeatedly bound to women's bodies by the poets and writers who invoked topknots and sidelocks to represent social disorder, and by the artists who created sumptuously attired women as objects of pleasure. Literary scholar Paul Rouzer has noted that "women became more interesting in the Tang" because "they begin to be represented in texts to a much greater extent, and the roles they play in those texts become more complex." This shift had to do with the simple fact that "literati themselves seem to find them more interesting."[2] This interpretation, however, hinges on the view that women and their forms of aesthetic play did not matter on their own terms. Since men dominated both the written and painted form, the visibility of Tang women—and their appeal as women—depended on the male authorial voice. The corollary of such a position, one that is certainly not specific to Tang history or Chinese society, is that historical women had few models for self-representation other than the one ascribed to them: fashion. This gendering of fashion as female has, in turn, yielded longstanding consequences for the study of it as a historical phenomenon, so that "the marginality of fashion as an issue or a research domain cannot be divorced from the marginality of the woman who is regarded as its prime target and object."[3]

Dress and adornment have been important in the lives of women, but matters of appearance and its change over time were important to men and women alike. Dress and adornment, then as now, mediated one's relationship to social and material environs. By bringing interpretative strategies to bear on the dressed figure, described in text or depicted in paint, viewers produced a complex range of readings that connected them to the material world and their historical context. That is, fashion was a practice of meaning-making that became a key form of metaphorical thinking about social structures, desire, gender, and the progress of time.

APPENDIX

Textile Basics

A BASIC TEXTILE (*ZHIPIN*) IS WOVEN ON A LOOM (*ZHIJI*) OF WARP (*JING*) threads running parallel to the length of the loom and weft (*wei*) threads that are drawn perpendicular to the warp and across the width of the loom. Warp "ends" (the individual threads) pass through loops of cords called heddles, which facilitate the passage of the weft through them. The weft threads are interlaced through the warp at a right angle to form a weave structure, also called a binding unit. When weaving a basic textile, first one half of the warp ends and then the other half are alternately raised by a shed stick and a heddle-rod, creating a wedge-shaped opening called a "shed" that allows the passage of a shuttle, bearing a weft thread, between the separated groups of warp ends. The heddle-rod is a stick with attached heddles, and the grouping of heddles together forms a shaft, used to raise and lower warp ends simultaneously. Each shuttle transports a weft thread, called a "pick," from one side to the other. By adding more heddle-rods, which act as pattern rods, the weaver can produce more complex weaves.

BINDING UNITS

There are three fundamental binding systems from which other weaves are derived: plain weave (*pingwen*) or tabby, twill (*xiewen*), and satin (*duanwen*) (fig. A.1). A plain weave or tabby is based on a unit of two ends and two picks, creating a simple crisscross pattern. The weaver interlaces the warp thread over one weft thread and then under one. With the next warp thread, the weaver alternates the pattern by going under and then over. A silk plain weave in the Tang dynasty was commonly referred to as *juan*; tabbies woven of plant fibers were called *bu*, while those woven of animal fibers were called *he* (fig. A.2). One of the most documented tax silks of the Tang dynasty, *shi*, a weft-ribbed silk, was a plain weave created with weft threads of varying thickness to produce a ribbed or striped effect on the surface (fig. A.3).

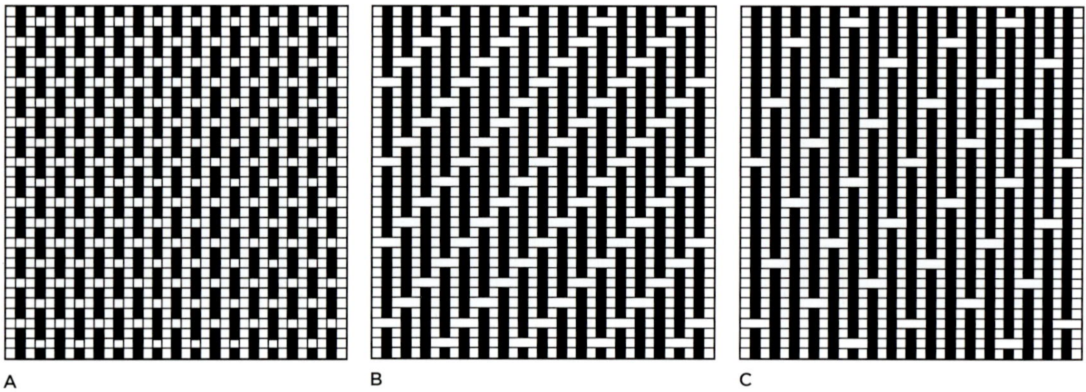

FIGURE A.1. Binding systems: (A) plain weave, (B) twill, and (C) satin. Drawn by Jennifer Shontz.

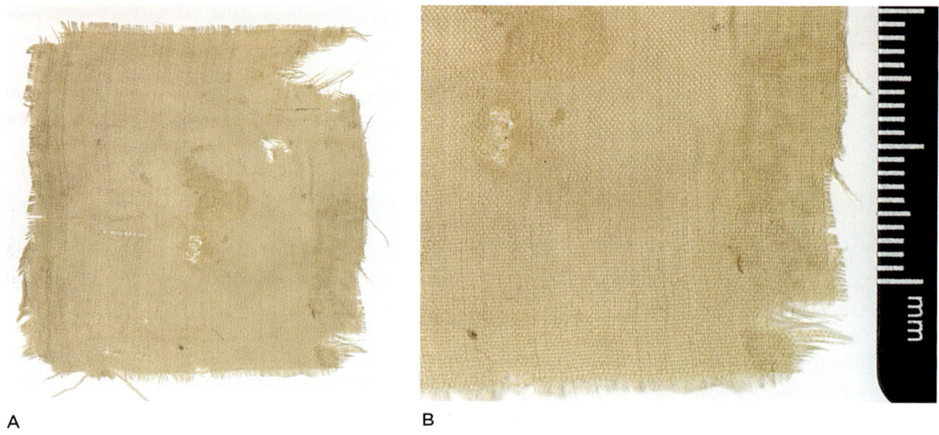

FIGURE A.2. (A) Square undyed plain weave fragment; (B) detail. Dated eighth to ninth century. Warp: silk, untwisted, single, undyed; weft: silk, untwisted, single, undyed. Weave structure: 1/1 plain weave. L. 5.2 cm, W. 5.2 cm. Found in Endere, Xinjiang. © Trustees of the British Museum.

A twill weave is a unit composed of three or more warp ends and three or more weft picks, in which each end passes over two or more adjacent picks and under the next one or more. By passing warp threads over two or more weft threads and then under one or more wefts, the weaver produces a chevron pattern. Satin, the third principal binding system, is based on a unit of five or more ends and five or more picks. The weaver either passes each warp end over four or more contiguous weft picks and under the next one, or passes the end under four or more picks and over the next one. The defining feature of a satin weave is its smooth lustrous appearance, an effect that results from floating

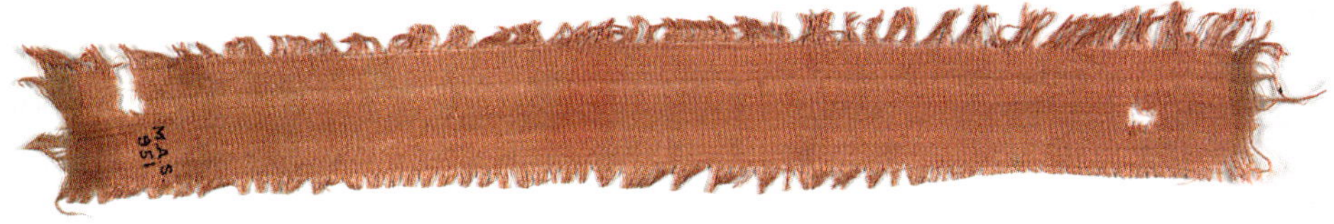

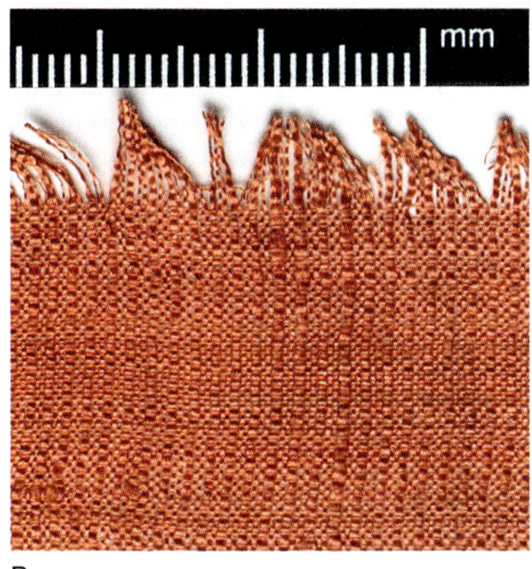

FIGURE A.3. (A) Fragment of red ribbed silk; (B) detail. Dated ninth to tenth century. Warp: silk, untwisted, single, red; weft: silk, untwisted, single, red. Weave structure: 1/1 ribbed plain weave. L. 26.3 cm, W. 3.4 cm. Excavated from Cave 17 of the Mogao Grottoes. © Trustees of the British Museum.

warp threads in long stretches over the weft. The earliest extant satin textiles unearthed in China date to the Song dynasty (960–1279), but references to satin appear in Tang dynasty textual sources, leading textile historian Zhao Feng to conclude that it might have been a Tang innovation.[1]

EARLY LOOMS

In early China, plain weaves were woven on a back-strap loom, in which the warp ends were attached to the strap at one end and to a fixed stick on the other end. When the strap was placed behind the weaver's back, she could use her body weight to keep the stretched warp threads taut for weaving.[2] During the Spring and Autumn period (771–476 BCE) a double-beam loom was introduced, displacing the back-strap loom. The double-beam loom, assumed to have originated in the state of Lu, improved on the back-strap loom by the addition of a supporting frame, a reed (a comb-like frame that separates the threads), and a warp beam.[3] An oblique loom with two treadles to allow mechanical control of shedding surfaced during the Warring States period (475–221 BCE). On the oblique loom, the warp is tilted at an angle causing the threads to be uniformly stretched between the warp beam and the cloth beam, thereby enhancing the smoothness of the woven cloth.[4] Twill damask or *ling* probably did not appear until the sixth century, when a second shaft was added to the two-treadle loom.

COMPOUND WEAVES

The three principal weaves can be developed into compound weaves with two or more series of warps and wefts: they can be self-patterned by using one set of warps and wefts to form the ground and pattern, or they can be brocaded, creating a pattern by weaving with a supplementary weft into the ground weave. Damasks are self-patterned monochrome textiles that can be categorized as twill damask (*ling*) or damask on plain weave (*qi*). Weavers made *qi* with lozenge or diamond designs by combining a plain ground weave with a twill pattern and manipulating the warp threads to form the pattern (fig. A.4). A weaver making warp-faced patterns (using the warp to produce the pattern) would need pattern heddle-rods added to the treadle loom to lift groups of warp ends and two assistants to clear the sheds. During the Tang, the production of twill damasks increased exponentially. Monochrome twill damasks, woven with warps and wefts dyed the same color, were the most common (fig. A.5). Archaeological sources suggest that real twill damask, in which a twill binding unit is used for the ground and pattern, did not appear until the Tang dynasty.

Weaving polychrome silks or *jin* required a more sophisticated loom that enabled the mechanical repetition of patterns. In addition to pattern-heddle rods, a device used to ease the separation of warp series would have been necessary.[5] *Jin* silks woven in early China featured warp-faced geometric patterns on a plain ground, formed by interlacing two series of warps of different colors with one set of wefts on a treadle loom with two shafts.[6] Excavated textiles bearing patterns of animals and auspicious symbols from the

A

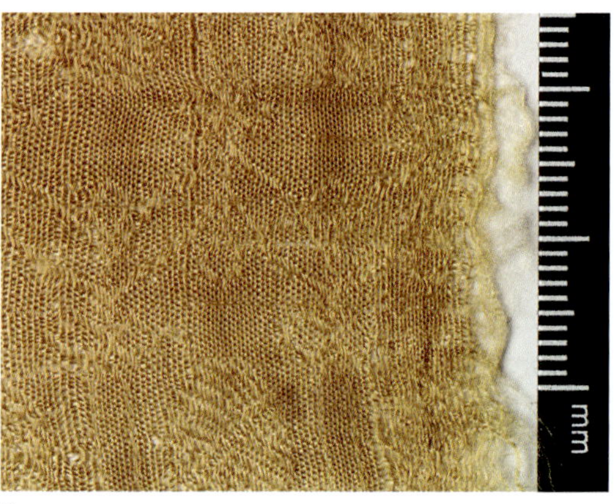

B

FIGURE A.4. (A) A yellow rectangular fragment of damask on tabby with a hexagon grid, enclosing a four-petal rosette in each cell; (B) detail. Dated ninth to tenth century. Warp: silk, untwisted, single, yellow; weft: silk, untwisted, single, yellow. Weave structure: 2-4 patterning weave for pattern on 1/1 plain weave for foundation. L: 16.5 cm, W. 15.5 cm. Excavated from Cave 17 of the Mogao Grottoes. © Trustees of the British Museum.

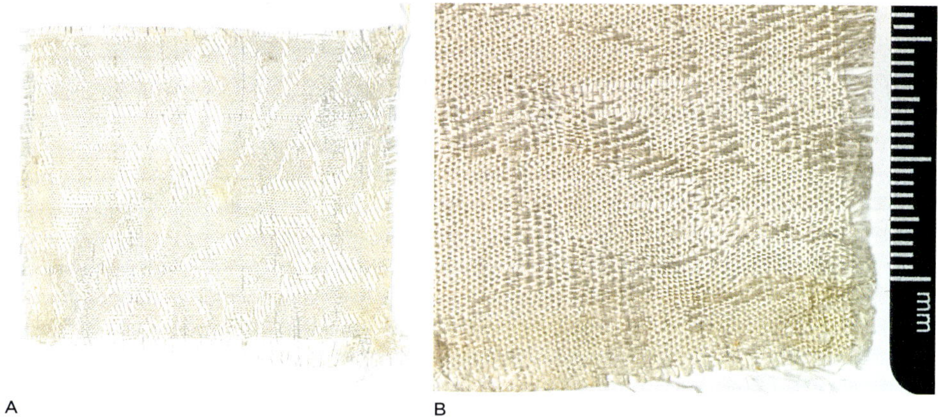

FIGURE A.5. (A) Rectangular fragment of monochrome patterned woven twill damask; (B) detail. Dated ninth to tenth century. Warp: silk, untwisted, single, white; weft: silk, untwisted, single, white. Weave structure: 2/1S twill for pattern on 1/5S twill for foundation. L. 6.8 cm, W. 7.6 cm. Excavated from Cave 17 of the Mogao Grottoes. © Trustees of the British Museum.

Han dynasty have hinted that a significant development in the production of *jin* silks took place by the second or third century CE. The 2013 discovery of the four wooden models of looms in Laoguangshan, Chengdu, in a tomb dated to the late second century BCE, have confirmed the early invention of a pattern loom with multiple shafts and heddles (fig. A.6). This early pattern loom—the earliest evidence of the pattern loom in the world—is related to development of *jin* silks (fig. A.7).

Unlike the tabby, twill, and satin binding systems, gauze is woven by looping or crossing warp and weft threads resulting in a loosely structured, lightweight weave with a pattern of square meshes (fig. A.8). In weaving plain gauze (*sha*), warp ends, called doup ends, cross to the right and left of stationary warp ends, called fixed ends (fig. A.9). Complex gauze (*luo*) is a cross-woven textile with square meshes resembling *sha* gauze, but required the skill and labor of more specialized artisans.[7] Whereas *sha* is formed by one fixed end and one doup end that fully cross, *luo* is woven with the doup ends alternating in position on successive rows. *Luo* can be patterned or nonpatterned, and patterned gauzes usually feature a lozenge or diamond repeat (fig. A.10). Patterned gauzes were created by combining gauze weaves with a plain weave or by floating warp ends.

THE PROBLEM OF TERMINOLOGY

The translation of textile terms found in transmitted historical texts remains a difficult endeavor as many terms do not have fixed meanings and may refer to different textiles or techniques across different historical eras. Excavation of archaeological textiles has

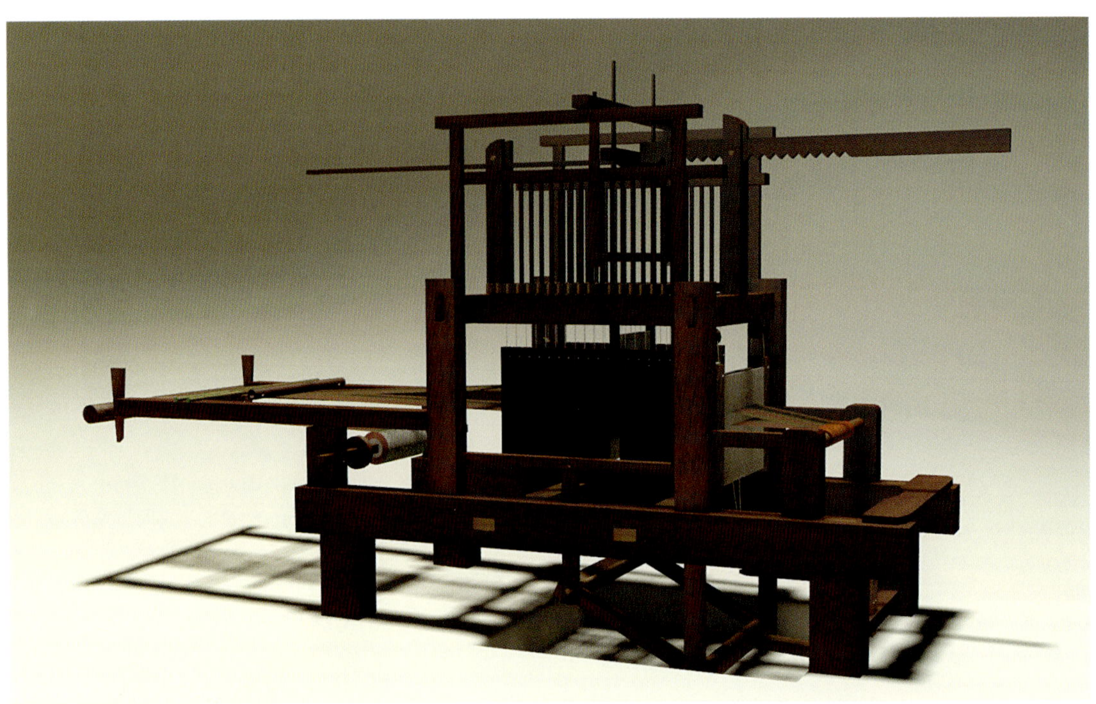

FIGURE A.6. Reconstruction of Laoguanshan loom. Courtesy of China National Silk Museum, Hangzhou.

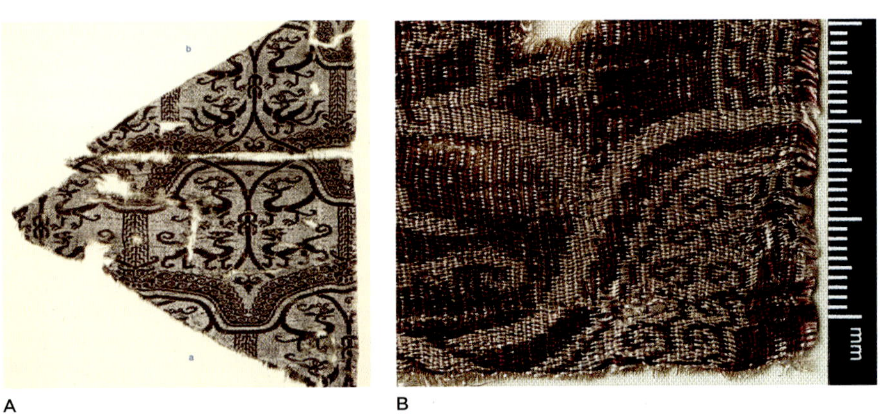

FIGURE A.7. (A) Fragment of warp-faced compound tabby (*jin*) with paired dragons and winged birds among interlacing borders; (B) detail. Dated fifth to sixth century. Warp: silk, untwisted, red and white; Inner weft: silk, untwisted, triple, white; Binding weft: silk, untwisted, single, white. Weave structure: 1/1 warp faced compound plain weave. L. 17 cm, W. 9.5 cm. Excavated from Cave 17 of the Mogao Grottoes. © Trustees of the British Museum.

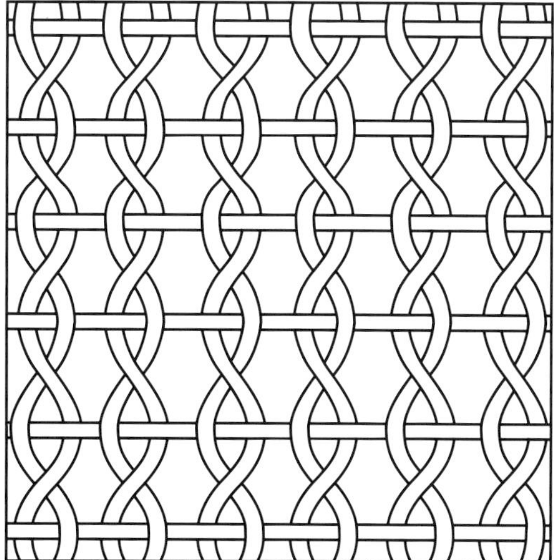

FIGURE A.8. Gauze binding unit. Drawn by Jennifer Shontz.

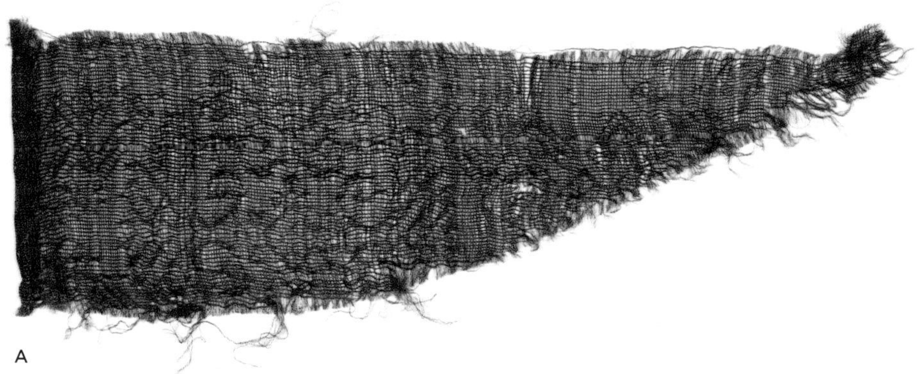

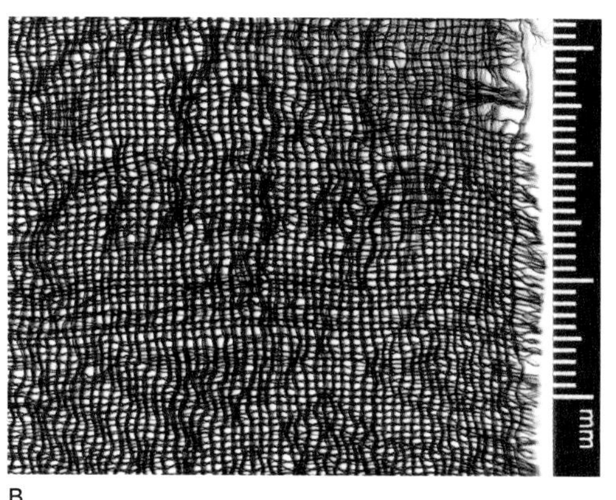

FIGURE A.9. (A) Fragment of monochrome patterned woven simple gauze (*sha*); (B) detail. Dated ninth to tenth century. Warp: silk, untwisted, single, purple; Weft: silk, untwisted, single but thick, purple. Weave structure: ground: 1:1 plain weave, doup warp crossing fixed warp in one direction; pattern: floating of doup ends on fixed ends. L. 6.5 cm, W. 21 cm. Excavated from Cave 17 of the Mogao Grottoes. © Trustees of the British Museum.

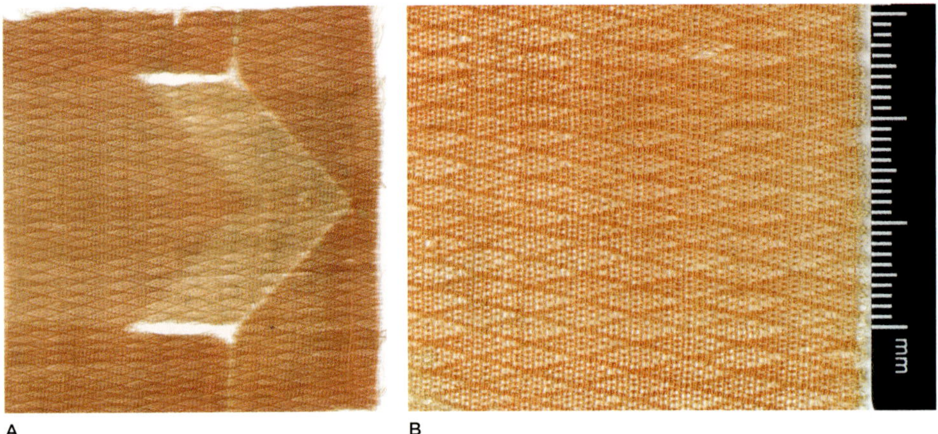

FIGURE A.10. (A) Fragment of complex gauze (*luo*) with lozenge pattern; (B) detail. Dated seventh to tenth century; Warp: silk, untwisted, single, red; Weft: silk, untwisted, paired or triple, red. Weave structure: complex gauze, ground: 4-end crossing weave; pattern: 2-end crossing weave. L. 9.7 cm, W. 10.3 cm. Excavated from Cave 17 of the Mogao Grottoes. © Trustees of the British Museum.

assisted in the research on technology and innovation, but the matching of terminology with artifact is beset with methodological challenges as well. Two recent publications, however, provide valuable glossaries of key textile terms that engage with both the textual and archaeological sources: Zhao Feng and Wang Le, "Glossary of Textile Terminology (Based on the Documents from Dunhuang and Turfan)," *Journal of the Royal Asiatic Society* 23 (2013): 349–87; and Dieter Kuhn, "Glossary," in *Chinese Silks*, ed. Kuhn et al. (New Haven: Yale University Press, 2012), 521–29.

GLOSSARY

An Lushan (703–757) 安祿山
Anbei 安北
Andong 安東
Anle, Princess (ca. 685–710) 安樂公主
Annan 安南
Anxi 安西
ao 襖

bacan si 八蠶絲
bai 白
bai guanjin 白綸巾
Bai Juyi (772–846) 白居易
baibian ling 白編綾
baihu 白縠
baihua 白畫
bainiao qun 百鳥裙
bailing 白綾
Ban Gu (32–92 BCE) 班固
banbi 半臂
banbi jin 半臂錦
baohua 寶花
Beili zhi 北里志
ben 本
benye 本業
bo 帛
bosi 波斯
biji 筆記
bixie 辟邪
bu 布

caibo hang 彩帛行
caoshi 草市
Chang'an 長安
Chang'an zhi 長安志
changfu 常服
Changhen ge 長恨歌
Changle, Princess (d. 643) 長樂公主
Changzhou 常州
chaofu 朝服
cheng 丞
chonglian ling 重蓮綾
chou 紬 (coarse plain weave from spun silk)
chou 綢 (plain weave silk)
choubu 绸布
chouxian 紬線
chuanqi 傳奇
chunfeng 淳風
chunluo 春羅
cishi 刺史
cun 寸

da duke ling 大獨窠綾
da lian 大練
da mian 大綿
da nü 大女
da shengjuan 大生絹
Da Tang Liudian 大唐六典
daishang 貸商
Daizong (r. 762–779) 代宗
dansi luo 單絲羅
dao 道
dayi hang 大衣行
Dezong (r. 779–805) 德宗
di 邸
diaobu 調布
didian 邸店
dingshen 丁身
Dingzhou 定州
dishui 地稅

Dou Shilun 竇師綸 (also known as Lingyang Gong, 陵陽公)
Dou Yi 竇乂
Du Mu (803–852) 杜牧
Du You (735–812) 杜佑
duan 段
duanwen 緞紋
duhu fu 都護府
duke xiling 獨窠細綾
duzhi 度支

Fan Zongshi (d. ca. 821) 樊宗師
fanghu 方縠
fangqi ling 方棋綾
fangwen 方紋
fangwen ling 方紋綾
fanke jinpao 蕃客錦袍
Fanyang ling 範陽綾
feiling 緋綾
fengyu shi 諷諭詩
fu 府
fubing 府兵
fugu 復古
fuyao 服妖

Gaochang 高昌
Gaoli 高麗
gaotou caolü 高頭草履
Gaozong (r. 649–83) 高宗
Gaozu (r. 618–626) 高祖
gexing 歌行
gong 貢
gongcheng 宮城
gongfu 公服
gongji 功績
gu 固 (solid, firm)
gu 古 (ancient)
guai 怪
guan 貫
Guan Zhong (ca. 720–645 BCE) 管仲
guandian 官典
Guannei 關內
gugong 雇工
guo 國
guqi 骨氣
guwen 古文
guyong 雇佣

Han Yu (768–824) 韓愈
hang 行
Hangzhou 杭州
he 褐
He Chou (540–620) 何稠
Hebei 河北
hedi 和糴
Hedong 河東
Hejiacun 何家村
Henan 河南
Hexi 河西
hong guanjin 紅綸巾
Hou Junji (d. 643) 侯君集
hu 縠
hu ji 胡姬
hua 華
huagu xiesha 花鼓歇沙
Huainan 淮南
Huan Kuan (fl. 60 BCE) 桓寬
huang 黃
Huang Chao (d. 884) 黃巢
huangcheng 皇城
huasha 花紗
huawen 花紋
huaxia 華夏
hubing 胡餅
hubu 戶部
hufu 胡服
Huihe 迴紇 (alternative transliteration of Uyghur)
Huihu 回鶻
hushi 互市
hushui 戶稅
Huzhou 湖州

ji 吉
jian 監 (supervisor)
jian 繝 (polychrome silk patterned with stripes)
jian 縑 (densely woven silk)
jian'er 健兒
jiang 絳
Jiangnan 江南
Jiannan 劍南
jiaobu 交布
jiaosuo 交梭
jiaosuo bailing 交梭白綾
jiaosuo hu 交梭縠

jiaosuo ling 交梭綾
jiaxie 夾纈
jie 借
jiedu shi 節度使
jieshi 街使
jifu 祭服
jimi fuzhou 羈縻府州
jin 錦
jinbei 錦被
jing 經
jingchai buqun 荊釵布裙
jingdu sheng 京都聲
jinghua ling 鏡花綾
Jingzong (r. 824–826) 敬宗
jinsha 緊紗
jinshi 進士
jisu 季俗
Jiu Tangshu 舊唐書
juan 絹
juntian 均田

Kaiyuan (reign era, 713–741) 開元
kesi 緙絲
kongque luo 孔雀羅
kuapao 袴袍
kuo 括
kuoshang 括商
kuxi 袴褶

Laoguanshan 老官山
Li Bai (701–762) 李白
Li Chui (711–736) 李倕
Li Deyu (787–850) 李德裕
Li Hua (715–766) 李華
Li Linfu (d. 752) 李林甫
Li Shanfu (fl. 9th cent.) 李山甫
Li Wa zhuan 李娃傳
Li Xian (654–684) 李賢 (posthumously Crown Prince Zhanghuai, 章懷太子)
Li Zhao (fl. 9th cent.) 李肇
Liangjing xinji 兩京新記
liangke xiling 兩窠細綾
liangshui 兩稅
lianran 練染
liaoling 繚綾
libu 禮部
Lidai minghua ji 歷代名畫記
Liji 禮記

ling 令 (statute, magistrate)
ling 綾 (twill silk)
Lingbiao 嶺表
lingjin fang 綾錦坊
lingjuan shan 綾絹扇
Lingnan 嶺南
lingzhi 靈芝
Liu Xu (887–946) 劉昫
liuwaiguan 流外官
liuxing 流行
Longyou 隴右
luo 羅
Lu Zhi (754–805) 陸贄
luoshan 羅衫
Luoyang 洛陽
lüfei 綠緋
lushi 錄事

manfei 縵緋
manzi 縵紫
Meng Jiao (751–814) 孟郊
menxia sheng 門下省
mian 綿
mianbu 綿布
mianchou 綿綢
mingfu 命婦
Minghuang zalu 明皇雜錄
Mingzhou 明州
minyuan kuang ye 愍怨旷也
mo 末
moli 末利
mu 畝
Muzong (r. 820–824) 穆宗

nangeng nüzhi 男耕女織
Nanzhao 南詔
nazi daiyi 納資代役
nei jiaofang 內教坊
neishi sheng 內侍省
neizuo 內作
nian nügong zhilao ye 念女工之勞也
niaoyan ling 鳥眼綾
Nishang yuyi qu 霓裳羽衣曲
nügong 女紅
nüyue 女樂

Ouyang Xiu (1007–1072) 歐陽修

pao 袍
pao'ao 袍襖
pibo 披帛
piduan 匹段
pingchou 平綢
pingsha 平紗
pingwen 平紋
pinnü 貧女
pinshi 貧士
putou 幞頭

qi 綺
qiandao 錢刀
qianqiu jie 千秋節
Qidan 契丹
qilin 麒麟
Qin Taoyu (fl. late 9th cent.) 秦韜玉
Qinfu yin 秦婦吟
qing 青
Qingbei yue 傾杯樂
qingrong 輕容
qingrong sha 清容紗
Qinzheng Lou 勤政樓
Qu, Lady (d. 688) 麴氏
Qujiang Chi 曲江池
qun 裙

ru 襦
ruijin 瑞錦
ruiling 瑞綾
Runzhou 润州
rushi 入時

sancai 三彩
Sang Hongyang (152–80 BCE) 桑弘羊
sangtian 桑田
seyi 色役
sha 紗
shan 衫 (short robe)
shan 山 (hill)
shangshu sheng 尚書省
Shangshu 尚書
Shangyang baifa ren 上陽白髮人
Shannan 山南
shanzhe 售者
shaofu jian 少府監
sheng 繩

shenghu 生縠
shi 市 (market)
shi 史 (scribe)
shi 絁 (ribbed plain weave silk)
shi 世 (world, generation)
Shi Daoluo (d. 658) 史道洛
Shi Hedan (d. 669) 史訶耽
Shi Jianwu (780–861) 施肩吾
Shi Shewu (d. 610) 史射勿
Shi Siming (703–761) 史思明
Shiji 史記
Shijing 詩經
shiling 市令
shishi 時世 ("of the times")
shishi 時勢 ("trend of the times")
shishifeng 食實封
Shishizhuang 時世妝
shiyang 時様
shiyang huawen ling 十樣花紋綾
shiye 世業
shoushi 手實
Shu 蜀
shuangceng jin 雙層錦
shuangmian jin 雙面錦
shuangpei 雙配
shuangsi ling 雙絲綾
shuipo ling 水波綾
shuiwen 水紋
shupu ling 樗蒲綾
si 肆
sibu 絲布
sige 絲葛
sihu canjun 司戶參軍
Sima Qian (ca. 145–86 BCE) 司馬遷
simian 絲綿
Song Minqiu (1019–1079) 宋敏求
Song Qi (998–1061) 宋祁
su 素
Sui Yangdi (r. 604–618) 隋煬帝
Sun Qi (fl. 884) 孫棨
Suzhou 苏州
Suzong (r. 756–762) 肅宗

taifu cheng 太府丞
taifu si 太府寺
Taiping, Princess (d. 713) 太平公主
Taiping guangji 太平廣記

taiyue shu 太樂署
Taizong (r. 626–649) 太宗
Tang guoshi bu 唐國史補
Tang liangjing chengfang kao 唐兩京城坊考
Tang lü 唐律
Tang yulin 唐語林
tao 緌
Tianbao (reign era, 742–756) 天寶
tianma 天馬
Tongdian 通典
Tufan 吐蕃
Tujue 突厥
tun 屯
tunjun 屯軍
tuntian 屯田

Wang Jian (ca. 767–830) 王建
Wang Ya (d. 835) 王涯
wanzi 卍字
wei 緯
Wei Shu (d. 757) 韋述
Wei Zhuang (836–910) 韋莊
weimao 帷帽
weiqi 圍棋
wen 文
wenling 紋綾
wensha 紋紗
wenxue 文學
wenzhang 文章
Wenzong (r. 826–840) 文宗
Wu Daozi (fl. 8th cent.) 吳道子
Wu Huifei (d. 737) 武惠妃
Wu juan 吳絹
Wu ling 吳綾
wu yuanjin 無遠近
Wu Zetian (ca. 624–705) 武則天
Wu zhusha 吳朱紗
Wuxing zhi 五行志
Wuzong (r. 840–846) 武宗

xian 縣 (county, district)
xian 線 (thread, yarn)
xiang 巷 (lane, alley)
xiang 緗 (light yellow silk)
xianwen ling 仙文綾
Xianzong (r. 806–820) 憲宗
xichi ling 鸂鶒綾
xiewen 斜紋
xiling 細綾
xin 心
Xin Tangshu 新唐書
Xin Yuefu 新樂府
Xincheng, Princess (d. 663) 新成長公主
xinggang 行綱
Xingyuan 杏園
xinjia jinpao 新加錦袍
xinyang 新樣
xiuye 繡葉
xiyu 西域
Xizhou 西州
Xu Hui (627–650) 徐惠
Xu Song (1781–1848) 徐松
Xuanzong (r. 712–756) 玄宗
Xue Jianxun (fl. 8th cent.) 薛兼訓
xunshi 巡使

Yan Liben (d. 673) 閻立本
Yang Guifei (719–756) 楊貴妃
Yangzhou 揚州
Yantie lun 鹽鐵輪
yi yi wenxiu 衣以文繡
Yide, Crown Princc (d. 701) 懿德太了
ying 纓
yingtian shi 營田使
Yinshan dao 陰山道
yiting ju 掖庭局
Yizhou 益州
yong 傭
yongdiao bu 庸調布
Yongtai, Princess (d. 701) 永泰公主
you pushe 右僕射
You suojiao 有所教
youshang shu 右尚署
Yu gong 禹貢
Yuan Zhen (779–831) 元稹
yuanhuan 圓鬟
Yuanhe shiti 元和詩體 *or* Yuanhe ti 元和體
yuefu 樂府
Yuezhou 越州
yufu 御服
yufu jian 御府监
Yufu zhi 輿服志
yukou 魚口
yushi daifu 御史大夫

zao 皂 (black)
zao 造 (to construct, to create)
zaoyi zhe 造意者 (*or* zaozhe 造者)
zashi 雜事
zeng 繒
zhang 丈
Zhang Ji (ca. 767–830) 張籍
Zhang Qian (d. 113 BCE) 張騫
Zhang Xiong (d. 633) 張雄
Zhang Yanyuan (fl. 9th cent.) 張彥遠
zhanggu 掌固
zhangye shu 掌冶署
Zhao Yigong (fl. 9th cent.) 趙逸公
Zheng Gu (ca. 851–910) 鄭谷
Zheng Rentai (d. 663) 鄭仁泰
zhenshi 鎮市
zhidu shi 支度使
zhifu 織婦
Zhifu ci 織婦詞
zhiguai 志怪
zhiji 織機
Zhijin qu 織錦曲
zhiku 質庫
zhipin 織品
zhiran shu 織染署
zhiren 織紝
zhizao hu 織造戶
zhong 鍾
zhongshang shu 中尚署
zhongshu menxia 中書門下
zhongshu sheng 中書省
zhou 州
Zhou Fang (ca. 730–800) 周昉
Zhouli 周禮
zhu 銖
zhuang 妝
zi 字 (courtesy name)
zi 紫 (purple)
zi guanjin 紫綸巾
zongguan 總管
zu 組
zuocang shu 左藏署
zuoshang shu 左尚署
zuoshiyi 左拾遺
zushou 組綬
zu-yong-diao 租庸調

NOTES

INTRODUCTION: TOWARD A DEFINITION OF FASHION IN TANG CHINA

1 *Xin Tangshu*, 34:878. In *New Standard History of the Tang*, concern about clothing habits as portents of disorder became systematized as a separate entry, entitled "Sartorial Anomalies," and incorporated into the "Treatise on the Five Phases" (Wuxing zhi). Inclusion in the treatise that organized calamities, omens, abnormal phenomena, and their correlation to political affairs bespeaks Ouyang Xiu's historiographic motives as a didactic Confucian scholar-official. See Huang Zhengjian, *Tangdai yishi zhuxing yanjiu*, 91–92.

2 Sombart, *Economic Life in the Modern Age*, 225, originally published in his article "The Emergence of Fashion."

3 See Sombart, *Luxury and Capitalism*; Veblen, "The Economic Theory of Woman's Dress," 198–205; Simmel, "Fashion," reprinted as "The Philosophy of Fashion" in 1957.

4 Bell, *On Human Finery*, 59.

5 Braudel, *The Structures of Everyday Life*, 312.

6 Eileen Chang [Zhang Ailing], "A Chronicle of Changing Clothes" (Gengyi ji), 427–41.

7 Clunas, *Superfluous Things*; Brook, *The Confusions of Pleasure*; Finnane, *Changing Clothes in China*. For work in European history, see Frick, *Dressing Renaissance Florence*; Vincent, *Dressing the Elite*; Sarah-Grace Heller, *Fashion in Medieval France*; Rublack, *Dressing Up*.

8 See Clunas, "Modernity Global and Local," 1497–1511. This trend was sparked by the cultural turn, which shifted focus from the industrial revolution to the consumer revolution as the seminal event in the rise of modernity. McKendrick et al., *The Birth of a Consumer Society*; Mukerji, *From Graven Images: Patterns of Modern Materialism*.

9 Jones and Stallybrass, *Renaissance Clothing and the Materials of Memory*, 2.

10 *Jiu Tangshu*, 51:2179; *Xin Tangshu*, 76:3494.

11 Mann, "Myths of Asian Womanhood," 835–62.

12 This turn of phrase is borrowed from Friedrich Schiller's *Letters on the Aesthetic Education of Man* (1795), and incorporates ideas from Hans-Georg Gadamer's *Truth and Method* (1960) and "The Play of Art" (1973). For Schiller, aesthetic play or the play drive reconciled the sensory drive with the formal drive and allowed for self-realization. Thus, it is aesthetic play that has made man human.

13 As Ulinka Rublack has argued, "dress was obviously experienced in dialogue with the body and its social meanings had to be lived with." Rublack, *Dressing Up*, 31.

1. HISTORY: CLOTH AND THE LOGICS OF COSMOPOLITAN EMPIRE

1 Turfan is located in today's Xinjiang Uyghur Autonomous Region in northwestern China.

2 Hansen, *The Silk Road: A New History*, see plate 8.

3 Another figurine of a dancer (73TAM206:42/9) with arms made from paper contained lists of debts and payments that documented a total of 608 transactions.

4 See Chen Guocan, "Cong Tulufan chutu de 'zhikuzhang' kan Tangdai," 316–43. For an English translation, see Hansen and Mata-Fink, "Records from a Seventh-Century Pawnshop in China," 54–64.

5 See Deng, "Women in Turfan during the Sixth to Eighth Centuries," 85–103.

6 Chen Guocan, "Cong Tulufan," 328–29. See also Xiong, *Sui-Tang Chang'an*, 269.

7 The pawnshop may be the oldest credit institution in Chinese history. One scholar has traced pawnbroking practices to Buddhist monasteries of the Six Dynasties era. Lien-sheng Yang, *Money and Credit in China*, 70.

8 *Jiu Tangshu*, 183:4740. See also *Xin Tangshu*, 83:3654, and *Zizhi Tongjian*, 210:6685.

9 "One hears that those in the court, no matter if they are descendants from esteemed families or if they are honest officials, privately establish pawnshops and stores to compete with people for profit. From this day forward, they are both prohibited [from doing so]." *Quan Tangwen*, 78:357.

10 Dudbridge, *The Tale of Li Wa*, 130–31.

11 Linda Feng has also suggested that the addresses documented in these slips, such as "the northern alley" and "the eastern end," show how Chang'an residents experienced and conceived of space relationally. See Feng, "Chang'an and Narratives of Experience in Tang Tales," 35–68.

12 In Mark Lewis's textbook history on the Tang dynasty, *China's Cosmopolitan Empire*, he describes the era as, "the most open, cosmopolitan period of Chinese history" (148).

13 Settlements in the Tarim Basin have been recorded with names in, but not limited to, Uyghur and Chinese, which mark both changes in political regimes and populations over time. For example, Gaochang (Ch.) is also referred to as Karakhoja (Uy.) and, alternatively, as the Kingdom of Qocho established in 843 under Tocharian-Uyghur rule.

14 These documents were published in ten volumes, *Tulufan chutu wenshu* (Documents excavated from Turfan). A folio-size edition containing photographic plates with the same title was published by the Chinese Institute of Cultural Relics in four volumes in 1992. Another two-volume set, compiled from new documents excavated from 1997 to 2006, was published in 2008. See also Rong Xinjiang et al., *Xin hou Tulufan chutu*.

15 For a close examination of Richtofen's invention, see Chin, "The Invention of the Silk Road, 1877," 194–219. David Christian has called attention to the Silk Roads as narrowly defined as east-west land and sea routes that transported luxury goods, technology, and religion, ignoring that the routes also served to transmit political culture. He has further argued for the importance of the transecological "Steppe Roads" that ran north to south, and linked Eurasian grassland and agricultural regions. Christian, "Silk Roads or Steppe Roads?" 1–26.

16 *Shiji*, 123.3171; Tamara Chin credits Richtofen's student, Sven Hedin (1865–1962), for popularizing both the term and the story of Zhang Qian's embassy to Fergana as the narrative beginnings of the Silk Road. She argues that the "Silk Road" entered the Chinese language as a neologism, appeared in limited circulation prior to 1949, and only became widely used during the second half of the twentieth century, when the *People's Daily* (Remin ribao) used the term to describe China's two-thousand-year-old ties with Afghanistan, Pakistan, and the Middle East. Chin, "The Invention of the Silk Road, 1877," 217.

17 See Rong, *Dunhuang xue shiba jiang*, 33–37. Zhang Qian was also the first to report on existing trade networks with India (Shendu). See Sen, *Buddhism, Diplomacy, and Trade.*

18 *Shiji*, 123:3171–4.

19 Ibid. The structure and ethnographic content of the "Account of Fergana" (Dayuan liezhuan) provided a template for later historical and literary accounts of the Western Regions, such as those compiled in the official dynastic histories. In addition to individual accounts of foreign territories, including the "Account of the Xiongnu" (Xiongnu zhuan), the *Standard History of the [Former] Han* (Hanshu) includes an "Account on the Western Regions" (Xiyu zhuan). See *Hanshu*, 96:3871–3932. See also Chin, *Savage Exchange.*

20 "The Han dispatched more than ten embassies to foreign countries outside of Dayuan in pursuit of exotic things." *Shiji*, 123:3174; see also *Hanshu*, 96a:3895.

21 *Shiji*, 123:3174.

22 Chin, *Savage Exchange*, 11–19.

23 See Lewis, *The Flood Myths of Early China.*

24 See Twitchett, ed., *The Cambridge History of China*, 3:48–149.

25 On the construction of the Grand Canal, see Xiong, *Emperor Yang of the Sui Dynasty*, 75–93.

26 The Li clan's ethnic makeup has been the source of much debate by historians of the Tang dynasty. Chen Yinke put forward a theory that the mixed Chinese-Turkic background of the Tang ruling clan was the key to understanding its style of rule. See Chen Yinke, *Tangdai zhengzhi shi shulun gao*; Twitchett, *The Cambridge History of China*, 3:150–87.

27 Twitchett, *Financial Administration*, see chap. 4, "Currency and Credit."

28 An edict dated to 732 encouraged the use of twill silk, gauze, plain tabby, and hemp to be used for commercial transactions, and made the exclusive use of coins a punishable offense. *Tang Huiyao*, 88:1618; *Da Tang liudian*, 3:48b (74).

29 For an overview of Sui-Tang China's relations with Inner Asia and, particularly, the debates at court about the resettlement of the Eastern Türks, see Skaff, *Sui-Tang China and its Turko-Mongol Neighbors.*

30 Skaff has tabulated the frequency of attacks on north China from 599 through 755, showing that under Taizong's rule less than one attack took place annually; under Gaozong, from 650 through 675, there was an average of less than one attack every five years. Skaff, *Sui-Tang China and Its Turko-Mongol Neighbors*, see tables 1.2 and 1.3 on p. 40 and p. 43 respectively.

31 Taizong initiated the attack in 639 on the pretext that the ruler had failed to fulfill its tributary obligations. See *Jiu Tangshu*, 198:5293–97.

32 Zhang and Rong, "A Concise History of the Turfan Oasis," 13–36; Hansen, "The Impact of the Silk Road Trade on a Local Community," 283–310; see also Hansen, *The Silk Road: A New History.*

33 Rong, "Beichao Sui Tang Sute ren zhi qianxi ji qi juluo," 27–86; Skaff, "The Sogdian Trade Diaspora," 475–524; de La Vaissière, *Sogdian Traders: A History.*

34 Jonathan Skaff has argued that the Chinese compound, which translates literally as, "horse bridle" and "ox halter," suggests that Tang official attitude toward foreigners was one that equated the Han Chinese to the "'humans' who use bridles and halters to control ethnic groups who are analogous to beasts of burden." Skaff, *Sui-Tang China and its Turko-Mongol Neighbors*, 61.

35 *Xin Tangshu*, 43b:1146–55.

36 Ibid.

37 Pan, *Son of Heaven and Heavenly Qaghan*, 197–202. As Zhang Qun has shown, the loose-rein commands prefectures were established on an ad-hoc basis, and the configurations and names of the protectorates changed over time. Zhang Qun, *Tangdai fanjiang yanjiu*, 120–42.

38 Zhang Guogang, "Tangdai de fanbu yu fanbing," 93–112.

39 The new dynasty adopted and adapted institutions, systems of land ownership and taxation, and legal codes from the regimes that had governed north China in the fifth and sixth centuries. Following the Sui model, the basic structure of the Tang central government consisted of the Secretariat (Zhongshu Sheng), Chancellery (Menxia Sheng), and the Department of State Affairs (Shangshu Sheng) and its six subordinate boards. The Secretariat prepared edicts, the Chancellery reviewed them, and the Department of State Affairs implemented them. After 723, the Secretariat and Chancellery functioned as a single government organ (Zhongshu Menxia). See Twitchett, *The Cambridge History of China*, 3:150–241; Twitchett, *Financial Administration under the T'ang Dynasty*; Chen Yinke, *Sui Tang zhidu yuanyuan lüelun gao.*

40 See Twitchett, *Financial Administration*, 1–6 and 24–28; Li Jinxiu, *Tangdai caizheng shigao*, vol. 1. I have followed Angela Sheng's calculations for the lengths of tax cloth, in Sheng, "Determining the Value of Textiles in the Tang Dynasty," 183.

41 See Francesca Bray's seminal work on the significance of women's textile production: *Technology and Gender: Fabrics of Power in Late Imperial China.*

42 In the 1930s, Japanese scholar Niida Noboru reconstructed the Tang statutes from various sources, including two commentaries on the Nara Japan code (Yōrō ritsuryō), the *Ryō no gige* and *Ryō no shuge*, in his now classic *Tōryō shūi* (Collection of the Tang statutes).

43 Twitchett, *Financial Administration*, 19. Taizong initiated the first systematic reworking of the Tang legal code in 637 and was followed by Gaozong in 651. In 653, a commentary was appended to the code to educate officials in the proper conduct of trials. Xuanzong promulgated the most extensive version of the Tang legal code in 725. See Wallace Johnson, trans., *The T'ang Code*, vol. 1, 39–40.

44 Twitchett, "Local Financial Administration," 82–114.

45 *Xin Tangshu*, 43b:1146–55; *Taxation Statues* are translated from Niida in Twitchett, *Financial Administration*, 140–47.

46 Twitchett, *Financial Administration*, 142.

47 Ibid, 144.

48 The earliest record of the equal-field system is dated to the ninth month of 640, only one month after the Tang army had defeated the Gaochang Kingdom, Tang Changru et al., *Tulufan chutu wenshu*, 4:71–73. The document is transcribed and translated in Xiong, "The Land-Tenure System of Tang China," 356. Lu Xiangqian has argued that the equal-field system was not implemented until after 624, Lu, "Tangdai Xizhou tudi de guanli fangshi," 385–408.

49 See Yamamoto and Dohi, *Tun-huang and Turfan Documents*, vol. 2.

50 Deng, "Women in Turfan during the Sixth to Eighth Centuries," 85–103.

51 See Ching, "Silk in Ancient Kucha," 63–82; Yoshida, *Kōtan shutsudo 8–9-seiki no Kōtan-go sezoku bunsho ni kansuru oboegaki*. For an abridged English version of Yoshida's book, see Yoshida, "On the Taxation System of Pre-Islamic Khotan," 95–126. A group of wooden tallies with Chinese-Khotanese inscriptions (Hetian) that record local tax collection by Tang officials dated to 722 have been recently rendered into English, see Rong and Wen, "Newly Discovered Chinese-Khotanese Bilingual Tallies," 99–118. See also Duan and Wang, "Were Textiles Used as Money in Khotan in the Seventh and Eighth Centuries?" 307–25.

52 *Tang liudian*, 3:44a (72).

53 Wang Binghua, "Tulufan chutu Tangdai yongdiao bu yanjiu," 56–62. An English translation of Wang's 1983 essay was published in a special issue of the *Journal of the Royal Asiatic Society*, edited by Valerie Hansen and Helen Wang. See Binghua Wang and Helen Wang, "A Study of the Tang Dynasty Tax Textiles (Yongdiao Bu) from Turfan," 263–80.

54 Discovered by Aurel Stein in 1915. See Hansen and Wang, "Introduction," 157–58.

55 Wang Binghua, "Tulufan chutu Tangdai yongdiao bu yanjiu," 59; see also Twitchett, *Financial Administration*, 102.

56 Wang Binghua notes that among the tax textiles documented by Aurel Stein was one hemp fragment dated to 684 that had been used as substitute payment for the gain (*zu*) tax, "Tulufan chutu Tangdai yongdiao bu yanjiu," 59.

57 This document records that Yizhou (Hami, Xinjiang) received 30,000 bolts (*duan*) of hemp and Guazhou (Gansu) received 10,000 bolts annually between 676 and 679. See Arakawa, "The Transportation of Tax Textiles," 245–61.

58 *Jiu Tangshu*, 38:1385.

59 Twitchett, *The Cambridge History of China*, 3:415–19.

60 Du, *Tongdian*, 6:111. Twitchett has translated Du's entry on state finances during the Tianbao era in appendix 2 of *Financial Administration*, 153–57.

61 Zhang Guogang has estimated that by the late Tang, the per capita cost was about 24 *guan* (a string of coins) for uniforms, grain, rewards and grants, and arms equipment and replacement. Zhang, *Tangdai fanzhen yanjiu*, 214–19.

62 Arakawa and Hansen, "The Transportation of Tax Textiles," 254–60.

63 Ikeda, *Chūgoku kodai sekichō kenkyū*, 447–62. See also Trombert and de La Vaissière, "Le prix des denrées sur le marché de Turfan en 743," 1–52.

64 I follow Victor Xiong's division of the city into six sectors: Northeast, East Central, Southeast, Northwest, West Central, and Southwest. See Xiong, *Sui-Tang Chang'an*, 217–34. Chang'an has been the subject of extensive scholarship. See, for example: Steinhardt, *Chinese Imperial City Planning*; and Kiang, *Cities of Aristocrats and Bureaucrats*. On changes to the ward system throughout the Tang, see Li Xiaocong, *Tangdai diyu jiegou yu yunzuo kongjian*, 248–306.

65 Kiang, *Cities of Aristocrats and Bureaucrats*, 2.

66 Heng Chye Kiang has been working on a digital reconstruction of Chang'an from archaeological and textual sources, which has offered new insights into the layout of the ward system. See Kiang, "Visualizing Everyday Life in the City," 91–117.

67 Ma Dezhi, "Tangdai Chang'an cheng kaogu jilue," 595–611.

68 Xiong, *Sui-Tang Chang'an*, 55–105. See also Chung, "A Study of the Daming Palace," 23–72.

69 Schafer, "The Last Years of Ch'ang-an," 133–79.

70 Victor Xiong has calculated this figure based on the numbers provided in the "Treatise on Geography" (Dili zhi) in the *Old Standard History of the Tang* (Jiu Tangshu, *juan* 38). See Xiong, *Sui-Tang Chang'an*, 197–98.

71 Niida, *Tangdai ling shiyi*, 644.

72 Niida, *Tangdai ling shiyi*, 276; Johnson, *The T'ang Code*, 2:469–70 (article 406).

73 See *Tang liudian*, 20:10b-14a (384–386); Twitchett, "The T'ang Market System," 202–48. Xiong has noted that according to transmitted sources, there were seven markets that operated during the dynasty at different times. *Sui-Tang Chang'an*, 167–68.

74 Ma Dezhi, "Tangdai Chang'an cheng kaogu jilue," 595–611.

75 Niida cites a stipulation that required each *hang* to display a sign above each lane with the name of the *hang*. Niida, *Tangdai ling shiyi*, 644.

76 Ma, "Tangdai Chang'an cheng kaogu jilue," 605–8.

77 Schafer, *Golden Peaches of Samarkand*, 20.

78 In the 1950s, Hiraoka Takeo compiled primary sources on Sui-Tang Chang'an and Luoyang, maps, and indexes in his monumental three-volume, *Chōan to Rakuyō* (Chang'an

and Luoyang), which remains invaluable to the historical study of Chang'an and Luoyang. Hiraoka, *Chōan to Rakuyō*, 3 vols.

79 Jack W. Chen, *The Poetics of Sovereignty*, see chap. 7.

80 Ibid., 352–75.

81 This exact phrasing comes from Nancy Steinhardt's *Chinese Imperial City Planning*, but similar or near-exact phrasing can be found across English-, Chinese-, and Japanese-language scholarship on the Tang. See Steinhardt, *Chinese Imperial City Planning*, 20.

82 This view was first pioneered by Xiang Da in the 1930s and picked up by Edward Schafer in the 1960s. Xiang Da, "Tangdai Chang'an yu Xiyu wenming" (1933); reprinted with other essays on Tang China's exchanges with Inner Asia in *Tangdai Chang'an yu xiyu wenming* (1957). Edward Schafer's *The Golden Peaches of Samarkand*, influenced by Xiang's work, narrated the cosmopolitanism of the Tang through the empire's material imports.

83 Some scholars date the discovery to 1623, others to 1625. See Yoshirō, *Keikyō hibun kenkyū*; Kahar Barat, "Aluoben, A Nestorian Missionary in 7th Century China," 184–98.

84 Yoshirō, *Keikyō hibun kenkyō*, 130.

85 Li Su's family may have fled to Tang China along with other members of the Sasanid royal family when their empire came to an end in 651. The heirs to the Sasanian empire, Peroz and his son, Narseh, famously sought refuge in the capital during Gaozong's reign. See Rong, *Zhonggu Zhongguo yu wailai wenming*, 238–57.

86 In 2006, a second Nestorian pillar dated to the Tang was unearthed in Luoyang. See Ge, ed., *Jingjiao yizhen*; Nicolini-Zani, "The Tang Christian Pillar from Luoyang," 99–140.

87 Rong, *Zhonggu Zhongguo yu wailai wenming*, 169–79.

88 Luo, *Guyuan nanjiao Sui-Tang mudi.*

89 Ibid., 7–30, and 57–60.

90 *Sui shu*, 68:1596–1598.

91 Taniichi, "Six-Lobed Tang Dynasty (AD 658) Glass Cups," 107–10.

92 An, "The Art of Glass Along the Silk Road," 57–65.

93 Shaanxi Provincial Museum, "Xi'an nanjiao Hejiacun faxian Tangdai jiaocang wenwu," 30–42. See Qi Dongfang's magisterial study of the silver and gold vessels. Qi, *Tangdai jinyin qi yanjiu*. Valerie Hansen has published a short essay about the discovery that includes a table of all of the items. See Hansen, "The Hejia Village Hoard," 14–19.

94 Two hypotheses have been put forward. In the initial report, it was suggested that the hoard was buried in the Xinghua Ward, south of the Imperial City and close to the West Market, sometime after 731. The first dating of the burial is based on the four silver ingots incised with information identifying them as tax payments. One is dated to 722 and the other three were paid in 731. Since ingots were melted down to form bigger lumps after they were collected, it is believed that the hoard was buried not long after 731—perhaps around the time of the An Lushan Rebellion. Duan Pengqi, based on subsequent research of the Chang'an's ward system and the stylistic properties of the silver vessels, contended that the hoard must date from the 780s and was buried in the Qinren Ward. Most recently, Qi Dongfang has advanced the theory that the hoard belonged to Liu Zhen, who served as special supply commissioner (*zuyong zhi*) during the reign of Emperor Dezong (r. 779–805), who buried the treasure before fleeing the 783 mutiny by frontier troops in the capital. See Shaanxi Provincial Museum, "Xi'an nanjiao Hejiacun faxian Tangdai jiaocang wenwu," 34; Duan Pengyi, "Xi'an nanjiao Hejiacun Tangdai jinyin qi xiaoyi," 536–43; Qi Dongfang, "Hejiacun yibao de mai cang didian he niandai," 70–74.

95 See Qi, *Tangdai jinyin qi yanjiu*, 49.

96 The discovery of a ninth-century shipwreck off the coast of Belitung Island in Indonesia

has provided further evidence of the extent of Tang China's commercial network. The ship, believed to have been an Arab trading vessel, was stocked with ceramics from the Changsha kilns of Hunan, the Yue kilns of Zhejiang, white wares from kilns in either Hebei or Henan, as well as bronze mirrors and gilt silverware. Excavated in 1998 and 1999, the Belitung shipwreck is the earliest evidence of direct trade between the western Indian Ocean and China. See Krahl et al., *Shipwrecked: Tang Treasures and Monsoon Winds.*

97 Zheng Chuhui (fl. 834), *Minghuang zalu*, 26.

98 Hino, *Tōdai teiten no kenkyū*, 2 vols. See also Xiong, *Sui-Tang Chang'an*, 183–92.

99 Cited in Xue, "Lun Sui Tang Chang'an de shangren," 69–75, see 74. Xue cites two other Li Bai poems with references to foreign girls (*hu ji*). The poem is also translated in Schafer, *Golden Peaches of Samarkand*, 21.

100 From Bai Juyi's preface to his famous poem, "Ballad of the Pipa Player" (Pipa xing). *Quan Tangshi*, 435.4822. On nostalgia in Bai Juyi's poems, see Shields, "Remembering When: The Uses of Nostalgia," 321–361.

101 Bossler, "Vocabularies of Pleasure," 71–99, see 81.

102 Sun Qi, "Beili zhi" (Anecdotes from the Northern Ward), 22.

103 See Xiong for a list of the East Central's prominent residents, *Sui-Tang Chang'an*, 219–24.

104 See Rouzer, *Articulated Ladies*, 249–83, and Yao, "The Status of Pleasure," 26–53. For a more recent study on Sun Qi's work and the literati-courtesan relationship, see Feng, *City of Marvel and Transformation*, 112–34. As Feng argues, "The courtesans mattered—even if their representations were penned by and shared among male literati. The living room where the conversations and banter took place—along with the nonliterati neighbors—mattered. The prices for banquets and entertainment mattered, even if they were seldom mentioned directly. Most of all, the location of all this within the urban social and commercial matrix of Chang'an mattered. Visitors to the Pingkang Ward, along with the women who inhabited it, were part of a social space that was the product of the newly emerging discourse of transformation for the cultural elite in Chang'an" (114).

105 On the Inner Court Entertainment Bureau, see Bossler, "Vocabularies of Pleasure," 76–77.

106 *Xin Tangshu*, 22:476–77.

107 *Minghuang zalu*, 45–6. See also Kroll, "The Dancing Horses of T'ang," 240–68.

108 I am drawing on arguments advanced by Ann Rosalind Jones and Peter Stallybrass in their seminal work on fashion, cloth, and the making of subjects in Renaissance Europe. Jones and Stallybrass, *Renaissance Clothing and the Materials of Memory*, see the introduction.

109 My discussion of luxury objects here follows Appadurai's analysis of them as "incarnated signs." Appadurai, *The Social Life of Things*, 38–39.

110 Conflicting stories about the composition of the tune have been transmitted in the textual sources. See Yang, *Yang Yinliu Yinyue Lunwen Xuanji*, 325–26.

111 *Quan Tangshi*, 435:4816–18.

112 *Quan Tangshi*, 444:4970–71.

113 *Minghuang zalu*, 45–46.

114 Li Zhao, *Tang guoshi bu*, 19.

115 See Naito, "A Comprehensive Look at the T'ang-Sung Period," 88–99; Katō, *Shina keizaishi kōshō*; Hartwell, "Demographic, Political, and Social Transformations of China, 750–1550," 365–442; and Skinner, ed., *The City in Late Imperial China*. On developments in intellectual thought, see Bol, *'This Culture of Ours'*; McMullen, *State and Scholars in T'ang China*; Ruoshi Chen, *Liu Tsung-yüan and Intellectual Change in T'ang China, 773–819*; DeBlasi, *Reform in the Balance*.

116 See Tackett, *The Destruction of the Medieval Chinese Aristocracy*.

2. DISCOURSE: FASHION AND SUMPTUARY REGULATION

1 See Yan, *Zhouli zhi mian*. David McMullen has argued that: "Though again the *Zhouli* was never the exclusive authority for Tang rituals, it functioned with other Confucian canonical texts, interpreted by the commentarial tradition, to supply an important sanction for prescriptions. Tang state ritual played an indispensable part in defining the very nature of the dynastic house, the official hierarchy, and the larger society." McMullen, "The Role of the *Zhouli* in Seventh- and Eighth-Century Civil Administrative Traditions," 184.

2 Appadurai, *The Social Life of Things*, 25. Also see Vincent, *Dressing the Elite*, 143. Vincent's discussion of symbolic legislation derives from Alan Hunt's study of the relationship between sumptuary law and political power, *Governance of the Consuming Passions*.

3 The statute, known as the *Wude ling*, was modeled after Sui Yangdi's clothing code. See Harada Yoshito's classic study on Tang dress, *Tōdai no fukushoku*, 18.

4 Johnson, tr., *The T'ang Code*, 1:23–29. See also Johnson, "Status and Liability for Punishment in the T'ang Code," 217–29.

5 Francesca Bray has argued that clothing served to mark "civilization" in the Confucian worldview: "Not only does it [clothing] distinguish ranks and provide ornament, it is linked to the reproduction of human society through descent, the care of the old, the raising of children, and the proper distinction and complementarity between the sexes." Bray, *Technology and Gender: Fabrics of Power in Late Imperial China*, 190.

6 Sun Ji and Harada Yoshito have completed the most comprehensive research on the two Tang treatises. My discussion of the contents of the wardrobe is drawn, in part, from their work. See Sun Ji, *Zhongguo gudai yufu luncong*; Harada, *Tōdai no fukushoku*.

7 According to *Tang Huiyao* (Gathered essential documents of the Tang), which details the structures of government institutions, the roles ascribed to women of the court depended on their classification as either "outer" (*wai*) or "inner" (*nei*). Women who fell under the category of *nei mingfu* (inner women of the court) included the emperor's consorts and the heir apparent's consorts, whereas *wai mingfu* (outer women of the court) were comprised of imperial princesses and princes' consorts. See *Tang Huiyao*, 26:573.

8 Gaozu's successors simplified the clothing code by opting to wear only one ceremonial suit and abandoning the rest. Emperor Taizong adopted the habit of dressing informally for all occasions with the exception of New Year's Day, winter solstice, holding court, and major rites. Of the twelve suits, Emperor Gaozong continued to wear the suit for performing the Fengshan ritual (*da qiumian*) and the suit for enthronement and important occasions (*qiumian*). Xuanzong disposed of the ritual ensembles, keeping only the suits for holding court and for ceremonial occasions. See *Jiu Tangshu*, 45:1937; also Huang Zhengjian, *Tangdai yishi zhuxing yanjiu*, 54–55.

9 Each rank was divided into two classes, and each class from rank four through nine was further separated into two grades. On the privileges afforded to ranking civil officials in the *Code*, see Johnson, *The T'ang Code*, 1:25.

10 Detailed regulatory ordinances governing colors, cuts, and fabrics issued during the successive reigns of the emperors were primarily collected in *Tang Huiyao* (Gathered essential documents of the Tang), *Tang da zhaoling ji* (Collected edicts of the Tang), *Quan Tangwen* (Complete prose of the Tang), *Zizhi tongjian* (Comprehensive mirror to aid in governance), and *Cefu yuangui* (Outstanding models from the storehouse of literature). "Treatise on Carriages and Dress" presents an outline of the types of ceremonial and everyday attire of the ruler and his subjects, supplemented by anecdotes of sartorial misconduct or aberrational behavior.

11 "On the fourteenth day of the eighth month of the fourth year of Zhenguan [631], [the

emperor] decreed: 'The system of ceremonial vestments [for the emperor] follows the [dress] statute, ordinary dress and adornments [for officials] has yet to be distinguished according to rank.' Thus, those of rank three and up [i.e., to rank one] wear robes of purple, ranks four and five wear red, ranks six and seven wear green, ranks eight and nine wear blue." *Tang Huiyao*, 31:663.

12 So-called *liuwaiguan* or "officials without rank" are also translated as "out-of-stream officials." *Xin Tangshu*, 24:527.

13 The edict, known as the "Decree Prohibiting Officials and Commoners from Transgressing Dress Regulations," was issued in 674 after Emperor Gaozong had heard that: "Among officials and commoners, there were those who did not comply with the rules imposed by the statue and so, they wear red, purple, blue, and green short robes under their outer robe. When they are in their villages, they even openly exposed the colored inner garment. With no distinction between noble and base, there is disorder in the realm [literally, there is an insect feeding on the cardinal principles]." *Quan Tangwen*, 13:159. See also *Jiu Tangshu*, 5:99; *Cefu yuangui*, 60:296 and 63:312 (recorded as the fifth year of the Xianheng reign period, 670–674); *Tang da zhaoling*, 108:515.

14 See *Tang Huiyao*, 32:680.

15 These occasions included the sericulture ritual (*congcan*), attending court (*chaohui*), important ceremonial rites, and receiving honored guests.

16 *Xin Tangshu*, 24:530.

17 "High-ranked women can dress in the colors of the lower rank, but the lower rank cannot appropriate the colors of the upper rank." See *Jiu Tangshu*, 45:1957.

18 *Jiu Tangshu*, 45:1957.

19 *Xin Tangshu*, 34:878.

20 Hunt, *Governance of the Consuming Passions*, 105.

21 As stated by article 449, "Violation of Statues" (Weiling) of "Miscellaneous Articles" (Zalü) in *Tang Code* (Tang lü), "all cases of violation are to be punished by fifty blows, and the violation of 'special regulations' is reduced by one degree." According to the subcommentary, transgressing dress regulations (such as wearing colors that did not correspond to one's ranks) was considered a violation of the "special regulations" and was to be punished by forty blows. See *Tang lü shuyi*, 521–22.

22 Under Emperor Taizong two edicts were passed, the first in 630 and the second in 631. Gaozong followed with an edict in 674, Xuanzong in 716, and Wenzong in 832 (as part of Wang Ya's recommended reforms).

23 Major reforms to regulations governing court dress took place in 684 under Emperor Ruizong, in 729 under Xuanzong, and in 791 under Dezong. *Tang Huiyao* records fifteen edicts, passed between 630 and 889, pertaining to the dress of court officials. See *Tang Huiyao*, 1:31–32.659–688.

24 Matthew Sommer has argued that "the guiding principle for the regulation of sexuality from at least the Tang through the early Qing Dynasty may be termed *status performance*: the assumption that one must perform the role conferred by a particular legal status." He extended the principle of status performance to sumptuary laws since they "imposed particular kinds of dress on different status groups, and adornment above one's station was a criminal offense." Sommer, *Sex, Law, and Society in Late Imperial China*, 6.

25 John Zou has claimed, "The generic writings of the *yufuzhi*, or 'records of carriages and garments,' in dynastic histories that covered nearly two millennia from the later Han to the Qing, bear testimony to the role a somewhat exaggerated concern with male dress played in

the political institutions of China's past. Sumptuary specifications regarding the color, kind, quality, patterns, cut, and combination of materials are the subject of detailed consideration in these texts and point to their grave relevance within the Confucian imperial order." Zou, "Cross-Dressed Nation," 79–97.

26 Catherine K. Killerby's study of medieval Italian sumptuary regulation provides an interesting contrast. She argues, "Men, by contrast, gained public recognition from their civil, professional, and military roles, and their elaborate clothing was easily justified by appeal to these same public roles" (114). Excessive ornamentation of women's dress, however, was equated with an unstable economy, decline in marriages, and falling birth rates. Killerby, *Sumptuary Law in Italy, 1200–1500*, see chap. 6.

27 One of the most cited arguments about sumptuary legislation, articulated by Arjun Appadurai, emphasizes the role of "taste" as the mechanism of social regulation in a fashion system in contrast to fashionless societies devoted to "stable status displays" such as China. Appadurai, *The Social Life of Things*, 3–63.

28 Relevant works include: Frances E. Baldwin, *Sumptuary Legislation and Personal Regulation in England*; H. Freudenberger, "Fashion, Sumptuary Laws, and Business"; N. B. Harte, "State Control of Dress and Social Change in Pre-Industrial England"; Daniel Roche, *The Culture of Clothing: Dress and Fashion in the Ancien Regime*; and Alan Hunt, *Governance of the Consuming Passions*. Echoing Hunt and Roche, Eiko Ikegami, in her study of elite culture in Tokugawa Japan (1600–1868), has proposed that sumptuary legislation indicates a transitional period when money rather than inheritance becomes the chief determinant of one's social status. She suggests, "sumptuary laws can be understood as a form of hegemonic resistance from an aristocratic order attempting to freeze the structural changes taking place in society." Ikegami, *Bonds of Civility*, 258.

29 Martha Howell, for example, has argued that, "sumptuary legislation both created new meanings for clothing and helped give birth to the discourse of the modern self," by driving a new self-consciousness about clothing as external trappings of an interior "self" during an era of intensifying commerce. Howell, *Commerce before Capitalism in Europe*, 260.

30 Dieter Kuhn has claimed that "the idea of agriculture as the basis of the nation's wealth may have originated in the justified and permanent fear of bad harvests and famine, a source of danger to the rulers and the government. And it may have been the care about the people's welfare which brought about the idealistic view that production of agricultural goods and their consumption should be looked on favourably. The same view was certainly held for the products of spinning, reeling and peasant weaving, works which were regarded as belonging to agricultural activity. When the 'natural' balance was lost due to incompetence, extravagance or luxury, everything was bound to get into disorder." Kuhn, *Textile Technology: Spinning and Reeling*, 5.

31 Tamara Chin has described *Debate on Salt and Iron* as a "first century BCE manifesto for classicism as well as an anti-imperialist, anti-market call for a return to traditional hierarchies." Chin, *Savage Exchange*, 21.

32 See Chin's discussion of the use of *ben* and *mo* in the *Debates on Salt Iron* in *Savage Exchange*, 48–58; for her interpretation of "women's work" and the *Debates*, see 206–13.

33 Huan, *Yantie lun*, 24–25.

34 Ibid., 25–26.

35 On the relationship between court power and craft, see Helms, *Craft and the Kingly Ideal*. I thank Jacob Eyferth for introducing me to this work.

36 The Tang regulated the training of artisans who were recruited into the official workshops. Length of training was determined by the amount of work, which presumably referred to the

number of tasks involved in the particular craft and the degree of difficulty. Four years was the maximum, while forty days was the minimum. At the top of the hierarchy of crafts was metalwork. *Tang liudian*, 22:11b–12a.

37 See article 403, "Violation of Statutes on Residences, Carriages, Clothing, Utensils, and Goods" of the Miscellaneous Statutes. Zhangsun Wuji, *Tanglü shuyi*, 488.

38 The document exists as Documents P.3078 and S.4637. Printed in Yamamoto, *Tun-huang and Turfan Documents*, 1:35.

39 *Jiu Tangshu*, 51:2167–9. See Kroll, "The Life and Writings of Xu Hui (627–650)," 35–64.

40 *Jiu Tangshu*, 51:2168.

41 Kroll makes the same claim about the inclusion of the petition in the official history. Kroll, "The Life and Writings of Xu Hui (627–650)," 62.

42 In 709 Wei Sili (654–719) submitted a memorial, petitioning Emperor Zhongzong (r. 705–710) to reduce the size of individual fiefs ("Memorial on reducing the size of lavish fiefs"). Wei claimed that more than 600,000 adult male taxpayers (*ding*) were assigned to the fiefs. With each adult male producing two bolts of tax silk, the fiefs collected more than 1.2 million bolts per year—significantly more than the Court of the Treasury. See *Quan Tangwen*, 236:2383.

43 Alternate title: "Imperial decree to burn jade, pearl, *jin*, and embroidered articles." *Quan Tangwen*, 254:2572; See also: *Cefu yuangui*, 1:56.72; *Wenyuan yinghua*, 465:2376; *Xin Tangshu*, 5:123; *Tang da zhaoling*, 108:516; *Zizhi tongjian*, 211:6702.

44 Xuanzong's edict erroneously attributes the decree to Emperor Wen (r. 180–157 BCE) of the Han dynasty. According to the *Standard History of the [Former] Han* (Hanshu), Emperor Jing instituted the ban on gold, pearls, and jade in the fourth month of 142 BCE with the declaration, "Carved ornaments and chiseled engravings are harmful to agriculture. *Jin* silks, embroidery, and vermillion silk ribbons are harmful to women's work. Injury to agriculture is the root of hunger; injury to women's work is the source of suffering from cold." *Hanshu*, 1.5.151.

45 Alternate title: "Prohibition on jade, pearl, *jin*, and embroidered articles." See *Quan Tangwen*, 26:300; *Cefu yuangui*, 56:72, 60:296; *Tang Huiyao*, 31:665; *Tang da zhaoling*, 108:516; *Zizhi tongjian*, 211:6702. On the second edict, see, See *Wenyuan yinghua*, 465:2375–76; *Tang da zhaoling*, 109.517; *Quan Tangwen*, 253:2556.

46 "Decree forbidding extravagance," see *Cefu yuangui*, 159:32; *Quan Tangwen*, 35:383–84.

47 Li Chui's tomb had not been robbed and is one of the few undisturbed Tang dynasty tombs to have been excavated. Shaanxi Provincial Institute of Archaeology et al., "Tang Li Chui mu fajue jianbao," 3–22; Greiff et al., The *Tomb of Li Chui*.

48 The Metropolitan Museum of Art in New York has ornaments in its collection, dated to the Tang dynasty, which may have also been used for these hanging bands. See accession nos. 20.38.1–20.38.3, and 20.38.6.

49 Gold and silver vessels and ornaments were made at an unprecedented scale in the Tang, a result of the mining of gold and silver in Lingnan circuit and the Annan protectorate (modern Guangdong, Guangxi, and Yunnan) and the migration of Sogdian artisans. See Schafer, *Golden Peaches of Samarkand*, 222–49 (Jewels) and 250–57 (Metals). On gold and silver, see Yang Yuan, *Tangdai de kuangchan*.

50 The size of tomb figurines (*yong*) was also subject to regulations. Figurines representing supernatural beings were not to exceed one *chi* (about 30 cm), whereas attendants, ceremonial guards, and musicians were restricted to seven *cun* (about 20 cm). Excavated figurines from elite tombs show that these regulations were consistently transgressed. *Tang liudian*, 23:18b–19a.

51 The epitaph is transcribed and translated in Greiff et al., The *Tomb of Li Chui*, 6–7. See also Li Ming, "Zhuan muzhi yu jinhua guan—'Tang Li muzhi' xuhou," 64–67.

52 See, for example, the recently excavated epitaph of Shangguan Wan'er, famous for her literary skills, patronage by Wu Zetian, and involvement in court intrigue that resulted in her death. Her literary talent is extolled through the metaphor of weaving. For an English translation of the full text, see Rothschild, "'Her Influence Great, Her Merit beyond Measure,'" 131–48.

53 See Twitchett, "Lands under State Cultivation under the T'ang," 162–203.

54 Xuanzong also made large payments of silk to the Khitan and the Qay between 720 and 732 as compensation for frontier defense and their military services against the Türk khanates of Mongolia. The largest recorded amount was 710,000 bolts paid to the Khitans in 720. See Skaff, *Sui-Tang China*, 256–58.

55 *Tang liudian*, 3:42b–46a.

56 *Quan Tangwen*, 35:387.

57 *Tang liudian*, 3:48a.

58 Compare with the Zhenguan period (627–649)—in 639, the number of households totaled three million and the population was about thirteen million. See Fei, *Tangdai renkou dili*, 39.

59 *Tongdian*, 6:111.

60 Ibid.

61 "For this expense: the purchase of rice and grains totaled 3.6 million bolts of cloth [Commentary: Shuofang and Hexi circuits, each 800,000; Longyou, 1 million; Yixi, Peiting, 80,000; Anxi, 120,000; Hedong commandery and pasture lands, each 400,000]. Provisioning of clothing totaled 5.2 million bolts [Commentary: Shuofang, 1.2 million; Longyou, 1.5 million; Hexi, 1 million; Yixi and Beiting, each 400,000; Anxi, 500,000; Hedong commandery, 400,000; pasture lands, 200,000]." See *Tongdian*, 6:111.

62 Pelliot no. 3348, Bibliothèque nationale de France. The document includes prices for each category of silk, including price per bolt and the total cost. For example: one bolt of plain silk was worth about 465 *wen* (coins), 5,600 bolts cost 2,604 *guan* (strings of coin; one guan equaled one thousand coins); one bolt of ribbed silk from Henan was worth about 620 *wen*, 550 bolts equaled 341 *guan*; and one bolt of dyed red silk was priced at 550 *wen*, 270 bolts cost 148 *guan* and 500 *wen*. See also Ikeda, *Chūgoku kodai sekichō kenkyū*, 463–66.

63 See Takahashi, "Tōdai orimono kōgyo zakkō," 341–59; Satō Taketoshi, "Tōdai ni okeru kinu-orimono no sanchi," 57–87.

64 A portion of this amount also paid the salaries of officials and the cost of the postal relay service in distant small prefectures. See *Tongdian*, 6:111.

65 Twitchett, "Merchant, Trade, and Government in Late T'ang," 75–76.

66 Monopoly taxes on salt and iron were first implemented under Emperor Wu (r. 140–87 BCE) of the Han.

67 See *Jiu Tangshu*, 195:5207; see also Beckwith, "The Impact of the Horse and Silk Trade," 187; and Mackerras, "Sino-Uighur Diplomatic and Trade Contacts," 215–40.

68 In 809 under Xianzong's command, Bai Juyi sent a letter to the Uyghur khagan complaining of a recently conducted horse-silk trade transaction: 500,000 bolts of plain tabby silk in exchange for 20,000 horses. Bai's letter states that having paid 250,000 bolts of silk for 6,500 horses (approximately 38.5 bolts per horse), the government could not afford an additional 250,000 for the remaining horses. See Mackerras, "Sino-Uighur Diplomatic and Trade Contacts," 219; cf. *Quan Tangwen*, 665:6759–60.

69 *Jiu Tangshu*, 11:298; see also *Quan Tangwen*, 47:518, *Tang da zhaoling*, 109:519; *Cefu yuangui*, 64:317.

70 The shafts mechanically raised warp threads for patterning, reducing labor-time in the production of complex weaves. See Sheng, "Determining the Value of Textiles," 184–88.

71 No figures exist for how long it took weavers to produce plain or complex silks in the Tang. In the Song dynasty, it took an artisan working in an imperial manufacture at Runzhou (Zhenjiang, Jiangsu) about twelve days to weave a bolt (twelve meters) of *luo*-gauze silk. See Sheng, "Textile Use, Technology, and Change in Rural Textile Production in Song China (960–1279)," 61. Another estimate of a skilled weaver's productivity can be found in the seventh-century compendium *Ten Classics of Mathematics* (*Suanjing shishu*), presented to the throne by Li Chunfeng (602–670) in 656. The text, *Zhang Qiujian Suanjing* (The mathematical classic of Zhang Qiujian), dated to the fifth century, claimed that a good weaver can produce nine *pi* and three *zhang* of plain silk cloth in a month. Cited in Zhao Feng, *Tangdai sichou yu sichou zhi lu*, 19. See also Yong, "*Zhang Qiujian Suanjing* (The mathematical classic of Zhang Qiujian)," 201–40.

72 Twitchett has argued that Daizong's edict of 771 was prompted by the inability of the post-rebellion government to manipulate silk prices and maintain the stable value of silk as a medium of currency. He claimed that "it was the currency function of silk cloth which lay behind the continual efforts of the government to preserve standard size, weave and quality of cloth presented as tax." Twitchett, "Provincial Autonomy and Central Finance in Late T'ang," 228, cf. 62.

73 According to Du You's estimates, there were only 1.3 million registered households by the middle of the Dali reign period. *Tongdian*, 7:157; see also Ikeda, "T'ang Household Registers and Related Documents," 121–50.

74 The supplementary taxes included green sprout tax (*qingmiao jian*), acreage tax (*ditou jian*), and household levy (*hushui*). Twitchett, *Financial Administration*, 37–39.

75 *Jiu Tangshu*, 18.3420–3422; also transmitted in *Tang Huiyao*, 83:1819–1820; *Cefu yuangui*, 488:2568–2569. For the "Act of Grace" (780), see *Cefu yuangui*, 89:466 and 488:2568; *Jiu Tangshu*, 12:324; *Tang Huiyao*, 78:1679–80, 83:1818–19; 780 edict recorded in *Cefu yuangui*, 162:353; *Tang da zhaoling*, 104:488; Twitchett, *Financial Administration*, 24–48.

76 *Cefu yuangui*, 169:895.

77 See *Tang Huiyao*, 84:1830–33; *Cefu yuangui*, 501:2644–45.

78 Lu states that one length of tax silk was fixed at 3,230 cash in 780; by 794, it had decreased to 1,560 cash. Following these calculations, in 780 three lengths of plain silk tabby was equivalent to ten thousand cash, and in 794 six lengths added up to that amount. See Lu's memorial, "Six-point proposal to reform taxation for the relief of the people," *Lu Xuan Gong ji*, 3:22.3a and 6b.

79 Three new decrees were promulgated in 804, 811, and 830. Twitchett, *Financial Administration*, 46–47. See also Twitchett, "Provincial Autonomy and Central Finance in Late T'ang," 228–30.

80 Lu maintained that under the twice-a-year tax, "those who deal in commerce and who wander the land constantly escape their share of the tax burden, while those who dedicate themselves to the fundamental profession [of agriculture] and set up permanent homes are continually hard-pressed to meet ever-increasing demands. This, then, will tempt the people to become crafty, and compel them to shirk their work. It is inevitable that productivity decline, customs degenerate, villages and towns deteriorate, and tax collections diminish." *Lu Xuan Gong ji*, 3:22.2b.

81 See *Cefu yuangui*, 504:2665; *Tang Huiyao*, 86:1874.

82 Twitchett, "Merchant, Trade and Government in Late T'ang," 94.

83 See Huang Zhengjian, *Zhongwan Tangdai shehui yu zhengzhi yanjiu*, 268–335.

84 Twitchett, ed., *The Cambridge History of China*, 3:28–31.

85 Twitchett has stressed that the breakdown of the controlled market system "is significant also in the history of Chinese fiscal institutions and economic theory. The abandonment by the government of their attempts to preserve a rigid and direct control over prices and markets coincides with the relaxation, in the late eighth and ninth centuries, of the extreme physiocratic theories which had led all administrations to adopt a generally repressive and hostile attitude toward trade and industry" ("The T'ang Market System," 205).

86 In 707, the central government banned the establishment of markets that did not have county or prefectural status. See *Tang Huiyao*, 2:86.1874. Bao Weimin has argued that the edict of 707 was intended to control the number of market officials and not the number of markets to bolster his larger claim that the Tang state did not institute rigid control over the markets. Bao, "Tangdai shizhi zai lun," 179–89.

87 See Wu Jianguo, "Tangdai shichang guanli zhidu yanjiu," 72–79; Kato, "Tang Song shidai de caoshi ji qi fazhan," 310–36.

88 From Li Hua (715–766), "Note on the Wall of the Hall of the Hangzhou Prefect," dated 765. *Wenyuan yinghua*, 800:4233.

89 Twitchett claimed that the term *caoshi* was only in use in northern and central China, whereas *xushi* was more common in the south. "The T'ang Market System," 234.

90 "Emperor Xuanzong, Dazhong reign period, fifth year, eighth month (851) decreed: 'In districts with three thousand and above households, one official and two deputies will be assigned to supervise the markets. [Districts that] do not reach three thousand and above households are prohibited from establishing markets." See *Cefu yuangui*, 3:504.2665.

91 Twitchett, "The T'ang Market System," 232–33.

92 *Lüdai* constituted a form of miscellaneous tax (*zashui*), in which the property and finances of wealthy merchants and affluent families were taxed 20 percent. *Jiu Tangshu*, 48:2087; *Tongdian*, 1:11.250; *Xin Tangshu*, 6:175. See also, Zhang, *Tangdai gongshang ye*, 405–6.

93 *Zizhi tongjian*, 227:7325–7326.

94 See Zhang Zexian, *Tangdai gongshang ye*, 409–17. Xue, "Lun Sui Tang Chang'an shangren," 69–75.

95 *Taiping guangji*, 243:1875–1879. See also Ning, "Lun Tangdai Chang'an linglei shangren yu shichang fayu," 71–78.

96 *Kaiyuan Tianbao yishi*, 17.

97 *Kaiyuan Tianbao yishi*, 37.

98 "During the Tang, He Mingyuan of Dingzhou had a great fortune. He was in charge of three government relay stations. Next to each station, he erected an inn to house merchants, solely to make a profit off of foreign [*hu*] merchants. His property and wealth exceeded tens of thousands. He owned five hundred looms for the weaving of twill damask in his house." See *Taiping Guangji*, 243:1875.

99 Zhang Zexian, *Tangdai gongshang ye*, 105 and 208. See also Du Wenyu, "Lun Tangdai guyong laodong," 40–45.

100 "In the eighth year [of the Dali reign period], in the first month, it was decreed: all laborers and craftsmen who would rather pay a levy in lieu of corvée service, must each pay two-thousand cash every month." *Cefu yuangui* 1984, 2:487.2568; See also Xue, "Lun Sui Tang shangren," 69.

101 Nicolas Tackett has shown that for a significant sector of provincial society in the late Tang, the accumulation of land and commercial wealth was equivalent to attaining bureaucratic office. Tackett has also proposed that in southern Hebei, the lower Yangzi, and the cities and towns along the Yongji Canal (Hebei) and Grand Canal, it was possible for private individuals

to accumulate substantial wealth owing to the smaller government and military presence. Compared to the capital and border regions, there were fewer representatives of the state who could forcibly acquire local resources for their own use in these regions. Tackett, "Great Clansmen, Bureaucrats, and Local Magnates," 113–14.

102 Han Yu wrote an essay in 803 claiming that the examinations and imperial university were full of the sons of rich merchants and artisans. Cited in Twitchett, "Merchant, Trade and Government in Late T'ang," 92–93.

103 *Jiu Tangshu*, 13:371. In *Tang Huiyao*, the decree is dated to the third year of the Zhenyuan reign period (787): "Zhenyuan, third year, third month, newly fabricated *shifu* [seasonal dress] was bestowed upon the military and surveillance commissioners. . . . That same year, in the eleventh month, on the ninth day, it was decreed that officials who attend regular court audiences must wear *ling*-twill robes with gold and jade belts. Up until the eleventh month of the eighth year, grand *ling*-twill robes were conferred upon civil and military officials who were in regular court attendance." See *Tang Huiyao*, 32:681.

104 *Tang Huiyao*, 59:1192.

105 The edict opens with the following premise, "Dress and carriages, utensils and buildings, have diverged considerably from the dictates of frugality and extravagance in recent times." *Quan Tangwen*, 70:743; see also *Tang Huiyao*, 31:668.

106 *Jiu Tangshu*, 17:545.

107 *Jiu Tangshu*, 17:546; *Quan Tangwen*, 448:4579–81.

108 *Cefu yuangui*, 61:299; *Quan Tangwen*, 72:757, and 448:4579–81; *Tang Huiyao*, 31:668–72.

109 "Princes of the first rank [of royal blood] to those of rank three, as well as enfeoffed descendants of the previous two dynasties [*er wanghou*], dress in the color purple with ornaments of jade. Rank five and up [to rank four] dress in red with ornaments of gold. Rank seven and up [to rank six] dress in green with ornaments of silver. Rank nine and up [to rank eight] dress in blue with ornaments of brass." See *Tang Huiyao*, 31:668.

110 "Officials without rank and commoners dress in yellow with ornaments of copper and iron." *Tang Huiyao*, 31:669.

111 "The trains of robes, outer cloaks, tunics, and so on, are not to exceed two *cun* in length. Sleeves are not to exceed one *chi* and three *cun* in width." *Tang Huiyao*, 31:669.

112 "The cut of women's skirts cannot be wider than five *fu*. The train of the skirt cannot exceed three *cun* in length. The sleeves of the jacket cannot exceed one *chi* and five *cun* in width." *Tang Huiyao*, 31:669. Calculations are taken from Sun Ji, who based his estimates on the measurements of bolts of cloth provided in the "Shihuo zhi" [Treatise on food and goods] from the *Jiu Tangshu*. Sun also mentions references to skirts composed of 7 or 8 *fu*, which would have measured 3.71 meters and 4.24 meters, respectively. See Sun Ji, *Zhongguo gudai yufu luncong*, 226.

113 See *Quan Tangwen*, 448:580.

114 *Xin Tangshu*, 24:532.

115 Wenzong ordered, "The princess entered court, wearing clothes that violated the regulations. In accordance with the principle of 'the wife must follow her husband,' her husband will be punished for her transgressions. Dou Huan will forfeit two months' salary" (*Jiu Tangshu*, 17:576).

116 "Kaicheng reign period, fourth year, second month: Li Deyu, surveillance commissioner of Huainan, submitted a memorial: 'The women in my circuit, their sleeves were wider than four *chi* at first, now I have ordered that they be one *chi* and five *cun* wide; the trains of skirts were four or five *cun* at the beginning, now I have ordered that they be reduced by five *cun*.' The emperor followed [his counsel]." *Tang Huiyao*, 31:673.

117 Huang Zhengjian has argued that Wenzong's regulation of dress and vehicles directly

addressed the structural changes in late Tang society, demonstrating the government's awareness of the shift from a capital-based court society to a bureaucratic society grounded in the ranking of officials. Wenzong's reform of 832 was the final attempt to restore the vertical relationship between the emperor and his officials through the standardization of official dress. See Huang Zhengjian, *Zhongwan Tangdai shehui yu zhengzhi yanjiu*, 307–11; Huang, "Wang Ya zouwen yu Tang houqi chefu zhidu de bianhua," 297–327.

118 See, for example, Ditter, "The Commerce of Commemoration," 21–46; Ditter, "Civil Examinations and Cover Letters in the Mid-Tang," 642–74; Nugent, *Manifest in Words, Written on Paper*; Shi, "'My Tomb Will Be Opened in Eight Hundred Years,'" 217–57.

119 Dagmar Schäfer has made a similar argument about the Ming court's relationship to craft production: "During the Ming period, emperors and scholars had full confidence in their rights to silk and their knowledge about it. They felt in line with a cultural tradition when they used the symbols and styles of clothing of their predecessors as a symbol for social status and political power. The Ming rulers relied on their hegemonial power and rights when they exerted pressure on artisanal production in their Southern provinces." (Schäfer, "Silken Strands," 50).

120 *Jiu Tangshu*, 174:4513–14; *Xin Tangshu*, 180:5329.

3. STYLE: FASHIONING THE TANG BEAUTY

1 "The Fashions Change in China Just as They Do Here," *New York Times*, Aug. 3, 1913, SM9.

2 Du Halde, *Description géographique, historique, chronologique, politique, et physique de l'empire de la Chine et la Tartarie chinoise* (1735).

3 From the preface to the original French edition. Ann Waltner has speculated that the sources for Humblot's drawings were export illustrations produced in Canton. Waltner, "Les Noces Chinoises: An Eighteenth-Century French Representation," 21–40.

4 Braudel, *The Structures of Everyday Life*, 312.

5 Nagel, "Fashion and the Now-Time of Renaissance Art," 32–52.

6 Anne Hollander has stressed that when viewing works of art to understand the construction of clothing, one must take into account the formal properties governing their depiction, arguing that "formal properties offer different but even more important evidence about changing assumptions and habits of actual seeing, and so of visual self-awareness. Such formal elements demonstrate not how clothes were made but how they and the bodies in them were supposed and believed to look" (Hollander, *Seeing through Clothes*, xii).

7 Examples of scholarship that treat pictorial sources as eyewitness accounts of sartorial change include Shen, *Zhongguo gudai fushi yanjiu*; Zhou and Gao, *Zhongguo lidai fushi*; Zhou Xibao, *Zhongguo gudai fushi shi*; Na, *Tangdai fushi shishang*.

8 Famous paintings of court ladies attributed to well-known Tang dynasty painters include: *Bunian tu* (Emperor Taizong receiving the Tibetan Envoy or The sedan chair), attributed to Yan Liben (d. 673); *Guoguo furen youchun tu* (Spring outing of the court ladies) and *Daolian tu* (Court ladies preparing newly woven silk) attributed to Zhang Xuan (ca. 710–748); *Zanhua shinü tu* (Court ladies pinning their hair with flowers), *Huishan shinü tu* (Court ladies waving fans), and *Neiren shuanglu tu* (Palace ladies playing double sixes) attributed to Zhou Fang (ca. 730–800); and *Gongzhong tu* (In the palace) attributed to Zhou Wenju (active late tenth century). For Dunhuang murals, see Duan Wenjie, ed., *Zhongguo meishu quanji 14, 15: Huihua bian Dunhuang bihua*.

9 The relevant Tang dynasty tomb sites (with the excavation report) include: Princess Changle (dated 643), see Zhaoling Museum, "Tang Zhaoling Changle gongzu mu"; Duan Jianbi

(dated 651), see Zhaoling Museum, "Tang Zhaoling Duan Jianbi mu qingli jianbao"; Princess Xincheng (dated 663), see Shaanxi Provincial Institute of Archaeology et al., "Tang Zhaoling Xincheng zhanggongzhu mu fajue jianbao"; Zheng Rentai (dated 664), see Shaanxi Provincial Museum et al., "Tang Zheng Rentai mu fajue jianbao"; Princess Fangling (dated 673), see An Zhengdi, "Tang Fangling da zhanggongzhu mu qingli jianbao"; Ashina Zhong (dated 675), see Shaanxi Provincial Cultural Relics Bureau et al., "Tang Ashina Zhong mu fajue jianbao"; Xue Yuanchao (dated 685), see Yang Zhengxing (Qianling Museum), "Tang Xue Yuanchao mu de sanfu bihua jieshao"; Princess Yongtai (dated 706), see Shaanxi Provincial Cultural Relics Bureau, "Tang Yongtai gongzhu mu fajue jianbao"; Prince Yide (dated 706), see Shaanxi Provincial Museum et al., "Tang Yide taizi mu fajue jianbao"; Prince Zhanghuai (dated 706), see Shaanxi Provincial Museum et al., "Tang Zhanghuai taizi mu fajue jianbao"; Prince Jiemin (dated 710), see Shaanxi Provincial Institute of Archaeology et al., *Tang Jiemin taizi mu fajue baogao*; Prince Huizhuang (dated 724), see Shaanxi Provincial Institute of Archaeology et al., "Tang Huizhuang taizi mu fajue jianbao"; Princess Jinxiang (dated 724), see Wang Zili and Sun Fuxi, *Tang Jinxiang xianzhu mu*; Princess Tang'an (dated 784), see Chen Anli and Ma Yongzhong, "Xi'an Wangjiafen Tangdai Tang'an gongzhu mu"; Astana Tomb 38 (latter half of the eighth century), see Xinjiang Uyghur Autonomous Region Museum, "Tulufan xian Asitana-Hala hezhuo gumu qun fajue jianbao"; Wang Chuzhi (dated 924), see Hebei Province Research Institute of Cultural Relics, *Wudai Wang Chuzhi mu*.

10 See Hay, "Seeing through Dead Eyes," 16–54.

11 Wu Hung has claimed that the substitution of figurines for human sacrifices also gave rise to the practice of painting murals in tombs. Wu, *The Art of the Yellow Springs*, 100.

12 Fraser, *Performing the Visual*, 104n73.

13 Li Xingming, *Tangdai mushi bihua yanjiu*, 253. The excavation report on Xincheng's tomb also provides a brief description of the painting protocol. Shaanxi Provincial Institute of Archaeology, *Tang Xincheng zhang gongzhu mu fajue baogao*, 74.

14 Mural paintings found in a tomb in Gansu suggest that the striped skirt dates back to the fourth or fifth centuries CE. The stripes or panels in these early representations are wider than what has been found in Tang murals. See Sun Ji, *Zhongguo gudai yufu*, 224.

15 Robert Thorp has suggested that the figures of women and servants were "ornaments tied to the status of others, marking the position of the deceased within the social and sumptuary hierarchy of the family." Thorp et al., *Chinese Art and Culture*, 195. Wu Hung, too, has claimed that "ancient Chinese tomb figures rarely, if at all, represented named individuals; what they were made to signify were certain general 'roles' considered essential to an ideal afterlife" (102). Claiming that "more than any other art form in traditional China, the tomb figurine is intimately linked with the notion of *verisimilitude*," Wu Hung has proposed two forms of "mimetic representation" that dictate the production of these figurines. The first is a sculptural program, in which the artisan directed sole attention to the external appearance of the figure such as bodily features, costume, and ornaments to signify the figure's gender, status, and social role. The production of doll-like figures with movable limbs and removable clothes to shift the focus onto the body underneath constitutes the second form of representation. The bulk of Tang dynasty pottery figurines belong to the first category. Wu, *The Art of the Yellow Springs*, 117–22.

16 In 712, Emperor Ruizong attempted to curb extravagant burials, citing the production of lifelike figurines (*yong*) as a transgression of Confucian ritual. *Jiu Tangshu*, 45:1958.

17 Medley, *T'ang Pottery and Porcelain* and *The Chinese Potter*; Eckfeld, *Imperial Tombs in Tang China*, 44–49.

18 Other figurines composed of a wooden body, miniaturized clothes, and ceramic heads have been excavated from the tomb of Zhang Xiong and Lady Qu. See the description in Cao and

Sun, eds., *Zhongguo gudai yong*, 264–67; "Figurine of a Eunuch" in Xinjiang Uyghur Autonomous Region Museum et al., *Gudai xiyu fushi xiecui*, 93; Xinjiang Uyghur Autonomous Region Museum, *Xinjiang Uyghur Autonomous Region Museum* [catalogue], see plate nos. 119–21.

19 Qi Dongfang has made the same observation about the decorative treatment of the figurines. See Qi, "Tang yong yu funü shenghuo," 333.

20 Hot wax is applied to the textile either by a patterned stamp or a pointed tool as a resist, so that the areas covered retain the original color of the fabric and the uncovered areas absorb the dye. This was a simple technique for creating basic floral and geometric patterns.

21 See Medley, *The Chinese Potter*, 34. Examples of *sancai* glaze and resist decoration are beautifully reproduced in S. J. Vainker, *Chinese Pottery and Porcelain.*

22 On the relationship between *sancai* and Central Asian metalwork techniques, see Rawson, "Inside Out," 25–45.

23 Chinese scholars have argued that this was largely due to the fact that the founding family of the Tang dynasty was of foreign-blood, favored martial culture, and thus preferred foreign dress and adornment. Kate Lingley has refuted this, claiming that by the Tang, these styles of dress were no longer marked as foreign, but instead had become linked to gender. Rong, "Nü ban nanzhuang," 740; Lingley, "Naturalizing the Exotic," 50–80.

24 Foreign dance (*huwu*), wind instruments (*hudi*), food (*hufan*), and furniture were imported alongside foreign attire. See Xiang, *Tangdai Chang'an yu Xiyu wenming.*

25 Rong Xinjiang has argued that during the early Tang dynasty, *hu* (胡) was mainly used to refer to peoples belonging to the Sasanid Persian empire, who had settled along the trade route in Central Asia—namely, Sogdians. Rong, "Nü ban nanzhuang," 740.

26 See Qi Dongfang's discussion of the gendering of Tang dynasty tomb figures. Qi and Zhang, "Tang mu bihua yu Gaosong zhong gufen bihua de bijiao yanjiu," 458.

27 Cahill, "Ominous Dress," 221–22.

28 *Jiu Tangshu*, 45:1958. *New Standard History of the Tang* offers a different date for the popularity of topknots, boots, and men's coats. The compilers instead linked the trend to the other infamous woman of the dynasty—Wu Zetian: "During the reign of Empress Wu, the *weimao* was exceptionally popular. After Zhongzhong, no one wore the *mili* again. The palace women and the emperor's attendants all wore *hu* hats to ride horses and all within the empire imitated this. Then the women exposed their hair, tied in topknots, to go horse riding and the *weimao* was abandoned. They dressed in men's robes and boots, similar to the dress of the Xi and Khitans" (*Xin Tangshu*, 24:529).

29 *Jiu Tangshu*, 45:1958.

30 See Abramson, *Ethnic Identity in Tang China*, 3–4.

31 *Xin Tangshu*, 24:529.

32 Zheng Rentai was buried in the Zhaoling Mausoleum, the imperial burial grounds of Emperor Taizong. Since Emperor Gaozong decreed that his tomb be built in Zhaoling, it is likely that the figurines and other furnishings were produced in the imperial workshops. Shaanxi Provincial Museum et al., "Tang Zheng Rentai mu fajue jianbao," 33–42.

33 Rong Xinjiang has cataloged the murals and figures of cross-dressing women in Tang dynasty tombs, showing that the majority of these images are distributed between the years 643 and 745. See chart in Rong, "Nü ban nanzhuang," 729–30.

34 In addition to Suzanne Cahill's groundbreaking essay, scholars in the U.S. and China have argued that the Tang dynasty was "fashionable" (*shishang*). This scholarship, however, does not provide a critical look into how Tang dress and adornment amounted to fashion beyond the paradigm of changing clothes. See Cahill, "Our Women Are Acting Like Foreigners'

Wives!"; Schafer, *Golden Peaches of Samarkand*; Huang Zhengjian, *Tangdai yishi zhuxing yanjiu*.

35 Zhang's *Record of Famous Painters of Successive Dynasties* is divided into ten sections (*juan*) with three sections devoted to discussions on the origins of painting, styles of painting, transmission of techniques from masters to pupils, collecting and connoisseurship, signatures and seals, and temple wall-paintings. The following seven sections provide short biographies of documented artists from the time of the Yellow Emperor through the Tang dynasty.

36 Translations from this text are based on William Acker with slight modifications. Zhang Yanyuan, *Lidai minghua ji*, 65; Acker, *Some T'ang and Pre-T'ang Texts*, 170.

37 Zhang Yanyuan, *Lidai minghua ji*, 65; Acker, *Some T'ang and Pre-T'ang Texts*, 170.

38 Zhang, *Lidai minghua ji*, 66; Acker, *Some T'ang and pre-T'ang Texts*, 173.

39 This was also articulated by the sixth-century scholar-critic, Yao Zui (535–602), who anticipated Zhang's emphasis on accuracy when he remarked on Xie He's (479–502) figure paintings, "Their festive robes and cosmetics changed according to the times, and he made straight eyebrows or curved forehead locks to suit the latest fashion," in *Xuhua pinlu* (Continuation of the classification of painters). Translated in Susan Bush and Hsio-yen Shih, eds., *Early Chinese Texts on Painting*, 31. Alexander Nagel has highlighted a similar relationship between perceptions about dress and attention to artistic style in the context of Renaissance painting. In his discussion on the intrusion of secular "now-time" (*jetztzeit*) into religious art, he noted that Renaissance treatises on painting—including Filanete (1464), Lodovico Dolce (1557), and Leonardo da Vinci (1650s)—likewise advised that garments of religious figures should be in "keeping with their age." Nagel, "Fashion and the Now-Time of Renaissance Art," 32–52.

40 Acker, *Some T'ang and pre-T'ang Texts*, 149–50.

41 Ibid.

42 In Yang Guifei's biography in *Old Standard History of the Tang*, she is described as "plump and beautiful in appearance and substance." See *Jiu Tangshu*, 52:2178. Wu Hung also insisted that "from 745 to 756 the most powerful figure in the country was Yang Guifei, Minghuang's celebrated consort and the most famous femme fatale in Chinese history. It is said that the fashion of portraying portly women owed much to Yang's well-known corpulence. Although this contention is questionable because such figures had appeared in the early eighth century and even before then, Yang Guifei did embody the very essence of this imagery and signify its culmination. As she came to dominate not only Chang'an high society but also contemporary male fantasy, a stereotyped palace lady developed into a cultural icon" (Barnhart et al., *Three Thousand Years of Chinese Painting*, 75).

43 Shaanxi Provincial Museum et al., "Tang Zhanghuai taizi mu fajue jianbao," 13–25.

44 Eckfeld interprets the scenes of women idling in the courtyard as having been tailored to reflect the life of Consort Fang, arguing that, "it emphasizes 'womanly virtue' through the recreation of what was thought to be the ideal domestic arrangement of Chinese palaces at the time" (Eckfeld, *Imperial Tombs in Tang China*, 44–49).

45 Li Xingming, *Tangdai mushi bihua yanjiu*, 282. The tomb of Prince Jiemin, constructed in 710, is an exception. Murals of women dressed in meticulously detailed black-and-white and green-and-black skirts, as well as patterned shawls and blouses adorn the walls. See plate nos. 95, 96.1, 105, 118, 120.1, 128, and 129 in Han and Zhang, eds., *Shaanxi xin chutu Tang mu bihua*; Shaanxi Provincial Institute of Archaeology, *Tang Jiemin taizi mu fajue baogao*.

46 Vincent makes an important case for critically reading the changes in vestimentary history, proposing: "The structure of garments and their techniques of assemblage and wear have certain implications for both the body within, and its relationship to other bodies, and to space. It is not enough to state merely that breeches were full or bodices were corseted, for this

distension and constriction meant something for the wearer, and influenced not only physical behaviours, but also such intangibles as perceptions of beauty, grace and health" (Vincent, *Dressing the Elite*, 29).

47 Zhang Yanyuan in *Record of Famous Painters of Successive Dynasties* distinguishes between detailed and sketchy brushwork using the terms *su* and *mi*. In book 2 of *Record of Famous Painters*, Zhang recalls a past conversation on the brushwork of Gu (Kaizhi), Lu (Tanwei), Zhang (Sengyou), and Wu (Daozi), in which he privileges the *su* over the *mi* style of painting: "The divine quality of Gu and Lu is that one cannot see the ends of the strokes, which is what you call 'thorough and exact brush-work.' But the subtle virtue of Zhang and Wu is that with one or two strokes, the image is already reflected. They left spaces between dots and strokes, and sometimes one sees breaks and omissions (in the lines). In these places, though the stroke may be incomplete, yet the intention is fully carried out. Only when you realize that there are two styles of painting, the free and the detailed, may you join in discussions about paintings." Translated by Acker, *Some T'ang and pre-T'ang Texts*, 183–84; Zhang, *Lidai minghua ji*, 71. Susan Bush and Hiso-yen Shih translate *su* and *mi* as "sparse" and "dense." Bush and Shih, *Early Chinese Texts on Painting*, 62. Also see Sarah Fraser's discussion on the practice of artistic sketching in the Tang dynasty and the influence of Wu Daozi. Fraser, *Performing the Visual*, 197–206.

48 Wu Hung has argued that the development of "the screen with women's images" was a shift from narrative to portraiture and, in turn, allowed the external viewer to claim a direct relation to the beauty. Wu, *The Double Screen*, 99.

49 See Zhao and Wang, "Chang'an xian nanliwangcun Tang mu bihua," 3–9.

50 Jonathan Hay has advanced an alternative timeline of Chinese painting, arguing that the two-century period from 765 to 970 constituted a distinct stage in the development of painting, in which both format and genre underwent significant changes. Hay states, "Between 765 and 970, painters gradually shifted their attention from a hierarchical cataloguing of experience to an articulation of the interconnections that make experience of the world continuous" (303). This shift in pictorial representation can be seen in the conflation of themes, like in *Court Ladies Pinning Their Hair with Flowers*. For Hay, these ninth-century compositions suggest an epistemic shift: "a new understanding of the order of the world, in which the basic unit is no longer an atomized element belonging to a distinct category but instead a *relation* between elements that is at the same time a relation between categories" (305). Hay, "Tenth-Century Painting before Song Taizong's Reign," 285–318.

51 Zhang, *Lidai minghua ji*, 323; Acker, *Some T'ang and Pre-T'ang Texts*, 2:290. Hay has proposed that the artist may have been an official named Dou Xiao, active in the final years of the dynasty. Hay, "Margins, Transitions, Interstices."

52 Scholars have disagreed on the exact dating of this work. Yang Renkai, curator of the Liaoning Provincial Museum, has argued that the piece is an original Zhou Fang painting from the Zhenyuan reign period (785–805). Xu Shucheng, using textual sources on late Tang dress supports Yang's position. In the other camp, Sun Ji and Xie Zhiliu have attributed the painting to the Southern Tang, insisting that the dress, hair accessories, and foliage are native to the south. Other scholars, including Shen Congwen, have suggested that the painting is a Northern Song copy. Most recently, Li Xingming has argued that the painting should be attributed to a late Tang follower of Zhou Fang. Yang, "Dui 'Tang Zhou Fang *Zanhua shinü tu* de shangque' de yijian," 44–45; Yang, *Zanhua shinütu yanjiu*; Xu, "Cong *Wanshan Shinü tu*, *Zanhua shinü tu* luetan Tangren shinü hua," 71–75; Xie, "Tang Zhou Fang *Zanhua shinü tu* de shangque," 25–26; Sun Ji, *Zhongguo gudai yufu*, 224–52; Shen, *Zhongguo gudai fushi yanjiu*, 344–48; Li, "*Zanhua shinü tu* niandai lijian," 65–71.

53 *Palace Ladies Playing Double Sixes* (Neiren shuanglu tu) is another "palace women" painting attributed to Zhou.
54 Hay, "Margins, Transitions, Interstices."
55 The female donor figures in this hanging and in the early tenth-century hanging, *Avalokitesvara as Guide of Souls* may be renderings of the Zhou Fang style as interpreted by Zhou's early tenth-century followers, Ruan Zhihui (active ca. 919–937) and his son Ruan Weide (dates unknown). Hay, "Tenth-Century Painting before Song Taizong's Reign," 299.
56 See Kyan, "Family Space," 61–82.
57 Jonathan Hay has noted that the eleventh-century text, *Record of Famous Painters of Yizhou* (Yizhou minghua lu), by Huang Xiufu, identified historical figures or "old-style figures" as an established genre in the late Tang and Five Dynasties era. Hay, "Tenth-century Painting before Song Taizong's Reign," 309.
58 Hay has also put forward the view that the period from 764 to 976, roughly the era following the end of the An Lushan Rebellion and extending into the first decade of the Song dynasty, was a time when painters engaged in a process of "disentanglement" and "re-engagement." This double process was evident in how painters updated or adapted older compositions and themes that resulted in "a high degree of self-consciousness about style." Hay, "Margins, Transitions, Interstices."
59 Acker, *Some T'ang and Pre-T'ang Texts*, 210.
60 Ibid.

4. DESIGN: SILK AND THE LOGICS OF FASHION

1 Zheng Gu, "Two Stanzas on *Jin*" (Jin ershou), *Quan Tangshi*, 675:7738.
2 Schuyler Cammann first hypothesized that *kesi* derived from Uyghur tapestry weaving techniques. Anima Malagò has proposed three different theories for the origins of *kesi*, which also emphasizes connections with West and Central Asian weaving traditions. Most recently, Angela Sheng has suggested that Turfan was an important site for textile innovation as Han Chinese and Sogdians in the region exchanged weaving techniques and skills. *Kesi* might have emerged from imitating wool tapestry weaving techniques. See Cammann, "Notes on the Origin of Chinese K'ossu Tapestry," 90–110; Malagò, "The Origin of Kesi, the Chinese Silk Tapestry," 279–97; Sheng, "Chinese Silk Tapestry," 166–71; Sheng, "Addendum to 'Chinese Silk Tapestry'," 225; Sheng, "Innovations in Textile Techniques on China's Northwest Frontier, 500–700 AD," 117–60.
3 Edward Schafer has argued that the Tang empire functioned as an important intermediary for the dissemination of foreign textiles and motifs in Asia, claiming that, "the handsome T'ang fabrics preserved in the Shōsō-in and Hōryūji at Nara in Japan, and the almost identical ones found near Turfan in Central Asia, display the popular images, designs, and symbols of Sasanian Persia, usually thoroughly adapted to T'ang culture" (Schafer, *Golden Peaches of Samarkand*, 197).
4 Compiled from the section on "Shangshu Hubu" (Ministry of Revenue) in *Da Tang liudian*; cross-referenced with Lu Huayu, *Tangdai cansang sichou yanjiu*, 10. See *Tang Liudian*, 3:6a–26b.
5 Niida, *Tangdai ling shiyi*, 588. Also translated in Twitchett, *Financial Administration under the T'ang Dynasty*, see appendix 2.
6 According to this calculation, silk-producing regions of the empire would have added up to 37 million *mu* with 370 million mulberry trees in the Tianbao era. The annual production would have totaled 18.5 million bolts—meaning 8,500 tons of silk thread were produced from 1.32 billion tons of silk cocoons. Zhao Feng, *Tangdai sichou yu sichou zhi lu*, 13–22.

7 *Tongdian*, 6:108; *Xin Tangshu*, 48:1263. The standard loom width is believed to have corresponded with this measurement, but documents from Dunhuang and Turfan mention bolts of silks with larger widths. See Ikeda, *Chūgoku kodai sekichō kenkyū*, 211.

8 *Tongdian*, 6:108.

9 Wu Zhen, "Tulufan chutu wenshu zhong de sizhipin kaobian," 101.

10 "Any persons found to be selling utensils, articles for use, and silk and hempen cloth that are defective [*lan*], too short, or too narrow, will receive sixty blows with a heavy stick." *Tanglu shuyi jianjie*, 26.1860; Johnson, *The Tang Code*, vol. 2, *Specific Articles*, 26.480.

11 Zhu, *Zhongguo sichou shi*, 146.

12 See Sheng's discussion of silk nomenclature in "Determining the Value of Textiles in the Tang," 175–95.

13 Prior to 604, the Court of Treasury (Taifu Si) managed nongrain revenues and provisions for the palace. Following the establishment of the Directorate of Imperial Workshops, the Court of Treasury was transformed into a fiscal agency of the government. During the Tang dynasty, the agency managed storehouses and vaults, disbursed payments to officials, supervised trade in the marketplaces, and collected fees and taxes on mercantile transactions. See *Xin Tangshu*, 48:1263; *Jiu Tangshu*, 44:1889; and *Tang Liudian*, 22:18a–21a.

14 *New Standard History of the Tang* lists only nine workshops, which were: *jin*, complex gauze, open weave gauze, crêpe (*hu*), ling damask, coarse silk, mixed fabrics, plain tabby weave silk, and bast-fiber cloth. *Xin Tangshu*, 48:1271.

15 *Xin Tangshu*, 48:1269.

16 *Xin Tangshu*, 47:1221–1223; *Tongdian*, 1:27.755–757. Each time the women finished a warp-faced *jin* textile, wine and mutton were sacrificed.

17 Zhao Feng, *Zhongguo sichou tongshi*, 193.

18 See *Taiping Guangji*, 243:1875.

19 Lu Huayu has compiled a list of silk textiles produced for tribute for each region that compares the early period to the late period (post-An Lushan). Lu, *Tangdai cansang sichou yanjiu*, 24–27.

20 Jonathan Hay has made this argument about luxury and decoration, claiming that "the specialty item that came from afar—the decorative object as much as food or tea or wine—had a plus-value that derived from geographic separation" (Hay, *Sensuous Surfaces*, 42).

21 See "Dili zhi" (Treatise on Geography) in *Xin Tangshu*, 37–43:959–1157; and "Fushui" (Taxes), *Tongdian*, 6:106–41. According to the section "Shangshu Hubu" (Ministry of Revenue) in the *Da Tang liudian*, the metropolitan prefecture (*jingzhao*) including the capital, Chang'an, also produced plain tabby and silk floss for tax. See *Tang Liudian*, 3:7a. For a comprehensive list of tribute items for both the Kaiyuan and Yuanhe reign periods, see Li Jifu, *Yuanhe junxian tuzhi*, 2 vols. See also Satō, *Chūgoku kodai kinuorimonoshi kenkyū*, 2:311–20.

22 *Dansi luo* or "single-thread gauze" was presented to the court as annual tribute. According to the *Tongdian*, "Shu Commandery: offers as tribute—twenty bolts of single-thread gauze and twenty bolts of high-grade ramie; now [known as] Yizhou." See *Tongdian*, 6:125.

23 *Jiu Tangshu*, 105:3222–5; *Xin Tangshu*, 134:4560–2.

24 "Boling Commandery: offers as tribute—1,270 bolts of tabby silk patterned in twill [*xiling*], fifteen bolts of tabby with two pattern units in twill [*liangke xiling*], 255 bolts of twill damask with auspicious patterns [*ruiling*], twenty-five bolts of twill damask with one large pattern unit [*da duke ling*], and ten bolts of twill with single pattern unit; now [known as] Dingzhou." See *Tongdian*, 6:117.

25 Du Mu, "On the appointment of Li Na to Surveillance Commissioner of Zhedong and Chief Censor," *Quan Tangwen*, 748:7753.

26 Lu Huayu, *Tangdai cansang sichou yanjiu*, 72.

27 Du Mu, "Letter to the Chief Minister seeking [the Prefectship of] Hangzhou," *Quan Tangwen*, 753:7805–7806; *Fanchuan wenji*, 2 vols., 16:1067.

28 See "Dili zhi" (Treatise on geography) in *Xin Tangshu*, 37–43:959–1157; *Yuanhe junxian tuzhi*, 25–26:289–641. See also Zhu Zude, "Tangdai Yuezhou jingji fazhan tanxi," 21–42; and Wang Yongxing, "Shilun Tangdai si fangzhi ye de diqu fenbu," 288–90.

29 Zhu Zude, "Tangdai Yuezhou jingji fazhan tanxi," 40.

30 See Li Zhao, *Tang guoshi bu*, 65.

31 Shi Jianwu (780–861), "Miscellaneous Ancient-Style Lyrics" (Zagu ci), *Quan Tangshi*, 494:5588.

32 In Du Huan's record of his experience in Kufa, the capital of the Abbāsid empire, he noted that Tang goldsmiths and silversmiths, painters from Chang'an, and weavers from Hedong were employed there. Du was captured by the Abbāsid army after they defeated the Tang army at the Battle of Talas in 751, and lived in Kufa as a prisoner of war for ten years. Upon his release and return to the Tang, he wrote down his experiences. *Tongdian*, 193:5280.

33 Here, I follow Zhao Feng's and Wang Le's translation of the term. Zhao and Wang, "Glossary of Textile Terminology," 349–87.

34 The kidnapping of textile workers as booty was not a new phenomenon. During the Warring States period, the state of Chu brokered peace with the state on Lu on the condition of receiving as compensation one hundred weavers, tailors, and woodcarvers each. See *Chunqiu Zuozhuan zhu*, 2:807.

35 "Nanman zhuan" (Account of the southern barbarians), in *Jiu Tangshu*, 163:4264; *Xin Tangshu*, 222:6282; and *Zizhi tongjian*, 244:7868. On the Nanzhao, see Backus, *The Nan-Chao Kingdom and T'ang China's Southwestern Frontier.*

36 The court held Du Yuanying (769–833), the inept military commissioner of Xichuan (modern Sichuan), responsible for the Nanzhao invasion. His corrupt government had failed to supply the local troops with adequate provisions and consequently they had grown restive. Du's unceasing requisition of valuable manufactures had exhausted the people. The invasion met with little resistance and the "barbarian soldiers plundered the city of Shu, taking jade, silk, young men and women, and tools, and left." What is noteworthy in the *Old Standard History* account is the mention of craft tools (*gongqiao zhi ju*) and labor, in the form of young men and women, but not artisans. *Jiu Tangshu*, 163:4264.

37 See Fan Chuo (act. 860–873), *Manshu*, 30:336; *Xin Tangshu*, 222:6282.

38 Just fifty years before the 829 incursion, in 779, the Tibetans forged an alliance with the Nanzhao to mount a massive invasion into Sichuan. In the biography of Cui Ning, commander of the Tang troops, the Tibetan king is recorded having declared, "I want to make Sichuan our eastern prefecture. Skilled artisans will all be taken to Lhasa, where each will be levied no more than one piece of thin silk each year" (*Jiu Tangshu*, 117:3200–3201).

39 See "Chengdu ji xu" (Preface to Records of Chengdu), in *Quan Tang wen*, 8:744.7701–03. On the connections between the invasion and the development of Buddhist art, see Howard, "Gilt Bronze Guanyin from the Nanzhao Kingdom of Yunnan," 1–12.

40 Sichuan was required to produce 8,167 bolts for tribute each year. There exist two estimates for the number of bolts produced: *Old Standard History of the Tang* states that Sichuan's annual tribute was reduced by 2,510 bolts, whereas *Outstanding Models from the Storehouse of Literature* records that it was only reduced by five hundred. See "Wenzong benji" [Basic annals of Emperor Wenzong], *Jiu Tangshu*, 2:17.537; *Cefu yuangui*, 484:1211.

41 Yokohari, "The Hōryū-ji Lion-Hunting Silk and Related Silks," 155–73.

42 Geijer, "A Silk from Antinoe and the Sasanian Textile Art," 3–36; Meister, "The Pearl Roundel in Chinese Textile Design," 255–67; Harper, *In Search of a Cultural Identity*; Trilling,

Ornament; Muthesius, *Studies in Byzantine and Islamic Silk Weaving*; Matsumoto, *Shōsōin-gire to Asuka Tenpyō no senshoku*; Schrenk, *Textilien des Mittelmeerraumes aus spätantiker bis frühislamischer Zeit.*

43 See Amy Heller, "Two Inscribed Fabrics and their Historical Context," 95–118.

44 Canepa, *The Two Eyes of the Earth*, 210. See also Canepa, "Distant Displays of Power," 121–54.

45 Ibid., 37.

46 See Watt and Wardwell, eds., *When Silk Was Gold*, catalogue entry no. 5, 34–37.

47 The story of He Chou is frequently cited in scholarship on the connections between Central Asian and Sui-Tang Chinese textiles. See, for example, Zhao and Simcox, "Silk Roundels from the Sui to the Tang," 80–85; Watt and Wardwell, *When Silk was Gold*, 23–24.

48 *Sui shu*, 68:1596–98; *Bei shi*, 90:2985–88.

49 Zhang, *Lidai minghua ji*, 309.

50 Wu Min has identified several patterned silks from the Turfan excavations, which she claimed were produced in Sichuan before the seventh century. Wu, "Tulufan chutu Shu jin de yanjiu," 70–80.

51 On this historical development, see Jones, *Sexing La Mode.*

52 *Tang Huiyao*, 31:668–72.

53 *Xin Tangshu*, 131:4514.

54 Tim Ingold has proposed that we think of design as "immanent in the activity itself, in the gestural synergy of human being, tool and raw material." Ingold, *The Perception of the Environment*, 352. I am grateful to Annapurna Mamidipudi for reminding me of this crucial argument.

55 Compareti, "The Role of the Sogdian Colonies in the Diffusion of the Pearl Roundel Design," 149–74.

56 As evidence of exchanges between Sogdians and Han Chinese weavers, Angela Sheng has presented an unusual group of *jin* silks featuring simple geometric designs, excavated in Turfan. Sheng, "Innovations in Textile Techniques on China's Northwestern Frontier, 500–700 AD," 117–60. Also see Sheng, "Textile Finds along the Silk Road," 42–48.

57 See essays by Angela Sheng, Wu Min, and Zhao Feng in Regula Schorta, ed., *Central Asian Textiles and their Contexts in the Early Middle Ages* (2006).

58 This structure is referred to as Liao style because silks woven with this technique were first discovered at Liao dynasty (907–1125) gravesites. Kuhn, ed., *Chinese Silks*, 223.

59 See Sheng, "Textiles from Astana," 117–27; and Zhao Feng "Weaving Methods for Western-Style *Samit* from the Silk Road in Northwestern China," 189–210.

60 Becker, *Pattern and Loom*, 55–79.

61 Dieter Kuhn has argued that an early form of the "drawloom," a loom in which the pattern is created by a mechanism that lifts individual or small groups of warp ends, emerged in the later Han dynasty (25–220 CE). According to Kuhn, this early manifestation of the drawloom may have developed from a combination of the treadle loom and the pattern-rod loom and was likely employed for the limited production of polychrome warp-patterned fabrics. See Kuhn, "Silk Weaving in Ancient China," 77–114.

62 Watt, *China*, see cat. no. 239, p. 340.

63 Xie et al., "Chengdu shi Tianhuizhen Laoguanshan Han mu," 59–70. See also Zhao et al., "The Earliest Evidence of Pattern Looms," 360–74.

64 Sheng, "Determining the Value of Textiles in the Tang Dynasty," 187.

65 In Ma and Yue, *Xinjiang Weiwu'erqi zizhiqu silu kaogu zhenpin*, cat. no. 54.

66 Yao Runeng, *An Lushan shiji*, 6–7.

67 Documents from the late ninth century, including an inventory of items presented to the Famen Temple (dated to 874) and a comprehensive checklist of items held in various Buddhist temples in Shazhou (dated to 873), mention clamp-resist dyed silks. See Kuhn, ed. *Chinese Silks*, 241.
68 Zhao Feng, "Woven Color in China," 5–8; Zhao Feng, *Sichou yishu shi*, 83–84; Weiji Chen, *History of Textile Technology*, 328–30.
69 Han Wei, "Famensi digong Tangdai 'Sui zhenshen yiwu zhang' kao," 27–37.
70 Wang Dang (fl. early twelfth century), *Tang yulin*, 4:149.
71 Zhao Feng, *Zhongguo sichou tongshi*, 229.
72 Han Jinke, "Silk and Gold Textiles from the Tang Underground Palace at Famen si," 129–45; Zhao Feng, *Zhongguo sichou tongshi*, 232.
73 Braudel, *The Structures of Everyday Life*, 317.
74 *Taiping guangji*, 257:2005.

5. DESIRE: MEN OF STYLE AND THE METRICS OF FASHION

1 Bai Juyi, "Adornment of the Times" (Shishizhuang), *Quan Tangshi*, 427:4705.
2 Bai was born in 772 to a low-ranking official family in Henan. In 798 he took the district-level examinations, followed by the exam given to men "presented in tribute for the examinations" (*gongju*) in 799, before receiving the *jinshi* degree. He was first appointed to the office of editor (*jiaoshu lang*) in the Palace Library (Mishu Sheng) in 803 and was quickly promoted to defender (*wei*) in 806. In 842, he retired from official life. See *Jiu Tangshu*, 166:4340–60; *Xin Tangshu*, 119:4300–4307. For Bai's biographical chronology, see Zhu Jincheng, *Bai Juyi nianpu*.
3 This line is from Bai's poem, "Re-sending six-rhyming couplets to Yuan Zhen (Weizhi) on my afterthoughts." *Quan Tangshi*, 446:5000.
4 See Twitchett, ed., *The Cambridge History of China*, 3:464–560; 561–681; Owen, "The Cultural Tang (650–1020)," 286–380.
5 Arguing for fashion's dominance in Europe, Braudel claimed that, "In fact one cannot really talk of fashion becoming all-powerful before about 1700. At that time the word gained a new lease of life and spread everywhere with its new meaning: 'keeping up with the times.' From then on fashion in the modern sense began to influence everything: the pace of change had never been as swift in earlier times." In Braudel's narrative, fashion gained momentum once the word acquired the connotation of "keeping up with the times" and became synonymous with change itself. Braudel, *The Structures of Everyday Life*, 316.
6 Scholarship on late eighth- and ninth-century intellectuals has been extensive. See McMullen, *State and Scholars in T'ang China*; Hartman, *Han Yu and the T'ang Search for Unity*; Bol, *'This Culture of Ours'*; Ruoshui Chen, *Liu Tsung-yüan and Intellectual Change in T'ang China, 773–819*; Deblasi, *Reform in the Balance: The Defense of Literary Culture in Mid-Tang Chin.*
7 Paul Rouzer has proposed that the "articulated" female voice found in Six Dynasties and Tang texts be read as a technique of male-gender identification and in light of "homosocial modes of desire," the latter referring to "the literatus' longing for the ruler's attention, his concern for his own position within the social order, or his desire to bond with or triumph over one's peers" (Rouzer, *Articulated Ladies*, see introduction and chap. 1).
8 Shields, "Gossip, Anecdote, and Literary History," 107–131.
9 *Tangguo shi bu*, 57.
10 See Shields, "Gossip, Anecdote, and Literary History," 113–17.
11 This appeared in a letter that accompanied a collection of poems sent to chief minister,

Linghu Chu, from whom Yuan sought patronage. Shields, "Gossip, Anecdote, and Literary History," 112.

12 Georg Simmel's theory of fashion is particularly apt here to describe the competition between postrebellion intellectuals. Simmel, "Fashion," (1904).

13 David McMullen has similarly argued that the generation of intellectuals that lived through the rebellion "no longer praised the court literary figures of the late seventh and early eighth centuries. Instead they demanded that writing be committed to the cause of political and social reform, and judged past writers by this standard. . . . They reformulated traditional definitions of verse and literature and emphasized that an individual's writing was the expression of his moral nature, as well as the reflection of the spirit of the age that had produced it" (McMullen, *State and Scholars*, 245).

14 See McMullen and Deblasi on the *guwen* movement.

15 Li Shen (772–846) also composed a set of "New Music Bureau" poems. In Yuan's preface to his collection, he states that his poems were composed in response to Li's. See "He Li Jiaoshu xinti Yuefu shi'er shou" (In Response to the Twelve Poems Composed by Li, the Collator of Texts), *Yuan Zhen* ji, 1:277–78.

16 "Letter to Yuan the Ninth" (Yu Yuan jiushu), *Jiu Tangshu*, 166:4347. Arthur Waley has produced a partial translation of the letter. See Waley, *The Life and Times of Po Chu-I*, chap. 8. Alternate translations can be found in Yu, *The Reading of Imagery in the Chinese Poetic Tradition*. For more recent studies on Bai Juyi's life and literary practices, see Chui, "Between the World and the Self"; Yao, "Women, Femininity, and Love in the Writings of Bo Juyi (772–846)."

17 *Jiu Tangshu*, 166:4347.

18 "Since I have taken up the post of the Reminder, there are some [poems] that record what I experienced and felt and pertain to *mei* (eulogistic), *ci* (critical), *xing* (allegorical), and *bi* (metaphorical). There are also some from the Wude to Yuanhe eras, for which I created titles [topics] based on real affairs, and which I have titled 'Xin Yuefu.' There are one hundred and fifty poems in total and I call them 'poems of remonstrance'" (*Jiu Tangshu*, 166:4347). In addition to the "New Music Bureau" poems, Bai's collection of pentasyllabic ancient-style poems entitled "Songs in *Qin*" (Qinzhong yin) have also been classified as "poems of remonstrance" (fengyu shi). Based on events between the Zhenyuan (785–805) and Yuanhe periods (806–820), this group of poems also addresses a range of social ills including marriage (*yihun*), taxation (*zhongfu*), and the extravagance of officials (*shangzhai*).

19 Chen Yinke, *Yuan Bai shijian zhenggao*, 121–35.

20 His poems on women include "The Girl Who Danced the Whirl" (Huxuan nü), "Concubine at the Imperial Tombs" (Lingyuan qie), "Lady Li" (Li furen), and "The Salt Merchant's Wife" (Yanshang fu).

21 Stephen Owen has argued that the "New Music Bureau" ballads of Bai and his friends followed the assumption of an "intense relation between verbal representations and the political or social order," so that "the clear representation of moral issues and their consequences for society would call forth and strengthen the innate moral sense of all readers, clarifying ethical issues and changing behavior" (Owen, *The End of the Chinese 'Middle Ages'*, 12).

22 Wang Ay-Ling provides a detailed explication of Bai's general preface (as well as an alternative translation) to the "New Music Bureau," see "Dramatic Elements in the Narrative Poetry of Bo Juyi (772–846) and Yuan Zhen (799–831)," 195–268.

23 Ma Zili has argued that Bai Juyi's literary works bring to light his heightened political consciousness as a *jianguan*, his adherence to the poetic traditions of *Shijing*, and his concern

for social issues that was inherited from the folk songs and ballads of the Han *yuefu*. See Ma, "Jianguan ji qi huodong yu zhong Tang wenxue," 16–30.

24 Deblasi, *Reform in the Balance*, 25–26.

25 Jonathan Hay has linked the developments in the post–An Lushan era to the development of a high-degree of self-consciousness about style among artists and viewers. Hay, "Margins, Transitions, Interstices."

26 *Quan Tangshi*, 426:4692.

27 "Petition to Select and Send Home Palace Women." *Quan Tangwen*, 667:6783. For English translations of all eighteen of Bai's memorials, see Eugene Feifel, *Po Chu-I as a Censor.*

28 One of the definitions of *shi* (世) provided in Morohashi Tetsuji's *Great Chinese-Japanese Dictionary* is "the world" (世の中) or *jinkan* 人間, citing Zhuangzi's story, "Heaven and Earth" (Tiandi) as an example of this usage. See the entry for 世 in Morohashi, *Dai Kan-Wa Jiten*, 1:268.

29 *Quan Tangshi*, 427:4705. Alternate translations include: Waley, "Foreign Fashions," 3; and "Styles of the Times," in Cahill, "'Our Women Are Acting Like Foreigners' Wives!'" 103.

30 Chen Yinke has argued that the *hu* styles of hair and makeup, which Bai described as belonging to the Yuanhe era, already existed by the end of the Zhenyuan era. See Chen, *Yuan Bai shijian zhenggao*, 268–69.

31 Clunas, *Empire of Great Brightness*, 38.

32 *Quan Tangshi*, 422:4643. This poem belongs to Yuan Zhen's collection of *Yanshi*, which were written as observations of the women of his generation, detailing their dress and ornamentation. See Shi Zhecun, *Tangshi baihua*, 510. For an in-depth study of Yuan's *Yanshi*, see Shields, "Defining Experience," 61–78.

33 "Vermillion silk ribbons and embroidery certainly harm women's work." See *Jiu Tangshu*, 11:298.

34 *Quan Tangshi*, 670:7657.

35 *Quan Tangshi*, 643:7364.

36 See Shi Zhecun, *Tangshi baihua*, 668–73.

37 Emperor Wenzong's sumptuary reform of 832 included a decree prohibiting women from removing their eyebrows, which suggests that it was a dominant trend of the ninth century. *Tang Huiyao*, 1:31.670.

38 From "On Marriage" (Yihun), taken from Bai's "Songs in Qin" (Qinzhong yin), his second collection of remonstrance poems. *Quan Tangshi*, 425:4674.

39 Gungwu Wang, *The Structure of Power in North China*, 85.

40 On receiving his degree in 882, Qin expressed his joy at gaining admission into the bureaucracy in a letter to his fellow graduates: "Beneath three candles, although I was barred from the literary enclosure, I lasted for several occasions beside its walls, until I was blessed to join you in this merciful land." Quoted from Moore, *Rituals of Recruitment in Tang China*, 153.

41 Qin Taoyu's poem has become canonized in the tradition of invoking the image of the poor girl (*pinnü*) to stand in for the poor literatus (*pinshi*). See Chen Wenzhong, *Zhongguo gudian shige jieshou shi yanjiu*, 162–82.

42 *Quan Tangshi*, 298:3389.

43 *Quan Tangshi*, 418:4607.

44 See Chin, *Savage Exchange*, 119–213.

45 *Quan Tangshi*, 419:4620. For Bai Juyi's poem of the same title, see *Quan Tangshi*, 427:4705. On the trade with the Uyghurs, see *Jiu Tangshu*, 195:5207.

46 See Drompp, *Tang China and the Collapse of the Uighur Empire*, 24–26.

47 Christopher Beckwith has calculated the total debt incurred in the Tang-Uighur horse trade: "When the Uighurs began selling horses to the T'ang in 760, they are supposed to have gotten

forty pieces of silk per horse. At then-current prices, this amount of silk was worth 400,000 cash. In 780, when the price of forty pieces of silk per horse was supposedly still in effect, but the price of silk had fallen, it would have amounted to 270,000 cash per horse. In 809 the Chinese paid 250,000 pieces for 6,500 horses, that is 38.46 pieces or 30,768 cash, per horse. By 838, the price of silk within China was back to normal—one thousand cash per piece—and the price of an imported horse, at thirty eight pieces of silk, was 38,000 cash" (Beckwith, "The Impact of the Horse and Silk Trade," 187). For further discussion on the impact of this trade on the Tang economy, see Saitō, "Tō, Uiguru kenba bōeki saikō," 33–58. Tan Mei Ah has also published a study of this poem, concluding that "Yinshan Circuit" and Yuan's other New Music Bureau poetry expressed primarily a concern about proper governance. Tan, "Exonerating the Horse Trade for the Shortage of Silk," 49–96.

48 See Zhao Feng's analysis of Bai's poem. Zhao, *Tangdai sichou yu sichou zhi lu*, 109–13.

49 *Quan Tangshi*, 247:4704.

EPILOGUE

1 Adapted from Robin Yates's translation in *Washing Silk*, 108–22. On the transmission of this poem and the surviving manuscripts, see Nugent, "The Lady and Her Scribes," 25–73.

2 Rouzer, *Articulated Ladies*, 201.

3 Tseëlon, "Ontological, Epistemological, and Methodological Clarifications in Fashion Research," 237.

APPENDIX: TEXTILE BASICS

1 Zhao Feng, *Sichou yishu shi*, 43–44.

2 Sheng, "The Disappearance of Silk Weaves with Weft Effects in Early China," 41–76, cf. 63.

3 Weiji Chen, *History of Textile Technology of Ancient China*, 74–76; Zhao Feng, *Sichou yishu shi*, 18.

4 Stone relief representations of this loom dating to the Han dynasty have been discovered in Shandong and Jiangsu. Weiji Chen, *History of Textile Technology of Ancient China*, 244–551; Zhao Feng, *Sichou yishu shi*, 17–18.

5 Becker, *Pattern and Loom*, 55–79.

6 Chen, *History of Textile Technology of Ancient China*, 384; Zhao Feng, *Sichou yishu shi*, 55–57.

7 Weiji Chen, *History of Textile Technology of Ancient China*, 116–17; Zhao Feng, *Sichou yishu shi*, 45; Kuhn, "Silk Weaving in Ancient China," 80–81. Some scholars have translated *luo* as "leno," which is a term applied to a general class of complex gauze weaves.

BIBLIOGRAPHY

Abramson, Marc S. *Ethnic Identity in Tang China.* Philadelphia: University of Pennsylvania Press, 2008.

Acker, William. *Some T'ang and Pre-T'ang Texts on Chinese Painting*, 2 vols. Leiden: E. J. Brill, 1954–74.

An, Jiayao. "The Art of Glass Along the Silk Road." In *China: Dawn of a Golden Age, 200–750*, edited by James C.Y. Watt, 57–65. New York: Metropolitan Museum of Art, 2004.

An Zhengdi 安崢地. "Tang Fangling da zhanggongzhu mu qingli jianbao" 唐房陵大長公主墓清理簡報. *Wenbo* 文博, no. 1 (1990): 2–6.

Appadurai, Arjun, ed. *The Social Life of Things: Commodities in Cultural Perspective.* New York: Cambridge University Press, 1988.

Arakawa, Masahiro, and Valerie Hansen. "The Transportation of Tax Textiles to the North-West as part of the Tang-Dynasty Military Shipment System." *Journal of the Royal Asiatic Society* 23, no. 2 (2013): 245–61.

Backus, Charles. *The Nan-Chao Kingdom and T'ang China's Southwestern Frontier.* New York: Cambridge University Press, 1981.

Baizerman, Suzanne, Joanne B. Eicher, and Catherine Cerny. "Eurocentrism in the Study of Ethnic Dress." *Dress* 20, no. 1 (1993): 19–32.

Baldwin, Frances Elizabeth. *Sumptuary Legislation and Personal Regulation in England.* Baltimore: Johns Hopkins University Press, 1926.

Ban Gu 班固. *Hanshu* 漢書, 8 vols. Edited by Yan Shigu 顏師古 (581–645). Beijing: Zhonghua shuju. Reprint, 2007.

Bao Weimin 包偉民. "Tangdai shizhi zai lun" 唐代市制再論. *Zhongguo shehui kexue* 中國社會科學, no. 4 (2011): 179–89.

Barat, Kahar. "Aluoben, A Nestorian Missionary in 7th Century China." *Journal of Asian History* 36, no. 2 (2002): 184–98.

Barnhart, Richard M., Xin Yang, Chongzheng Nie, James Cahill, Shaojun Lang, and Hung Wu. *Three Thousand Years of Chinese Painting.* New Haven: Yale University Press, 1997.

Becker, John. *Pattern and Loom: A Practical Study of the Development of Weaving Techniques in China, Western Asia and Europe*, 2nd ed. Copenhagen: Rhodos International Publishers, 2009.

Beckwith, Christopher I. "The Impact of the Horse and Silk Trade on the Economies of T'ang China and the Uighur Empire: On the Importance of International Commerce in the Early Middle Ages." *Journal of the Economic and Social History of the Orient* 34, no. 3 (1991): 183–98.

Belfanti, Carlo. "Was Fashion a European Invention?" *Journal of Global History* 3, no. 3 (2008): 419–43.

Bell, Quentin. *On Human Finery*. London: Allison and Busby, 1992.
Benjamin, Walter. *The Arcades Project*. Edited by Rolf Tiedemann. Translated by Howard Eiland and Kevin McLaughlin. Cambridge, Mass.: Belknap Press of Harvard University Press, 1999.
———. *Illuminations: Essays and Reflections*. Edited by Hannah Arendt. Translated by Harry Zohn. New York: Shocken Books, 1988.
Berger, John. *Ways of Seeing*. London: Penguin Books, 1972.
Bol, Peter. *'This Culture of Ours': Intellectual Transitions in T'ang and Sung China*. Stanford: Stanford University Press, 1992.
Bossler, Beverly. "Vocabularies of Pleasure: Categorizing Female Entertainers in the Late Tang Dynasty." *Harvard Journal of Asiatic Studies* 72, no. 1 (2012): 71–99.
Bourdieu, Pierre. *Distinction: A Social Critique of the Judgment of Taste*. Translated by Richard Nice. Cambridge, Mass.: Harvard University Press, 1984.
Brandauer, Frederick P., and Chün-chieh Huang. *Imperial Rulership and Cultural Change in Traditional China*. Seattle: University of Washington Press, 1994.
Braudel, Fernand. *Civilization and Capitalism, 15th–18th Centuries*. Vol. 1, *The Structures of Everyday Life*. Translated by Sian Reynolds. London: Collins, 1981.
Bray, Francesca. *Technology and Gender: Fabrics of Power in Late Imperial China*. Berkeley: University of California Press, 1997.
Brook, Timothy. *The Confusions of Pleasure: Commerce and Culture in Ming China*. Berkeley: University of California Press, 1998.
Burnham, Dorothy. *Warp and Weft: A Dictionary of Textile Terms*. New York: Scribner, 1981.
Bush, Susan, and Hsio-yen Shih, eds. *Early Chinese Texts on Painting*. Cambridge, Mass.: Harvard University Press, 1985.
Cahill, Suzanne. "Material Culture and the Dao: Textiles, Boats, and Zithers in the Poetry of Yu Xuanji (844–868)." In *Daoist Identity: Cosmology, Lineage, and Ritual*, edited by Livia Kohn and Harold D. Roth, 101–126. Honolulu: University of Hawai'i Press, 2002.
———. "Ominous Dress: Hufu 胡服 ('Barbarian Clothing') during the Tang Dynasty (618–907)." In *China and Beyond in the Mediaeval Period: Cultural Crossings and Inter-Regional Connections*, edited by Dorothy C. Wong and Gustav Heldt, 219–28. Amherst, Mass.: Cambria Press, 2014.
———. "Our Women Are Acting Like Foreigners' Wives!: Western Influences on Tang Dynasty Women's Fashion." In *China Chic: East Meets West*, edited by Valerie Steele and John S. Major, 103–17. New Haven: Yale University Press, 1999.
Cammann, Schuyler V. R. *China's Dragon Robes*. New York: Ronald Press, 1952.
———. "Notes on the Origin of Chinese K'ossu Tapestry." *Artibus Asiae* 11 (1948): 90–110.
Campbell, Colin. *The Romantic Ethic and the Spirit of Modern Consumerism*. New York: Basil Blackwell, 1987.
Canepa, Matthew P. "Distant Displays of Power: Understanding Cross-Cultural Interaction Among the Elites of Rome, Sasanian Iran, and Sui-Tang China." *Ars Orientalis* 38 (2010): 121–54.
———. *The Two Eyes of the Earth: Art and Ritual of Kingship between Rome and Sasanian Iran*. Berkeley: University of California Press, 2009.
Cao Zhezhi 曹者祉, and Sun Binggen 孫秉根, eds. *Zhongguo gudai yong* 中國古代俑. Shanghai: Shanghai wenhua chubanshe, 1996.
Chan, Chui M. "Between the World and the Self: Orientations of Pai Chu-I's (772–846) Life and Writings." PhD diss., University of Wisconsin, 1991.
Chang, Eileen [Zhang Ailing]. "Chinese Life and Fashions." *XXth Century* 4, no. 1 (1943): 54–61.
———. "A Chronicle of Changing Clothes." Translated by Andrew F. Jones. *positions: east asia cultures critique* 11, no. 2 (2003): 427–41.

Chen, Fan Pen. "Yang Kuei-Fei in 'Tales From The T'ien-Pao Era: A Chu-Kung-Tiao Narrative.'" *Journal of Song-Yuan Studies*, no. 22 (1990): 1–22.

Chen, Jack W. *The Poetics of Sovereignty: On Emperor Taizong of the Tang Dynasty.* Cambridge, Mass.: Harvard University Asia Center, 2010.

———. "Social Networks, Court Factions, Ghosts, and Killer Snakes: Reading Anyi Ward." *Tang Studies* 2011, no. 29 (2011): 45–61.

Chen, Jack W., and David Schaberg, eds. *Idle Talk: Gossip and Anecdote in Traditional China.* Berkeley: University of California Press, 2014.

Chen, Ruoshui. *Liu Tsung-yüan and Intellectual Change in T'ang China, 773–819.* New York: Cambridge University Press, 1992.

Chen, Song. "Managing the Territories from Afar: The Imperial State and Elites in Sichuan, 755–1279." PhD diss., Harvard University, 2011.

Chen, Tina Mai, and Paola Zamperini. "Guest Editors' Introduction." *positions: east asia cultures critique* 11, no. 2, Special Issue: *Fabrications* (2003): 261–69.

Chen, Weiji. *History of Textile Technology of Ancient China.* New York: Science Press, 2002.

Chen Anli 陳安利 and Ma Yongzhong 馬咏鐘. "Xi'an Wangjiafen Tangdai Tang'an gongzhu mu" 西安王家墳唐代唐安公主墓. *Wenwu* 文物, no. 9 (1991): 15–27.

Chen Guocan 陳國燦. "Cong Tulufan chutu de 'zhikuzhang' kan Tangdai de zhizhang zhidu" 從吐魯番出土的質庫帳看唐代的質帳制度. In *Dunhuang Tulufan wenshu chutan* 敦煌吐魯番文書初探, edited by Tang Changru 唐長孺, 316–43. Wuhan: Wuhan daxue chubanshe, 1983.

Chen Jinhua. "The Statues and Monks of Shengshan Monastery: Money and Maitreyan Buddhism in Tang China." *Asia Major*, Third Series 19, no. 1/2 (2006): 111–60.

Chen Ruoshi 陳弱水. *Tangdai de funu wenhua yu jiating shenghuo* 唐代的婦女文化與家庭生活. Taipei: Yunchen wenhua, 2007.

Chen Wenzhong 陳文忠. *Zhongguo gudian shige jieshou shi yanjiu* 中國古典詩歌接受史研究. Hefei: Anhui daxue chubanshe, 1998.

Chen Yinke 陳寅恪. *Sui Tang zhidu yuanyuan lüelun gao* 隋唐制度淵源略論稿. Beijing: Shenghuo, dushu, xinzhi sanlian shudian, 1954.

———. *Tangdai zhengzhi shi shulun gao* 唐代政治史述論稿. Beijing: Shenghuo, xushu, xinzhi sanlian shudian, 1956.

———. *Yuan Bai shijian zhenggao* 元白詩箋證稿. Beijing: Shenghuo, dushu, xinzhi sanlian shudian, 2001.

Chen Yong 陳勇. *Tangdai changjiang xiayou jingji fazhan yanjiu* 唐代長江下游經濟發展研究. Shanghai: Shanghai renmin chubanshe, 2006.

Chin, Tamara T. "The Invention of the Silk Road, 1877." *Critical Inquiry* 40, no. 1 (2013): 194–219.

———. *Savage Exchange: Han Imperialism, Chinese Literary Style, and the Economic Imagination.* Cambridge, Mass.: Harvard University Asia Center, 2014.

Ching Chao-jung. "Silk in Ancient Kucha: On the Toch. B word *kaum** found in the documents of the Tang period." *Tocharian and Indo-European Studies* 12 (2011): 63–82.

Choo, Jessey J. C. "Historicized Ritual and Ritualized History—Women's Lifecycle Rituals in Late Medieval China (600–1000 AD)." PhD diss., Princeton University, 2009.

———. "Shall We Profane the Service of the Dead? Burial Divinations, Untimely Burials, and Remembrance in Tang *Muzhiming.*" *Tang Studies* 33, no. 1 (2015): 1–37.

Christian, David. "Silk Roads or Steppe Roads? The Silk Roads in World History." *Journal of World History* 11, no. 1 (2000): 1–26.

Chung, Saehyang P. "A Study of the Daming Palace: Documentary Sources and Recent Excavations." *Artibus Asiae* 50, no. 1/2 (1990): 23–72.

Clark, Hugh R. "Bridles, Halters, and Hybrids: A Case Study in T'ang Frontier Policy." *Tang Studies*, no. 6 (1988): 49–68.

Clunas, Craig. *Empire of Great Brightness: Visual and Material Cultures of Ming China, 1368–1644*. London: Reaktion Books, 2007.

———. "Modernity Global and Local: Consumption and the Rise of the West." *American Historical Review*, no. 104 (1999): 1497–511.

———. "Regulation of Consumption and the Institution of Correct Morality by the Ming State." In *Norms and the State in China*, edited by Chun-Chien Huang and Erik Zurcher, 39–49. Leiden: Brill, 1993.

———. *Superfluous Things: Material Culture and Social Status in Early Modern China*. Honolulu: University of Hawai'i Press, 1991.

Compareti, Matteo. "The Role of the Sogdian Colonies in the Diffusion of the Pearl Roundel Design." In Ērān *ud Anērān: Studies Presented to Boris I. Maršak on the Occasion of His 70th Birthday*, part 2, edited by M. Compareti, P. Raffetta, and G. Scarcia, 149–74. Venice: Cafoscarina, 2006.

Craik, Jennifer. *The Face of Fashion: Cultural Studies in Fashion*. New York: Routledge, 1994.

Davis, Fred. *Fashion, Culture, and Identity*. Chicago: University of Chicago Press, 1992.

de La Vaissière, Étienne. *Sogdian Traders: A History*. Translated by James Ward. Leiden: Brill, 2005.

de Tarde, Gabriel. *The Laws of Imitation*. Translated by Elsie C. Parsons. New York: Henry Holt, 1903.

DeBlasi, Anthony. *Reform in the Balance: The Defense of Literary Culture in Mid-Tang China*. Albany: State University of New York Press, 2002.

Deng, Xiaonan. "Women in Turfan during the Sixth to Eighth Centuries: A Look at Their Activities Outside the Home." *Journal of Asian Studies* 58, no. 1 (1999): 85–103.

Ditter, Alexei. "Civil Examinations and Cover Letters in the Mid-Tang: A Close Reading of Dugu Yu's 獨孤郁 (776–815) 'Letter Submitted to Attendant Gentleman Quan of the Ministry of Rites 上禮部權侍郎.'" In *History of Chinese Epistolary Culture*, edited by Antje Richter, 643–74. Leiden: Brill, 2015.

———. "The Commerce of Commemoration: Commissioned *Muzhiming* in the Mid- to Late Tang." *Tang Studies* 32, no. 1 (2014): 21–46.

———. "Conceptions of Urban Space in Duan Chengshi's 'Record of Monasteries and Stupas.'" *Tang Studies* 2011, no. 29 (2011): 62–83.

Dong Gao 董誥 (1740–1818) et al., comps. *Quan Tangwen* 全唐文, 11 vols. Beijing: Zhonghua shuju. Reprint, 1987.

Doran, Rebecca Esther. "Insatiable Women and Transgressive Authority: Constructions of Gender and Power in Early Tang China." PhD diss., Harvard University, 2011.

Douglas, Mary, and Baron Isherwood. *The World of Goods: Towards an Anthropology of Consumption*. New York: Basic Books, 1979.

Drompp, Michael R. *Tang China and the Collapse of the Uighur Empire*. Leiden: Brill, 2005.

du Halde, Jean-Baptiste (1674–1743). *Description géographique, historique, chronologique, politique, et physique de l'empire de la Chine et la Tartarie chinoise*, 4 vols. Paris: P. G. Lemercier, 1735.

Du Mu 杜牧. *Fanchuan wenji* 樊川文集, 2 vols. Chengdu: Ba shu shushe, 2007.

Du Wenyu 杜文玉. "Lun Tangdai guyong laodong" 論唐代雇傭勞動. *Weinan shifan xueyuan xuebao* 渭南師範學院學報, no. 1 (1986): 40–45.

Du You 杜佑, comp. *Tongdian* 通典, 5 vols. Beijing: Zhonghua shuju, 1988.

Duan, Qing, and Helen Wang. "Were Textiles Used as Money in Khotan in the Seventh and Eighth Centuries?" *Journal of the Royal Asiatic Society* 23, no. 2 (2013): 307–25.

Duan Pengqi 段鵬琦. "Xi'an nanjiao Hejiacun Tangdai jinyin qi xiaoyi" 西安南郊何家村唐代金銀器小議. *Kaogu* 考古 6 (1980): 536–41.

Duan Wenjie 段文傑. *Dunhuang shiku yishu yanjiu* 敦煌石窟藝術研究. Lanzhou: Gansu renmin chubanshe, 2007.

———. *Zhongguo meishu quanji 14: Huihua bian Dunhuang bihua shang.* 中國美術全集14: 繪畫編, 敦煌壁畫上. Shanghai: Renmin meishu chubanshe, 1985.

———. *Zhongguo meishu quanji 15: Huihua bian Dunhuang bihua xia.* 中國美術全集15: 繪畫編, 敦煌壁畫下. Shanghai: Renmin meishu chubanshe, 1985.

Dudbridge, Glen. *The Tale of Li Wa: Study and Critical Edition of a Chinese Story from the Ninth Century.* London: Ithaca Press, 1983.

Ebrey, Patricia B. *The Aristocratic Families of Early Imperial China: A Case Study of the Po-Ling Ts'ui Family.* New York: Cambridge University Press, 1978.

Eckfeld, Tonia. *Imperial Tombs in Tang China, 618–907: The Politics of Paradise.* New York: Routledge, 2005.

Eicher, Joanne B. *Dress and Ethnicity: Change Across Space and Time.* Oxford: Berg, 1995.

Eicher, Joanne B., and Ruth Barnes, eds. *Dress and Gender: Making and Meaning in Cultural Contexts.* Oxford: Berg, 1992.

Elias, Norbert. *The Civilizing Process I: The History of Manners.* Translated by Edmund Jephcott. Oxford: Basil Blackwell, 1978.

———. *The Civilizing Process II: State Formation and Civilization.* Translated by Edmund Jephcott. Oxford: Basil Blackwell, 1982.

———. *The Court Society.* Translated by Edmund Jephcott. Oxford: Basil Blackwell, 1983.

Entwistle, Joanne. "Fashion and the Fleshy Body: Dress as Embodied Practice." *Fashion Theory* 4, no. 3 (2000): 323–48.

———. *The Fashioned Body: Fashion, Dress, and Modern Social Theory.* Cambridge: Polity Press, 2000.

Fan Chuo 樊綽 (active 860–873). *Manshu* 蠻書. Beijing: Zhonghua shudian. Reprint, 2007.

Fei Sheng 費省. *Tangdai renkou dili* 唐代人口地理. Xi'an: Xibei daxue chubanshe, 1996.

Feifel, Eugene. *Po Chu-I as a Censor: His Memorials Presented to Emperor Hsien-Tsung during the Years 808–810.* Hague: Mouton, 1961.

Feng, Linda Rui. "Chang'an and Narratives of Experience in Tang Tales." *Harvard Journal of Asiatic Studies* 71, no. 1 (2011): 35–68.

———. *City of Marvel and Transformation: Chang'an and Narratives of Experience in Tang Dynasty China.* Honolulu: University of Hawai'i Press, 2015.

———. "Unmasking 'Fengliu' in Urban Chang'an: Rereading 'Beili Zhi' (Anecdotes from the Northern Ward)." *Chinese Literature: Essays, Articles, Reviews (CLEAR)* 32 (2010): 1–21.

Fernald, Helen E. *Chinese Court Costumes.* Toronto: Royal Ontario Museum of Archaeology, 1946.

Finnane, Antonia. *Changing Clothes in China: Fashion, History, Nation.* New York: Columbia University Press, 2008.

Flugel, J. C. *The Psychology of Clothes.* London: Hogarth, 1930.

Fong, Adam C. "'Together They Might Make Trouble': Cross-Cultural Interactions in Tang Dynasty Guangzhou, 618–907 CE." *Journal of World History* 25, no. 4 (2015): 475–92.

Fong, Mary H. "Tang Tomb Murals Reviewed in the Light of Tang Texts on Painting." *Artibus Asiae* 45, no. 1 (1984): 35–72.

Fraser, Sarah. *Performing the Visual: The Practice of Buddhist Wall Painting in China and Central Asia, 618–960.* Stanford: Stanford University Press, 2004.

Freudenberger, Herman. "Fashion, Sumptuary Laws, and Business." *Business History Review* 37, no. 1/2 (Spring/Summer 1963): 37–48.

Frick, Carole Collier. *Dressing Renaissance Florence: Families, Fortunes, and Fine Clothing.* Baltimore: Johns Hopkins University Press, 2002.

Fu Shaoliang 傅紹良. *Tangdai jianyi zhidu yu wenren* 唐代諫議制度與文人. Beijing: Zhongguo shehui kexue chubanshe, 2003.

Ge Chengyong 葛承雍, ed. *Jingjiao yizhen: Luoyang xin chu Tangdai jingjiao jingchuang yanjiu* 景教遺珍—洛陽新出唐代景教經幢研究. Beijing: Wenwu chubanshe, 2009.

Geijer, Agnes. "A Silk from Antinoe and the Sasanian Textile Art," *Orientalia Suecana* 12 (1963): 2–36.

Giles, Lionel. "A Chinese Geographical Text of the Ninth Century." *Bulletin of the School of Oriental Studies* 6, no. 4 (1932): 825–46.

———. "Dated Chinese Manuscripts in the Stein Collection: I. Fifth and Sixth Centuries A.D." *Bulletin of the School of Oriental Studies* 7, no. 4 (1935): 809–36.

———. "Dated Chinese Manuscripts in the Stein Collection: II. Seventh Century A.D." *Bulletin of the School of Oriental Studies* 8, no. 1 (1935): 1–26.

———. "Dated Chinese Manuscripts in the Stein Collection: IV. Ninth Century A.D." *Bulletin of the School of Oriental Studies* 9, no. 4 (1939): 1023–46.

———. "Dated Chinese Manuscripts in the Stein Collection: V. Tenth Century A.D." *Bulletin of the School of Oriental Studies* 10, no. 2 (1940): 317–44.

———. "Dated Chinese Manuscripts in the Stein Collection: VI. Tenth Century (A.D. 947–995)." *Bulletin of the School of Oriental and African Studies* 11, no. 1 (1943): 148–219.

———. "The Lament of the Lady of Chin." *T'oung Pao* 24, no. 4/5 (1925): 305–80.

———. "A Topographical Fragment from Tunhuang." *Bulletin of the School of Oriental Studies* 7, no. 3 (1934): 545–72.

———. "Tun Huang Lu: Notes on the District of Tun-Huang." *Journal of the Royal Asiatic Society of Great Britain and Ireland* (1914): 703–28.

———. "The Tun Huang Lu Re-Translated." *Journal of the Royal Asiatic Society of Great Britain and Ireland* (1915): 41–47.

Graff, David A. "Provincial Autonomy and Frontier Defense in Late Tang: The Case of the Lulong Army." In *Battlefronts Real and Imagined*, edited by Don J. Wyatt, 43–58. New York: Palgrave Macmillan, 2008.

Greiff, Susanne, Romina Schiavone, Zhang Jianlin, Hou Gailing, and Yang Junchang, eds. *The Tomb of Li Chui: Interdisciplinary Studies into a Tang Period Finds Assemblage.* Mainz: Verlag des Romisch-Germanischen Zentralmuseums, 2014.

Guojia wenwuju guwenxian yanjiushi 國家文物局古文獻研究室 et al., eds. *Tulufan chutu wenshu* 吐魯番出土文書, 10 vols. Beijing: Wenwu chubanshe, 1981–91.

Han, Jinke. "Silk and Gold Textiles from the Tang Underground Palace at Famen Si." In *Central Asian Textiles and Their Contexts in the Early Middle Ages*, edited by Regula Schorta, 129–45. Riggisberg, Switzerland: Abegg-Stiftung, 2006.

Han Wei 韓偉. "Famensi digong Tangdai 'Sui zhenshen yiwu zhang' kao" 法門寺地宮唐代隨真身衣物帳考. *Wenwu* 文物, no. 5 (1991): 27–37.

Han Wei 韓偉, and Zhang Jianlin 張建林. *Shaanxi xin chutu Tang mu bihua* 陝西新出土唐墓壁畫. Chongqing: Chongqing chubanshe, 1998.

Hansen, Valerie. "A Brief History of the Turfan Oasis." *Orientations* 30, no. 4 (1999): 24–27.

———. "The Hejia Village Hoard: A Snapshot of China's Silk Road Trade." *Orientations* 34, no. 2 (2003): 14–19.

———. "The Impact of the Silk Road Trade on a Local Community: The Turfan Oasis, 500–800." In *Les Sogdiens en Chine*, edited by Étienne de La Vaissière and Eric Trombert, 283–310. Paris: École française d'Extrême-Orient, 2005.

———. "Introduction: Turfan as a Silk Road Community." *Asia Major*, Third Series 11, no. 2 (1998): 1–12.

———. *Negotiating Daily Life in Traditional China: How Ordinary People Used Contracts, 600–1400.* New Haven: Yale University Press, 1995.

———. "New Work on the Sogdians, the Most Important Traders on the Silk Road, A.D. 500–1000." *T'oung Pao* 89, no. 1/3 (2003): 149–61.

———. *The Silk Road: A New History*. New York: Oxford University Press, 2012.

———. "The Tribute Trade with Khotan in Light of Materials Found at the Dunhuang Library Cave." *Bulletin of the Asia Institute* 19 (2005): 37–46.

Hansen, Valerie, and Anna Mata-Fink. "Records from a Seventh-Century Pawnshop in China." In *The Origins of Value: The Financial Innovations that Created Modern Capital Markets*, edited by William N. Goetzmann and K. Geert Rouwenhorst, 54–64. New York: Oxford University Press, 2005.

Hansen, Valerie, and Xinjiang Rong. "How the Residents of Turfan Used Textiles as Money." Journal of the Royal Asiatic Society 23, no. 2 (2013): 281–305.

Hansen, Valerie, and Helen Wang. "Introduction." *Journal of the Royal Asiatic Society* 23, no. 2 (2013): 155–63.

Harada Yoshito 原田淑人. *Chinese Dress and Personal Ornaments in the Han and Six Dynasties.* Tokyo: Tōyō Bunko, 1937.

———. *Shina Tōdai no fukushoku* 支那唐代の服飾. Tokyo: Tokyo Teikoku Daigaku, 1921.

———. *Tōdai no fukushoku* 唐代の服飾. Tokyo: Tōyō Bunko, 1970.

Harper, Prudence O. *In Search of a Cultural Identity: Monuments and Artifacts of the Sasanian Near East, Third to Seventh Century A.D.* New York: Bibliotheca Persica, 2006.

Harte, Negley B. "State Control of Dress and Social Change in Pre-Industrial England." In *Trade, Government, and Economy in Pre-Industrial England: Essays Presented to E. J. Fisher*, edited by D. C. Coleman and A. H. John, 132–65. London: Weidenfeld and Nicolson, 1976.

Hartman, Charles. *Han Yu and the T'ang Search for Unity*. Princeton: Princeton University Press, 1986.

Hartwell, Robert. "Demographic, Political, and Social Transformations of China, 750–1550." *Harvard Journal of Asiatic Studies* 42, no. 2 (1982): 365–442.

Hay, John. "The Body Invisible in Chinese Art?" In *Body, Subject, & Power in China*, edited by Angela Zito and Tani Barlow, 42–77. Chicago: University of Chicago Press, 1994.

Hay, Jonathan. "Margins, Transitions, Interstices: How to Look at Chinese Paintings." Class lecture at Institute of Fine Arts, New York University, February 24, 2015.

———. "Seeing through Dead Eyes: How Early Tang Tombs Staged the Afterlife." *RES: Anthropology and Aesthetics*, no. 57/58 (2010): 16–54.

———. *Sensuous Surfaces: The Decorative Object in Early Modern China*. London: Reaktion Books, 2009.

———. "Tenth-Century Painting before Song Taizong's Reign: A Macrohistorical View." In *Tenth-Century China and Beyond: Art and Visual Culture in a Multi-Centered Age*, edited by Wu Hung, 285–318. Chicago: University of Chicago Press, 2013.

Hebei Province Research Institute of Cultural Relics 河北省文物研究所. *Wudai Wang Chuzhi mu* 五代王處直墓. Beijing: Wenwu chubanshe, 1998.

Heller, Amy. "Two Inscribed Fabrics and their Historical Context: Some Observations on Esthetics and Silk Trade in Tibet, 7th to 9th Century." In *Entlang der Seidenstrasse. Frühmittelalterliche Kunst zwischen Persien und China in der Abegg-Stiftung*, edited by K. Otavsky, 95–118. Riggisberg, Switzerland: Riggisberger Berichte 6, 1998.

Heller, Sarah-Grace. "Anxiety, Hierarchy, and Appearance in Thirteenth-Century Sumptuary Laws and the Roman de La Rose." *French Historical Studies* 27, no. 2 (2004): 311–48.

———. *Fashion in Medieval France*. Oxford: Boydell and Brewer, 2007.

Helms, Mary. W. *Craft and the Kingly Ideal: Art, Trade, and Power*. Austin: University of Texas Press, 1993.

Hino Kasaiburō 日野開三郎. *Tōdai teiten no kenkyū* 唐代邸店の研究. Fukuoka: Kyushu Daigaku Bungakubu Tōyōshi Kenkyūshitsu, 1968.

———. *Zoku Tōdai teiten no kenkyū* 続唐代邸店の研究. Fukuoka: Kyushu Daigaku Bungakubu Tōyōshi Kenkyūshitsu, 1970.

Hiraoka Takeo 平岡武夫. *Chōan to Rakuyō: Shiryō* 長安と洛陽: 資料. Kyoto: Kyoto Daigaku Jinbun Kagaku Kenkyūjo Sakuin Henshū Iinkai, 1956.

Hirth, Friedrich. "The Story of Chang K'ién, China's Pioneer in Western Asia: Text and Translation of Chapter 123 of Ssï-Ma Ts'ién's Shï-Ki." *Journal of the American Oriental Society* 37 (1917): 89–152.

Ho, Norman P. "Understanding Traditional Chinese Law in Practice: The Implementation of Criminal Law in the Tang Dynasty (618–907)." *Pacific Basin Law Journal* 32, no. 2 (2015): 145–80.

Hoffman, Eva. "Pathways of Portability: Islamic and Christian Interchange from the Tenth to the Twelfth Century." *Art History* 24, no. 1 (2001): 17–50.

Hollander, Anne. *Seeing through Clothes*. Berkeley: University of California Press, 1993.

Howard, Angela. "Gilt Bronze Guanyin from the Nanzhao Kingdom of Yunnan: Hybrid Art from the Southwestern Frontier." *The Journal of the Walters Art Gallery* 48 (1990): 1–12.

Howell, Martha. *Commerce before Capitalism in Europe, 1300–1600*. New York: Cambridge University Press, 2010.

Hu, Suh [Hu Shi]. "Notes on Dr. Lionel Giles' Article on 'Tun Huang Lu.'" *Journal of the Royal Asiatic Society of Great Britain and Ireland* (1915): 35–39.

Huan Kuan 桓寬, comp. *Yantie lun* 鹽鐵論. Beijing: Zhonghua shuju, 1991.

Huang Nengfu 黄能馥 and Chen Juanjuan 陳娟娟. *Zhongguo fuzhuang shi* 中國服裝史. Beijing: Beijing lüyou chubanshe, 1995.

Huang Zhengjian 黄正建. *Tangdai yishi zhuxing yanjiu* 唐代衣食住行研究. Beijing: Shoudu shifan daxue chubanshe, 1998.

———. "Wang Ya zouwen yu Tang houqi chefu zhidu de bianhua" 王涯奏文與唐後期車服制度的變化. *Tang Yanjiu* 唐研究, no. 10 (2004): 297–327.

———. *Zhongwan Tangdai shehui yu zhengzhi yanjiu* 中晚唐代社會與政治研究. Beijing: Zhongguo shehui kexue chubanshe, 2006.

Hucker, Charles O. *A Dictionary of Official Titles in Imperial China*. Stanford: Stanford University Press, 1985.

Hunt, Alan. *Governance of the Consuming Passions*. New York: St. Martin's Press, 1996.

Ikeda On 池田温. *Chūgoku kodai sekichō kenkyū* 中国古代籍帳研究. Tokyo: Tōyō Bunko, 1979.

———. "T'ang Household Registers and Related Documents." In *Perspectives on the T'ang*, edited by Denis Twitchett and Arthur F. Wright, 121–50. New Haven: Yale University Press, 1973.

Ikegami, Eiko. *Bonds of Civility: Aesthetic Networks and the Political Origins of Japanese Culture*. New York: Cambridge University Press, 2005.

Ingold, Tim. "Materials against Materiality." *Archaeological Dialogues* 14, no. 1 (2007): 1–16.

———. *The Perception of the Environment: Essays on Livelihood, Dwelling and Skill*. New York: Routledge, 2000.
———. "The Textility of Making." *Cambridge Journal of Economics* 34, no. 1 (2010): 91–102.
Ji, Minkyung. "Commoditizing Tombs: Materialism in the Funerary Art of Middle Imperial China and Korea." PhD diss., University of Pennsylvania, 2014.
Jia, Yiliang, and Wenjuan Ma. "The Costume of Wuji in the Dunhuang Murals of Tang Dynasty." *Asian Social Science* 9, no. 1 (2013): 299–305.
Johnson, David G. "The Last Years of a Great Clan: The Li Family of Chao cün in Late T'ang and Early Sung." *Harvard Journal of Asiatic Studies* 37, no. 1 (1977): 5–102.
———. *The Medieval Chinese Oligarchy*. Boulder: Westview Press, 1977.
Johnson, Wallace. "Status and Liability for Punishment in the T'ang Code." *Chicago-Kent Law Review* 71 (1995): 217–29.
———, ed. and trans. *The T'ang Code*. Vol. 1, *General Principles*. Princeton: Princeton University Press, 1979.
———. *The T'ang Code*. Vol. 2, *Specific Articles*. Princeton: Princeton University Press, 1997.
Jones, Ann Rosalind, and Peter Stallybrass. *Renaissance Clothing and the Materials of Memory*. New York: Cambridge University Press, 2000.
Jones, Jennifer. *Sexing La Mode: Gender, Fashion and Commercial Culture in Old Regime France*. Oxford: Berg, 2004.
Kang, Xiaofei. "The Fox [hu] and the Barbarian [hu]: Unraveling Representations of the Other in Late Tang Tales." *Journal of Chinese Religions* 27, no. 1 (1999): 35–67.
Karetzky, Patricia. "The Representation of Women in Medieval China: Recent Archaeological Evidence." *T'ang Studies*, no. 17 (1999): 213–71.
Katō Shigeshi 加藤繁. "On the Hang or Association of Merchants in China, with Special Reference to the Institution in the Tang and Song Periods." *Memoirs of the Research Department of the Tōyō Bunko* 9 (1936): 45–83.
———. *Shina keizaishi kōshō* 支那経済史考證, 2 vols. Tokyo: Tōyō Bunko, 1953.
———. "Tang Song shidai de caoshi ji qi fazhan" 唐宋時代的草市及其發展. In *Zhongguo jingjishi kaozheng* 中國經濟史考證. Translated by Wu Jie, 367–74. Beijing: Shangwu yinshuguan, 1959.
Kennedy, Philip F. and Shawkat M. Toorawa, eds. *Two Arabic Travel Books*. New York: New York University Press, 2014.
Kesner, Ladislav. "Face as Artifact in Early Chinese Art." *RES: Anthropology and Aesthetics*, no. 51 (2007): 33–56.
Kiang, Heng Chye. *Cities of Aristocrats and Bureaucrats: The Development of Medieval Chinese Cityscapes*. Honolulu: University of Hawai'i Press, 1999.
———. "Visualizing Everyday Life in the City: A Categorization System for Residential Wards in Tang Chang'an." *Journal of the Society of Architectural Historians* 73, no. 1 (2014): 91–117.
Killerby, Catherine K. *Sumptuary Law in Italy, 1200–1500*. New York: Clarendon, 2002.
Knechtges, David R. "Gradually Entering the Realm of Delight: Food and Drink in Early Medieval China." *Journal of the American Oriental Society* 117, no. 2 (1997): 229–39.
Krahl, Regina, et al. *Shipwrecked: Tang Treasures and Monsoon Winds*. Washington, DC: Arthur M. Sackler Gallery, Smithsonian Institution Press, 2010.
Kroll, Paul W. "The Dancing Horses of T'ang." *T'oung Pao* 67, no. 3/5 (1981): 240–68.
———. *Essays in Medieval Chinese Literature and Cultural History*. Burlington, Vt.: Ashgate, 2009.
———. "The Life and Writings of Xu Hui (627–650), Worthy Consort, at the Early Tang Court." *Asia Major*, Third Series 22, no. 2 (2009): 35–64.

———. "Nostalgia and History in Mid-Ninth-Century Verse: Cheng Yü's Poem on 'The Chin-Yang Gate.'" *T'oung Pao* 89, no. 4/5 (2003): 286–366.
———. "The Significance of the *fu* in the History of T'ang Poetry." *Tang Studies*, no. 18–19 (2000): 87–105.
Kuchta, David. "The Making of the Self-Made Man: Class, Clothing, and English Masculinity, 1688–1832." In *The Sex of Things: Gender and Consumption in Historical Perspective*, edited by Victoria de Grazia, 54–78. Berkeley: University of California Press, 1996.
Kuhn, Dieter, ed. *Chinese Silks*. New Haven: Yale University Press, 2012.
———. *Science and Civilisation in China*. Vol. 5, pt. 9, *Textile Technology: Spinning and Reeling*. Edited by Joseph Needham. Cambridge: Cambridge University Press, 1988.
———. "Silk Weaving in Ancient China: From Geometric Figures to Patterns of Pictorial Likeness." *Chinese Science*, no. 12 (1995): 77–114.
Kyan, Winston. "Family Space: Buddhist Materiality and Ancestral Fashioning in Mogao Cave 231." *The Art Bulletin* 92, no. 1/2 (2010): 61–82.
Laver, James. *Style in Costume*. London: Oxford University Press, 1949.
———. *Taste and Fashion: From the French Revolution until Today*. London: G. G. Harrap, 1937.
Lee, Jen-Der. "Gender and Medicine in Tang China." *Asia Major*, Third Series 16, no. 2 (2003): 1–32.
Leslie, Donald Daniel. "Persian Temples in T'ang China." *Monumenta Serica* 35 (1981): 275–303.
Levy, Howard S. "The Career of Yang Kuei-Fei." *T'oung Pao* 45, no. 4/5 (1957): 451–89.
Lewis, Mark E. *China's Cosmopolitan Empire*. Cambridge, Mass.: Harvard University Press, 2009.
———. *The Flood Myths of Early China*. Albany: State University of New York Press, 2006.
Li Bozhong 李伯重. *Tangdai Jiangnan nongye de fazhan* 唐代江南農業的發展. Beijing: Nongye chubanshe, 1990.
Li Fang 李昉 (925–996) et al., comps. *Taiping guangji* 太平廣記, 5 vols. Beijing: Renmin wenxue chubanshe, 1959.
———. *Wenyuan yinghua* 文苑英華, 6 vols. Beijing: Zhonghua shuju, 1966.
Li Jiankun 李建崑, ed. *Zhang Ji shiji xiaozhu* 張籍詩集校注. Taipei: Huatai wenhua, 2001.
Li Jifu 李吉甫 (758–814), comp. *Yuanhe junxian tuzhi* 元和郡縣圖志, 2 vols. Beijing: Zhonghua shuju, 1983.
Li Jinxiu 李錦繡. *Tangdai caizheng shigao* 唐代財政史稿, 5 vols. Beijing: Shehui kexue wenxian chubanshe, 2007.
Li Linfu 李林甫 and Li Longji 李隆基, eds. *Da Tang liudian* 大唐六典. Revised by Konoe Iehiro 近衛家熙 (1667–1736). Edited by Uchida Tomoo 内田智雄 and Hiroike Chikurō 广池千九郎. Xi'an: Sanqin chubanshe, 1991.
Li Ming 李明. "Zhuan muzhi yu jinhua guan—'Tang Li muzhi' xuhou" 磚墓誌與金花冠—《唐李墓誌》讀後. *Wenbo* 文博, no. 3 (2015): 64–67.
Li Xiaocong 李孝聰. Tangdai diyu jiegou yu yunzuo kongjian 唐代地域結構與運作空間. Shanghai: Shanghai cishu chubanshe, 2003.
Li Xingming 李星明. *Tangdai mushi bihua yanjiu* 唐代墓室壁畫. Shaanxi: Shaanxi renmin meishu chubanshe, 2005.
———. "*Zanhua shinü tu* niandai lijian" 《簪花仕女圖》年代蠡見. *Hubei meishu xueyuan xuebao* 湖北美術學院學報, no. 1 (2006): 65–71.
Li Yanshou 李延壽 (active seventh century) et al., comps. *Bei shi* 北史, 10 vols. Beijing: Zhonghua shuju, 1995.
Li Zhao 李肇 (fl. early ninth century). *Tang guoshi bu* 唐國史補. Shanghai: Gudian wenxue chubanshe, 1957.
Lien, Y. Edmund. "Dunhuang Gazetteers of the Tang Period." *Tang Studies*, no. 27 (2009): 19–39.

Lingley, Kate A. “Naturalizing The Exotic: On the Changing Meanings of Ethnic Dress in Medieval China.” *Ars Orientalis* 38 (2010): 50–80.

Lipovetsky, Gilles. *The Empire of Fashion: Dressing Modern Democracy.* Translated by Catherine Porter. Princeton: Princeton University Press, 1994.

Liu, James T. C. “Polo and Cultural Change: From T’ang to Sung China.” *Harvard Journal of Asiatic Studies* 45, no. 1 (1985): 203–24.

Liu Xu 劉昫 et al., comps. *Jiu Tangshu* 舊唐書, 16 vols. Shanghai: Zhonghua shuju. Reprint, 1995.

Louis, François. “The Hejiacun Rhyton and the Chinese Wine Horn (*gong*): Intoxicating Rarities and Their Antiquarian History.” *Artibus Asiae* 67, no. 2 (2007): 201–42.

Lu Huayu 盧華語. *Tangdai cansang sichou yanjiu* 唐代蠶桑絲綢研究. Beijing: Shoudu shifan daxue chubanshe, 1995.

Lu Xiangqian 盧向前. “Tangdai Xizhou tudi de guanli fangshi: Tangdai Xizhou tianzhi yanjiu zhi san” 唐代西州土地的管理方式—唐代西州田制研究之三. *Tang yanjiu* 唐研究 1 (1995): 385–408.

Lu Yang. “Dynastic Revival and Political Transformation in Late T’ang China: A Study of Emperor Hsien-Tsung (805–820) and His Reign.” PhD diss., Princeton University, 1999.

Lu Zhi 陸贄 (754–805). Lu Xuan Gong ji 陸宣公集, 3 vols. Shanghai: Zhonghua shuju, 1936.

Luo Feng 羅豐. *Guyuan nanjiao Sui-Tang mudi* 固原南郊隋唐墓地. Beijing: Wenwu chubanshe, 1996.

Ma Chengyuan 馬承源 and Yue Feng 岳峰, eds. *Xinjiang Weiwu’erqi zizhiqu silu kaogu zhenpin* 新疆维吾尔自治区絲路考古珎品. Shanghai: Shanghai yiwen chubanshe, 1998.

Ma Dezhi 馬得志. “Tangdai Chang’an cheng kaogu jilue” 唐代長安城考古紀略. *Kaogu* 考古, no. 11 (1963): 595–611.

Ma Zili 馬自力. “Jianguan ji qi huodong yu zhong Tang wenxue” 諫官及其活動與中唐文學. *Wenxue yichan* 文學遺產 6 (2005): 16–30.

———. *Zhong Tang wenren zhi shehui jiaose yu wenxue huodong* 中唐文人之社會角色與文學活動. Beijing: Zhongguo shehui kexue chubanshe, 2005.

Mackerras, Colin. “Sino-Uighur Diplomatic and Trade Contacts.” *Central Asiatic Journal* 13, no. 3 (1969): 215–40.

Malagò, Amina. “The Origin of Kesi, the Chinese Silk Tapestry.” *Annali di Ca’ Foscari* 27, no. 3 (1988): 279–97.

Mann, Susan. “Myths of Asian Womanhood.” *Journal of Asian Studies* 59, no. 4 (2000): 835–62.

Matsumoto Kaneo 松本包夫. *Shōsōin-gire to Asuka Tenpyō no senshoku* 正倉院裂と飛鳥天平の染織. Kyoto: Shikōsha, 1984.

Mauss, Marcel. *The Gift: The Form and Reason for Exchange in Archaic Societies.* Translated by W. D. Halls. London: Routledge, 1990.

Mckendrick, Neil, John Brewer, and John H. Plumb, eds. *The Birth of a Consumer Society: The Commercialization of Eighteenth Century England.* Bloomington: Indiana University Press, 1982.

McMullen, David. “Devolution in Chinese History: The Fengjian Debate Revisited.” *International Journal of China Studies* 2, no. 2 (2011): 135–54.

———. “Disorder in the Ranks: A Political Analysis of Tang Court Assemblies.” *Tang Studies*, no. 28 (2010): 1–60.

———. “The Emperor, the Princes, and the Prefectures: A Political Analysis of the Pu’an Decree of 756 and the Fengjian Issue.” *Tang Studies* 32, no. 1 (2014): 47–97.

———. “The Role of the Zhouli in Seventh- and Eighth-Century Civil Administrative Traditions.” In *Statecraft and Classical Learning: The Rituals of Zhou in East Asian History*, edited by Benjamin Elman and Martin Kern, 179–228. Leiden: Brill, 2010.

———. *State and Scholars in T'ang China*. Cambridge: Cambridge University Press, 1988.
Medley, Margaret. *The Chinese Potter: A Practical History of Chinese Ceramics*. 3rd ed. Oxford: Phaidon, 1989.
———. *T'ang Pottery and Porcelain*. London: Faber and Faber, 1981.
Meister, Michael W. "The Pearl Roundel in Chinese Textile Design." *Ars Orientalis* 8 (1970): 255–67.
Meng Erdong 孟二冬. *Zhong Tang shige zhi kaituo yu xinbian* 中唐詩歌之開拓與新變. Beijing: Beijing daxue chubanshe, 1998.
Minneapolis Institute of Arts. *Catalogue of an Exhibition of Imperial Robes and Textiles of the Chinese Court*. Minneapolis: Minneapolis Institute of Arts, 1943.
Moore, Oliver J. *Rituals of Recruitment in Tang China: Reading an Annual Programme in the Collected Statements by Wang Dingbao (870–940)*. Leiden: Brill, 2004.
Morohashi Tetsuji 諸橋轍次. Dai Kan-Wa Jiten 大漢和辭典, 13 vols. Tokyo: Taishūkan Shoten, 1984.
Mukerji, Chandra. *From Graven Images: Patterns of Modern Materialism*. New York: Columbia University Press, 1983.
Muthesius, Anna. *Studies in Byzantine and Islamic Silk Weaving*. London: Pindar, 1995.
Na Chunying 納春英. *Tangdai fushi shishang* 唐代服飾時尚. Beijing: Zhongguo shehui kexue chubanshe, 2009.
Nagel, Alexander. "Fashion and the Now-Time of Renaissance Art." *RES: Anthropology and Aesthetics*, no. 46 (2004): 32–52.
Naito, Torajiro. "A Comprehensive Look at the T'ang-Sung Period." Translated by Joshua A. Fogel. *Chinese Studies in History* 17, no. 1 (1983): 88–99.
Nicolini-Zani, Matteo. "The Tang Christian Pillar from Luoyang and its Jingjiao Inscription." *Monumenta Serica* 57, no. 1 (2009): 99–140.
Niessen, Sandra. "Afterword: Re-Orienting Fashion Theory." In *Re-Orienting Fashion: The Globalization of Asian Dress*, edited by Sandra Niessen, Ann Marie Leshkowich, and Carla Jones, 243–66. New York: Berg, 2003.
Niida Noboru 仁井田陞, comp. *Tangdai ling shiyi* 唐令拾遺. Edited by Li Jing 栗劲. Chinese edition. Changchun: Changchun chubanshe, 1989.
Ning Xin 寧欣. "Lun Tangdai Chang'an linglei shangren yu shichang fayu—yi 'Dou Yi zhuan' wei zhongxin" 論唐代長安另類商人與市場發育—以《竇乂傳》爲中心. *Xibei shidaxuebao* 西北師大學報, no. 4 (2006): 71–78.
———. *Tang Song ducheng shehui jiegou yanjiu: Dui chengshi jingji yu shehui de guanzhu* 唐宋都城社會結構研究: 對城市經濟與社會的關注. Beijing: Shangwu yinshuguan, 2009.
Nugent, Christopher M. B. "The Lady and Her Scribes: Dealing with the Multiple Dunhuang Copies of Wei Zhuang's 'Lament of the Lady of Qin.'" *Asia Major*, Third Series 20, no. 2 (2007): 25–73.
———. *Manifest in Words, Written on Paper: Producing and Circulating Poetry in Tang Dynasty China*. Cambridge, Mass.: Harvard University Asia Center. 2010.
Ouyang Xiu 歐陽修 and Song Qi 宋祁 et al., comps. *Xin Tangshu* 新唐書, 20 vols. Shanghai: Zhonghua shuju. Reprint, 2006.
Owen, Stephen. "The Cultural Tang (650–1020)." In *The Cambridge History of Chinese Literature: Volume 1*, edited by Kang-I. Sun Chang and Stephen Owen, 286–380. Cambridge: Cambridge University Press, 2010.
———. "The Difficulty of Pleasure." *Extrême-Orient Extrême-Occident*, no. 20 (1998): 9–30.
———. *The End of the Chinese 'Middle Ages': Essays in Mid-Tang Literary Culture*. Stanford: Stanford University Press, 1996.
Pan, Yihong. "Integration of the Northern Ethnic Frontiers in Tang China." *The Chinese Historical Review* 19, no. 1 (2012): 3–26.

———. *Son of Heaven and Heavenly Qaghan: Sui-Tang China and Its Neighbors*. Bellingham: Center for East Asian Studies, Western Washington University Press, 1997.

Peng Dingqiu 彭定求 (1645–1719) et al., comps. *Quan Tangshi* 全唐詩, 25 vols. Shanghai: Zhonghua shuju. Reprint, 1960.

Perrot, Philippe. *Fashioning the Bourgeoisie: A History of Clothing in the Nineteenth Century*. Translated by Richard Bienvenu. Princeton: Princeton University Press, 1994.

Picken, L. E. R. "T'ang Music and Musical Instruments." *T'oung Pao* 55, no. 1/3 (1969): 74–122.

Polhemus, Ted, and Lynne Proctor, eds. *Fashion and Anti-Fashion: Anthropology of Clothing and Adornment*. London: Thames and Hudson, 1978.

Priest, Alan. *Costumes from the Forbidden City*. New York: Metropolitan Museum of Art, 1945.

Qi Dongfang 齊東方. "Hejiacun yibao de mai cang didian he niandai" 何家村遺寶的埋藏地點和年代. *Kaogu yu wenwu* 考古與文物 2 (2003): 70–74.

———. "Tang yong yu funü shenghuo" 唐俑與婦女生活. In *Tang Song nüxing yu shehui* 唐宋女性與社會, vol. 2, edited by Deng Xiaonan, 322–37. Shanghai: Shanghai cishu chubanshe, 2003.

———. *Tangdai jinyin qi yanjiu* 唐代金銀器研究. Beijing: Zhongguo shehui kexue chubanshe, 1999.

Qi Dongfang 齊東方 and Zhang Jing 張靜. "Tang mu bihua yu Gaosong zhong gufen [Takamatsuzuka kofun] bihua de bijiao yanjiu" 唐墓壁畫與高松冢古墳壁畫的比較研究. *Tang Yanjiu* 唐研究 1 (1995): 447–72.

Rawson, Jessica. "Inside Out: Creating the Exotic within Early Tang Dynasty China in the Seventh and Eighth Centuries." *World Art* 2, no. 1 (2012): 25–45.

Reischauer, Edwin O. "Notes on T'ang Dynasty Sea Routes." *Harvard Journal of Asiatic Studies* 5, no. 2 (1940): 142–64.

Roche, Daniel. *The Culture of Clothing: Dress and Fashion in the Ancien Regime*. Translated by Jean Birrell. New York: Cambridge University Press, 1994.

Rong, Xinjiang, and Xin Wen. "Newly Discovered Chinese-Khotanese Bilingual Tallies." *Journal of Inner Asian Art and Archaeology* 3 (2008): 99–118.

Rong Xinjiang 榮新江. "Beichao Sui Tang Sute ren zhi qianxi ji qi juluo" 北朝隋唐粟特人之遷徙及其聚落. *Guoxue yanjiu* 國學研究 6 (1999): 27–85.

———. *Dunhuang xue shiba jiang* 敦煌學十八講. Beijing: Beijing daxue chubanshe, 2001.

———. "Nü ban nanzhuang—Tangdai qianqi de xingbie yishi" 女扮男裝—唐代前期的性別意識. In *Tang Song nüxing yu shehui* 唐宋女性與社會, edited by Deng Xiaonan, 2:723–50. Shanghai: Shanghai cishu chubanshe, 2003.

———. *Zhonggu Zhongguo yu wailai wenming* 中古中國與外來文明. Beijing: Shenghuo, tushu, xinzhi sanlian shudian, 2001.

Rong Xinjiang 榮新江, Li Xiao 李肖, and Meng Xianshi 孟憲實, eds. *Xinhuo Tulufan chutu wenxian* 新獲吐魯番出土文獻. 2 vols. Beijing: Zhonghua shuju, 2008.

Rothschild, Norman Harry. "'Her Influence Great, Her Merit beyond Measure': A Translation and Initial Investigation of the Epitaph of Shangguan Wan'er." *Studies in Chinese Religions* 1, no. 2 (2015): 131–48.

———. "An Inquiry into Reign Era Changes under Wu Zhao, China's Only Female Emperor." *Early Medieval China* 12 (2006): 123–49.

Rouzer, Paul F. *Articulated Ladies: Gender and the Male Community in Early Chinese Texts*. Cambridge, Mass.: Harvard University Asia Center, 2001.

———. "Watching the Voyeurs: Palace Poetry and the Yuefu of Wen Tingyun." *Chinese Literature: Essays, Articles, Reviews (CLEAR)* 11 (1989): 13–34.

Rublack, Ulinka. *Dressing Up: Cultural Identity in Renaissance Europe*. New York: Oxford University Press, 2010.

Saitō, Masaru. "Tō, Uiguru kenba bōeki saikō" 唐, 回鶻絹馬交易再考. *Shigaku-Zasshi* 史学雑誌 108, no. 10 (1999): 33–58.
Satō Taketoshi 佐藤武敏. *Chūgoku kodai kinuorimonoshi kenkyū* 中国古代絹織物史研究. 2 vols. Tokyo: Kazama Shobu, 1977–78.
———. "Tōdai ni okeru kinuorimono no sanchi" 唐代における絹織物の産地. *Jinbun Kenkyū* 人文研究 25, no. 10 (1973): 57–87.
Schäfer, Dagmar. "Silken Strands: Making Technology Work in China." In Cultures of Knowledge: Technology in Chinese History, edited by Dagmar Schäfer, 45–73. Leiden: Brill, 2011.
Schafer, Edward. *The Golden Peaches of Samarkand: A Study of T'ang Exotics.* Berkeley: University of California Press, 1963.
———. "The Last Years of Ch'ang-An." *Oriens Extremus* 10, no. 2 (1963): 133–79.
Schmid, Neil. "The Material Culture of Exegesis and Liturgy and a Change in the Artistic Representations in Dunhuang Caves, ca. 700–1000." *Asia Major*, Third Series 19, no. 1/2 (2006): 171–210.
Schrenk, Sabine. *Textilien des Mittelmeerraumes aus spätantiker bis frühislamischer Zeit.* Riggisberg: Abegg-Stiftung, 2004.
Sen, Tansen. *Buddhism, Diplomacy, and Trade: The Realignment of Sino-Indian Relations, 600–1400.* Honolulu: University of Hawai'i Press, 2003.
Sewell, William H. "The Empire of Fashion and the Rise of Capitalism in Eighteenth-Century France." *Past and Present*, no. 206 (2010): 81–120.
Shaanxi Provincial Cultural Relics Bureau et al. 陝西省文物管理委員會等. "Tang Ashina Zhong mu fajue jianbao" 唐阿史那忠墓發掘簡報. *Kaogu* 考古, no. 2 (1977): 132–38.
———. "Tang Yongtai gongzhu mu fajue jianbao" 唐永泰公主墓發掘簡報. *Wenwu*文物, no. 1 (1964): 7–33.
Shaanxi Provincial Institute of Archaeology 陝西省考古研究所 et al. *Tang Huizhuang taizi Li Hui mu fajue baogao* 唐惠庄太子李撝墓發掘報告. Beijing: Kexue chubanshe, 2004.
———. "Tang Huizhuang taizi mu fajue jianbao" 唐惠庄太子墓發掘簡報. *Kaogu yu wenwu* 考古與文物, no. 2 (1999): 3–21.
———. *Tang Jiemin taizi mu fajue baogao* 唐節愍太子墓發掘報告. Beijing: Kexue chubanshe, 2004.
———. "Tang Li Chui mu fajue jianbao" 唐李倕墓發掘簡報. *Kaogu yu wenwu* 考古與文物, no. 6 (2015): 3–22.
———. *Tang Li Xian mu fajue baogao* 唐李憲墓發掘報告. Beijing: Kexue chubanshe, 2004.
———. *Tang Xincheng zhanggongzhu mu fajue baogao* 唐新城長公主墓發掘報告. Beijing: Kexue chubanshe, 2004.
———. "Tang Zhaoling Xincheng zhanggongzhu mu fajue jianbao" 唐昭陵新城長公主墓發掘簡. *Kaogu yu wenwu* 考古與文物, no. 3 (1997): 3–24.
———. *Tangdai Xue Jing mu fajue baogao* 唐代薛儆墓發掘報告. Beijing: Kexue chubanshe, 2000.
Shaanxi Provincial Museum et al. 陝西省博物館等. *Tang mu bihua guoji xueshu yantaohui lunwen ji* 唐墓壁畫國際學術研討會論文集. Xi'an: Sanqin chubanshe, 2006.
———. "Tang Yide taizi mu fajue jianbao" 唐懿德太子墓發掘簡報. *Wenwu* 文物, no. 7 (1972): 26–32.
———. "Tang Zheng Rentai mu fajue jianbao" 唐鄭仁泰墓發掘簡報. *Wenwu* 文物, no. 7 (1972): 33–42.
———. "Xi'an nanjiao Hejiacun faxian Tangdai jiaocang wenwu" 西安南郊何家村發現唐代窖藏文物. *Wenwu* 文物, no. 1 (1972): 30–42.
Shaanxi Provincial Museum 陝西省博物館 and Qian Country Bureau of Culture and Education 乾縣文教局唐墓發掘組. "Tang Zhanghuai taizi mu fajue jianbao" 唐章懷太子墓發掘簡報. *Wenwu* 文物, no. 7 (1972): 13–25.

Shen Congwen 沈從文. *Zhongguo gudai fushi yanjiu* 中國古代服飾研究. Hong Kong: Shangwu yinshuguan, 1981.

Sheng, Angela. "Addendum to 'Chinese Silk Tapestry: A Brief Social Historical Perspective of Its Early Development.'" In *Chinese and Central Asian Textiles: Selected Articles from Orientations 1973–1997*, 225. Hong Kong: Orientations Magazine, 1998.

———. "Chinese Silk Tapestry: A Brief Social Historical Perspective of Its Early Development." *Orientations* 26, no. 5 (1995): 70–75. Reprinted in *Chinese and Central Asian Textiles: Selected Articles from Orientations 1973–1997*, 166–71. Hong Kong: Orientations Magazine, 1998.

———. "Determining the Value of Textiles in the Tang Dynasty, in Memory of Professor Denis Twitchett (1925–2006)." *Journal of the Royal Asiatic Society* 23, no. 2 (2013): 175–95.

———. "The Disappearance of Silk Weaves with Weft Effects in Early China." *Chinese Science*, no. 12 (1995): 41–76.

———. "Innovations in Textile Techniques on China's Northwest Frontier, 500–700 AD." *Asia Major*, Third Series 11, no. 2 (1998): 117–60.

———. "Textile Finds along the Silk Road." In *The Glory of the Silk Road: Art from Ancient China*, edited by Li Jian, 42–48. Dayton, Ohio: Dayton Art Institute, 2003.

———. "Textiles from Astana: Art, Technology, and Social Change." In *Central Asian Textiles and Their Contexts in the Early Middle Ages*, edited by Regula Schorta, 117–28. Riggisberg, Switzerland: Abegg-Stiftung, 2006.

———. "Textile Use, Technology, and Change in Rural Textile Production in Song China (960–1279)." PhD diss., University of Pennsylvania, 1990.

Shi, Jie. "'My Tomb Will Be Opened in Eight Hundred Years': A New Way of Seeing the Afterlife in Six Dynasties China." *Harvard Journal of Asiatic Studies* 72, no. 2 (2012): 217–57.

Shi Zhecun 施蟄存. *Tangshi baihua* 唐詩白話. Shanghai: Shanghai guji chubanshe, 1987.

Shields, Anna M. "Defining Experience: The Poems of Seductive Allure (*Yanshi*) of the Mid-Tang Poet Yuan Zhen (779–831)." *Journal of the American Oriental Society* 122, no. 1 (2002): 61–78.

———. "Gossip, Anecdote, and Literary History: Representations of the Yuanhe Era in Tang Anecdote Collections." In *Idle Talk: Gossip and Anecdote in Traditional China*, edited by Jack W. Chen and David Schaberg, 107–31. Berkeley: University of California Press, 2014.

———. "Remembering When: The Uses of Nostalgia in the Poetry of Bai Juyi and Yuan Zhen." *Harvard Journal of Asiatic Studies* 66, no. 2 (2006): 321–61.

Sima Guang 司馬光 (1019–1086) et al. *Zizhi tongjian* 資治通鑑, 10 vols. Annotated by Hu Sanxing 胡三省 (1230–1302). Taipei: Tiangong shuju. Reprint, 1988.

Sima Qian 司馬遷. *Shiji* 史記, 10 vols. Beijing: Zhonghua shuju. Reprint, 2013.

Simmel, Georg. "Fashion." *International Quarterly*, no. 10 (1904): 130–55.

———. "The Philosophy of Fashion." *The American Journal of Sociology* 62, no. 6 (1957): 541–58.

Skaff, Jonathan Karam. "The Sogdian Trade Diaspora in East Turkestan during the Seventh and Eighth Centuries." *Journal of the Economic and Social History of the Orient* 46, no. 4 (2003): 475–524.

———. *Sui-Tang China and Its Turko-Mongol Neighbors: Culture, Power, and Connections, 580–800.* New York: Oxford University Press, 2012.

Skinner, G. William, ed. *The City in Late Imperial China.* Stanford: Stanford University Press, 1977.

Sombart, Werner. "Economic Life in the Modern Age." Edited by Nico Stehr and Reiner Grundmann. New Brunswick: Transaction Publishers, 2001.

———. *Luxury and Capitalism.* Translated by W. R. Dittmar. Ann Arbor: University of Michigan Press, 1967.

Sommer, Matthew H. *Sex, Law, and Society in Late Imperial China.* Stanford: Stanford University Press, 2000.

Song Minqui 宋敏求 (1019–1079), comp. *Tang da zhaoling ji* 唐大詔令集. Shanghai: Xuelin chubanshe. Reprint, 1992.
Soper, Alexander Coburn. "Yen Li-Pen, Yen Li-Te, Yen P'i, Yen Ch'ing: Three Generations in Three Dynasties." *Artibus Asiae* 51, no. 3/4 (1991): 199–206.
Spencer, Herbert. *The Principles of Sociology*. New Brunswick: Transaction Publishers, 2002.
Spring, Madeline K. "Fabulous Horses and Worthy Scholars in Ninth-Century China." *T'oung Pao* 74, no. 4/5 (1988): 173–210.
Steinhardt, Nancy Shatzman. *Chinese Imperial City Planning*. Honolulu: University of Hawai'i Press, 1990.
———. "Why Were Chang'an and Beijing So Different?" *Journal of the Society of Architectural Historians* 45, no. 4 (1986): 339–57.
Stuard, Susan. *Gilding the Market: Luxury and Fashion in Fourteenth-Century Italy*. Philadelphia: University of Pennsylvania Press, 2006.
Sun Ji 孫機. *Zhongguo gudai yufu luncong* 中國古代輿服論叢. Beijing: Wenwu chubanshe, 1993.
Sun Qi 孫棨. "Beili zhi" 北里志. In *Jiaofang ji, Beili zhi, Qinglou ji* 教坊記 · 北里志 ·青樓集. By Cui Lingqin 崔令欽, Sun Qi 孫棨, and Xia Bohe 夏伯和. Shanghai: Gudian wenxue chubanshe, 1957.
Tackett, Nicolas. *The Destruction of the Medieval Chinese Aristocracy*. Cambridge, Mass.: Harvard University Asia Center, 2014.
———. "Great Clansmen, Bureaucrats, and Local Magnates: The Structure and Circulation of the Elite in Late-Tang China." *Asia Major*, Third Series, 21, no. 2 (2008): 101–52.
———. "The Transformation of Medieval Chinese Elites." PhD diss., Columbia University, 2006.
Takahashi Tairo 高橋泰郎. "Tōdai orimono kōgyo zakkō" 唐代織物工業雑考. *Tōa ronso* 東亜論叢, no. 5 (1941): 341–59.
Tan, Mei Ah. "Exonerating the Horse Trade for the Shortage of Silk: Yuan Zhen's 'Yin Mountain Route.'" *Zhongguo wenhua yanjiusuo xuebao* 中國文化研究所學報, no. 57 (2013): 49–95.
———. "A Study of Yuan Zhen's Life and Verse 809–810: Two Years That Shaped His Politics and Prosody." PhD diss., University of Wisconsin, Madison, 2008.
Tang Changru 唐長孺 et al., eds. *Tulufan chutu wenshu* 吐魯番出土文書, 4 vols. Beijing: Wenwu chubanshe, 1992–96.
Taniichi, Takashi. "Six-Lobed Tang Dynasty (AD 658) Glass Cups Recently Excavated in China." *Annales du 15e Congrès de l'Association Internationale pour l'Histoire du Verre: New York-Corning 2001*, 107–10. Nottingham: AIHV, 2003.
Thirsk, Joan. "The Fantastical Folly of Fashion: The English Stocking Knitting Industry, 1500–1700." In *Textile History and Economic History: Essays in Honour of Miss Julia de Lacy Mann*, edited by N. B. Harte and K. G. Ponting, 50–73. Manchester: Manchester University Press, 1973.
Thorp, Robert, and Richard Ellis Vinograd, eds. *Chinese Art and Culture*. New York: Abrams, 2001.
Trilling, James. *Ornament: A Modern Perspective*. Seattle: University of Washington Press, 2003.
Trombert, Eric, and Étienne de La Vaissière. "Le prix des denrées sur le marché de Turfan en 743." In Études de Dunhuang et Turfan, edited by J. P. Drège and O. Venture, 1–53. Geneva: Droz, 2007.
Tsai, Kevin S. C. "Ritual and Gender in the 'Tale of Li Wa.'" *Chinese Literature: Essays, Articles, Reviews (CLEAR)* 26 (2004): 99–127.
Tseëlon, Efrat. "Ontological, Epistemological, and Methodological Clarifications in Fashion Research: From Critique to Empirical Suggestions." In *Through the Wardrobe: Women's Relationships with their Clothes*, edited by Ali Guy, Eileen Green, and Maura Banim, 237–54. Oxford: Berg, 2001.
Tunstall, Alexandra. "Beyond Categorization: Zhu Kerou's Tapestry Painting 'Butterfly and Camellia.'" *East Asian Science, Technology, and Medicine*, no. 36 (2012): 39–76.

Tuotuo 脫脫 (Toghto, 1313–1355) et al., comps. *Songshi* 宋史, 40 vols. Beijing: Zhonghua shuju. Reprint, 2007.

Twitchett, Denis, ed. *The Cambridge History of China*. Vol. 3, *Sui and T'ang China, 586–906 AD, Part I*. New York: Cambridge University Press, 1979.

———. "Chinese Social History from the Seventh to the Tenth Centuries. The Tunhuang Documents and Their Implications." *Past & Present*, no. 35 (1966): 28–53.

———. "A Confucian's View of the Taxation of Commerce: Ts'ui Jung's Memorial of 703." *Bulletin of the School of Oriental and African Studies, University of London* 36, no. 2 (1973): 429–45.

———. *Financial Administration under the T'ang Dynasty*. Cambridge: Cambridge University Press, 1963.

———. "How to Be an Emperor: T'ang T'ai-Tsung's Vision of His Role." *Asia Major*, Third Series 9, no. 1/2 (1996): 1–102.

———. "Lands under State Cultivation under the T'ang." *Journal of the Economic and Social History of the Orient* 2, no. 2 (1959): 162–203.

———. "Lands under State Cultivation under the T'ang: Some Central Asian Documents concerning Military Colonies." *Journal of the Economic and Social History of the Orient* 2, no. 3 (1959): 335–36.

———. "Merchant, Trade, and Government in Late T'ang." *Asia Major*, New Series 14, no. 1 (1968): 63–95.

———. "Provincial Autonomy and Central Finance in Late T'ang." *Asia Major*, New Series 11, no. 2 (1965): 211–32.

———. "The Seamy Side of Late T'ang Political Life: Yü Ti and His Family." *Asia Major*, Third Series 1, no. 2 (1988): 29–63.

———. "The T'ang Imperial Family." *Asia Major*, Third Series 7, no. 2 (1994): 1–61.

———. "The T'ang Market System." *Asia Major*, New Series 12, no. 2 (1966): 202–48.

Vainker, S. J. *Chinese Pottery and Porcelain*, 2nd ed. London: British Museum Press, 2005.

Veblen, Thorstein. "The Economic Theory of Woman's Dress." *The Popular Science Monthly* 46 (1894): 198–205.

———. *The Theory of the Leisure Class*. New York: Modern Library, 2001.

Vedal, Nathan. "Never Taking a Shortcut: Examination Poetry of the Tang Dynasty." *Tang Studies* 33, no. 1 (2015): 38–61.

Vincent, Susan. *Dressing the Elite: Clothes in Early Modern England*. New York: Berg, 2003.

Waley, Arthur. *The Life and Times of Po Chu-I*. London: George Allen and Unwin, 1951.

Waltner, Ann. "Les Noces Chinoises: An Eighteenth-Century French Representation of a Chinese Wedding Procession." In *Gender & Chinese History: Transformative Encounters*, edited by Beverly Bossler, 21–39. Seattle: University of Washington Press, 2015.

Wang, Binghua, and Helen Wang. "A Study of the Tang Dynasty Tax Textiles (Yongdiao bu) from Turfan." *Journal of the Royal Asiatic Society* 23, no. 2 (2013): 263–80.

Wang, Gungwu. *The Structure of Power in North China During the Five Dynasties*. Stanford: Stanford University Press, 1967.

Wang, Zhenping. "Ideas Concerning Diplomacy and Foreign Policy under the Tang Emperors Gaozu and Taizong." *Asia Major*, Third Series 22, no. 1 (2009): 239–85.

Wang Ay-Ling 王璦玲. "Dramatic Elements in the Narrative Poetry of Bo Juyi (772–846) and Yuan Zhen (799–831)." *Zhongguo wenzhe yanjiu jikan* 中國文哲研究集刊 5 (1994): 195–272.

Wang Binghua 王炳華. "Tulufan chutu Tangdai yongdiaobu yanjiu" 吐魯番出土唐代庸調布研究. *Wenwu* 文物, no. 1 (1981): 56–62.

Wang Dang 王讜 (active twelfth century). *Tang yulin* 唐語林. Shanghai: Shanghai guji chubanshe. Reprint, 1985.

Wang Pu 王溥 (922–982), comp. *Tang Huiyao* 唐會要, 2 vols. Shanghai: Shanghai guji chubanshe, 1991.

Wang Qinruo 王欽若 (962–1065) et al. *Songben Cefu yuangui* 宋本冊府元龜. 4 vols. Beijing: Zhonghua shuju. Reprint, 1989.

Wang Renyu 王仁裕 (880–956), comp. *Kaiyuan Tianbao yishi* 開元天寶遺事. Beijing: Zhonghua shuju. Reprint, 2006.

Wang Yongxing 王永興. "Shilun Tangdai si fangzhi ye de diqu fenbu" 試論唐代絲紡織業的地區分布. In *Chen men wenxue conggao* 陳門問學叢稿, edited by Wang Yongxing, 269–92. Nanchang: Jiangxi chubanshe, 1993.

Wang Yuqing 王宇清. *Lidai funü paofu kaoshi* 歷代婦女袍服考實. Taipei: Zhongguo qipao yanjiuhui, 1975.

———. *Zhongguo fuzhuang shigang* 中國服裝史綱. Taipei: Zhonghua dadian bianyinhui, 1967.

Wang Zili 王自力 and Sun Fuxi 孫福喜. *Tang Jinxiang xianzhu mu* 唐金鄉縣主墓. Beijing: Wenwu chubanshe, 2002.

Watt, James C. Y., ed. *China: Dawn of a Golden Age, 200–750 AD*. New York: Metropolitan Museum of Art, 2004.

Watt, James C. Y., and Anne E. Wardwell, eds. *When Silk Was Gold: Central Asian and Chinese Textiles*. New York: Metropolitan Museum of Art, 1997.

Wei, Shuya, Erwin Rosenberg, and Yarong Wang. "Analysis and Identification of Dyestuffs in Historic Chinese Textiles." *Studies in Conservation* 59, no. 1 (2014): 275–76.

Wei Zheng 魏徵 (580–643) et al., comps. *Sui shu* 隋書. 6 vols. Beijing: Zhonghua shuju, 1973.

Weiner, Annette, and Jane Schneider, eds. *Cloth and Human Experience*. Washington, DC: Smithsonian Institution Press, 1989.

Wilson, Verity. *Chinese Dress*. London: Victoria and Albert Museum, 1986.

Wong, Kwok-Yiu. "The White Horse Massacre and Changing Literati Culture in Late-Tang and Five Dynasties China." *Asia Major*, Third Series 23, no. 2 (2010): 33–75.

Wright, Arthur F. "Symbolism and Function: Reflections on Chang'an and Other Great Cities." *The Journal of Asian Studies* 24, no. 4 (1965): 667–79.

Wu, Min. "The Exchange of Weaving Technologies between China and Central and Western Asia." In *Central Asian Textiles and Their Contexts in the Early Middle Ages*, edited by Regula Schorta, 211–242. Riggisberg, Switzerland: Abegg-Stiftung, 2006.

Wu Hung. *The Art of the Yellow Springs: Understanding Chinese Tombs*. Honolulu: University of Hawai'i Press, 2010.

———. *The Double Screen: Medium and Representation in Chinese Painting*. Chicago: University of Chicago Press, 1996.

———. "Enlivening the Soul in Chinese Tombs." *RES: Anthropology and Aesthetics*, no. 55/56 (2009): 21–41.

———. "Han Sarcophagi: Surface, Depth, Context." *RES: Anthropology and Aesthetics*, no. 61/62 (2012): 196–212.

———. "On Tomb Figurines: The Beginning of a Visual Tradition." In *Body and Face in Chinese Visual Culture*, edited by Wu Hung and Katherine Tsiang, 13–48. Cambridge, Mass.: Harvard University Asia Center, 2005.

Wu Jianguo 武建國. "Tangdai shichang guanli zhidu yanjiu" 唐代市場管理制度研究. *Sixiang zhanxian* 思想戰線, no. 3 (1988): 72–79.

Wu Min 武敏. "Tulufan chutu Shu jin de yanjiu" 吐魯番出土蜀錦的研究. *Wenwu* 文物 6 (1984): 70–80.

Wu Zhen 吳震. "Tulufan chutu wenshu zhong de sizhipin kaobian" 吐魯番出土文書中的絲織

品考辨. In *Tulufan diyu yu chutu juan zhiwu* 吐魯番地域與出土絹織物, edited by Xinjiang Uygur Autonomous Region Museum and Nara Research Center for Silk Roadology, 84–103. Nara: Shiruku Rōdo-gaku Kenkyū Sentā, 2000.

Xiang Da 向達. *Tangdai Chang'an yu Xiyu wenming* 唐代長安與西域文明. Chongqing: Chongqing chubanshe, 2009.

Xie Tao 谢涛 et al. "Chengdu shi Tianhuizhen Laoguanshan Han mu" 成都市天回鎮老官山漢墓. *Kaogu* 考古 7, no. 1 (2014): 59–70.

Xie Zhiliu 謝稚柳. "Tang Zhou Fang *Zanhua shinü tu* de shangque" 唐周昉《簪花仕女圖》的商榷. *Wenwu cankao ziliao* 文物參考資料, no. 6 (1958): 25–26.

Xinjiang Uyghur Autonomous Region Museum et al. 新疆維吾爾自治區博物館. *Gudai xiyu fushi xiecui* 古代西域服飾擷萃. Beijing: Wenwu chubanshe, 2009.

———. "Tulufan xian Asitana-Hala hezhuo gumu qun fajue jianbao" 吐魯番縣阿斯塔那–哈拉和卓古墓群發掘簡報. *Wenwu* 文物, no. 10 (1973): 7–27.

———. *Xinjiang weiwu'er zizhiqu bowuguan* 新疆維吾爾自治區博物館 [Catalogue]. Beijing: Wenwu chubanshe, 1991.

Xiong, Victor. *Emperor Yang of the Sui Dynasty: His Life, Times, and Legacy.* Albany: State University of New York Press, 2006.

———. "The Land-Tenure System of Tang China: A Study of the Equal-Field System and the Turfan Documents." *T'oung Pao* 85, no. 4/5 (1999): 328–90.

———. *Sui-Tang Chang'an: A Study in the Urban History of Medieval China.* Ann Arbor: Center for Chinese Studies, University of Michigan Press, 2000.

Xu, Chang, and Helen Wang. "Managing a Multicurrency System in Tang China: The View from the Centre." *Journal of the Royal Asiatic Society* 23, no. 2 (2013): 223–44.

Xu Shucheng 徐書城. "Cong *Wanshan Shinü tu, Zanhua shinü tu* luetan Tangren shinü hua" 從《紈扇仕女圖》《簪花仕女圖》略談唐人仕女畫. *Wenwu* 文物, no. 7 (1980): 71–75.

Xue Pingshan 薛平栓. "Lun Sui Tang Chang'an de shangren" 論隋唐長安的商人. *Shaanxi shifan daxue xuebao* 陝西師範大學學報 33, no. 2 (2004): 69–75.

Yamamoto, Tatsuro, Ikeda On, Okana Makoto, eds. *Tun-Huang and Turfan Documents Concerning Social and Economic History.* Vol. 1, *Legal Texts.* Tokyo: Committee for the Studies of the Tun-huang Manuscripts, 1978.

Yamamoto, Tatsuro, and Yoshikazu Dohi. *Tun-huang and Turfan Documents Concerning Social and Economic History.* Vol. 2, *Census Registers.* Tokyo: Committee for the Studies of the Tun-huang Manuscripts, 1984.

Yan Buke 閻步克. *Zhouli zhi mian: "Zhouli" liumian li zhidu de xingshuai bianyi* 服周之冕:《周禮》六冕禮制度的興衰變異. Beijing: Zhonghua shuju, 2009.

Yang, Jidong. "The Making, Writing, and Testing of Decisions in the Tang Government: A Study of the Role of the 'Pan' in the Literary Bureaucracy of Medieval China." *Chinese Literature: Essays, Articles, Reviews (CLEAR)* 29 (2007): 129–67.

Yang, Lien-sheng. "Buddhist Monasteries and Four Money-Raising Institutions in Chinese History." *Harvard Journal of Asiatic Studies* 13, no. 1/2 (1950): 174–91.

———. *Money and Credit in China: A Short History.* Cambridge, Mass.: Harvard University Press, 1952.

Yang Bojun 楊伯峻, ed. *Chunqiu Zuozhuan zhu* 春秋左传注. 4 vols. Beijing: Zhonghua shuju, 1995.

Yang Renkai. 楊仁愷. "Dui 'Tang Zhou Fang *Zanhua shinü tu* de shangque' de yijian" 對「唐周昉簪花仕女圖的商榷」的意見. *Wenwu* 文物, no. 2 (1959): 44–45.

———. *Zanhua shinütu yanjiu* 簪花仕女圖研究. Beijing: Zhaohua meishu chubanshe, 1962.

Yang Yinliu 楊蔭瀏. *Yang Yinliu yinyue lunwen xuanji* 楊蔭瀏音樂論文選集. Shanghai: Shanghai wenyi chubanshe, 1986.

Yang Yuan 楊遠. *Tangdai de kuangchan* 唐代的礦產. Taipei: Taiwan xuesheng shuju, 1982.
Yang Zhengxing 楊正興. “Tang Xue Yuanchao mu de sanfu bihua jieshao” 唐薛元超墓的三幅壁畫介紹. *Kaogu yu wenwu* 考古與文物, no. 6 (1983): 104–5.
Yao, Ping. “Historicizing Great Bliss: Erotica in Tang China (618–907).” *Journal of the History of Sexuality* 22, no. 2 (2013): 207–29.
———. “The Status of Pleasure: Courtesan and Literati Connections in T’ang China (618–907).” *Journal of Women’s History* 14, no. 2 (2002): 26–53.
———. “Women, Femininity, and Love in the Writings of Bo Juyi (772–846).” PhD diss., University of Illinois, Urbana-Champaign, 1997.
Yao Ping 姚平. *Tangdai funü de shengming licheng* 唐代婦女的生命歷程. Shanghai: Shanghai guji chubanshe, 2004.
Yao Runeng 姚汝能 (dates unknown). *An Lushan shiji* 安祿山事蹟. Shanghai: Shanghai guji chubanshe, 1983.
Yates, Robin S. *Washing Silk: The Life and Selected Poetry of Wei Chuang (834?–910).* Cambridge, Mass.: Harvard Council on East Asian Studies, 1988.
Ye, Wa. “Mortuary Practice in Medieval China: A Study of the Xingyuan Tang Cemetery.” PhD diss., University of California, Los Angeles, 2005.
Yokohari, Kazuko. “The Hōryū-ji Lion-Hunting Silk and Related Silks.” In *Central Asian Textiles and Their Contexts in the Early Middle Ages*, edited by Regula Schorta, 155–73. Riggisberg: Abegg-Stiftung, 2006.
Yong, Lam Lay. “Zhang Qiujian Suanjing (The Mathematical Classic of Zhang Qiujian): An Overview.” *Archive for History of Exact Sciences* 50, no. 3/4 (1997): 201–40.
Yoshida Yukata 吉田豊. *Kōtan shutsudo 8–9-seiki no Kōtan-go sezoku monjo ni kansuru oboe gaki* コータン出土8–9世紀のコータン語世俗文書に関する覚え書き. Kobe: Kobe-shi gaikokugo daigaku gaikokugaku kenkyūjo, 2006.
———. “On the Taxation System of Pre-Islamic Khotan.” *Acta Asiatica* 94 (2008): 95–126.
Yoshirō Saeki 佐伯好郎. *Keikyō Hibun Kenkyū* 景教碑文研究. Tokyo: Tairō Shoin, 1911.
Yu, Pauline. *The Reading of Imagery in the Chinese Poetic Tradition.* Princeton: Princeton University Press, 1987.
Yuan Zhen 元稹. *Yuan Zhen ji* 元稹集. 2 vols. Edited by Ji Qin 冀勤. Beijing: Zhonghua shuju, 1982.
Zamperini, Paola. “On Their Dress They Wore a Body: Fashion and Identity in Late Qing Shanghai.” *positions: east asia cultures critique* 11, no. 2 (2003): 301–30.
Zhang, Guangda, and Xinjiang Rong. “A Concise History of the Turfan Oasis and Its Exploration.” *Asia Major*, Third Series 11, no. 2 (1998): 13–36.
Zhang Guogang 張國剛. “Tangdai de fanbu yu fanbing” 唐代蕃部與蕃兵. In *Tangdai zhengzhi zhidu yanjiu lunji* 唐代政治制度研究論集, edited by Zhang Guogang, 93–112. Taibei: Wenjin chubanshe, 1994.
———. *Tangdai fanzhen yanjiu* 唐代蕃镇研究. Changsha: Hunan jiaoyu chubanshe, 1987.
Zhang Moyuan 張末元. *Hanchao fuzhuang tuyang ziliao* 漢朝服裝圖樣資料. Hong Kong: Taiping shuju, 1963.
———. *Handai fushi cankao ziliao* 漢代服飾參考資料. Beijing: Renmin meishu chubanshe, 1959.
Zhang Qun 章群. *Tangdai fanjiang yanjiu* 唐代蕃將研究. Taipei: Lianjing chubanshe, 1986.
Zhang Yanyuan 張彥遠 (fl. ninth century). *Lidai minghua ji* 歷代名畫記. Beijing: Zhonghua shuju, 1985.
Zhang Zexian 張澤咸. *Tangdai gongshang ye* 唐代工商業. Beijing: Zhongguo shehui kexue chubanshe, 1995.

Zhangsun Wuji 長孫無忌 (d. 659) et al., comps. *Tanglü shuyi* 唐律疏議. Annotated by Liu Junwen 劉俊文. Beijing: Zhonghua shuju, 1983.

Zhao, Feng. *Recent Excavations of Textiles in China*. Hong Kong: ISAT/Costume Squad, 2002.

———. "Weaving Methods for Western Style *Samit* from the Silk Road in Northwestern China." In *Central Asian Textiles and Their Contexts in the Early Middle Ages*, edited by Regula Schorta, 189–210. Riggisberg, Switzerland: Abegg-Stiftung, 2006.

———. "Woven Color in China: The Five Colors in Chinese Culture and Polychrome Woven Textiles." *Textile Society of America Symposium Proceedings*, no. 63 (2010): 1–11.

Zhao, Feng, and Jacqueline Simcox. "Silk Roundels from the Sui to the Tang." *Hali* 92 (1997): 80–85.

Zhao, Feng, and Le Wang. "Glossary of Textile Terminology (Based on the Documents from Dunhuang and Turfan)." *Journal of the Royal Asiatic Society* 23, no. 2 (2013): 349–87.

Zhao, Feng, Wang Yi, Luo Qun, Long Bo, Zhang Baichun, Xia Yingchong, Xie Tao, Wu Shunqing, and Xiao Lin. "The Earliest Evidence of Pattern Looms: Han Dynasty Tomb Models from Chengdu, China," *Antiquity* 91, no. 356 (2017): 360–74.

Zhao Feng 趙豐. *Sichou yishu shi* 絲綢藝術史. Hangzhou: Zhejiang meishu xueyuan chubanshe, 1992.

———. *Tangdai sichou yu sichou zhi lu* 唐代絲綢與絲綢之路. Xi'an: Sanqin chubanshe, 1992.

———, ed. *Zhongguo sichou tongshi* 中國絲綢通史. Suzhou: Suzhou daxue chubanshe, 2005.

Zhao Liguang 趙力光 and Wang Jiugang 王九剛. "Chang'an xian nanliwangcun Tang mu bihua" 長安縣南里王村唐墓壁畫. *Wenbo* 文博, no. 4 (1989): 3–9.

Zhaoling Museum 昭陵博物館. "Tang Zhaoling Changle gongzu mu" 唐昭陵長樂公主墓. *Wenbo* 文博, no. 3 (1988): 10–30.

———. "Tang Zhaoling Duan Jianbi mu qingli jianbao" 唐昭陵段簡璧墓清理簡報. *Wenbo* 文博, no. 6 (1989): 3–12.

Zheng, Yan, Marianne P. Y. Wong, and Shi Jie. "Western Han Sarcophagi and the Transformation of Chinese Funerary Art." RES: Anthropology and Aesthetics, no. 61/62 (2012): 65–79.

Zheng Chuhui 鄭處誨 (fl. 834). *Minghuang zalu* 明皇雜錄. Edited by Tian Tingzhu 田廷柱, and printed with *Dongguan zouji* 東觀奏記 by Pei Tingyu 裴庭裕. Beijing: Zhonghua shuju, 1994.

Zhou Tianyou 周天游, ed. *Xincheng, Fangling, Yongtai gongzhu mu bihua* 新城, 房陵, 永泰公主墓壁畫. Beijing: Wenwu chubanshe, 2002.

———. *Zhanghuai taizi mu bihua* 章懷太子墓壁畫. Beijing: Wenwu chubanshe, 2002.

Zhou Xibao 周錫保. *Zhongguo gudai fushi shi* 中國古代服飾史. Beijing: Zhongguo xiju chubanshe, 1984.

Zhou Xun 周汛, and Gao Chunming 高春明 et al. *Zhongguo lidai fushi* 中國歷代服飾. Shanghai: Xuelin chubanshe, 1984.

Zhu Jincheng 朱金城. *Bai Juyi nianpu* 白居易年譜. Shanghai: Shanghai guji chubanshe, 1982.

Zhu Xinyu 朱新予, ed. *Zhongguo sichou shi* 中國絲綢史. Beijing: Fangzhi gongye chubanshe, 1992.

Zhu Zude 朱祖德. "Tangdai Yuezhou jingji fazhan tanxi" 唐代越州經濟發展探析. *Danjiang Shixue* 淡江史學, no. 18 (1996): 21–42.

Zou, John. "Cross-Dressed Nation: Mei Lanfang and the Clothing of Modern Chinese Men." In *Embodied Modernities: Corporeality, Representation, and Chinese Cultures*, edited by Larissa Heinrich and Fran Martin, 79–97. Honolulu: University of Hawai'i Press, 2006.

INDEX

NOTE: Page numbers in italics refer to figures, maps, and captions; those followed by "n" and "t" indicate endnotes and tables, respectively.

C

D

T

W

X

Y

Z